# CAMBRIDGE LIBR

*Books of endurin*



## Literary S

This series provides a high-quality selection of early printings of literary works, textual editions, anthologies and literary criticism which are of lasting scholarly interest. Ranging from Old English to Shakespeare to early twentieth-century work from around the world, these books offer a valuable resource for scholars in reception history, textual editing, and literary studies.

## The Life of Charles Dickens

John Forster (1812–76), an exact contemporary of Charles Dickens, was one of his closest friends, and acted for him (as for many other authors) as advisor, editor, proofreader, agent and marketing manager: according to Thackeray, 'whenever anyone is in a scrape we all fly to him for refuge. He is omniscient and works miracles.' Forster was Dickens' literary executor, and was left the manuscripts of many of the novels, which he in turn left (along with the rest of his magnificent library) to the South Kensington Museum (later the Victoria and Albert Museum). He was ideally placed to write a biography of Dickens, having known him since the 1830s, and having been involved in deeply private matters such as Dickens' separation from his wife. This three-volume account was first published between 1872 and 1874; the version of Volume 2 reissued here is the 'tenth thousand' of 1873.

Cambridge University Press has long been a pioneer in the reissuing of out-of-print titles from its own backlist, producing digital reprints of books that are still sought after by scholars and students but could not be reprinted economically using traditional technology. The Cambridge Library Collection extends this activity to a wider range of books which are still of importance to researchers and professionals, either for the source material they contain, or as landmarks in the history of their academic discipline.

Drawing from the world-renowned collections in the Cambridge University Library, and guided by the advice of experts in each subject area, Cambridge University Press is using state-of-the-art scanning machines in its own Printing House to capture the content of each book selected for inclusion. The files are processed to give a consistently clear, crisp image, and the books finished to the high quality standard for which the Press is recognised around the world. The latest print-on-demand technology ensures that the books will remain available indefinitely, and that orders for single or multiple copies can quickly be supplied.

The Cambridge Library Collection will bring back to life books of enduring scholarly value (including out-of-copyright works originally issued by other publishers) across a wide range of disciplines in the humanities and social sciences and in science and technology.

# The Life of Charles Dickens

Volume 2: 1842–1852

John Forster

Cambridge
University Press

CAMBRIDGE UNIVERSITY PRESS

Cambridge, New York, Melbourne, Madrid, Cape Town,
Singapore, São Paolo, Delhi, Tokyo, Mexico City

Published in the United States of America by Cambridge University Press, New York

www.cambridge.org
Information on this title: www.cambridge.org/9781108039369



This edition first published 1873
This digitally printed version 2011

ISBN 978-1-108-03936-9 Paperback

# THE LIFE

OF

W. P. Frith, R. A. R. Graves. A.R.A.

CHARLES DICKENS.

ÆT 47.

# THE LIFE

OF

# CHARLES DICKENS.

BY JOHN FORSTER.

VOLUME THE SECOND.

1842—1852.

TENTH THOUSAND.

LONDON:
CHAPMAN AND HALL, 193, PICCADILLY.
1873.

LONDON:
BRADBURY, EVANS, AND CO., PRINTERS, WHITEFRIARS.

# CORRECTIONS MADE IN THE LATER EDITIONS OF THE FIRST VOLUME.

A NOTICE written under date of the 23rd December, 1871, appeared with the Tenth Edition. 'Such has been the rapidity of the demand for successive impres-'sions of this book, that I have found it impossible, until now, to correct at pages '11, 66, and 76 three errors of statement made in the former editions; and some 'few other mistakes, not in themselves important, at pages 75, 80, and 81. I 'take the opportunity of adding, that the mention at p. 62 is not an allusion to 'the well-known "Penny" and "Saturday" magazines, but to weekly periodicals 'of some years' earlier date resembling them in form. One of them, I have since 'found from a later mention by Dickens himself, was presumably of a less whole-'some and instructive character. "I used," he says, "when I was at school, to '"take in the *Terrific Register*, making myself unspeakably miserable, and '"frightening my very wits out of my head, for the small charge of a penny '"weekly; which, considering that there was an illustration to every number '"in which there was always a pool of blood, and at least one body, was cheap." 'An obliging correspondent writes to me upon my reference to the Fox-under-'the-hill, at pp. 42–3: "Will you permit me to say, that the house, shut up '"and almost ruinous, is still to be found at the bottom of a curious and most '"precipitous court, the entrance of which is just past Salisbury-street. . . . '"It was once, I think, the approach to the halfpenny boats. The house is '"now shut out from the water-side by the Embankment."' I proceed to state in detail what the changes thus referred to were.

The passage about James Lamert, beginning at the seventh line of p. 11, now stands: 'His chief ally and encourager in these displays was a youth of some 'ability, much older than himself, named James Lamert, stepson to his mother's 'sister and therefore a sort of cousin, who was his great patron and friend in his 'childish days. Mary, the eldest daughter of Charles Barrow, himself a lieutenant 'in the navy, had for her first husband a commander in the navy called Allen; 'on whose death by drowning at Rio Janeiro she had joined her sister, the navy-'pay clerk's wife, at Chatham; in which place she subsequently took for her 'second husband Doctor Lamert, an army-surgeon, whose son James, even after 'he had been sent to Sandhurst for his education, continued still to visit Chatham 'from time to time. He had a turn for private theatricals; and as his father's 'quarters were in the ordnance-hospital there, a great rambling place otherwise 'at that time almost uninhabited, he had plenty of room in which to get up his 'entertainments.' Two other corrections were consequent on this change. At the 21st line of page 18, for 'the elder cousin read 'the cousin by marriage;' and at the 19th line of p. 29, 'cousin by his mother's side should be 'cousin by 'his aunt's marriage.'

At the 14th line of the 21st page, 'his bachelor-uncle, fellow-clerk,' &c. should be 'the uncle who was at this time fellow-clerk,' &c. At the 7th line of page 34, 'Charles-court' should be 'Clare-court.' The allusion to one of his favourite localities at the 29th line of page 42 should stand thus: 'a little public-house by 'the water-side called the Fox-under-the-hill, approached by an underground 'passage which we once missed in looking for it together.'

The passage at pp. 65–6, having reference to an early friend who had been with him, as I supposed, at his first school, should run thus: 'In this however I have 'since discovered my own mistake: the truth being that it was this gentleman's 'connection, not with the Wellington-academy, but with a school kept by Mr. 'Dawson in Hunter-street, Brunswick-square, where the brothers of Dickens were 'subsequently placed, which led to their early knowledge of each other. I fancy 'that they were together also, for a short time, at Mr. Molloy's in New-square, 'Lincoln's-inn; but, whether or not this was so, Dickens certainly had not quitted 'school many months before his father had made sufficient interest with an attorney 'of Gray's-inn, Mr. Edward Blackmore, to obtain him regular employment in his 'office.' There is subsequent allusion to the same gentleman (at p. 159) as his 'school-companion at Mr. Dawson's in Henrietta-street,' which ought to stand as 'having known him when himself a law-clerk in Lincoln's-inn.'

At p. 75 I had stated that Mr. John Dickens reported for the *Morning Chronicle;* and at p. 80 that Mr. Thomas Beard reported for the *Morning Herald;* whereas Mr. Dickens, though in the gallery for other papers, did not report for the *Chronicle*, and Mr. Beard did report for that journal; and where (at p. 81) Dickens was spoken of as associated with Mr. Beard in a reporting party which represented respectively the *Chronicle* and *Herald*, the passage ought simply to have described him as 'connected with a reporting party, being Lord John Rus-'sell's Devonshire contest above-named, and his associate chief being Mr. Beard, 'entrusted with command for the *Chronicle* in this particular express.'

At p. 76 I had made a mistake about his 'first published piece of writing, in too hastily assuming that he had himself forgotten what the particular piece was. It struck an intelligent and kind correspondent as very unlikely that Dickens should have fallen into error on such a point; and, making personal search for himself (as I ought to have done), discovered that what I supposed to be another piece was merely the same under another title. The description of his first printed sketch should therefore be '(Mr. Minns and his Cousin, as he afterwards 'entitled it, but which appeared in the magazine as A Dinner at Poplar Walk).' There is another mistake at p. 136, of 'bandy-legged' instead of 'bulky-legged;' and, at p. 155, of 'fresh fields' for 'fresh woods.'

Those several corrections were made in the Tenth Edition. To the Eleventh these words were prefixed (under date of the 23rd of January, 1872): 'Since the 'above mentioned edition went to press, a published letter has rendered necessary 'a brief additional note to the remarks made at pp. 133-4.' The remark occurs in my notice of the silly story of Mr. Cruikshank having originated *Oliver Twist*, and, with the note referred to, now stands in the form subjoined. 'Whether all 'Sir Benjamin's laurels however should fall to the person by whom the tale is 'told,* or whether any part belongs to the authority alleged for it, is unfortunately 'not quite clear. There would hardly have been a doubt, if the fable had been 'confined to the other side of the Atlantic; but it has been reproduced and widely 'circulated on this side also; and the distinguished artist whom it calumniates 'by attributing the invention to him has been left undefended from its slander. 'Dickens's letter spares me the necessity of characterizing, by the only word which 'would have been applicable to it, a tale of such incredible and monstrous absur-'dity as that one of the masterpieces of its author's genius had been merely an 'illustration of etchings by Mr. Cruikshank!' Note to the words 'person by 'whom the tale is told:' '* This question has been partly solved, since my last 'edition, by Mr. Cruikshank's announcement in the *Times*, that, though Dr. 'Mackenzie had "confused some circumstances with respect to Mr. Dickens look-'"ing over some drawings and sketches," the substance of his information as to 'who it was that originated *Oliver Twist*, and all its characters, had been derived 'from Mr. Cruikshank himself. The worst part of the foregoing fable, therefore, 'has not Dr. Mackenzie for its author; and Mr. Cruikshank is to be congratulated 'on the prudence of his rigid silence respecting it as long as Mr. Dickens lived.'

In the Twelfth Edition I mentioned, in the note at p. 128, a little work of which all notice had been previously omitted; and the close of that note now runs: 'He 'had before written for them, without his name, *Sunday under Three Heads;* and 'he added subsequently a volume of *Young Couples.*' At p. 135, 'parish abuses' is corrected in the same edition to 'parish practices;' and at p. 151, 'in his 'later works' to 'in his latest works.'

I have received letters from several obliging correspondents, among them three or four who were scholars at the Wellington-house Academy before or after Dickens's time, and one who attended the school with him; but such remark as they suggest will more properly accompany my third and closing volume.

PALACE GATE HOUSE, KENSINGTON,
*29th of October*, 1872.

## ILLUSTRATIONS.

# TABLE OF CONTENTS.

## CHAPTER I. 1842.

Pages 1–18.

AMERICAN NOTES. ÆT. 30.



## CHAPTER II. 1843.

Pages 19-40.

FIRST YEAR OF MARTIN CHUZZLEWIT. ÆT. 31.



## CHAPTER III. 1843-1844.

Pages 41-69.

CHUZZLEWIT DISAPPOINTMENTS AND CHRISTMAS CAROL. ÆT. 31-32.

## CHAPTER IV. 1844.

Pages 70–86.

YEAR OF DEPARTURE FOR ITALY. ÆT. 32.



## CHAPTER V. 1844.

Pages 87–113.

IDLENESS AT ALBARO: VILLA BAGNERELLO. ÆT. 32.

## CHAPTER VI. 1844.

Pages 114–137.

WORK IN GENOA : PALAZZO PESCHIERE. ÆT. 32.



## CHAPTER VII. 1844.

Pages 138–153.

ITALIAN TRAVEL. ÆT. 32.

## CHAPTER X. 1846.

Pages 196–216.

A Home in Switzerland. Æt. 34.



## CHAPTER XI. 1846.

Pages 217–233.

Swiss People and Scenery. Æt. 34.

## CHAPTER XII. 1846.

Pages 234–249.

SKETCHES CHIEFLY PERSONAL.

ÆT. 34.



## CHAPTER XIII. 1846.

Pages 250–267.

LITERARY LABOUR AT LAUSANNE.

ÆT. 34.

## CHAPTER XIV. 1846.

Pages 268–288.

REVOLUTION AT GENEVA, CHRISTMAS BOOK, AND LAST DAYS IN SWITZERLAND. ÆT. 34.



## CHAPTER XV. 1846-1847.

Pages 289–308.

THREE MONTHS IN PARIS. ÆT. 34-35.

CHAPTER XVI. 1846–1848.

Pages 309–338.

DOMBEY AND SON. ÆT. 34-36.

## CHAPTER XVII. 1847–1852.

Pages 338–372.

SPLENDID STROLLING. ÆT. 35–40.

## CHAPTER XVIII. 1848-1851.

Pages 373–411.

SEASIDE HOLIDAYS. ÆT. 36–39.

## CHAPTER XIX. 1848–1850.

Pages 412–425.

HAUNTED MAN AND HOUSEHOLD WORDS. ÆT. 36–40.



## CHAPTER XX. 1848–1851.

Pages 426–462.

LAST YEARS IN DEVONSHIRE TERRACE. ÆT. 36-39.

THE

# LIFE OF CHARLES DICKENS.

## CHAPTER I.

### AMERICAN NOTES.

1842.

LONDON: 1842.

Return from America.

THE reality did not fall short of the anticipation of home. His return was the occasion of unbounded enjoyment; and what he had planned before sailing as the way we should meet, received literal fulfilment. By the sound of his cheery voice I first knew that he was come; and from my house we went together to Maclise, also 'without 'a moment's warning.' A Greenwich dinner in which several friends (Talfourd, Milnes, Procter, Maclise, Stanfield, Marryat, Barham, Hood, and Cruikshank among them) took part, and other immediate greetings, followed; but the most special celebration was reserved for autumn, when, by way of challenge to what he had seen while abroad, a home-journey was arranged with Stanfield, Maclise, and myself for his companions, into such of the most striking scenes of a picturesque English county as the majority of us might not before have visited: Cornwall being ultimately chosen.

Page 387 of Vol. I.

LONDON: 1842.

Before our departure he was occupied by his preparation of the *American Notes;* and to the same interval belongs the arrival in London of Mr. Longfellow, who became his guest, and (for both of us I am privileged to add) our attached friend. Longfellow's name was not then the pleasant and familiar word it has since been in England; but he had already written several of his most felicitous pieces, and he possessed all the qualities of delightful companionship, the culture and the charm, which have no higher type or example than the accomplished and genial American. He reminded me, when lately again in England, of two experiences out of many we had enjoyed together this quarter of a century before. One of them was a day at Rochester, when, met by one of those prohibitions which are the wonder of visitors and the shame of Englishmen, we overleapt gates and barriers, and, setting at defiance repeated threats of all the terrors of law coarsely expressed to us by the custodian of the place, explored minutely the castle ruins. The other was a night among those portions of the population which outrage law and defy its terrors all the days of their lives, the tramps and thieves of London; when, under guidance and protection of the most trusted officers of the two great metropolitan prisons afforded to us by Mr. Chesterton and Lieut. Tracey, we went over the worst haunts of the most dangerous classes. Nor will it be unworthy of remark, in proof that attention is not drawn vainly to such scenes, that, upon Dickens going over them a dozen years later when he wrote a paper about them for his *Household Words,* he found important changes effected whereby these human dens, if not less dangerous, were

Longfellow in England.

At Rochester Castle.

Among London tramps and thieves.

Page 255 of Vol. I.

become certainly more decent. On the night of our earlier visit, Maclise, who accompanied us, was struck with such sickness on entering the first of the Mint lodging-houses in the borough, that he had to remain, for the time we were in them, under guardianship of the police outside. Longfellow returned home by the Great Western from Bristol on the 21st of October, enjoying as he passed through Bath the hospitality of Landor; and at the end of the following week we started on our Cornish travel.

LONDON: 1842.

Thirty years ago.

But what before this had occupied Dickens in the writing way must now be told. Not long after his reappearance amongst us, his house being still in the occupation of Sir John Wilson, he went to Broadstairs, taking with him the letters from which I have quoted so largely to help him in preparing his *American Notes;* and one of his first announcements to me (18th of July) shows not only this labour in progress, but the story he was under engagement to begin in November working in his mind. 'The subjects 'at the beginning of the book are of that kind that I can't '*dash* at them, and now and then they fret me in conse- 'quence. When I come to Washington, I am all right. 'The solitary prison at Philadelphia is a good subject, 'though; I forgot that for the moment. Have you seen 'the Boston chapter yet? . . . I have never been in Corn- 'wall either. A mine certainly; and a letter for that 'purpose shall be got from Southwood Smith. I have 'some notion of opening the new book in the lantern of 'a lighthouse!' A letter a couple of months later (16th of Sept.) recurs to that proposed opening of his story which after all he laid aside; and shows how rapidly he was

AT BROAD-STAIRS.

Pages 257-8 of Vol. I.

Preparing *Notes*.

BROADSTAIRS: 1842.

Thanet races.

getting his *American Notes* into shape. 'At the Isle of 'Thanet races yesterday I saw—oh! who shall say what 'an immense amount of character in the way of incon-'ceivable villainy and blackguardism! I even got some 'new wrinkles in the way of showmen, conjurors, pea-and-'thimblers, and trampers generally. I think of opening 'my new book on the coast of Cornwall, in some terribly 'dreary iron-bound spot. I hope to have finished the 'American book before the end of next month; and we 'will then together fly down into that desolate region.' Our friends having Academy engagements to detain them, we had to delay a little; and I meanwhile turn back to his letters to observe his progress with his *Notes*, and other employments or enjoyments of the interval. They require no illustration that they will not themselves supply: but I may remark that the then collected *Poems* of Tennyson had become very favourite reading with him; and that while in America Mr. Mitchell the comedian had given him a small white shaggy terrier, who bore at first the imposing name of Timber Doodle, and became a great domestic pet and companion.

Fancy for the opening of *Chuzzlewit*.

A domestic friend.

'I have been reading' (7th of August) 'Tennyson all 'this morning on the seashore. Among other trifling 'effects, the waters have dried up as they did of old, and 'shown me all the mermen and mermaids, at the bottom 'of the ocean; together with millions of queer creatures, 'half-fish and half-fungus, looking down into all manner of 'coral caves and seaweed conservatories; and staring in 'with their great dull eyes at every open nook and loop-'hole. Who else, too, could conjure up such a close to the

'Merman' and 'mer-'maid.'

'extraordinary and as Landor would say "most woonderful" 'series of pictures in the "dream of fair women," as—

BROADSTAIRS: 1842.

Reading Tennyson.

> 'Squadrons and squares of men in brazen plates,
> 'Scaffolds, still sheets of water, divers woes,
> 'Ranges of glimmering vaults with iron grates,
> 'And hushed seraglios!

'I am getting on pretty well, but it was so glittering and 'sunshiny yesterday that I was forced to make holiday.' Four days later: 'I have not written a word this blessed 'day. I got to New York yesterday, and think it goes 'as it should . . . Little doggy improves rapidly, and now 'jumps over my stick at the word of command. I have 'changed his name to Snittle Timbery, as more sonorous 'and expressive. He unites with the rest of the family 'in cordial regards and loves. *Nota Bene.* The Margate 'theatre is open every evening, and the Four Patagonians '(see Goldsmith's *Essays*) are performing thrice a week at 'Ranelagh . . .'

Little doggy.

Attractions at Margate.

A visit from me was at this time due, to which these were held out as inducements; and there followed what it was supposed I could not resist, a transformation into the broadest farce of a deep tragedy by a dear friend of ours. 'Now you really must come. Seeing only is believing, very 'often isn't that, and even Being the thing falls a long way 'short of believing it. Mrs. Nickleby herself once asked 'me, as you know, if I really believed there ever was such 'a woman; but there'll be no more belief, either in me or 'my descriptions, after what I have to tell of our excellent 'friend's tragedy, if you don't come and have it played 'again for yourself "by particular desire." We saw it

Being, not always Believing.

BROAD-STAIRS: 1842.

'last night, and oh! if you had but been with us! Young 'Betty, doing what the mind of man without my help 'never *can* conceive, with his legs like padded boot-trees 'wrapped up in faded yellow drawers, was the hero. The 'comic man of the company enveloped in a white sheet, 'with his head tied with red tape like a brief and greeted 'with yells of laughter whenever he appeared, was the 'venerable priest. A poor toothless old idiot at whom the 'very gallery roared with contempt when he was called a 'tyrant, was the remorseless and aged Creon. And Ismene 'being arrayed in spangled muslin trowsers very loose in 'the legs and very tight in the ankles, such as Fatima would 'wear in *Blue Beard*, was at her appearance immediately 'called upon for a song. After this, can you longer . . . ?'

Burlesque of classic tragedy.

With the opening of September I had renewed report of his book, and of other matters. 'The Philadelphia chapter 'I think very good, but I am sorry to say it has not made 'as much in print as I hoped . . . In America they have 'forged a letter with my signature, which they coolly 'declare appeared in the *Chronicle* with the copyright 'circular; and in which I express myself in such terms 'as you may imagine, in reference to the dinners and 'so forth. It has been widely distributed all over the 'States; and the felon who invented it is a "smart man" 'of course. You are to understand that it is not done as 'a joke, and is scurrilously reviewed. Mr. Park Benjamin 'begins a lucubration upon it with these capitals, DICKENS 'IS A FOOL, AND A LIAR. . . . . I have a new protégé, in 'the person of a wretched deaf and dumb boy whom I 'found upon the sands the other day, half dead, and have

Page 389 of Vol. I.

Smart man and forged letter.

A new protégé.

'got (for the present) into the union infirmary at Minster. 'A most deplorable case.'

BROADSTAIRS: 1842.

On the 14th he told me: 'I have pleased myself very 'much to-day in the matter of Niagara. I have made 'the description very brief (as it should be), but I fancy 'it is good. I am beginning to think over the introductory 'chapter, and it has meanwhile occurred to me that I 'should like, at the beginning of the volumes, to put what 'follows on a blank page. *I dedicate this Book to those 'friends of mine in America, who, loving their country, 'can bear the truth, when it is written good humouredly 'and in a kind spirit.* What do you think? Do you see 'any objection?'

Proposed Dedication.

My reply is to be inferred from what he sent back on the 20th. 'I don't quite see my way towards an expres'sion in the dedication of any feeling in reference to the 'American reception. Of course I have always intended 'to glance at it, gratefully, in the end of the book; and it 'will have its place in the introductory chapter, if we decide 'for that. Would it do to put in, after "friends in America," '*who giving me a welcome I must ever gratefully and 'proudly remember, left my judgment free, and* who, 'loving, &c. If so, so be it.'

As to American reception.

Before the end of the month he wrote: 'For the last 'two or three days I have been rather slack in point of 'work; not being in the vein. To-day I had not written 'twenty lines before I rushed out (the weather being 'gorgeous) to bathe. And when I have done that, it is all 'up with me in the way of authorship until to-morrow. 'The little dog is in the highest spirits; and jumps, as

Sea-bathing and authorship.

BROAD-STAIRS: 1842.

'Mr. Kenwigs would say, perpetivally. I have had letters 'by the Britannia from Felton, Prescott, Mr. Q, and others, 'all very earnest and kind. I think you will like what 'I have written on the poor emigrants and their ways as 'I literally and truly saw them on the boat from Quebec 'to Montreal.'

Emigrants in Canada.

This was a passage, which, besides being in itself as attractive as any in his writings, gives such perfect expression to a feeling that underlies them all, that I subjoin it in a note.* On board this Canadian steamboat he

C. D. *loq.*

Patient Poor and easy-living Rich.

* 'Cant as we may, and as we shall to the end of all things, it is very much 'harder for the poor to be virtuous than it is for the rich; and the good that 'is in them, shines the brighter for it. In many a noble mansion lives a man, 'the best of husbands and of fathers, whose private worth in both capacities 'is justly lauded to the skies. But bring him here, upon this crowded deck. 'Strip from his fair young wife her silken dress and jewels, unbind her braided 'hair, stamp early wrinkles on her brow, pinch her pale cheek with care and 'much privation, array her faded form in coarsely patched attire, let there 'be nothing but his love to set her forth or deck her out, and you shall put it 'to the proof indeed. So change his station in the world that he shall see, 'in those young things who climb about his knee, not records of his wealth 'and name, but little wrestlers with him for his daily bread; so many poachers 'on his scanty meal; so many units to divide his every sum of comfort, and 'farther to reduce its small amount. In lieu of the endearments of childhood 'in its sweetest aspect, heap upon him all its pains and wants, its sicknesses 'and ills, its fretfulness, caprice, and querulous endurance: let its prattle be, 'not of engaging infant fancies, but of cold, and thirst, and hunger: and if 'his fatherly affection outlive all this, and he be patient, watchful, tender; 'careful of his children's lives, and mindful always of their joys and sorrows; 'then send him back to parliament, and pulpit, and to quarter sessions, and 'when he hears fine talk of the depravity of those who live from hand to mouth, 'and labour hard to do it, let him speak up, as one who knows, and tell those 'holders-forth that they, by parallel with such a class, should be high angels 'in their daily lives, and lay but humble siege to heaven at last. . . . Which 'of us shall say what he would be, if such realities, with small relief or 'change all through his days, were his! Looking round upon these people: 'far from home, houseless, indigent, wandering, weary with travel and 'hard living: and seeing how patiently they nursed and tended their young 'children: how they consulted ever their wants first, then half supplied their

encountered crowds of poor emigrants and their children; and such was their patient kindness and cheerful endurance, in circumstances where the easy-living rich could hardly fail to be monsters of impatience and selfishness, that it suggested to him a reflection than which it was not possible to have written anything more worthy of observation, or more absolutely true. Jeremy Taylor has the same philosophy in his lesson on opportunities, but here it was beautified by the example with all its fine touches. It made us read Rich and Poor by new translation.

BROADSTAIRS: 1842.

Rich and Poor by new translation.

The printers were now hard at work, and in the last week of September he wrote: 'I send you proofs as far 'as Niagara . . . I am rather holiday-making this week '. . . taking principal part in a regatta here yesterday, 'very pretty and gay indeed. We think of coming up 'in time for Macready's opening, when perhaps you will 'give us a chop; and of course you and Mac will dine 'with *us* the next day? I shall leave nothing of the 'book to do after coming home, please God, but the 'two chapters on slavery and the people which I could 'manage easily in a week, if need were . . . The police-'man who supposed the Duke of Brunswick to be one of 'the swell mob, ought instantly to be made an inspector. 'The suspicion reflects the highest credit (I seriously think) 'on his penetration and judgment.' Three days later:

Coming to the end.

Drury-lane opening.

A shrewd guess.

'own; what gentle ministers of hope and faith the women were; how the 'men profited by their example; and how very, very seldom even a moment's 'petulance or harsh complaint broke out among them: I felt a stronger love 'and honour of my kind come glowing on my heart, and wished to God there 'had been many atheists in the better part of human nature there, to read 'this simple lesson in the book of life.'

C. D. *loq.*

BROAD-STAIRS: 1842.

'For the last two days we have had gales blowing from 'the north-east, and seas rolling on us that drown the pier. 'To-day it is tremendous. Such a sea was never known 'here at this season, and it is running in at this moment 'in waves of twelve feet high. You would hardly know 'the place. But we shall be punctual to your dinner 'hour on Saturday. If the wind should hold in the same 'quarter, we may be obliged to come up by land; and in 'that case I should start the caravan at six in the morning. '. . . What do you think of this for my title—*American 'Notes for General Circulation;* and of this motto?

Heavy seas.

Rejected motto for *Notes.*

'In reply to a question from the Bench, the Solicitor for the Bank observed, that 'this kind of notes circulated the most extensively, in those parts of the world 'where they were stolen and forged. *Old Bailey Report.*'

The motto was omitted, objection being made to it; and on the last day of the month I had the last of his letters during this Broadstairs visit. 'Strange as it may 'appear to you' (25th of September), 'the sea is running 'so high that we have no choice but to return by land. 'No steamer can come out of Ramsgate, and the Margate 'boat lay out all night on Wednesday with all her pas-'sengers on board. You may be sure of us therefore on 'Saturday at 5, for I have determined to leave here to-'morrow, as we could not otherwise manage it in time; 'and have engaged an omnibus to bring the whole caravan 'by the overland route. . . . We cannot open a window, 'or a door; legs are of no use on the terrace; and the 'Margate boats can only take people aboard at Herne 'Bay!' He brought with him all that remained to be done of his second volume except the last two chapters,

A gale of wind.

including that to which he has referred as 'introductory;' and on the following Wednesday (5th of October) he told me that the first of these was done. 'I want you very 'much to come and dine to-day that we may repair to 'Drury-lane together; and let us say half-past four, or 'there is no time to be comfortable. I am going out to 'Tottenham this morning, on a cheerless mission I would 'willingly have avoided. Hone, of the *Every Day Book*, 'is dying; and sent Cruikshank yesterday to beg me to 'go and see him, as, having read no books but mine of 'late, he wanted to see and shake hands with me before '(as George said) "he went." There is no help for it, 'of course; so to Tottenham I repair, this morning. I 'worked all day, and till midnight; and finished the slavery 'chapter yesterday.'

Hone of the *Every Day Book*.

Cheerless visit.

The cheerless visit had its mournful sequel before the next month closed, when he went with the same companion to poor Hone's funeral; and one of his letters written at the time to Mr. Felton has so vividly recalled to me the tragi-comedy of an incident of that day, as for long after he used to describe it, and as I have heard the other principal actor in it good-naturedly admit to be perfectly true, that two or three sentences may be given here. The wonderful neighbourhood in this life of ours, of serious and humorous things, constitutes in itself very much of the genius of Dickens's writing; the laughter close to the pathos, but never touching it with ridicule; and this small occurrence may be taken in farther evidence of its reality.

The mingled yarn.

'We went into a little parlour where the funeral party 'was, and God knows it was miserable enough, for the

C. D. *loq.*

LONDON: 1842.

'widow and children were crying bitterly in one corner, 'and the other mourners (mere people of ceremony, who 'cared no more for the dead man than the hearse did) 'were talking quite coolly and carelessly together in an-'other; and the contrast was as painful and distressing 'as anything I ever saw. There was an independent 'clergyman present, with his bands on and a bible under 'his arm, who, as soon as we were seated, addressed C thus, 'in a loud emphatic voice. "Mr. C, have you seen a para-'"graph respecting our departed friend, which has gone the '"round of the morning papers?" "Yes, sir," says C, "I '"have:" looking very hard at me the while, for he had 'told me with some pride coming down that it was his 'composition. "Oh!" said the clergyman. "Then you '"will agree with me, Mr. C, that it is not only an insult '"to me, who am the servant of the Almighty, but an insult '"to the Almighty, whose servant I am." "How is that, '"sir?" says C. "It is stated, Mr. C, in that paragraph," 'says the minister, "that when Mr. Hone failed in business '"as a bookseller, he was persuaded by *me* to try the pulpit; '"which is false, incorrect, unchristian, in a manner blas-'"phemous, and in all respects contemptible. Let us pray." 'With which, and in the same breath, I give you my word, 'he knelt down, as we all did, and began a very miserable 'jumble of an extemporary prayer. I was really pene-'trated with sorrow for the family' (he exerted himself zealously for them afterwards, as the kind-hearted C also did), 'but when C, upon his knees and sobbing for the loss 'of an old friend, whispered me "that if that wasn't a '"clergyman, and it wasn't a funeral, he'd have punched

Scene at a funeral.

Shop and pulpit.

'"his head," I felt as if nothing but convulsions could 'possibly relieve me.'

LONDON: 1842.

An introductory chapter suppressed.

On the 10th of October I heard from him that the chapter intended to be introductory to the *Notes* was written, and waiting our conference whether or not it should be printed. We decided against it; on his part so reluctantly, that I had to undertake for its publication when a more fitting time should come. This in my judgment has arrived, and the chapter first sees the light on this page. There is no danger at present, as there would have been when it was written, that its proper self-assertion should be mistaken for an apprehension of hostile judgments which he was anxious to deprecate or avoid. He is out of reach of all that now; and reveals to us here, as one whom fear or censure can touch no more, his honest purpose in the use of satire even where his humorous temptations were strongest. What he says will on other grounds also be read with unusual interest, for it will be found to connect itself impressively not with his first experiences only, but with his second visit to America at the close of his life. He held always the same high opinion of what was best in that country, and always the same contempt for what was worst in it.

'INTRODUCTORY. AND NECESSARY TO BE READ.

Chapter now first printed.

'I have placed the foregoing title at the head of this page, 'because I challenge and deny the right of any person to 'pass judgment on this book, or to arrive at any reasonable 'conclusion in reference to it, without first being at the trou- 'ble of becoming acquainted with its design and purpose.

'It is not statistical. Figures of arithmetic have already

LONDON: 1842.

Suppressed chapter.

'been heaped upon America's devoted head, almost as 'lavishly as figures of speech have been piled above Shake-'speare's grave.

'It comprehends no small talk concerning individuals, 'and no violation of the social confidences of private life. 'The very prevalent practice of kidnapping live ladies and 'gentlemen, forcing them into cabinets, and labelling and 'ticketing them whether they will or no, for the grati-'fication of the idle and the curious, is not to my taste. 'Therefore I have avoided it.

Intentions and plan for book.

'It has not a grain of any political ingredient in its 'whole composition.

Why silent as to personal reception.

'Neither does it contain, nor have I intended that it 'should contain, any lengthened and minute account of 'my personal reception in the United States: not because 'I am, or ever was, insensible to that spontaneous effusion 'of affection and generosity of heart, in a most affectionate 'and generous-hearted people; but because I conceive that 'it would ill become me to flourish matter necessarily 'involving so much of my own praises, in the eyes of my 'unhappy readers.

*Notes* described.

'This book is simply what it claims to be—a record of 'the impressions I received from day to day, during my 'hasty travels in America, and sometimes (but not always) 'of the conclusions to which they, and after-reflection on 'them, have led me; a description of the country I passed 'through; of the institutions I visited; of the kind of 'people among whom I journeyed; and of the manners 'and customs that came within my observation. Very 'many works having just the same scope and range, have 'been already published, but I think that these two 'volumes stand in need of no apology on that account. 'The interest of such productions, if they have any, lies 'in the varying impressions made by the same novel things 'on different minds; and not in new discoveries or extra-'ordinary adventures.

LONDON: 1842.

Suppressed chapter.

'I can scarcely be supposed to be ignorant of the hazard 'I run in writing of America at all. I know perfectly well 'that there is, in that country, a numerous class of well-'intentioned persons prone to be dissatisfied with all 'accounts of the Republic whose citizens they are, which 'are not couched in terms of exalted and extravagant 'praise. I know perfectly well that there is in America, 'as in most other places laid down in maps of the great 'world, a numerous class of persons so tenderly and deli-'cately constituted, that they cannot bear the truth in any 'form. And I do not need the gift of prophecy to discern 'afar off, that they who will be aptest to detect malice, 'ill-will, and all uncharitableness in these pages, and to 'show, beyond any doubt, that they are perfectly incon-'sistent with that grateful and enduring recollection which 'I profess to entertain of the welcome I found awaiting 'me beyond the Atlantic—will be certain native journalists, 'veracious and gentlemanly, who were at great pains to 'prove to me, on all occasions during my stay there, that 'the aforesaid welcome was utterly worthless.

Risks incurred.

Native critics.

'But, venturing to dissent even from these high 'authorities, I formed my own opinion of its value in the 'outset, and retain it to this hour; and in asserting (as 'I invariably did on all public occasions) my liberty and

LONDON: 1842.

Suppressed chapter.

'freedom of speech while I was among the Americans, and 'in maintaining it at home, I believe that I best show 'my sense of the high worth of that welcome, and of the 'honourable singleness of purpose with which it was ex- 'tended to me. From first to last I saw, in the friends 'who crowded round me in America, old readers, over- 'grateful and over-partial perhaps, to whom I had happily 'been the means of furnishing pleasure and entertainment; 'not a vulgar herd who would flatter and cajole a stranger 'into turning with closed eyes from all the blemishes of 'the nation, and into chaunting its praises with the discri- 'mination of a street ballad-singer. From first to last I saw, 'in those hospitable hands, a home-made wreath of laurel; 'and not an iron muzzle disguised beneath a flower or two.

Own estimate of American welcome.

'Therefore I take—and hold myself not only justified 'in taking, but bound to take—the plain course of saying 'what I think, and noting what I saw; and as it is not 'my custom to exalt what in my judgment are foibles and 'abuses at home, so I have no intention of softening down, 'or glozing over, those that I have observed abroad.

Probable reception of *Notes*.

'If this book should fall into the hands of any sensitive 'American who cannot bear to be told that the working of 'the institutions of his country is far from perfect; that 'in spite of the advantage she has over all other nations 'in the elastic freshness and vigour of her youth, she is far 'from being a model for the earth to copy; and that even 'in those pictures of the national manners with which he 'quarrels most, there is still (after the lapse of several 'years, each of which may be fairly supposed to have had 'its stride in improvement) much that is just and true at 'this hour; let him lay it down, now, for I shall not please 'him. Of the intelligent, reflecting, and educated among 'his countrymen, I have no fear; for I have ample reason 'to believe, after many delightful conversations not easily 'to be forgotten, that there are very few topics (if any) on 'which their sentiments differ materially from mine.

LONDON: 1842.

Suppressed chapter.

'I may be asked—"If you have been in any respect '"disappointed in America, and are assured beforehand '"that the expression of your disappointment will give '"offence to any class, why do you write at all?" My 'answer is, that I went there expecting greater things 'than I found, and resolved as far as in me lay to do justice 'to the country, at the expense of any (in my view) mis- 'taken or prejudiced statements that might have been 'made to its disparagement. Coming home with a cor- 'rected and sobered judgment, I consider myself no less 'bound to do justice to what, according to my best means 'of judgment, I found to be the truth.'

Why write the book at all.

Of the book for whose opening page this matter introductory was written, it will be enough merely to add that it appeared on the 18th of October; that before the close of the year four large editions had been sold; and that in my opinion it thoroughly deserved the estimate formed of it by one connected with America by the strongest social affections, and otherwise in all respects an honourable, high-minded, upright judge. 'You have been very tender,' wrote Lord Jeffrey, 'to our sensitive friends beyond sea, 'and my whole heart goes along with every word you have 'written. I think that you have perfectly accomplished 'all that you profess or undertake to do, and that the world

Jeffrey's opinion of it.

LONDON: 1842.

'has never yet seen a more faithful, graphic, amusing, 'kind-hearted narrative.'

---

Later page anticipated.

I permit myself so far to anticipate a later page as to print here a brief extract from one of the letters of the last American visit. Without impairing the interest with which the narrative of that time will be read in its proper place, I shall thus indicate the extent to which present impressions were modified by the experience of twenty-six years later. He is writing from Philadelphia on the fourteenth of January, 1868.

Experience of America in 1868.

'I see *great changes* for the better, socially. Politically, 'no. England governed by the Marylebone vestry and 'the penny papers, and England as she would be after 'years of such governing; is what I make of *that*. Socially, 'the change in manners is remarkable. There is much 'greater politeness and forbearance in all ways. . . On the 'other hand there are still provincial oddities wonderfully 'quizzical; and the newspapers are constantly expressing 'the popular amazement at "Mr. Dickens's extraordinary '"composure." They seem to take it ill that I don't 'stagger on to the platform overpowered by the spectacle 'before me, and the national greatness. They are all so 'accustomed to do public things with a flourish of trum-'pets, that the notion of my coming in to read without 'somebody first flying up and delivering an "Oration" 'about me, and flying down again and leading me in, is so 'very unaccountable to them, that sometimes they have no 'idea until I open my lips that it can possibly be Charles 'Dickens.'

# CHAPTER II.

## FIRST YEAR OF MARTIN CHUZZLEWIT.

1843.

THE Cornish trip had come off, meanwhile, with such unexpected and continued attraction for us that we were well into the third week of absence before we turned our faces homeward. Railways helped us then not much; but where the roads were inaccessible to post-horses, we walked. Tintagel was visited, and no part of mountain or sea consecrated by the legends of Arthur was left unexplored. We ascended to the cradle of the highest tower of Mount St. Michael, and descended into several mines. Land and sea yielded each its marvels to us; but of all the impressions brought away, of which some afterwards took forms as lasting as they could receive from the most delightful art, I doubt if any were the source of such deep emotion to us all as a sunset we saw at Land's-end. Stanfield knew the wonders of the Continent, the glories of Ireland were native to Maclise, I was familiar from boyhood with border and Scottish scenery, and Dickens was fresh from Niagara; but there was something in the sinking of the sun behind the Atlantic that autumn afternoon, as we viewed it together from the top of the rock projecting

CORNWALL: 1842.

A sunset at Land's-end.

CORNWALL: 1842.

farthest into the sea, which each in his turn declared to have no parallel in memory.

But with the varied and overflowing gladness of those three memorable weeks it would be unworthy now to associate only the saddened recollection of the sole survivor. 'Blessed star of morning!' wrote Dickens to Felton while yet the glow of its enjoyment was upon him. 'Such a 'trip as we had into Cornwall just after Longfellow went 'away! .. Sometimes we travelled all night, sometimes all 'day, sometimes both... Heavens! If you could have seen 'the necks of bottles, distracting in their immense varieties

C. D.'s description.

'of shape, peering out of the carriage pockets! If you 'could have witnessed the deep devotion of the post-boys, 'the wild attachment of the hostlers, the maniac glee of the 'waiters! If you could have followed us into the earthy 'old churches we visited, and into the strange caverns on 'the gloomy sea-shore, and down into the depths of mines, 'and up to the tops of giddy heights where the unspeak-'ably green water was roaring, I don't know how many 'hundred feet below! If you could have seen but one 'gleam of the bright fires by which we sat in the big 'rooms of ancient inns at night, until long after the small

A holiday party.

'hours had come and gone... I never laughed in my life 'as I did on this journey. It would have done you good to 'hear me. I was choking and gasping and bursting the 'buckle off the back of my stock, all the way. And Stan-'field got into such apoplectic entanglements that we were 'often obliged to beat him on the back with portmanteaus 'before we could recover him. Seriously, I do believe 'there never was such a trip. And they made such 'sketches, those two men, in the most romantic of our 'halting-places, that you would have sworn we had the 'Spirit of Beauty with us, as well as the Spirit of Fun.' *

CORNWALL: 1842.

Sketches by Maclise and Stanfield.

The Logan Stone, by Stanfield, was one of them; and it laughingly sketched both the charm of what was seen and the mirth of what was done, for it perched me on the top of the stone. It is historical, however, the ascent having been made; and of this and other examples of steadiness at heights which deterred the rest, as well as of a subject suggested for a painting of which Dickens became the unknown purchaser, Maclise reminded me in some pleasant allusions many years later, which, notwithstanding their tribute to my athletic achievements, the good-natured reader must forgive my printing. They complete the little picture of our trip. Something I had written to him of recent travel among the mountain scenery of the wilder coasts of Donegal had touched the chord of these old remembrances. 'As to your clambering,' he replied, 'don't I know what happened of old? Don't I still see 'the Logan Stone, and you perched on the giddy top, 'while we, rocking it on its pivot, shrank from all that 'lay concealed below! Should I ever have blundered on 'the waterfall of St. Wighton, if you had not piloted the 'way? And when we got to Land's-end, with the green 'sea far under us lapping into solitary rocky nooks where 'the mermaids live, who but you only had the courage to 'stretch over, to see those diamond jets of brightness that

Maclise to J. F.

* Printed in the *Atlantic Monthly* shortly after his death, and since collected, by Mr. James T. Fields of Boston, with several of later date addressed to himself, and much correspondence having reference to other writers, into a pleasing volume entitled *Yesterdays with Authors.*

CORNWALL: 1842.

Maclise to J. F.

'I swore then, and believe still, were the flappings of their 'tails! And don't I recall you again, sitting on the tip-top 'stone of the cradle-turret over the highest battlement 'of the castle of St. Michael's Mount, with not a ledge or 'coigne of vantage 'twixt you and the fathomless ocean 'under you, distant three thousand feet? Last, do I forget 'you clambering up the goat-path to King Arthur's castle 'of Tintagel, when, in my vain wish to follow, I grovelled 'and clung to the soil like a Caliban, and you, in the man-'ner of a tricksy spirit and stout Ariel, actually danced up 'and down before me!'

Maclise's 'Girl at 'the Wa-'terfall.'

The waterfall I led him to was among the records of the famous holiday, celebrated also by Thackeray in one of his pen-and-ink pleasantries, which were sent by both painters to the next year's Academy; and so eager was Dickens to possess this landscape by Maclise which included the likeness of a member of his family, yet so anxious that our friend should be spared the sacrifice which he knew would follow an avowal of his wish, that he bought it under a feigned name before the Academy opened, and steadily refused to take back the money which on discovery of the artifice Maclise pressed upon him.* Our friend, who already had munificently given him a charming drawing of his four eldest children to accompany him and his wife to America, had his generous way nevertheless; and, as a voluntary offering four years later, painted Mrs. Dickens on a canvas of the same size as the picture of her husband in 1839.

Portrait of Mrs. Dickens.

'Behold finally the title of the new book,' was the first

* This is mentioned in Mr. O. Driscoll's agreeable little Memoir, but supposed to refer to Maclise's portrait of Dickens.

note I had from Dickens (12th of November) after our return; 'don't lose it, for I have no copy.' Title and even story had been undetermined while we travelled, from the lingering wish he still had to begin it among those Cornish scenes; but this intention had now been finally abandoned, and the reader lost nothing by his substitution for the lighthouse or mine in Cornwall, of the Wiltshire-village forge on the windy autumn evening which opens the tale of *Martin Chuzzlewit*. Into that name he finally settled, but only after much deliberation, as a mention of his changes will show. Martin was the prefix to all, but the surname varied from its first form of Sweezleden, Sweezleback, and Sweezlewag, to those of Chuzzletoe, Chuzzleboy, Chubblewig, and Chuzzlewig; nor was Chuzzlewit chosen at last until after more hesitation and discussion. What he had sent me in his letter as finally adopted, ran thus: 'The 'Life and Adventures of Martin Chuzzlewig, his family, 'friends, and enemies. Comprising all his wills and his 'ways. With an historical record of what he did and what 'he didn't. The whole forming a complete key to the house 'of Chuzzlewig.' All which latter portion of the title was of course dropped as the work became modified, in its progress, by changes at first not contemplated; but as early as the third number he sent me the plan of 'old 'Martin's plot to degrade and punish Pecksniff,' and the difficulties he encountered in departing from other portions of his scheme were such as to render him, in his subsequent stories, more bent upon constructive care at the outset, and adherence as far as might be to any design he had formed.

Names first given to *Chuzzlewit*.

Title chosen.

LONDON: 1842.

First No. of *Chuzzlewit.*

The first number, which appeared in January 1843, had not been quite finished when he wrote to me on the 8th of December: 'The Chuzzlewit copy makes so much more 'than I supposed, that the number is nearly done. Thank 'God!' Beginning so hurriedly as at last he did, altering his course at the opening and seeing little as yet of the main track of his design, perhaps no story was ever begun by him with stronger heart or confidence. Illness kept me to my rooms for some days, and he was so eager to try the effect of Pecksniff and Pinch that he came down with the ink hardly dry on the last slip to read the manuscript to me. Well did Sydney Smith, in writing to say how very much the number had pleased him, foresee the promise there was in those characters. 'Pecksniff and 'his daughters, and Pinch, are admirable—quite first-rate 'painting, such as no one but yourself can execute!' And let me here at once remark that the notion of taking Pecksniff for a type of character was really the origin of the book; the design being to show, more or less by every person introduced, the number and variety of humours and vices that have their root in selfishness.

Sydney Smith's opinion.

Origin of the book.

Prologue to a play

Another piece of his writing that claims mention at the close of 1842 was a prologue contributed to the *Patrician's Daughter,* Mr. Westland Marston's first dramatic effort, which had attracted him by the beauty of its composition less than by the courage with which its subject had been chosen from the actual life of the time.

> 'Not light its import, and not poor its mien;
> 'Yourselves the actors, and your homes the scene.'

This was the date, too, of Mr. Browning's tragedy of the

*Blot on the 'Scutcheon*, which I took upon myself, after reading it in the manuscript, privately to impart to Dickens; and I was not mistaken in the belief that it would profoundly touch him. 'Browning's play,' he wrote (25th of November), 'has thrown me into a perfect passion 'of sorrow. To say that there is anything in its subject 'save what is lovely, true, deeply affecting, full of the best 'emotion, the most earnest feeling, and the most true and 'tender source of interest, is to say that there is no light 'in the sun, and no heat in blood. It is full of genius, 'natural and great thoughts, profound and yet simple and 'beautiful in its vigour. I know nothing that is so affect-'ing, nothing in any book I have ever read, as Mildred's 'recurrence to that "I was so young—I had no mother." 'I know no love like it, no passion like it, no moulding of 'a splendid thing after its conception, like it. And I 'swear it is a tragedy that MUST be played; and must be 'played, moreover, by Macready. There are some things 'I would have changed if I could (they are very slight, 'mostly broken lines); and I assuredly would have the 'old servant *begin his tale upon the scene*; and be taken 'by the throat, or drawn upon, by his master, in its com-'mencement. But the tragedy I never shall forget, or less 'vividly remember than I do now. And if you tell 'Browning that I have seen it, tell him that I believe 'from my soul there is no man living (and not many dead) 'who could produce such a work.—Macready likes the 'altered prologue very much.' . . . There will come a more convenient time to speak of his general literary likings, or special regard for contemporary books; but I will say now

LONDON: 1842.

MS. shown to him.

A tragedy by Browning.

Other opinions books.

LONDON: 1842.

No petty jealousies.

that nothing interested him more than successes won honestly in his own field, and that in his large and open nature there was no hiding-place for little jealousies. An instance occurs to me which may be named at once, when, many years after the present date, he called my attention very earnestly to two tales then in course of publication in *Blackwood's Magazine*, and afterwards collected under the title of *Scenes of Clerical Life*. 'Do 'read them,' he wrote. 'They are the best things I have 'seen since I began my course.'

'George 'Eliot's' first book.

Eighteen hundred and forty-three* opened with the most vigorous prosecution of his *Chuzzlewit* labour. 'I 'hope the number will be very good,' he wrote to me of number two (8th of January). 'I have been hammering 'away, and at home all day. Ditto yesterday; except for 'two hours in the afternoon, when I ploughed through 'snow half a foot deep, round about the wilds of Wil-'lesden.' For the present, however, I shall glance only briefly from time to time at his progress with the earlier portions of the story on which he was thus engaged until the midsummer of 1844. Disappointments arose in connection with it, unexpected and strange, which had im-

Accompaniments of work.

* In one of the letters to his American friend Mr. Felton there is a glimpse of Christmas sports which had escaped my memory, and for which a corner may be found here, inasmuch as these gambols were characteristic of him at the pleasant old season, and were frequently renewed in future years. 'The 'best of it is' (31 Dec. 1842) 'that Forster and I have purchased between 'us the entire stock-in-trade of a conjuror, the practice and display whereof 'is entrusted to me. . . . In those tricks which require a confederate I am 'assisted (by reason of his imperturbable good humour) by Stanfield, who 'always does his part exactly the wrong way, to the unspeakable delight of 'all beholders. We come out on a small scale to-night, at Forster's, where 'we see the old year out and the new one in.' *Atlantic Monthly*, July 1871.

Christmas sports.

Maclise. R.A. C.H.Jeens.

CHARLES DICKENS, HIS WIFE, & HER SISTER.

DRAWN BY MACLISE IN 1842.

portant influence upon him: but I reserve the mention of these for awhile, that I may speak of the leading incidents of 1843.

LONDON: 1843.

'I am in a difficulty,' he wrote (12th of February), 'and 'am coming down to you some time to-day or to-night. 'I couldn't write a line yesterday; not a word, though I 'really tried hard. In a kind of despair I started off at 'half-past two with my pair of petticoats to Richmond; 'and dined there!! Oh what a lovely day it was in 'those parts.' His pair of petticoats were Mrs. Dickens and her sister Georgina: the latter, since his return from America, having become part of his household, of which she remained a member until his death; and he had just reason to be proud of the steadiness, depth, and devotion of her friendship. In a note-book begun by him in January 1855, where, for the first time in his life, he jotted down hints and fancies proposed to be made available in future writings, I find a character sketched of which, if the whole was not suggested by his sister-in-law, the most part was applicable to her. 'She—sacrificed to 'children, and sufficiently rewarded. From a child her- 'self, always "the children" (of somebody else) to engross her. And so it comes to pass that she is never married; never herself has a child; is always devoted "to the '"children" (of somebody else); and they love her; and 'she has always youth dependent on her till her death— 'and dies quite happily." Not many days after that holiday at Richmond, a slight unstudied outline in pencil was made by Maclise of the three who formed the party there, as we all sat together; and never did a touch so

Miss Georgina Hogarth.

C. D.'s MS. note-book.

Pencil drawing by Maclise.

LONDON: 1843.

light carry with it more truth of observation. The likenesses of all are excellent; and I here preserve the drawing because nothing ever done of Dickens himself has conveyed more vividly his look and bearing at this yet youthful time. He is in his most pleasing aspect; flattered, if you will; but nothing that is known to me gives a general impression so lifelike and true of the then frank, eager, handsome face.

Help in sickness.

It was a year of much illness with me, which had ever helpful and active sympathy from him. 'Send me word 'how you are,' he wrote, two days later. 'But not so 'much for that I now write, as to tell you, peremptorily, 'that I insist on your wrapping yourself up and coming 'here in a hackney-coach, with a big portmanteau, to-'morrow. It surely is better to be unwell with a Quick 'and Cheerful (and Co) in the neighbourhood, than in 'the dreary vastness of Lincoln's-inn-fields. Here is the 'snuggest tent-bedstead in the world, and there you are 'with the drawing-room for your workshop, the Q and C 'for your pal, and "everythink in a concatenation ac-'"cordingly." I begin to have hopes of the regeneration 'of mankind after the reception of Gregory last night, 'though I have none of the *Chronicle* for not denouncing 'the villain. Have you seen the note touching my *Notes* 'in the blue and yellow?'

Q and C and Co.

A public scandal.

The first of these closing allusions was to the editor of th. ...mous *Satirist* having been hissed from the Drury-lane stage, on which he had presented himself in the character of Hamlet; and I remember with what infinite pleasure I afterwards heard Chief Justice Tindal in court, charging the jury in an action brought by this malefactor against a publican of St. Giles's for having paid men to take part in the hissing of him, avow the pride he felt in 'living in the same parish with a man of that humble 'station of life of the defendant's,' who was capable of paying money out of his own pocket to punish what he believed to be an outrage to decency. The second allusion was to a statement of the reviewer of the *American Notes* in the *Edinburgh* to the effect, that, if he had been rightly informed, Dickens had gone to America as a kind of missionary in the cause of international copyright; to which a prompt contradiction had been given in the *Times*. 'I deny it,' wrote Dickens, 'wholly. He is wrongly in-'formed; and reports, without enquiry, a piece of infor-'mation which I could only characterize by using one of 'the shortest and strongest words in the language.'

LONDON: 1843.

Tindal, C.J.

A public benefactor.

C. D. and international copyright.

The disputes that had arisen out of the American book, I may add, stretched over great part of the year. It will quite suffice, however, to say here that the ground taken by him in his letters written on the spot, and printed in my former volume, which in all the more material statements his book invited public judgment upon and which he was moved to reopen in *Chuzzlewit*, was so kept by him against all comers, that none of the counter-statements or arguments dislodged him from a square inch of it. But the controversy is dead now; and he took occasion, on his later visit to America, to write its epitaph.

American controversy.

Though I did not, to revert to his February letter, obey its cordial bidding by immediately taking up quarters with him, I soon after joined him at a cottage he rented

LONDON: 1843.

Cottage at Finchley.

in Finchley; and here, walking and talking in the green lanes as the midsummer months were coming on, his introduction of Mrs. Gamp, and the uses to which he should apply that remarkable personage, first occurred to him. In his preface to the book he speaks of her as a fair representation, at the time it was published, of the hired attendant on the poor in sickness: but he might have added that the rich were no better off, for Mrs. Gamp's original was in reality a person hired by a most distinguished friend of his own, a lady, to take charge of an invalid very dear to her; and the common habit of this nurse in the sick room, among other Gampish peculiarities, was to rub her nose along the top of the tall fender. Whether or not, on that first mention of her, I had any doubts whether such a character could be made a central figure in his story, I do not now remember; but if there were any at the time, they did not outlive the contents of the packet which introduced her to me in the flesh a few weeks after our return. 'Tell me,' he wrote from Yorkshire, where he had been meanwhile passing pleasant holiday with a friend, 'what you think of Mrs. Gamp? You'll 'not find it easy to get through the hundreds of misprints 'in her conversation, but I want your opinion at once. I 'think you know already something of mine. I mean to 'make a mark with her.' The same letter enclosed me a clever and pointed little parable in verse which he had written for an annual edited by Lady Blessington.*

Mrs. Gamp.

From whom taken.

What he will do with her.

Service for a friend.

* 'I have heard, as you have, from Lady Blessington, for whose behoof I 'have this morning penned the lines I send you herewith. But I have only 'done so to excuse myself, for I have not the least idea of their suiting her;

Another allusion in the February letter reminds me of the interest which his old work for the *Chronicle* gave him in everything affecting its credit, and that this was the year when Mr. John Black ceased to be its editor, in circumstances reviving strongly all Dickens's sympathies. 'I am deeply grieved' (3rd of May 1843) 'about 'Black. Sorry from my heart's core. If I could find him

LONDON: 1843.

Change of editorship at *Chronicle.*

Page 85 of Vol. I.

'and I hope she will send them back to you for the *Ex.*' C. D. to J. F. July 1843. The lines are quite worth preserving.

A WORD IN SEASON.

Parable in verse by C. D.

They have a superstition in the East,
  That Allah, written on a piece of paper,
Is better unction than can come of priest,
  Of rolling incense, and of lighted taper:
Holding, that any scrap which bears that name
  In any characters its front impress'd on,
Shall help the finder thro' the purging flame,
  And give his toasted feet a place to rest on.

Accordingly, they make a mighty fuss
  With every wretched tract and fierce oration,
And hoard the leaves—for they are not, like us
  A highly civilized and thinking nation:
And, always stooping in the miry ways
  To look for matter of this earthly leaven,
They seldom, in their dust-exploring days,
  Have any leisure to look up to Heaven.

So have I known a country on the earth
  Where darkness sat upon the living waters,
And brutal ignorance, and toil, and dearth
  Were the hard portion of its sons and daughters:
And yet, where they who should have oped the door
  Of charity and light, for all men's finding,
Squabbled for words upon the altar-floor,
  And rent The Book, in struggles for the binding.

The gentlest man among those pious Turks
  God's living image ruthlessly defaces;
Their best High-Churchman, with no faith in works,
  Bowstrings the Virtues in the market-places.
The Christian Pariah, whom both sects curse
  (They curse all other men, and curse each other),
Walks thro' the world, not very much the worse,
  Does all the good he can, and loves his brother.

LONDON: 1843.

Dinner to John Black.

'out, I would go and comfort him this moment.' He did find him out; and he and a certain number of us did also comfort this excellent man after a fashion extremely English, by giving him a Greenwich dinner on the 20th of May; when Dickens had arranged and ordered all to perfection, and the dinner succeeded in its purpose, as in other ways, quite wonderfully. Among the entertainers were Sheil and Thackeray, Fonblanque and Charles Buller, Southwood Smith and William Johnson Fox, Macready and Maclise, as well as myself and Dickens.

Macready bound for America.

There followed another similar celebration, in which one of these entertainers was the guest and which owed hardly less to Dickens's exertions, when, at the Star-and-garter at Richmond in the autumn, we wished Macready good-speed on his way to America. Dickens took the chair at that dinner; and with Stanfield, Maclise, and myself, was in the following week to have accompanied the great actor to Liverpool to say good-bye to him on board the Cunard ship, and bring his wife back to London after their leave-taking; when a word from our excellent friend Captain Marryat, startling to all of us except Dickens himself, struck him out of our party. Marryat thought that Macready might suffer in the States by any public mention of his having been attended on his way by the author of the *American Notes* and *Martin Chuzzlewit*, and our friend at once agreed with him. 'Your main and foremost reason,' he wrote to me, 'for doubting Marryat's judgment, I can 'at once destroy. It has occurred to me many times; I 'have mentioned the thing to Kate more than once; and 'I had intended *not* to go on board, charging Radley to

A doubt of Marryat's as to C. D.

'let nothing be said of my being in his house. I have 'been prevented from giving any expression to my fears 'by a misgiving that I should seem to attach, if I did so, 'too much importance to my own doings. But now that 'I have Marryat at my back, I have not the least hesita-'tion in saying that I am certain he is right. I have very 'great apprehensions that the *Nickleby* dedication will 'damage Macready. Marryat is wrong in supposing it is 'not printed in the American editions, for I have myself 'seen it in the shop windows of several cities. If I were 'to go on board with him, I have not the least doubt that 'the fact would be placarded all over New York, before 'he had shaved himself in Boston. And that there are 'thousands of men in America who would pick a quarrel 'with him on the mere statement of his being my friend, 'I have no more doubt than I have of my existence. You 'have only doubted Marryat because it is impossible for '*any man* to know what they are in their own country, 'who has not seen them there.'

Apprehended disservice to Macready.

This letter was written from Broadstairs, whither he had gone in August, after such help as he only could give, and never took such delight as in giving, to a work of practical humanity. Earlier in the year he had presided at a dinner for the Printers' Pension-fund, which Thomas Hood, Douglas Jerrold, and myself attended with him; and upon the terrible summer-evening accident at sea by which Mr. Elton the actor lost his life, it was mainly by Dickens's unremitting exertions, seconded admirably by Mr. Serle and warmly taken up by Mr. Elton's own profession (the most generous in the world), that ample provision

Works of charity and mercy.

Mr. Elton's family.

BROADSTAIRS: 1843.

was made for the many children. At the close of August I had news of him from his favourite watering-place, too characteristic to be omitted. The day before had been a day of 'terrific heat,' yet this had not deterred him from doing what he was too often suddenly prone to do in the midst of his hardest work. 'I performed an insane match against 'time of eighteen miles by the milestones in four hours 'and a half, under a burning sun the whole way. I could 'get' (he is writing next morning) 'no sleep at night, and 'really began to be afraid I was going to have a fever. 'You may judge in what kind of authorship-training I am 'to-day. I could as soon eat the cliff as write about any-'thing.' A few days later, however, all was well again; and another sketch from himself, to his American friend, will show his sea-side life in ordinary. 'In a bay-window 'in a one-pair sits, from nine o'clock to one, a gentleman 'with rather long hair and no neckcloth, who writes and 'grins as if he thought he were very funny indeed. At one 'he disappears, presently emerges from a bathing-machine, 'and may be seen, a kind of salmon-coloured porpoise, 'splashing about in the ocean. After that he may be viewed 'in another bay-window on the ground floor, eating a 'strong lunch; and after that, walking a dozen miles or 'so, or lying on his back in the sand reading a book. 'Nobody bothers him unless they know he is disposed to 'be talked to; and I am told he is very comfortable indeed. 'He's as brown as a berry, and they *do* say is a small 'fortune to the innkeeper who sells beer and cold punch. 'But this is mere rumour. Sometimes he goes up to 'London (eighty miles or so away), and then I'm told

Foolish match against time.

Sea-side life in ordinary.

C. D. *loq.*

'there is a sound in Lincoln's-inn-fields at night, as of 'men laughing, together with a clinking of knives and 'forks and wine-glasses.' *

MANCHESTER: 1843.

He returned to town 'for good' on Monday the 2nd of October, and from the Wednesday to the Friday of that week was at Manchester, presiding at the opening of its great Athenæum, when Mr. Cobden and Mr. Disraeli also 'assisted.' Here he spoke mainly on a matter always nearest his heart, the education of the very poor. He protested against the danger of calling a little learning dangerous; declared his preference for the very least of the little over none at all; proposed to substitute for the old a new doggerel,

Opening of the Athenæum

> Though house and lands be never got,
> Learning can give what they can *not*;

told his listeners of the real and paramount danger we had lately taken Longfellow to see in the nightly refuges of London, 'thousands of immortal creatures condemned 'without alternative or choice to tread, not what our 'great poet calls the primrose path to the everlasting bon-'fire, but one of jagged flints and stones laid down by 'brutal ignorance;' and contrasted this with the unspeakable consolation and blessings that a little knowledge had shed on men of the lowest estate and most hopeless means, 'watching the stars with Ferguson the shepherd's 'boy, walking the streets with Crabbe, a poor barber 'here in Lancashire with Arkwright, a tallow-chandler's 'son with Franklin, shoe-making with Bloomfield in his

Speech on education of the poor.

* C. D. to Professor Felton (1st Sept. 1843), in *Atlantic Monthly* for July 1871.

LONDON: 1843.

'garret, following the plough with Burns, and, high above 'the noise of loom and hammer, whispering courage in the 'ears of workers I could this day name in Sheffield and in 'Manchester.'

Ragged schools.

The same spirit impelled him to give eager welcome to the remarkable institution of Ragged schools, which, begun by a shoemaker of Southampton and a chimney-sweep of Windsor and carried on by a peer of the realm, has had results of incalculable importance to society. The year of which I am writing was its first, as this in which I write is its last; and in the interval, out of three hundred thousand children to whom it has given some sort of education, it is computed also to have given to a third of that number the means of honest employment.* 'I sent 'Miss Coutts,' he had written (24th of September), 'a 'sledge-hammer account of the Ragged schools; and as 'I saw her name for two hundred pounds in the clergy 'education subscription-list, took pains to show her that

C. D.'s interest in education.

Results of Ragged schools.

* 'After a period of 27 years, from a single school of five small infants, 'the work has grown into a cluster of some 300 schools, an aggregate of nearly '30,000 children, and a body of 3000 voluntary teachers, most of them the 'sons and daughters of toil. . . . Of more than 300,000 children which, on 'the most moderate calculation, we have a right to conclude have passed 'through these schools since their commencement, I venture to affirm that 'more than 100,000 of both sexes have been placed out in various ways, in 'emigration, in the marine, in trades, and in domestic service. For many 'consecutive years I have contributed prizes to thousands of the scholars; and 'let no one omit to call to mind what these children were, whence they came, 'and whither they were going without this merciful intervention. They would 'have been added to the perilous swarm of the wild, the lawless, the wretched, 'and the ignorant, instead of being, as by God's blessing they are, decent and 'comfortable, earning an honest livelihood, and adorning the community to 'which they belong.' *Letter of Lord Shaftesbury in the Times of the* 13*th of November* 1871.

'religious mysteries and difficult creeds wouldn't do for 'such pupils. I told her, too, that it was of immense 'importance they should be *washed*. She writes back to 'know what the rent of some large airy premises would 'be, and what the expense of erecting a regular bathing 'or purifying place; touching which points I am in cor-'respondence with the authorities. I have no doubt she 'will do whatever I ask her in the matter. She is a most 'excellent creature, I protest to God, and I have a most 'perfect affection and respect for her.'

LONDON: 1843.

A great lady's beneficence.

One of the last things he did at the close of the year, in the like spirit, was to offer to describe the Ragged schools for the *Edinburgh Review*. 'I have told Napier,' he wrote to me, 'I will give a description of them in a 'paper on education, if the *Review* is not afraid to take 'ground against the church catechism and other mere for-'mularies and subtleties, in reference to the education of 'the young and ignorant. I fear it is extremely improbable 'it will consent to commit itself so far.' His fears were well-founded; but the statements then made by him give me opportunity to add that it was his impatience of differences on this point with clergymen of the Established Church that had led him, for the past year or two, to take sittings in the Little Portland-street Unitarian chapel; for whose officiating minister, Mr. Edward Tagart, he had a friendly regard which continued long after he had ceased to be a member of his congregation. That he did so quit it, after two or three years, I can distinctly state; and of the frequent agitation of his mind and thoughts in connection with this all-important theme, there will be other

Proposed paper on Ragged schools:

Declined by *Ed. Rev.*

Unitarianism.

London: 1843.

Return to Church of England.

occasions to speak. But upon essential points he had never any sympathy so strong as with the leading doctrine and discipline of the Church of England; to these, as time went on, he found himself able to accommodate all minor differences; and the unswerving faith in Christianity itself, apart from sects and schisms, which had never failed him at any period of his life, found expression at its close in the language of his will. Twelve months before his death, these words were written. 'I direct that my name be inscribed 'in plain English letters on my tomb . . . I conjure my 'friends on no account to make me the subject of any 'monument, memorial, or testimonial whatever. I rest my 'claim to the remembrance of my country on my published 'works, and to the remembrance of my friends upon their 'experience of me in addition thereto. I commit my soul 'to the mercy of God, through our Lord and Saviour Jesus 'Christ; and I exhort my dear children humbly to try to guide themselves by the teaching of the New Testament 'in its broad spirit, and to put no faith in any man's narrow 'construction of its letter here or there.'

Language of his Will.

Active as he had been in the now ending year, and great as were its varieties of employment; his genius in its highest mood, his energy unwearied in good work, and his capacity for enjoyment without limit; he was able to signalize its closing months by an achievement supremely fortunate, which but for disappointments the year had also brought might never have been thought of. He had not begun until a week after his return from Manchester, where the fancy first occurred to him, and before the end of November he had finished, his memorable *Christmas*

*Christmas Carol.*

*Carol.* It was the work of such odd moments of leisure as were left him out of the time taken up by two numbers of his *Chuzzlewit;* and though begun with but the special design of adding something to the *Chuzzlewit* balance, I can testify to the accuracy of his own account of what befell him in its composition, with what a strange mastery it seized him for itself, how he wept over it, and laughed, and wept again, and excited himself to an extraordinary degree, and how he walked thinking of it fifteen and twenty miles about the black streets of London, many and many a night after all sober folks had gone to bed. And when it was done, as he told our friend Mr. Felton in America, he let himself loose like a madman. 'Forster 'is out again,' he added, by way of illustrating our practical comments on his celebration of the jovial old season, 'and 'if he don't go in again after the manner in which we 'have been keeping Christmas, he must be very strong indeed. Such dinings, such dancings, such conjurings, such blind-man's-buffings, such theatre-goings, such kiss- 'ings-out of old years and kissings-in of new ones, never 'took place in these parts before.'

LONDON: 1843.

Origin of *Carol.*

Practical commentary.

Yet had it been to him, this closing year, a time also of much anxiety and strange disappointments of which I am now to speak; and before, with that view, we go back for a while to its earlier months, one step into the new year may be taken for what marked it with interest and importance to him. Eighteen hundred and forty-four was but fifteen days old when a third son (his fifth child, which received the name of its godfather Francis Jeffrey) was born; and here is an answer sent by him,

An anxious time.

Third son born.

LONDON: 1843.

two days later, to an invitation from Maclise, Stanfield, and myself to dine with us at Richmond. 'DEVONSHIRE 'LODGE, *Seventeenth of January*, 1844. FELLOW COUN-'TRYMEN! The appeal with which you have honoured me, 'awakens within my breast emotions that are more easily 'to be imagined than described. Heaven bless you. I 'shall indeed be proud, my friends, to respond to such a 'requisition. I had withdrawn from Public Life—I fondly 'thought for ever—to pass the evening of my days in 'hydropathical pursuits, and the contemplation of virtue. 'For which latter purpose, I had bought a looking-glass. '—But, my friends, private feeling must ever yield to a 'stern sense of public duty. The Man is lost in the 'Invited Guest, and I comply. Nurses, wet and dry; 'apothecaries; mothers-in-law; babbies; with all the 'sweet (and chaste) delights of private life; these, my 'countrymen, are hard to leave. But you have called 'me forth, and I will come. Fellow countrymen, your 'friend and faithful servant, CHARLES DICKENS.'

Amusing letter.

## CHAPTER III.

### CHUZZLEWIT DISAPPOINTMENTS AND CHRISTMAS CAROL.

1843—1844.

*CHUZZLEWIT* had fallen short of all the expectations formed of it in regard to sale. By much the most masterly of his writings hitherto, the public had rallied to it in far less numbers than to any of its predecessors. The primary cause of this, there is little doubt, had been the change to weekly issues in the form of publication of his last two stories; for into everything in this world mere habit enters more largely than we are apt to suppose. Nor had the temporary withdrawal to America been favourable to an immediate resumption by his readers of their old and intimate relations. This also is to be added, that the excitement by which a popular reputation is kept up to the highest selling mark, will always be subject to lulls too capricious for explanation. But whatever the causes, here was the undeniable fact of a grave depreciation of sale in his writings, unaccompanied by any falling off either in themselves or in the writer's reputation. It was very temporary; but it was present, and to be dealt with accordingly. The forty and fifty thousand purchasers of *Pickwick* and *Nickleby*, the sixty and seventy thousand

LONDON: 1843.

Sale of *Chuzzlewit*:

Less than that of former books.

LONDON: 1843.

of the early numbers of the enterprize in which the *Old Curiosity Shop* and *Barnaby Rudge* appeared, had fallen to little over twenty thousand. They rose somewhat on Martin's ominous announcement, at the end of the fourth number, that he'd *go to America;* but though it was believed that this resolve, which Dickens adopted as suddenly as his hero, might increase the number of his readers, that reason influenced him less than the challenge to make good his *Notes* which every mail had been bringing him from unsparing assailants beyond the Atlantic. The substantial effect of the American episode upon the sale was yet by no means great. A couple of thousand additional purchasers were added, but the highest number at any time reached before the story closed was twenty-three thousand. Its sale, since, has ranked next after *Pickwick* and *Copperfield.*

Effect of American episode.

Publishers and authors.

We were now, however, to have a truth brought home to us which few that have had real or varied experience in such matters can have failed to be impressed by—that publishers are bitter bad judges of an author, and are seldom safe persons to consult in regard to the fate or fortunes that may probably await him. Describing the agreement for this book in September 1841, I spoke of a provision against the improbable event of its profits proving inadequate to certain necessary repayments. In this unlikely case, which was to be ascertained by the proceeds of the first five numbers, the publishers were to have power to appropriate fifty pounds a month out of the two hundred pounds payable for authorship in the expenses of each number; but though this had been introduced with my

Pages 257-8 of Vol. I.

Unlucky clause in *Chuzzlewit* agreement.

knowledge, I knew also too much of the antecedent relations of the parties to regard it as other than a mere form to satisfy the attorneys in the case. The fifth number, which landed Martin and Mark in America, and the sixth, which described their first experiences, were published; and on the eve of the seventh, in which Mrs. Gamp was to make her first appearance, I heard with infinite pain that from Mr. Hall, the younger partner of the firm which had enriched itself by *Pickwick* and *Nickleby*, and a very kind well-disposed man, there had dropped an inconsiderate hint to the writer of those books that it might be desirable to put the clause in force. It had escaped him without his thinking of all that it involved; certainly the senior partner, whatever amount of as thoughtless sanction he had at the moment given to it, always much regretted it, and made endeavours to exhibit his regret; but the mischief was done, and for the time was irreparable.

Critical time for the story.

Premature fears.

'I am so irritated,' Dickens wrote to me on the 28th of June, 'so rubbed in the tenderest part of my eyelids with 'bay-salt, by what I told you yesterday, that a wrong kind 'of fire is burning in my head, and I don't think I *can* 'write. Nevertheless, I am trying. In case I should suc'ceed, and should not come down to you this morning, 'shall you be at the club or elsewhere after dinner? I am 'bent on paying the money. And before going into the 'matter with anybody I should like you to propound from 'me the one preliminary question to Bradbury and Evans. 'It is more than a year and a half since Clowes wrote to 'urge me to give him a hearing, in case I should ever

Resentment.

Resolve to have other publishers.

LONDON: 1843.

'think of altering my plans. A printer is better than a 'bookseller, and it is quite as much the interest of one (if 'not more) to join me. But whoever it is, or whatever, 'I am bent upon paying Chapman and Hall *down*. And 'when I have done that, Mr. Hall shall have a piece of 'my mind.'

Pages 103, 141, and 201-2 of Vol. I.

What he meant by the proposed repayment will be understood by what formerly was said of his arrangements with these gentlemen on the repurchase of his early copyrights. Feeling no surprise at this announcement, I yet prevailed with him to suspend proceedings until his return from Broadstairs in October; and what then I had to say led to memorable resolves. The communication he had desired me to make to his printers had taken them too much by surprise to enable them to form a clear judgment respecting it; and they replied by suggestions which were in effect a confession of that want of confidence in themselves. They enlarged upon the great results that would follow a re-issue of his writings in a cheap form; they strongly urged such an undertaking; and they offered to invest to any desired amount in the establishment of a magazine or other periodical to be edited by him. The possible dangers, in short, incident to their assuming the position of publishers as well as printers of new works from his pen, seemed at first to be so much greater than on closer examination they were found to be, that at the outset they shrank from encountering them. And hence the remarkable letter I shall now quote (1st of November, 1843).

A proposal to his printers.

Their reception of it.

'Don't be startled by the novelty and extent of my pro- 'ject. Both startled *me* at first; but I am well assured of 'its wisdom and necessity. I am afraid of a magazine—'just now. I don't think the time a good one, or the 'chances favourable. I am afraid of putting myself before 'the town as writing tooth and nail for bread, headlong, after 'the close of a book taking so much out of one as *Chuzzle-'wit.* I am afraid I could not do it, with justice to myself. 'I know that whatever we may say at first, a new magazine, 'or a new anything, would require so much propping, that 'I should be *forced* (as in the *Clock*) to put myself into it, 'in my old shape. I am afraid of Bradbury and Evans's 'desire to force on the cheap issue of my books, or any of 'them, prematurely. I am sure if it took place yet awhile, 'it would damage me and damage the property, *enormously.* 'It is very natural in them to want it; but, since they do 'want it, I have no faith in their regarding me in any 'other respect than they would regard any other man in a 'speculation. I see that this is really your opinion as well; 'and I don't see what I gain, in such a case, by leaving 'Chapman and Hall. If I had made money, I should un-'questionably fade away from the public eye for a year, and 'enlarge my stock of description and observation by seeing 'countries new to me; which it is most necessary to me 'that I should see, and which with an increasing family I 'can scarcely hope to see at all, unless I see them now. 'Already for some time I have had this hope and inten-'tion before me; and though not having made money 'yet, I find or fancy that I can put myself in the posi-'tion to accomplish it. And this is the course I have 'before me. At the close of *Chuzzlewit* (by which time 'the debt will have been materially reduced) I purpose

His own view of his position.

Doubts as to cheap edition now.

Desire to travel again.

Page 201 of Vol. I.

LONDON: 1843.

'drawing from Chapman and Hall my share of the sub-'scription—bills, or money, will do equally well. I design 'to tell them that it is not likely I shall do anything for 'a year; that, in the meantime, I make no arrangement 'whatever with any one; and our business matters rest '*in statu quo*. The same to Bradbury and Evans. I 'shall let the house if I can; if not, leave it to be let.

A plan for seeing foreign cities.

'I shall take all the family, and two servants—three at 'most—to some place which I know beforehand to be 'CHEAP and in a delightful climate, in Normandy or 'Brittany, to which I shall go over, first, and where I shall 'rent some house for six or eight months. During that 'time, I shall walk through Switzerland, cross the Alps, 'travel through France and Italy; take Kate perhaps to 'Rome and Venice, but not elsewhere; and in short see 'everything that is to be seen. I shall write my descrip-'tions to you from time to time, exactly as I did in America; 'and you will be able to judge whether or not a new 'and attractive book may not be made on such ground.

Other books in his mind.

'At the same time I shall be able to turn over the story 'I have in my mind, and which I have a strong notion 'might be published with great advantage, *first in Paris* '—but that's another matter to be talked over. And 'of course I have not yet settled, either, whether any book 'about the travel, or this, should be the first. "All very '"well," you say, "if you had money enough." Well, but

Ways and means.

'if I can see my way to what would be necessary without 'binding myself in any form to anything; without paying 'interest, or giving any security but one of my Eagle 'five thousand pounds; you would give up that objection.

'And I stand committed to no bookseller, printer, money-'lender, banker, or patron whatever; and decidedly 'strengthen my position with my readers, instead of 'weakening it, drop by drop, as I otherwise must. Is it 'not so? and is not the way before me, plainly this? I 'infer that in reality you do yourself think, that what I 'first thought of is *not* the way? I have told you my 'scheme very baldly, as I said I would. I see its great 'points, against many prepossessions the other way—as, 'leaving England, home, friends, everything I am fond of '—but it seems to me, at a critical time, *the* step to set 'me right. A blessing on Mr. Mariotti my Italian master, 'and his pupil!—If you have any breath left, tell Topping 'how you are.'

Self-dependance.

I had certainly not much after reading this letter, written amid all the distractions of his work, with both the *Carol* and *Chuzzlewit* in hand; but such insufficient breath as was left to me I spent against the project, and in favour of far more consideration than he had given to it, before anything should be settled. 'I expected you,' he wrote next day (the 2nd of November), 'to be startled. 'If I was startled myself, when I first got this project of 'foreign travel into my head, MONTHS AGO, how much 'more must you be, on whom it comes fresh: numbering 'only hours! Still, I am very resolute upon it—very. I 'am convinced that my expenses abroad would not be 'more than half of my expenses here; the influence of 'change and nature upon me, enormous. You know, as 'well as I, that I think *Chuzzlewit* in a hundred points 'immeasurably the best of my stories. That I feel my

Objections to the scheme.

His own opinion of *Chuzzlewit*.

LONDON: 1843.

Confidence in himself.

'power now, more than I ever did. That I have a greater 'confidence in myself than I ever had. That I *know*, if I 'have health, I could sustain my place in the minds of 'thinking men, though fifty writers started up to-morrow. 'But how many readers do *not* think! How many take 'it upon trust from knaves and idiots, that one writes too 'fast, or runs a thing to death! How coldly did this very 'book go on for months, until it forced itself up in 'people's opinion, without forcing itself up in sale! If I 'wrote for forty thousand Forsters, or for forty thousand 'people who know I write because I can't help it, I should 'have no need to leave the scene. But this very book 'warns me that if I *can* leave it for a time, I had better 'do so, and must do so. Apart from that again, I feel that 'longer rest after this story would do me good. You say 'two or three months, because you have been used to see 'me for eight years never leaving off. But it is not rest 'enough. It is impossible to go on working the brain to 'that extent for ever. The very spirit of the thing, in 'doing it, leaves a horrible despondency behind, when it 'is done; which must be prejudicial to the mind, so soon 'renewed, and so seldom let alone. What would poor 'Scott have given to have gone abroad, of his own free 'will, a young man, instead of creeping there, a driveller, 'in his miserable decay! I said myself in my note to you '—anticipating what you put to me—that it was a ques'tion *what* I should come out with, first. The travel-book, 'if to be done at all, would cost me very little trouble; and 'surely would go very far to pay charges, whenever pub'lished. We have spoken of the baby, and of leaving it

Want of confidence in others.

Brainwork.

'here with Catherine's mother. Moving the children into 'France could not, in any ordinary course of things, do 'them anything but good. And the question is, what it 'would do to that by which they live: not what it would 'do to them.—I had forgotten that point in the B. and E. 'negociation; but they certainly suggested instant publi-'cation of the reprints, or at all events of some of them; 'by which of course I know, and as you point out, I could 'provide of myself what is wanted. I take that as putting 'the thing distinctly as a matter of trade, and feeling it so. 'And, as a matter of trade with them or anybody else, 'as a matter of trade between me and the public, should 'I not be better off a year hence, with the reputation of 'having seen so much in the meantime? The reason 'which induces you to look upon this scheme with dis-'like—separation for so long a time—surely has equal 'weight with me. I see very little pleasure in it, beyond 'the natural desire to have been in those great scenes; I 'anticipate no enjoyment at the time. I have come to 'look upon it as a matter of policy and duty. I have a 'thousand other reasons, but shall very soon myself be 'with you.'

LONDON: 1843.

A suggestion of his printers.

Not acceptable.

Bent on his own plan.

There were difficulties, still to be strongly urged, against taking any present step to a final resolve; and he gave way a little. But the pressure was soon renewed. 'I have 'been,' he wrote (10th of November), 'all day in *Chuzzle-'wit* agonies—conceiving only. I hope to bring forth to-'morrow. Will you come here at six? I want to say a word 'or two about the cover of the *Carol* and the advertising, 'and to consult you on a nice point in the tale. It will

Preparation of *Carol.*

LONDON: 1843.

'come wonderfully I think. Mac will call here soon after, 'and we can then all three go to Bulwer's together. And 'do, my dear fellow, do for God's sake turn over about Chap-'man and Hall, and look upon my project as *a settled thing*. 'If you object to see them, I must write to them.' My reluctance as to the question affecting his old publishers was connected with the little story, which, amid all his perturbations and troubles and '*Chuzzlewit* agonies,' he was steadily carrying to its close; and which remains a splendid proof of how thoroughly he was borne out in the assertion just before made, of the sense of his power felt by him, and his confidence that it had never been greater than when his readers were thus falling off from him. He had entrusted the *Carol* for publication on his own account, under the usual terms of commission, to the firm he had been so long associated with; and at such a moment to tell them, short of absolute necessity, his intention to quit them altogether, I thought a needless putting in peril of the little book's chances. He yielded to this argument; but the issue, as will be found, was less fortunate than I hoped.

Anxiety to change his publishers.

Counsel for delay.

Let disappointments or annoyances, however, beset him as they might, once heartily in his work and all was forgotten. His temperament of course coloured everything, cheerful or sad, and his present outlook was disturbed by imaginary fears; but it was very certain that his labours and successes thus far had enriched others more than himself, and while he knew that his mode of living had been scrupulously governed by what he believed to be his means, the first suspicion that these might be inadequate

Turning-point of his career.

LONDON: 1843.

made a change necessary to so upright a nature. It was the turning-point of his career; and the issue, though not immediately, ultimately justified him. Much of his present restlessness I was too ready myself to ascribe to that love of change in him which was always arising from his passionate desire to vary and extend his observation; but even as to this the result showed him right in believing that he should obtain decided intellectual advantage from the mere effects of such farther travel. Here indeed he spoke from experience, for already he had returned from America with wider views than when he started, and with a larger maturity of mind. The money difficulties on which he dwelt were also, it is now to be admitted, unquestionable. Beyond his own domestic expenses necessarily increasing, there were many, never-satisfied, constantly-recurring claims from family quarters, not the more easily avoidable because unreasonable and unjust; and it was after describing to me one such with great bitterness, a few days following the letter last quoted, that he thus replied on the following day (19th of November) to the comment I had made upon it. 'I was 'most horribly put out for a little while; for I had got up 'early to go at it, and was full of interest in what I had to 'do. But having eased my mind by that note to you, and 'taken a turn or two up and down the room, I went at it 'again, and soon got so interested that I blazed away till '9 last night; only stopping ten minutes for dinner! I 'suppose I wrote eight printed pages of *Chuzzlewit* yester-'day. The consequence is that I *could* finish to-day, but 'am taking it easy, and making myself laugh very much.'

Not restlessness merely.

Solid grounds for course taken.

Work and its interruptions.

LONDON: 1843-4.

The very next day, unhappily, there came to himself a repetition of precisely similar trouble in exaggerated form, and to me a fresh reminder of what was gradually settling into a fixed resolve. 'I am quite serious and sober when 'I say, that I have very grave thoughts of keeping my 'whole menagerie in Italy, three years.'

---

As to *Martin Chuzzlewit.*

Of the book which awoke such varied feelings and was the occasion of such vicissitudes of fortune, some notice is now due; and this, following still as yet my former rule, will be not so much critical as biographical. He had left for Italy before the completed tale was published, and its reception for a time was exactly what his just-quoted letter prefigures. It had forced itself up in public opinion without forcing itself up in sale. It was felt generally to be an advance upon his previous stories, and his own opinion is not to be questioned that it was in a hundred points immeasurably the best of them thus far; less upon the surface, and going deeper into springs of character. Nor would it be difficult to say, in a single word, where the excellence lay that gave it this superiority. It had brought his highest faculty into play: over and above other qualities it had given scope to his imagination; and it first expressed the distinction in this respect between his earlier and his later books. Apart wholly from this, too, his letters will have confirmed a remark already made upon the degree to which his mental power had been altogether deepened and enlarged by the effect of his visit to America.

Superiority to former books.

Defects in story.

In construction and conduct of story *Martin Chuzzlewit* is defective, character and description constituting the chief part of its strength. But what it lost as a story by the American episode it gained in the other direction; young Martin, by happy use of a bitter experience, casting off his slough of selfishness in the poisonous swamp of Eden. Dickens often confessed, however, the difficulty it had been to him to have to deal with this gap in the main course of his narrative; and I will give an instance from a letter he wrote to me when engaged upon the number in which Jonas brings his wife to her miserable home. 'I write in 'haste' (28th of July 1843), 'for I have been at work all 'day; and, it being against the grain with me to go back 'to America when my interest is strong in the other parts 'of the tale, have got on but slowly. I have a great notion 'to work out with Sydney's favourite,* and long to be at 'him again.' But obstructions of this kind with Dickens measured only and always the degree of readiness and resource with which he rose to meet them, and never had his handling of character been so masterly as in *Chuzzlewit.* The persons delineated in former books had been more agreeable, but never so interpenetrated with meanings brought out with a grasp so large, easy, and firm. As well in this as in the passionate vividness of its descriptions, the imaginative power makes itself felt. The windy autumn night, with the mad desperation of the hunted leaves and the roaring mirth of the blazing village forge; the market-day at Salisbury; the winter walk, and the coach journey to London by night; the ship voyage over the Atlantic; the stormy midnight travel before the murder,

American portions.

Handling of character.

Descriptions.

* Chuffey. Sydney Smith had written to Dickens on the appearance of his fourth number (early in April): 'Chuffey is admirable . . . . I never read a 'finer piece of writing: it is deeply pathetic and affecting.'

LONDON: 1843-4.

Imaginative insight.

the stealthy enterprise and cowardly return of the murderer; these are all instances of first-rate description, original in the design, imaginative in all the detail, and very complete in the execution. But the higher power to which I direct attention is even better discerned in the persons and dialogue. With nothing absent or abated in its sharp impressions of reality, there are more of the subtle requisites which satisfy reflection and thought. We have in this book for the most part, not only observation but the outcome of it, the knowledge as well as the fact. While we witness as vividly the life immediately passing, we are more conscious of the permanent life above and beyond it. Nothing nearly so effective therefore had yet been achieved by him. He had scrutinised as truly and satirised as keenly; but had never shown the imaginative insight with which he now sent his humour and his art into the core of the vices of the time.

News from America.

Sending me the second chapter of his eighth number on the 15th of August, he gave me the latest tidings from America. 'I gather from a letter I have had this morn-'ing that Martin has made them all stark staring raving 'mad across the water. I wish you would consider this. 'Don't you think the time has come when I ought to 'state that such public entertainments as I received in 'the States were either accepted before I went out, or in 'the first week after my arrival there; and that as soon 'as I began to have any acquaintance with the country, 'I set my face against any public recognition whatever 'but that which was forced upon me to the destruction of 'my peace and comfort—and made no secret of my real

Page 306 of Vol. I.

'sentiments.' We did not agree as to this, and the notion was abandoned; though his correspondent had not overstated the violence of the outbreak in the States when those chapters exploded upon them. But though an angry they are a good humoured and a very placable people; and, as time moved on a little, the laughter on that side of the Atlantic became quite as great as our amusement on this side, at the astonishing fun and comicality of these scenes. With a little reflection the Americans had doubtless begun to find out that the advantage was not all with us, nor the laughter wholly against them.

American anger short-lived.

Its consolations.

They had no Pecksniff at any rate. Bred in a more poisonous swamp than their Eden, of greatly older standing and much harder to be drained, Pecksniff was all our own. The confession is not encouraging to national pride, but this character is so far English, that though our countrymen as a rule are by no means Pecksniffs, the ruling weakness is to countenance and encourage the race. When people call the character exaggerated, and protest that the lines are too broad to deceive any one, they only refuse, naturally enough, to sanction in a book what half their lives is passed in tolerating if not in worshipping. Dickens, illustrating his never-failing experience of being obliged to subdue in his books what he knew to be real for fear it should be deemed impossible, had already made the remark in his preface to *Nickleby*, that the world, which is so very credulous in what professes to be true, is most incredulous in what professes to be imaginary. They agree to be deceived in a reality, and reward themselves by refusing to be deceived in a

A worse swamp than Eden.

Difficulties that attend reality.

LONDON: 1843-4.

Critical compromises.

fiction. That a great many people who might have sat for Pecksniff, should condemn him for a grotesque impossibility, as Dickens averred to be the case, was no more than might be expected. A greater danger he has exposed more usefully in showing the greater numbers, who, desiring secretly to be thought better than they are, support eagerly pretensions that keep their own in countenance, and, without being Pecksniffs, render Pecksniffs possible. All impostures would have something too suspicious or forbidding in their look if we were not prepared to meet them half way.

Toleration of imposture.

There is one thing favourable to us however, even in this view, which a French critic has lately suggested. Informing us that there are no Pecksniffs to be found in France, Mr. Taine explains this by the fact that his countrymen have ceased to affect virtue, and pretend only to vice; that a charlatan setting up morality would have no sort of following; that religion and the domestic virtues have gone so utterly to rags as not to be worth putting on for a deceitful garment; and that, no principles being left to parade, the only chance for the French modern Tartuffe is to confess and exaggerate weaknesses.

Why no Pecksniff in France.

We seem to have something of an advantage here. We require at least that the respectable homage of vice to virtue should not be omitted. 'Charity, my dear,' says our English Tartuffe, upon being bluntly called what he really is, 'when I take my chamber-candlestick to-night, remind me to be more than usually particular in praying 'for Mr. Anthony Chuzzlewit, who has done me an injus- 'tice.' No amount of self-indulgence weakens or lowers

Why Tartuffes in England.

his pious and reflective tone. 'Those are her daughters,' he remarks, making maudlin overtures to Mrs. Todgers in memory of his deceased wife. 'Mercy and Charity, Charity 'and Mercy, not unholy names I hope. She was beau-'tiful. She had a small property.' When his condition has fallen into something so much worse than maudlin that his friends have to put him to bed, they have not had time to descend the staircase when he is seen to be "fluttering" on the top landing, desiring to collect their sentiments on the nature of human life. 'Let us be moral. 'Let us contemplate existence.' He turns his old pupil out of doors in the attitude of blessing him, and when he has discharged that social duty retires to shed his personal tribute of a few tears in the back garden. No conceivable position, action, or utterance finds him without the vice in which his being is entirely steeped and saturated. Of such consummate consistency is its practice with him, that in his own house with his daughters he continues it to keep his hand in; and from the mere habit of keeping up appearances, even to himself, falls into the trap of Jonas. Thackeray used to say that there was nothing finer in rascaldom than this ruin of Pecksniff by his son-in-law at the very moment when the oily hypocrite believes himself to be achieving his masterpiece of dissembling over the more vulgar avowed ruffian. '"Jonas!" 'cried Mr. Pecksniff much affected, "I am not a diplo-'"matical character; my heart is in my hand. By far '"the greater part of the inconsiderable savings I have '"accumulated in the course of—I hope—a not disho-'"nourable or useless career, is already given, devised, or

LONDON: 1843-4.

Pecksniff and Jonas.

'"bequeathed (correct me, my dear Jonas, if I am technically wrong), with expressions of confidence which I "will not repeat; and in securities which it is unnecessary to mention; to a person whom I cannot, whom I "will not, whom I need not, name." Here he gave the 'hand of his son-in-law a fervent squeeze, as if he would 'have added, "God bless you: be very careful of it when "you get it!"'

Uncon-scious growths.

Certainly Dickens thus far had done nothing of which, as in this novel, the details were filled in with such minute and incomparable skill; where the wealth of comic circumstance was lavished in such overflowing abundance on single types of character; or where generally, as throughout the story, the intensity of his observation of individual humours and vices had taken so many varieties of imaginative form. Everything in *Chuzzlewit* indeed had grown under treatment, as will be commonly the case in the handling of a man of genius, who never knows where any given conception may lead him, out of the wealth of resource in development and incident which it has itself created. 'As to the way,' he wrote to me of its two most prominent figures, as soon as all their capabilities were revealed to him, 'As to the way in which these characters 'have opened out, that is, to me, one of the most surprising 'processes of the mind in this sort of invention. Given what 'one knows, what one does not know springs up; and I 'am as absolutely certain of its being true, as I am of the 'law of gravitation—if such a thing be possible, more so.' The remark displays exactly what in all his important characters was the very process of creation with him.

Creating by becoming organ of creation.

Nor was it in the treatment only of his present fiction, but also in its subject or design, that he had gone higher than in preceding efforts. Broadly what he aimed at, he would have expressed on the title-page if I had not dissuaded him, by printing there as its motto a verse altered from that prologue of his own composition to which I have formerly referred: 'Your homes the scene. Yourselves, 'the actors, here!' Debtors' prisons, parish Bumbledoms, Yorkshire schools, were vile enough, but something much more pestiferous was now the aim of his satire; and he had not before so decisively shown vigour, daring, or discernment of what lay within reach of his art, as in taking such a person as Pecksniff for the central figure in a tale of existing life. Setting him up as the glass through which to view the groups around him, we are not the less moved to a hearty detestation of the social vices they exhibit, and pre-eminently of selfishness in all its forms, because we see more plainly than ever that there is but one vice which is quite irremediable. The elder Chuzzlewits are bad enough, but they bring their self-inflicted punishments; the Jonases and Tigg Montagues are execrable, but the law has its halter and its penal servitude; the Moulds and Gamps have plague-bearing breaths, from which sanitary wisdom may clear us; but from the sleek, smiling, crawling abomination of a Pecksniff, there is no help but self-help. Every man's hand should be against him, for his is against every man; and, as Mr. Taine very wisely warns us, the virtues have most need to be careful that they do not make themselves panders to his vice. It is an amiable weakness to put the best face on the worst things, but there is none more

Intended motto for the story.

Grand purpose of its satire.

The vice beyond reach of law.

LONDON: 1843-4.

dangerous. There is nothing so common as the mistake of Tom Pinch, and nothing so rare as his excuses.

Tom Pinch.

The art with which that delightful character is placed at Mr. Pecksniff's elbow at the beginning of the story, and the help he gives to set fairly afloat the falsehood he innocently believes, contribute to an excellent management of this part of the design; and the same prodigal wealth of invention and circumstance which gives its higher imaginative stamp to the book, appears as vividly in its lesser as in its leading figures. There are wonderful touches of this suggestive kind in the household of Mould the undertaker; and in the vivid picture presented to us by one of Mrs. Gamp's recollections, we are transported to the youthful games of his children. 'The sweet creeturs! 'playing at berryins down in the shop, and follerin' the 'order-book to its long home in the iron safe!' The American scenes themselves are not more full of life and fun and freshness, and do not contribute more to the general hilarity, than the cockney group at Todgers's; which is itself a little world of the qualities and humours that make up the interest of human life, whether it be high or low, vulgar or fine, filled in with a master's hand. Here, in a mere byestroke as it were, are the very finest things of the earlier books superadded to the new and higher achievement that distinguished the later productions. No part indeed of the execution of this remarkable novel is inferior. Young Bailey and Sweedlepipes are in the front rank of his humorous creations; and poor Mrs. Todgers, worn but not depraved by the cares of gravy and solicitudes of her establishment, with calculation shining

Mould the undertaker.

The Todgers group.

Young Bailey and Sweedlepipes.

out of one eye but affection and goodheartedness still beaming in the other, is in her way quite as perfect a picture as even the portentous Mrs. Gamp with her grim grotesqueness, her filthy habits and foul enjoyments, her thick and damp but most amazing utterances, her moist clammy functions, her pattens, her bonnet, her bundle, and her umbrella. But such prodigious claims must have a special mention.

Mrs. Gamp.

This world-famous personage has passed into and become one with the language, which her own parts of speech have certainly not exalted or refined. To none even of Dickens's characters has there been such a run of popularity; and she will remain among the everlasting triumphs of fiction, a superb masterpiece of English humour. What Mr. Mould says of her in his enthusiasm, that she's the sort of woman one would bury for nothing, and do it neatly too, every one feels to be an appropriate tribute; and this, by a most happy inspiration, is exactly what the genius to whom she owes her existence did, when he called her into life, to the foul original she was taken from. That which enduringly stamped upon his page its most mirth-moving figure, had stamped out of English life for ever one of its disgraces. The mortal Mrs. Gamp was handsomely put into her grave, and only the immortal Mrs. Gamp survived. Age will not wither this one, nor custom stale her variety. In the latter point she has an advantage over even Mr. Pecksniff. She has a friend, an alter ego, whose kind of service to her is expressed by her first utterance in the story; and with this, which introduces her, we may leave her most fitly. '"Mrs. Harris," I says, 'at the very last case as ever

A masterpiece.

Fiction and reality.

Mrs. Harris.

LONDON: 1843-4.

'I acted in, which it was but a young person, "Mrs. '"Harris," I says, "leave the bottle on the chimley-piece, '"and don't ask me to take none, but let me put my lips '"to it when I am so dispoged." "Mrs. Gamp," she says 'in answer, "if ever there was a sober creetur to be got at '"eighteen pence a day for working people, and three and '"six for gentlefolks—night watching," said Mrs. Gamp 'with emphasis, "being a extra charge—you are that in- '"wallable person." "Mrs. Harris," I says to her, "don't '"name the charge, for if I could afford to lay all my '"fellow-creeturs out for nothink, I would gladly do it, '"sich is the love I bears 'em."' To this there is nothing to be added, except that in the person of that astonishing friend every phase of fun and comedy in the character is repeated, under fresh conditions of increased appreciation and enjoyment. By the exuberance of comic invention which gives his distinction to Mr. Pecksniff, Mrs. Gamp profits quite as much; the same wealth of laughable incident which surrounds that worthy man is upon her heaped to overflowing; but over and above this, by the additional invention of Mrs. Harris, it is all reproduced, acted over with renewed spirit, and doubled and quadrupled in her favour. This on the whole is the happiest stroke of humorous art in all the writings of Dickens.

Uses of Mrs. Gamp's friend.

---

Publication of *Christmas Carol.*

But this is a chapter of disappointments, and I have now to state, that as *Martin Chuzzlewit's* success was to seem to him at first only distant and problematical so even the prodigious immediate success of the *Christmas Carol* itself was not to be an unmitigated pleasure.

Never had little book an outset so full of brilliancy of promise. Published but a few days before Christmas, it was hailed on every side with enthusiastic greeting. The first edition of six thousand copies was sold the first day, and on the third of January 1844 he wrote to me that 'two thousand of the three printed for second 'and third editions are already taken by the trade.' But a very few weeks were to pass before the darker side of the picture came. 'Such a night as I have passed!' he wrote to me on Saturday morning the 10th of February. 'I really believed I should never get up again, until I had 'passed through all the horrors of a fever. I found the '*Carol* accounts awaiting me, and they were the cause of 'it. The first six thousand copies show a profit of £230! 'And the last four will yield as much more. I had set 'my heart and soul upon a Thousand, clear. What a 'wonderful thing it is, that such a great success should 'occasion me such intolerable anxiety and disappoint-'ment! My year's bills, unpaid, are so terrific, that all 'the energy and determination I can possibly exert will 'be required to clear me before I go abroad; which, if 'next June come and find me alive, I shall do. Good 'Heaven, if I had only taken heart a year ago! Do come 'soon, as I am very anxious to talk with you. We can 'send round to Mac after you arrive, and tell him to join 'us at Hampstead or elsewhere. I was so utterly knocked 'down last night, that I came up to the contemplation of 'all these things quite bold this morning. If I can let 'the house for this season, I will be off to some seaside 'place as soon as a tenant offers. I am not afraid, if I

LONDON: 1844.

Sale and accounts.

Unrealized hopes.

Confirmed resolves.

LONDON: 1844.

'reduce my expenses; but if I do not, I shall be ruined 'past all mortal hope of redemption.'

Results.

The ultimate result was that his publishers were changed, and the immediate result that his departure for Italy became a settled thing; but a word may be said on these *Carol* accounts before mention is made of his new publishing arrangements.* Want of judgment had

* It may interest the reader, and be something of a curiosity of literature, if I give the expenses of the first edition of 6000, and of the 7000 more which constituted the five following editions, with the profit of the remaining 2000 which completed the sale of fifteen thousand:

Publishers' accounts:

CHRISTMAS CAROL.

1st Edition, 6000 No.

| | | £ | s. | d. |
|---|---|---|---|---|
| 1843. Dec. | Printing | 74 | 2 | 9 |
| | Paper | 89 | 2 | 0 |
| | Drawings and Engravings | 49 | 18 | 0 |
| | Two Steel Plates | 1 | 4 | 0 |
| | Printing Plates | 15 | 17 | 6 |
| | Paper for do. | 7 | 12 | 0 |
| | Colouring Plates | 120 | 0 | 0 |
| | Binding | 180 | 0 | 0 |
| | Incidents and Advertising | 168 | 7 | 8 |
| | Commission | 99 | 4 | 6 |
| | | £805 | 8 | 5 |

2nd to the 7th Edition, making 7000 Copies.

| | | £ | s. | d. |
|---|---|---|---|---|
| 1844. Jan. | Printing | 58 | 18 | 0 |
| | Paper | 103 | 19 | 0 |
| | Printing Plates | 17 | 10 | 0 |
| | Paper | 8 | 17 | 4 |
| | Colouring Plates | 140 | 0 | 0 |
| | Binding | 199 | 18 | 2 |
| | Incidents and Advertising | 83 | 5 | 8 |
| | Commission | 107 | 18 | 10 |
| | | £720 | 7 | 0 |

On sale of 15,000 copies.

Two thousand more, represented by the last item in the subjoined balance, were sold before the close of the year, leaving a remainder of 70 copies.

| | | | | £ | s. | d. |
|---|---|---|---|---|---|---|
| 1843. Dec. | Balance of a/c to Mr. Dickens's credit | | | 186 | 16 | 7 |
| 1844. Jan. to April. | Do. | Do. | | 349 | 12 | 0 |
| May to Dec. | Do. | Do. | | 189 | 11 | 5 |
| | Amount of Profit on the Work | | | £726 | 0 | 0 |

LONDON: 1844.

been shown in not adjusting the expenses of production with a more equable regard to the selling price, but even as it was, before the close of the year, he had received £726 from a sale of fifteen thousand copies; and the difference between this and the amount realised by the same proportion of the sale of the successor to the *Carol*, undoubtedly justified him in the discontent now expressed. Of that second tale, as well as of the third and fourth, more than double the numbers of the *Carol* were at once sold, and of course there was no complaint of any want of success: but the truth really was, as to all the Christmas stories issued in this form, that the price charged, while too large for the public addressed by them, was too little to remunerate their outlay; and when in later years he put forth similar fancies for Christmas, charging for them fewer pence than the shillings required for these, he counted his purchasers, with fairly corresponding gains to himself, not by tens but by hundreds of thousands.*

The *Carol* profits.

Mistakes in form and price.

It was necessary now that negotiations should be resumed with his printers, but before any step was taken Messrs. Chapman and Hall were informed of his intention not to open fresh publishing relations with them after *Chuzzlewit* should have closed. Then followed deliberations and discussions, many and grave, which settled themselves at last into the form of an agreement with Messrs. Bradbury and Evans executed on the first of June 1844; by which, upon advance made to him of

Renewed negotiations with printers.

* In November 1865 he wrote to me that the sale of his Christmas fancy for that year (*Doctor Marigold's Prescriptions*) had gone up, in the first week, to 250,000.

LONDON: 1844.

Agreement with Bradbury and Evans.

£2800, he assigned to them a fourth share in whatever he might write during the next ensuing eight years, to which the agreement was to be strictly limited. There were the usual protecting clauses, but no interest was to be paid, and no obligations were imposed as to what works should be written, if any, or the form of them; the only farther stipulation having reference to the event of a periodical being undertaken whereof Dickens might be only partially editor or author, in which case his proprietorship of copyright and profits was to be two thirds instead of three fourths. There was an understanding, at the time this agreement was signed, that a successor to the *Carol* would be ready for the Christmas of 1844; but no other promise was asked or made in regard to any other book, nor had he himself decided what form to give to his experiences of Italy, if he should even finally determine to publish them at all.

Proposed periodical.

Books.

Between this agreement and his journey six weeks elapsed, and there were one or two characteristic incidents before his departure: but mention must first be interposed of the success quite without alloy that also attended the little book, and carried off in excitement and delight every trace of doubt or misgiving.

As to the *Carol*.

'Blessings on your kind heart!' wrote Jeffrey to the author of the *Carol*. 'You should be happy yourself, for 'you may be sure you have done more good by this little 'publication, fostered more kindly feelings, and prompted 'more positive acts of beneficence, than can be traced to 'all the pulpits and confessionals in Christendom since 'Christmas 1842.' 'Who can listen,' exclaimed Thackeray,

LONDON: 1844.

Jeffrey and Thackeray.

'to objections regarding such a book as this? It seems 'to me a national benefit, and to every man or woman who 'reads it a personal kindness.' Such praise expressed what men of genius felt and said; but the small volume had other tributes, less usual and not less genuine. There poured upon its author daily, all through that Christmas time, letters from complete strangers to him which I remember reading with a wonder of pleasure; not literary at all, but of the simplest domestic kind; of which the general burden was to tell him, amid many confidences about their homes, how the *Carol* had come to be read aloud there, and was to be kept upon a little shelf by itself, and was to do them all no end of good. Anything more to be said of it will not add much to this.

Letters from strangers.

Message of the little book.

There was indeed nobody that had not some interest in the message of the *Christmas Carol*. It told the selfish man to rid himself of selfishness; the just man to make himself generous; and the good-natured man to enlarge the sphere of his good nature. Its cheery voice of faith and hope, ringing from one end of the island to the other, carried pleasant warning alike to all, that if the duties of Christmas were wanting no good could come of its outward observances; that it must shine upon the cold hearth and warm it, and into the sorrowful heart and comfort it; that it must be kindness, benevolence, charity, mercy, and forbearance, or its plum pudding would turn to bile, and its roast beef be indigestible.* Nor could

* A characteristic letter of this date, which will explain itself, has been kindly sent to me by the gentleman it was written to, Mr. James Verry Staples, of Bristol:—'Third of April, 1844. I have been very much gratified

LONDON: 1844.

C. D. identified with Christmas.

any man have said it with the same appropriateness as Dickens. What was marked in him to the last was manifest now. He had identified himself with Christmas fancies. Its life and spirits, its humour in riotous abundance, of right belonged to him. Its imaginations as well as kindly thoughts, were his; and its privilege to light up with some sort of comfort the squalidest places, he had made his own. Christmas Day was not more social or welcome: New Year's Day not more new: Twelfth Night not more full of characters. The duty of diffusing enjoyment had never been taught by a more abundant, mirthful, thoughtful, ever-seasonable writer.

Old nursery tales in higher form.

Something also is to be said of the spirit of the book, and of the others that followed it, which will not anticipate special allusions to be made hereafter. No one was more intensely fond than Dickens of old nursery tales, and he had a secret delight in feeling that he was here only giving them a higher form. The social and manly virtues he desired to teach, were to him not less the charm of the ghost, the goblin, and the fairy fancies of his childhood; however rudely set forth in those earlier days. What now were to be conquered were the more formidable

'by the receipt of your interesting letter, and I assure you that it would have 'given me heartfelt satisfaction to have been in your place when you read my 'little *Carol* to the Poor in your neighbourhood. I have great faith in the 'poor; to the best of my ability I always endeavour to present them in a 'favourable light to the rich; and I shall never cease, I hope, until I die, 'to advocate their being made as happy and as wise as the circumstances of 'their condition, in its utmost improvement, will admit of their becoming. I 'mention this to assure you of two things. Firstly, that I try to deserve their 'attention; and secondly, that any such marks of their approval and confi'dence as you relate to me are most acceptable to my feelings, and go at once 'to my heart.'

dragons and giants which had their places at our own hearths, and the weapons to be used were of a finer than the 'ice-brook's temper.' With brave and strong restraints, what is evil in ourselves was to be subdued; with warm and gentle sympathies, what is bad or unreclaimed in others was to be redeemed; the Beauty was to embrace the Beast, as in the divinest of all those fables; the star was to rise out of the ashes, as in our much-loved Cinderella; and we were to play the Valentine with our wilder brothers, and bring them back with brotherly care to civilization and happiness. Nor is it to be doubted, I think, that, in that largest sense of benefit, great public and private service was done; positive, earnest, practical good; by the extraordinary popularity, and nearly universal acceptance, which attended these little holiday volumes. They carried to countless firesides, with new enjoyment of the season, better apprehension of its claims and obligations; they mingled grave with glad thoughts, much to the advantage of both; what seemed almost too remote to meddle with they brought within reach of the charities, and what was near they touched with a dearer tenderness; they comforted the generous, rebuked the sordid, cured folly by kindly ridicule and comic humour, and, saying to their readers *Thus you have done, but it were better Thus,* may for some have realised the philosopher's famous experience, and by a single fortunate thought revised the whole manner of a life. Criticism here is a second-rate thing, and the reader may be spared such discoveries as it might have made in regard to the *Christmas Carol.*

**LONDON: 1844.**

**New faces to familiar friends.**

**Something better than literature.**

# CHAPTER IV.

## YEAR OF DEPARTURE FOR ITALY.

1844.

LONDON: 1844.

AND now, before accompanying Dickens on his Italian travel, one or two parting incidents will receive illustration from his letters. A thoughtful little poem written during the past summer for Lady Blessington has been quoted on a previous page: and it may remind me to say here what warmth of regard he had for her, and for all the inmates of Gore-house; how uninterruptedly joyous and pleasurable were his associations with them; and what valued help they now gave in his preparations for Italy. The poem, as we have seen, was written during a visit made in Yorkshire to the house of Mr. Smithson, already named as the partner of his early companion, Mr. Mitton; and this visit he repeated in sadder circumstances during the present year, when (April 1844) he attended Mr. Smithson's funeral. With members or connections of the family of this friend, his intercourse long continued.

Gore-house.

Yorkshire friends.

In the previous February, on the 26th and 28th respectively, he had taken the chair at two great meetings, in Liverpool of the Mechanics' Institution, and in Birmingham of the Polytechnic Institution, to which reference is made by him in a letter of the 21st. I quote the

Liverpool and Birmingham Institutes.

allusion because it shows thus early the sensitive regard to his position as a man of letters, and his scrupulous consideration for the feelings as well as interest of the class, which he manifested in many various and often greatly self-sacrificing ways all through his life. 'Advise me on 'the following point. And as I must write to-night, having 'already lost a post, advise me by bearer. This Liverpool 'Institution, which is wealthy and has a high grammar-'school the masters of which receive in salaries upwards 'of £2000 a year (indeed its extent horrifies me; I am 'struggling through its papers this morning), writes me 'yesterday by its secretary a business letter about the 'order of the proceedings on Monday; and it begins thus. '"I beg to send you prefixed, with the best respects of our '"committee, a bank order for twenty pounds in payment '"of the expenses contingent on your visit to Liverpool." '—And there, sure enough, it is. Now my impulse was, '*and is*, decidedly to return it. Twenty pounds is not of 'moment to me; and any sacrifice of independence is worth 'it twenty times' twenty times told. But haggling in my 'mind is a doubt whether that would be proper, and not 'boastful (in an inexplicable way); and whether as an 'author, I have a right to put myself on a basis which the 'professors of literature in other forms *connected with the* '*Institution* cannot afford to occupy. Don't you see? 'But of course you do. The case stands thus. The Man-'chester Institution, being in debt, appeals to me as it 'were *in formâ pauperis*, and makes no such provision 'as I have named. The Birmingham Institution, just 'struggling into life with great difficulty, applies to me

A question of receiving payment.

Sensitive for his calling.

LONDON: 1844.

'on the same grounds. But the Leeds people (thriving) 'write to me, making the expenses a distinct matter of 'business; and the Liverpool, as a point of delicacy, say 'nothing about it to the last minute, and then send the 'money. Now, what in the name of goodness ought I 'to do?—I am as much puzzled with the cheque as 'Colonel Jack was with his gold. If it would have settled 'the matter to put it in the fire yesterday, I should cer-'tainly have done it. Your opinion is requested. I think 'I shall have grounds for a very good speech at Brum-'magem; but I am not sure about Liverpool: having 'misgivings of over-gentility.' My opinion was clearly for sending the money back, which accordingly was done.

A troublesome cheque.

Both speeches, duly delivered to enthusiastic listeners at the places named, were good, and both, with suitable variations, had the same theme: telling his popular audience in Birmingham that the principle of their institute, education comprehensive and unsectarian, was the only safe one, for that without danger no society could go on punishing men for preferring vice to virtue without giving them the means of knowing what virtue was; and reminding his genteeler audience in Liverpool, that if happily they had been themselves well taught, so much the more should they seek to extend the benefit to all, since, whatever the precedence due to rank, wealth, or intellect, there was yet a nobility beyond them, expressed unaffectedly by the poet's verse and in the power of education to confer.

Education speeches: in Birmingham: in Liverpool.

Howe'er it be, it seems to me,
'Tis only noble to be good:
True hearts are more than coronets,
And simple faith than Norman blood.

He underwent some suffering, which he might have spared himself, at his return. 'I saw the *Carol* last night,' he wrote to me of a dramatic performance of the little story at the Adelphi. 'Better than usual, and Wright 'seems to enjoy Bob Cratchit, but *heart-breaking* to me. 'Oh Heaven! if any forecast of *this* was ever in my mind! 'Yet O. Smith was drearily better than I expected. It is a 'great comfort to have that kind of meat under done; and 'his face is quite perfect.' Of what he suffered from these adaptations of his books, multiplied remorselessly at every theatre, I have forborne to speak, but it was the subject of complaint with him incessantly; and more or less satisfied as he was with individual performances, such as Mr. Yates's Quilp or Mantalini and Mrs. Keeley's Smike or Dot, there was only one, that of Barnaby Rudge by the Miss Fortescue who became afterwards Lady Gardner, on which I ever heard him dwell with a thorough liking. It is true that to the dramatizations of his next and other following Christmas stories he gave help himself; but, even then, all such efforts to assist special representations were mere attempts to render more tolerable what he had no power to prevent, and, with a few rare exceptions, they were never very successful. Another and graver wrong was the piracy of his writings, every one of which had been reproduced with merely such colourable changes of title, incidents, and names of characters, as were believed to be sufficient to evade the law and adapt them to 'penny' purchasers. So shamelessly had this been going on ever since the days of *Pickwick*, in so many outrageous ways*

LONDON: 1844.

*Carol* at the Adelphi.

Sufferings from stage-adaptations.

His own share in them.

Wrongs from piracy.

* In a letter on the subject of copyright published by Thomas Hood after

LONDON: 1844.

Proceedings in Chancery.

and with all but impunity, that a course repeatedly urged by Talfourd and myself was at last taken in the present year with the *Christmas Carol* and the *Chuzzlewit* pirates. Upon a case of such peculiar flagrancy, however, that the vice-chancellor would not even hear Dickens's counsel; and what it cost our dear friend Talfourd to suppress his speech exceeded by very much the labour and pains with which he had prepared it. 'The pirates,' wrote Dickens to me, after leaving the court on the 18th of January, 'are 'beaten flat. They are bruised, bloody, battered, smashed,

Judge and counsel.

'squelched, and utterly undone. Knight Bruce would not 'hear Talfourd, but instantly gave judgment. He had in-'terrupted Anderdon constantly by asking him to produce 'a passage which was not an expanded or contracted idea 'from my book. And at every successive passage he cried 'out, "That is Mr. Dickens's case. Find another!" He 'said that there was not a shadow of doubt upon the 'matter. That there was no authority which would bear 'a construction in their favour; the piracy going beyond 'all previous instances. They might mention it again in 'a week, he said, if they liked, and might have an issue if 'they pleased; but they would probably consider it un-'necessary after that strong expression of his opinion. Of

End of Chancery suit.

'course I will stand by what we have agreed as to the only 'terms of compromise with the printers. I am determined

A pirate's plea.

Dickens's return from America, he described what had passed between himself and one of these pirates who had issued a Master Humphrey's Clock edited by Bos. 'Sir,' said the man to Hood, 'if you had observed the name, it was '*Bos*, not *Boz*; s, sir, not z; and, besides, it would have been no piracy, sir, 'even with the z, because *Master Humphrey's Clock*, you see, sir, was not 'published as by Boz, but by Charles Dickens!'

'that I will have an apology for their affidavits. The other 'men may pay their costs and get out of it, but I will 'stick to my friend the author.' Two days later he wrote: 'The farther affidavits put in by way of extenuation by 'the printing rascals *are* rather strong, and give one a 'pretty correct idea of what the men must be who hold on 'by the heels of literature. Oh! the agony of Talfourd at 'Knight Bruce's not hearing him! He had sat up till 'three in the morning, he says, preparing his speech; and 'would have done all kinds of things with the affidavits. 'It certainly was a splendid subject. We have heard 'nothing from the vagabonds yet. I once thought of print-'ing the affidavits without a word of comment, and sewing 'them up with *Chuzzlewit*. Talfourd is strongly disinclined 'to compromise with the printers on any terms. In which 'case it would be referred to the master to ascertain what 'profits had been made by the piracy, and to order the 'same to be paid to me. But wear and tear of law is my 'consideration.' The undertaking to which he had at last to submit was, that upon ample public apology, and payment of all costs, the offenders should be let go; but the real result was that, after infinite vexation and trouble, he had himself to pay all the costs incurred on his own behalf; and, a couple of years later, upon repetition of the wrong he had suffered in so gross a form that proceedings were again advised by Talfourd and others, he wrote to me from Switzerland the condition of mind to which his experience had brought him. 'My feeling about the —— 'is the feeling common, I suppose, to three fourths of the 'reflecting part of the community in our happiest of all

LONDON: 1844.

Hangers-on of literature.

Wear and tear of law.

Result of Chancery experience.

LONDON: 1844.

Never again to resort to it.

'possible countries; and that is, that it is better to suffer 'a great wrong than to have recourse to the much greater 'wrong of the law. I shall not easily forget the expense, 'and anxiety, and horrible injustice of the *Carol* case, 'wherein, in asserting the plainest right on earth, I was 'really treated as if I were the robber instead of the 'robbed. Upon the whole, I certainly would much rather 'NOT proceed. What do you think of sending in a grave 'protest against what has been done in this case, on account 'of the immense amount of piracy to which I am daily ex'posed, and because I have been already met in the court 'of chancery with the legal doctrine that silence under 'such wrongs barred my remedy: to which Talfourd's 'written opinion might be appended as proof that we 'stopped under no discouragement. It is useless to affect 'that I don't know I have a morbid susceptibility of ex'asperation to which the meanness and badness of the 'law in such a matter would be stinging in the last degree. 'And I know of nothing that *could* come, even of a suc'cessful action, which would be worth the mental trouble 'and disturbance it would cost.' *

Piracy preferred.

A confession.

* The reader may be amused if I add in a note what he said of the pirates in those earlier days when grave matters touched him less gravely. On the eve of the first number of *Nickleby* he had issued a proclamation. 'Whereas we 'are the only true and lawful Boz. And whereas it hath been reported to us, 'who are commencing a new work, that some dishonest dullards resident in 'the by-streets and cellars of this town impose upon the unwary and cre'dulous, by producing cheap and wretched imitations of our delectable works. 'And whereas we derive but small comfort under this injury from the know'ledge that the dishonest dullards aforesaid cannot, by reason of their mental 'smallness, follow near our heels, but are constrained to creep along by dirty 'and little-frequented ways, at a most respectful and humble distance behind. 'And whereas, in like manner, as some other vermin are not worth the killing

Proclamation on the eve of *Nickleby*.

A few notes of besetting temptations during his busiest days at *Chuzzlewit*, one taken from each of the first four months of the year when he was working at its masterly closing scenes, will amusingly exhibit, side by side, his powers of resistance and capacities of enjoyment. 'I had 'written you a line' (16th of January), 'pleading Jonas 'and Mrs. Gamp, but this frosty day tempts me sorely. I 'am distractingly late; but I look at the sky, think of 'Hampstead, and feel hideously tempted. Don't come 'with Mac, and fetch me. I couldn't resist if you did.' In the next (18th of February), he is not the tempted, but the tempter. 'Stanfield and Mac have come in, 'and we are going to Hampstead to dinner. I leave 'Betsey Prig as you know, so don't you make a scruple 'about leaving Mrs. Harris. We shall stroll leisurely up, to 'give you time to join us, and dinner will be on the table 'at Jack Straw's at four.... In the very improbable (surely 'impossible?) case of your not coming, we will call on you

Reliefs to work.

The tempted.

The tempter.

'for the sake of their carcases, so these kennel pirates are not worth the 'powder and shot of the law, inasmuch as whatever damages they may com-'mit they are in no condition to pay any. This is to give notice, that we 'have at length devised a mode of execution for them, so summary and ter-'rible, that if any gang or gangs thereof presume to hoist but one shred of 'the colours of the good ship *Nickleby*, we will hang them on gibbets so lofty 'and enduring that their remains shall be a monument of our just vengeance 'to all succeeding ages; and it shall not lie in the power of any lord high 'admiral, on earth, to cause them to be taken down again.' The last paragraph of the proclamation informed the potentates of Paternoster-row, that from the then ensuing day of the thirtieth of March, until farther notice, 'we shall hold our Levees, as heretofore, on the last evening but one of every 'month, between the hours of seven and nine, at our Board of Trade, number 'one hundred and eighty-six in the Strand, London; where we again request 'the attendance (in vast crowds) of their accredited agents and ambassadors. 'Gentlemen to wear knots upon their shoulders; and patent cabs to draw up 'with their doors towards the grand entrance, for the convenience of loading.'

Warning to pirates.

Invitation to booksellers.

LONDON: 1844.

'at a quarter before eight, to go to the ragged school.' The next (5th of March) shows him in yielding mood, and pitying himself for his infirmity of compliance. 'Sir, 'I will—he—he—he—he—he—he—I will NOT eat with 'you, either at your own house or the club. But the 'morning looks bright, and a walk to Hampstead would 'suit me marvellously. If you should present yourself at 'my gate (bringing the R. A.'s along with you) I shall 'not be sapparized. So no more at this writing from Poor 'MR. DICKENS.' But again the tables are turned, and he is tempter in the last; written on that Shakespeare day (23rd of April) which we kept always as a festival, and signed in character expressive of his then present unfitness for any of the practical affairs of life, including the very pressing business which at the moment ought to have occupied him, namely, attention to the long deferred nuptials of Miss Charity Pecksniff. 'November blasts! Why 'it's the warmest, most genial, most intensely bland, de'licious, growing, springy, songster-of-the-grovy, bursting'forth-of-the-buddy, day as ever was. At half-past four I 'shall expect you. Ever, MODDLE.'

Shakespeare-day.

A favourite bit of humour:

Moddle, the sentimental noodle hooked by Miss Pecksniff who flies on his proposed wedding-day from the frightful prospect before him, the reader of course knows; and has perhaps admired for his last supreme outbreak of common sense. It was a rather favourite bit of humour with Dickens; and I find it pleasant to think that he never saw the description given of it by a trained and skilful French critic, who has been able to pass under his review the whole of English literature without any apparent sense or understanding of one of its most important as well as richest elements. A man without the perception of humour taking English prose literature in hand, can of course set about it only in one way. Accordingly, in Mr. Taine's decisive judgments of our last great humourist, which proceed upon a principle of psychological analysis which it is only fair to say he applies impartially to everybody, *Pickwick, Oliver Twist,* and *The Old Curiosity Shop* are not in any manner even named or alluded to; Mrs. Gamp is only once mentioned as always talking of Mrs. Harris; and Mr. Micawber also only once as using always the same emphatic phrases; the largest extracts are taken from the two books in all the Dickens series that are weakest on the humorous side, *Hard Times* and the *Chimes; Nickleby,* with its many laughter-moving figures, is dismissed in a line and a half; Mr. Toots, Captain Cuttle, Susan Nipper, Toodles, and the rest have no place in what is said of *Dombey;* and, to close with what has caused and must excuse my digression, Mr. Augustus Moddle is introduced as a gloomy maniac who makes us laugh and makes us shudder, and as drawn so truly for a madman that though at first sight agreeable, he is in reality horrible! *

criticized without humour.

M. Henri Taine on C. D.

Moddle as a maniac.

* This might seem not very credible if I did not give the passage literally, and I therefore quote it from the careful translation of *Taine's History of English Literature* by Mr. Van Laun, one of the masters of the Edinburgh Academy, where I will venture to hope that other authorities on English Literature are at the same time admitted. 'Jonas' (also in *Chuzzlewit*) 'is on the verge 'of madness. There are other characters quite mad. Dickens has drawn 'three or four portraits of madmen, very agreeable at first sight, but so true 'that they are in reality horrible. It needed an imagination like his, ir'regular, excessive, capable of fixed ideas, to exhibit the derangements of 'reason. Two especially there are, which make us laugh, and which make

Taine on English literature.

LONDON: 1844.

A month before the letter subscribed by Dickens in the character, so happily unknown to himself, of this gloomy maniac, he had written to me from amidst his famous chapter in which the tables are turned on Pecksniff; but here I quote the letter chiefly for noticeable words at its close. 'I heard from Macready by the 'Hibernia. I have been slaving away regularly, but the 'weather is against rapid progress. I altered the verbal 'error, and substituted for the action you didn't like some 'words expressive of the hurry of the scene. Mac'ready sums up slavery in New Orleans in the way of 'a gentle doubting on the subject, by a "but" and a 'dash. I believe it is in New Orleans that the man is 'lying under sentence of death, who, not having the fear 'of God before his eyes, did not deliver up a captive slave 'to the torture? The largest gun in that country has not 'burst yet—*but it will.* Heaven help us, too, from 'explosions nearer home! I declare I never go into 'what is called "society" that I am not aweary of it, 'despise it, hate it, and reject it. The more I see of its 'extraordinary conceit, and its stupendous ignorance of what is passing out of doors, the more certain I am that 'it is approaching the period when, being incapable of 'reforming itself, it will have to submit to be reformed 'by others off the face of the earth.' Thus we see that

Macready in New Orleans.

Slavery in America.

Society in England.

'us shudder. Augustus, the gloomy maniac, who is on the point of marry'ing Miss Pecksniff; and poor Mr. Dick, half an idiot, half a monomaniac, 'who lives with Miss Trotwood . . . . The play of these shattered reasons 'is like the creaking of a dislocated door; it makes one sick to hear it.' (Vol. ii. p. 346.) The original was published before Dickens's death, but he certainly never saw it.

the old radical leanings were again rather strong in him at present, and I may add that he had found occasional recent vent for them by writing in the *Morning Chronicle*.

Writing in the *Chronicle*.

Some articles thus contributed by him having set people talking, the proprietors of the paper rather eagerly mooted the question what payment he would ask for contributing regularly; and ten guineas an article was named. Very sensibly, however, the editor who had succeeded his old friend Black pointed out to him, that though even that sum would not be refused in the heat of the successful articles just contributed, yet (I quote his own account in a letter of the 7th of March 1844) so much would hardly be paid continuously; and thereupon an understanding was come to, that he would write as a volunteer and leave his payment to be adjusted to the results. 'Then said the 'editor—and this I particularly want you to turn over in 'your mind, at leisure—supposing me to go abroad, could 'I contemplate such a thing as the writing of a letter 'a week under any signature I chose, with such scraps 'of descriptions and impressions as suggested themselves 'to my mind? If so, would I do it for the *Chronicle*? 'And if so again, what would I do it for? He thought 'for such contributions Easthope would pay anything. 'I told him that the idea had never occurred to me; but 'that I was afraid he did not know what the value of such 'contributions would be. He repeated what he had said 'before; and I promised to consider whether I could 'reconcile it to myself to write such letters at all. The 'pros and cons need to be very carefully weighed. I will 'not tell you to which side I incline, but if we should

Conference with its new editor.

Proposal to write letters from abroad.

LONDON: 1844.

'disagree, or waver on the same points, we will call 'Bradbury and Evans to the council. I think it more 'than probable that we shall be of exactly the same 'mind, but I want you to be in possession of the facts and 'therefore send you this rigmarole.' The rigmarole is not unimportant; because, though we did not differ on the wisdom of saying No to the *Chronicle*, the 'council' spoken of was nevertheless held, and in it lay the germ of another newspaper enterprise he permitted himself to engage in twelve months later, to which he would have done more wisely to have also answered No.

Doubts as to newspaper writing.

Preparations for departure.

The preparation for departure was now actively going forward, and especially his enquiries for two important adjuncts thereto, a courier and a carriage. As to the latter it occurred to him that he might perhaps get for little money 'some good old shabby devil of a coach—one 'of those vast phantoms that hide themselves in a corner 'of the Pantechnicon;' and exactly such a one he found there; sitting himself inside it, a perfect Sentimental Traveller, while the managing man told him its history. 'As for comfort—let me see—it is about the size of your 'library; with night-lamps and day-lamps and pockets 'and imperials and leathern cellars, and the most extraor-'dinary contrivances. Joking apart, it is a wonderful 'machine. And when you see it (if you *do* see it) you will 'roar at it first, and will then proclaim it to be "perfectly '"brilliant, my dear fellow."' It was marked sixty pounds; he got it for five-and-forty; and my own emotions respecting it he had described by anticipation quite correctly. In finding a courier he was even more

Travelling carriage.

Courier.

fortunate; and these successes were followed by a third apparently very promising, but in the result less satisfactory. His house was let to not very careful people.

LONDON: 1844.

The tenant having offered herself for Devonshire-terrace unexpectedly, during the last week or two of his stay in England he went into temporary quarters in Osnaburgh-terrace; and here a domestic difficulty befell of which the mention may be amusing, when I have disposed of an incident that preceded it too characteristic for omission. The Mendicity Society's officers had caught a notorious begging-letter writer, had identified him as an old offender against Dickens of which proofs were found on his person, and had put matters in train for his proper punishment; when the wretched creature's wife made such appeal before the case was heard at the police-court, that Dickens broke down in his character of prosecutor, and at the last moment, finding what was said of the man's distress at the time to be true, relented. 'When the Mendicity officers themselves told me 'the man was in distress, I desired them to suppress what 'they knew about him, and slipped out of the bundle (in 'the police office) his first letter, which was the greatest 'lie of all. For he looked wretched, and his wife had been 'waiting about the street to see me, all the morning. It 'was an exceedingly bad case however, and the imposition, 'all through, very great indeed. Insomuch that I could not '*say* anything in his favour, even when I saw him. Yet I 'was not sorry that the creature found the loophole for escape. 'The officers had taken him illegally without any warrant; 'and really they messed it all through, quite facetiously.'

In temporary quarters.

Page 205 of Vol. I.

Begging-letter case.

He will himself also best relate the small domestic diffi-

LONDON: 1844.

culty into which he fell in his temporary dwelling, upon his unexpectedly discovering it to be unequal to the strain of a dinner party for which invitations had gone out just before the sudden 'let' of Devonshire-terrace. The letter is characteristic in other ways, or I should hardly have gone so far into domesticities here; and it enables me to add that with the last on its list of guests, Mr. Chapman the chairman of Lloyd's, he held much friendly intercourse, and that few things more absurd or unfounded have been invented, even of Dickens, than that he found any part of the original of Mr. Dombey in the nature, the appearance, or the manners of this estimable gentleman. 'Advise, advise,' he wrote (9 Osnaburgh-terrace, 28th of May 1844), 'advise 'with a distracted man. Investigation below stairs renders 'it, as my father would say, "manifest to any person of or-'"dinary intelligence, if the term may be considered allow-'"able," that the Saturday's dinner cannot come off here 'with safety. It would be a toss-up, and might come down 'heads, but it would put us into an agony with that kind of 'people .. Now, I feel a difficulty in dropping it altogether, 'and really fear that this might have an indefinably sus-'picious and odd appearance. Then said I at breakfast this 'morning, I'll send down to the Clarendon. Then says Kate, 'have it at Richmond. Then I say, that might be inconve-'nient to the people. Then she says, how could it be if we 'dine late enough? Then I am very much offended with-'out exactly knowing why; and come up here, in a state of 'hopeless mystification .. What do you think? Ellis would 'be quite as dear as anybody else; and unless the weather 'changes, the place is objectionable. I must make up my

A family difficulty.

The farewell dinner-party.

'mind to do one thing or other, for we shall meet Lord 'Denman at dinner to-day. Could it be dropped decently? 'That, I think very doubtful. Could it be done for a couple 'of guineas apiece at the Clarendon?.. In a matter of more 'importance I could make up my mind. But in a matter of 'this kind I bother and bewilder myself, and come to no 'conclusion whatever. Advise! Advise!.. List of the In-'vited. There's Lord Normanby. And there's Lord Den-'man. There's Easthope, wife, and sister. There's Sydney 'Smith. There's you and Mac. There's Babbage. There's 'a Lady Osborne and her daughter. There's Southwood 'Smith. And there's Quin. And there are Thomas Chapman 'and his wife. So many of these people have never dined 'with us, that the fix is particularly tight. Advise! Advise!' My advice was for throwing over the party altogether, but additional help was obtained and the dinner went off very pleasantly. It was the last time we saw Sydney Smith.

Bothered and bewildered.

The Invited.

Of one other characteristic occurrence he wrote before he left; and the very legible epigraph round the seal of his letter, 'It is particularly requested that if Sir James 'Graham should open this, he will not trouble himself to 'seal it again,' expresses both its date and its writer's opinion of a notorious transaction of the time. 'I wish' (28th of June) 'you would read this, and give it me again 'when we meet at Stanfield's to-day. Newby has written 'to me to say that he hopes to be able to give Overs more 'money than was agreed on.' The enclosure was the proof-sheet of a preface written by him to a small collection of stories by a poor carpenter dying of consumption, who hoped by their publication, under protection of such a

Letter-opening.

'The Evenings of a Working-man.'

LONDON: 1844.

Doctor Elliotson.

name, to leave behind him some small provision for his ailing wife and little children.* The book was dedicated to the kind physician, Doctor Elliotson, whose name was for nearly thirty years a synonym with us all for unwearied, self-sacrificing, beneficent service to every one in need.

Greenwich dinner.

The last incident before Dickens's departure was a farewell dinner to him at Greenwich, which took also the form of a celebration for the completion of *Chuzzlewit*, or, as the Ballantynes used to call it in Scott's case, a christening dinner; when Lord Normanby took the chair, and I remember sitting next the great painter Turner, who had come with Stanfield, and had enveloped his throat, that sultry summer day, in a huge red belcher-handkerchief which nothing would induce him to remove. He was not otherwise demonstrative, but enjoyed himself in a quiet silent way, less perhaps at the speeches than at the changing lights on the river. Carlyle did not come; telling me in his reply to the invitation that he truly loved Dickens, having discerned in the inner man of him a real music of the genuine kind, but that he'd rather testify to this in some other form than that of dining out in the dogdays.

J. M. W. Turner.

Death of John Overs.

* He wrote from Marseilles (17th Dec. 1844). 'When poor Overs was dying 'he suddenly asked for a pen and ink and some paper, and made up a little 'parcel for me which it was his last conscious act to direct. She (his wife) 'told me this and gave it me. I opened it last night. It was a copy of his 'little book in which he had written my name, "With his devotion." I 'thought it simple and affecting of the poor fellow.' From a later letter a few lines may be added. 'Mrs. Overs tells me' (Monte Vacchi, 30th March, 1845) 'that Miss Coutts has sent her, at different times, sixteen pounds, has 'sent a doctor to her children, and has got one of the girls into the Orphan 'School. When I wrote her a word in the poor woman's behalf, she wrote me 'back to the effect that it was a kindness to herself to have done so, "for '"what is the use of my means but to try and do some good with them?"'

# CHAPTER V.

## IDLENESS AT ALBARO: VILLA BAGNERELLO.

1844.

THE travelling party arrived at Marseilles on the evening of Sunday the 14th of July. Not being able to get vetturino horses in Paris, they had come on, post; paying for nine horses but bringing only four, and thereby saving a shilling a mile out of what the four would have cost in England. So great thus far, however, had been the cost of travel, that 'what with distance, 'caravan, sight-seeing, and everything,' two hundred pounds would be nearly swallowed up before they were at their destination. The success otherwise had been complete. The children had not cried in their worst troubles, the carriage had gone lightly over abominable roads, and the courier had proved himself a perfect gem. 'Surrounded 'by strange and perfectly novel circumstances,' Dickens wrote to me from Marseilles, 'I feel as if I had a new 'head on side by side with my old one.'

MARSEILLES: 1844.

The travel.

New experiences.

To what shrewd and kindly observation the old one had helped him at every stage of his journey, his published book of travel tells, and of all that there will be nothing here; but a couple of experiences at his outset, of which

MARSEILLES: 1844.

he told me afterwards, have enough character in them to be worth mention.

Shortly before there had been some public interest about the captain of a Boulogne steamer apprehended on a suspicion of having stolen specie, but reinstated by his owners after a public apology to him on their behalf; and Dickens had hardly set foot on the boat that was to carry them across, when he was attracted by the look of its captain, and discovered him after a few minutes' talk to be that very man. 'Such an honest, simple, good 'fellow, I never saw,' said Dickens, as he imitated for me the homely speech in which his confidences were related. The Boulogne people, he said, had given him a piece of plate, 'but Lord bless us! it took a deal more than 'that to get him round again in his own mind; and for 'weeks and weeks he was uncommon low to be sure. 'Newgate, you see! What a place for a sea-faring man 'as had held up his head afore the best on 'em, and had 'more friends, I mean to say, and I do tell you the day-'light truth, than any man on this station—ah! or any 'other, I don't care where!'

A character: honesty under cloud.

His first experience in a foreign tongue he made immediately on landing, when he had gone to the bank for money, and after delivering with most laborious distinctness a rather long address in French to the clerk behind the counter, was disconcerted by that functionary's cool enquiry in the native-born Lombard-street manner, 'How would you like to take it, sir?' He took it, as everybody must, in five-franc pieces, and a most inconvenient coinage he found it; for he required so much that

French thrown away.

he had to carry it in a couple of small sacks, and was always 'turning hot about suddenly' taking it into his head that he had lost them. ALBARO: 1844.

The evening of Tuesday the 16th of July saw him in a villa at Albaro, the suburb of Genoa in which, upon the advice of our Gore-house friends, he had resolved to pass the summer months before taking up his quarters in the city. His wish was to have had Lord Byron's house there, but it had fallen into neglect and become the refuge of a third-rate wineshop. The matter had then been left to Angus Fletcher who just now lived near Genoa, and he had taken at a rent absurdly above its value* an unpicturesque and uninteresting dwelling, which at once impressed its new tenant with its likeness to a pink jail. 'It is,' he said to me, 'the most perfectly lonely, rusty, stagnant old stag-'gerer of a domain that you can possibly imagine. What 'would I give if you could only look round the courtyard! '*I* look down into it, whenever I am near that side of the 'house, for the stable is so full of "vermin and swarmers"

Villa taken for him.

Page 237 of Vol. I.

Account of it.

* He regretted one chance missed by his eccentric friend, which he described to me just before he left Italy. 'I saw last night an old palazzo 'of the Doria, six miles from here, upon the sea, which De la Rue urged 'Fletcher to take for us, when he was bent on that detestable villa Bagne-'rello; which villa the Genoese have hired, time out of mind, for one fourth 'of what I paid, as they told him again and again before he made the agree-'ment. This is one of the strangest old palaces in Italy, surrounded by beautiful '*woods* of great trees (an immense rarity here) some miles in extent: and has 'upon the terrace a high tower, formerly a prison for offenders against the 'family, and a defence against the pirates. The present Doria lets it as it 'stands for £40 English—for the year . . . And the grounds are no expense; 'being proudly maintained by the Doria, who spends this rent, when he gets 'it, in repairing the roof and windows. It is a wonderful house; full of the 'most unaccountable pictures and most incredible furniture: every room in 'it like the most quaint and fanciful of Cattermole's pictures; and how many 'rooms I am afraid to say.' 2nd of June 1845.

A house he might have had.

ALBARO: 1844.

'(pardon the quotation from my inimitable friend) that I 'always expect to see the carriage going out bodily, with 'legions of industrious fleas harnessed to and drawing it 'off, on their own account. We have a couple of Italian 'work-people in our establishment; and to hear one or 'other of them talking away to our servants with the ut-'most violence and volubility in Genoese, and our servants 'answering with great fluency in English (very loud: as if 'the others were only deaf, not Italian), is one of the most 'ridiculous things possible. The effect is greatly enhanced 'by the Genoese manner, which is exceedingly animated 'and pantomimic; so that two friends of the lower class 'conversing pleasantly in the street, always seem on the 'eve of stabbing each other forthwith. And a stranger 'is immensely astonished at their not doing it.'

Italian and English.

Pantomimic talk.

Heat.

The heat tried him less than he expected, excepting always the sirocco, which, near the sea as they were, and right in the course of the wind as it blew against the house, made everything hotter than if there had been no wind. 'One feels it most, on first getting up. Then, it is 'really so oppressive that a strong determination is neces-'sary to enable one to go on dressing; one's tendency 'being to tumble down anywhere and lie there.' It seemed to hit him, he said, behind the knee, and made his legs so shake that he could not walk or stand. He had unfortunately a whole week of this without intermission, soon after his arrival; but then came a storm, with wind from the mountains; and he could bear the ordinary heat very well. What at first had been a home-discomfort, the bare walls, lofty ceilings, icy floors, and lattice

Sirocco.

blinds, soon became agreeable; there were regular afternoon breezes from the sea; in his courtyard was a well of very pure and very cold water; there were new milk and eggs by the bucketful, and, to protect from the summer insects these and other dainties, there were fresh vine-leaves by the thousand; and he satisfied himself, by the experience of a day or two in the city, that he had done well to come first to its suburb by the sea. What startled and disappointed him most were the frequent cloudy days.* He opened his third letter (3rd of August) by telling me there was a thick November fog, that rain was pouring incessantly, and that he did not remember to have seen in his life, at that time of year, such cloudy weather as he had seen beneath Italian skies.

Country pleasures.

Cloudy weather.

'The story goes that it is in autumn and winter, when 'other countries are dark and foggy, that the beauty and 'clearness of this are most observable. I hope it may 'prove so; for I have postponed going round the hills 'which encircle the city, or seeing any of the sights, until 'the weather is more favourable.† I have never yet seen

* 'We have had a London sky until to-day,' he wrote on the 20th of July, 'grey and cloudy as you please: but I am most disappointed, I think, in the 'evenings, which are as commonplace as need be; for there is no twilight, 'and as to the stars giving more light here than elsewhere, that is humbug.' The summer of 1844 seems to have been, however, an unusually stormy and wet season. He wrote to me on the 21st of October that they had had, so far, only four really clear days since they came to Italy.

London skies.

† 'My faith on that point is decidedly shaken, which reminds me to ask 'you whether you ever read Simond's Tour in Italy. It is a most charming 'book, and eminently remarkable for its excellent sense, and determination 'not to give in to conventional lies.' In a later letter he says: 'None of the 'books are unaffected and true but Simond's, which charms me more and 'more by its boldness, and its frank exhibition of that rare and admirable 'quality which enables a man to form opinions for himself without a miserable

Simond's *Tour in Italy*.

ALBARO: 1844.

Sunsets and scenery.

'it so clear, for any long time of the day together, as 'on a bright, lark-singing, coast-of-France-discerning day 'at Broadstairs; nor have I ever seen so fine a sunset, '*throughout*, as is very common there. But the scenery 'is exquisite, and at certain periods of the evening and 'the morning the blue of the Mediterranean surpasses all 'conception or description. It is the most intense and 'wonderful colour, I do believe, in all nature.'

In his second letter from Albaro there was more of this subject; and an outbreak of whimsical enthusiasm in it, meant especially for Maclise, is followed by some capital description. 'I address you, my friend,' he wrote, 'with something of the lofty spirit of an exile, a banished commoner, 'a sort of Anglo-Pole. I don't exactly know what I have 'done for my country in coming away from it, but I feel it 'is something; something great; something virtuous and 'heroic. Lofty emotions rise within me, when I see the 'sun set on the blue Mediterranean. I am the limpet on 'the rock. My father's name is Turner, and my boots are 'green . . . Apropos of blue. In a certain picture called 'the Serenade for which Browning wrote that verse * in 'Lincoln's-inn-fields, you, O Mac, painted a sky. If you

Address to Maclise.

'and slavish reference to the pretended opinions of other people. His notices 'of the leading pictures enchant me. They are so perfectly just and faithful, 'and so whimsically shrewd.' Rome, 9th of March, 1845.

* I send my heart up to thee, all my heart
In this my singing!
For the stars help me, and the sea bears part;
The very night is clinging
Closer to Venice' streets to leave one space
Above me, whence thy face
May light my joyous heart to thee its dwelling-place.

Written to express Maclise's subject in the Academy catalogue.

ALBARO: 1844.

'ever have occasion to paint the Mediterranean, let it be 'exactly of that colour. It lies before me now, as deeply 'and intensely blue. But no such colour is above me. 'Nothing like it. In the south of France, at Avignon, at 'Aix, at Marseilles, I saw deep blue skies; and also in 'America. But the sky above me is familiar to my sight. 'Is it heresy to say that I have seen its twin brother 'shining through the window of Jack Straw's—that down 'in Devonshire-terrace I have seen a better sky? I dare 'say it is; but like a great many other heresies, it is true. '... But such green, green, green, as flutters in the vine-'yard down below the windows, *that* I never saw; nor yet 'such lilac and such purple as float between me and the 'distant hills; nor yet in anything, picture, book, or vestal 'boredom, such awful, solemn, impenetrable blue, as in 'that same sea. It has such an absorbing, silent, deep, 'profound effect, that I can't help thinking it suggested 'the idea of Styx. It looks as if a draught of it, only 'so much as you could scoop up on the beach in the 'hollow of your hand, would wash out everything else, and 'make a great blue blank of your intellect ... When the 'sun sets clearly, then, by Heaven, it is majestic. From 'any one of eleven windows here, or from a terrace over-'grown with grapes, you may behold the broad sea, villas, 'houses, mountains, forts, strewn with rose leaves. Strewn 'with them? Steeped in them! Dyed, through and 'through and through. For a moment. No more. The 'sun is impatient and fierce (like everything else in these 'parts), and goes down headlong. Run to fetch your hat '—and it's night. Wink at the right time of black night

French and Italian skies.

The Mediterranean.

Sun upon the sea.

ALBARO: 1844.

The cicala:

'—and it's morning. Everything is in extremes. There 'is an insect here that chirps all day. There is one out-'side the window now. The chirp is very loud: some-'thing like a Brobdingnagian grasshopper. The creature 'is born to chirp; to progress in chirping; to chirp louder, 'louder, louder; till it gives one tremendous chirp and 'bursts itself. That is its life and death. Everything is '"in a concatenation accordingly." The day gets brighter, 'brighter, brighter, till it's night. The summer gets hotter, 'hotter, hotter, till it explodes. The fruit gets riper, riper, 'riper, till it tumbles down and rots . . . Ask me a question 'or two about fresco: will you be so good? All the houses 'are painted in fresco, hereabout (the outside walls I mean, 'the fronts, backs, and sides), and all the colour has run 'into damp and green seediness; and the very design has 'straggled away into the component atoms of the plaster. 'Beware of fresco! Sometimes (but not often) I can make 'out a Virgin with a mildewed glory round her head, hold-'ing nothing in an undiscernible lap with invisible arms; 'and occasionally the leg or arm of a cherub. But it is 'very melancholy and dim. There are two old fresco-'painted vases outside my own gate, one on either hand, 'which are so faint that I never saw them till last night; 'and only then, because I was looking over the wall after 'a lizard who had come upon me while I was smoking a 'cigar above, and crawled over one of these embellishments 'in his retreat . . .'

typical in life and death.

A warning.

Perishing frescoes.

That letter sketched for me the story of his travel through France, and I may at once say that I thus received, from week to week, the 'first sprightly runnings' of every description in his *Pictures from Italy*. But my rule as to the American letters must be here observed yet more strictly; and nothing resembling his printed book, however distantly, can be admitted into these pages. Even so my difficulty of rejection will not be less; for as he had not actually decided, until the very last, to publish his present experiences at all, a larger number of the letters were left unrifled by him. He had no settled plan from the first, as in the other case.

ALBARO: 1844.

Nothing in print repeated here.

His most valued acquaintance at Albaro was the French consul-general, a student of our literature who had written on his books in one of the French reviews, and who with his English wife lived in the very next villa, though so oddly shut away by its vineyard that to get from the one adjoining house to the other was a mile's journey.* Describing, in that August letter, his first call from this new friend thus pleasantly self-recommended, he makes the visit his excuse for breaking off from a facetious description of French inns to introduce to me a sketch, from a pencil outline by Fletcher, of what bore the imposing name of the Villa di Bella vista, but which he called by the homelier one of its proprietor, Bagnerello. 'This, my friend, is quite accurate. Allow me to explain 'it. You are standing, sir, in our vineyard, among the 'grapes and figs. The Mediterranean is at your back as 'you look at the house: of which two sides, out of four, 'are here depicted. The lower story (nearly concealed by

French Consul of Genoa.

Pencil sketch by Angus Fletcher.

* 'Their house is next to ours on the right, with vineyard between; but 'the place is so oddly contrived that one has to go a full mile round to get to 'their door.'

ALBARO: 1844.

'the vines) consists of the hall, a wine-cellar, and some 'store-rooms. The three windows on the left of the first 'floor belong to the sala, lofty and whitewashed, which 'has two more windows round the corner. The fourth 'window *did* belong to the dining-room, but I have 'changed one of the nurseries for better air; and it now 'appertains to that branch of the establishment. The 'fifth and sixth, or two right-hand windows, sir, admit 'the light to the inimitable's (and uxor's) chamber; to 'which the first window round the right-hand corner, 'which you perceive in shadow, also belongs. The next 'window in shadow, young sir, is the bower of Miss H. 'The next, a nursery window; the same having two more 'round the corner again. The bowery-looking place 'stretching out upon the left of the house is the terrace, 'which opens out from a French window in the drawing-'room on the same floor, of which you see nothing: and 'forms one side of the court-yard. The upper windows 'belong to some of those uncounted chambers upstairs; 'the fourth one, longer than the rest, being in F.'s bed-'room. There is a kitchen or two up there besides, and 'my dressing-room; which you can't see from this point 'of view. The kitchens and other offices in use are down 'below, under that part of the house where the roof is 'longest. On your left, beyond the bay of Genoa, about 'two miles off, the Alps stretch off into the far horizon; 'on your right, at three or four miles distance, are moun-'tains crowned with forts. The intervening space on both 'sides is dotted with villas, some green, some red, some 'yellow, some blue, some (and ours among the number)

Rooms in villa described.

Surrounding scenery.

ALBARO: 1844.

'pink. At your back, as I have said, sir, is the ocean; 'with the slim Italian tower of the ruined church of St. 'John the Baptist rising up before it, on the top of a pile 'of savage rocks. You go through the court-yard, and out 'at the gate, and down a narrow lane to the sea. Note. 'The sala goes sheer up to the top of the house; the 'ceiling being conical, and the little bedrooms built round

Church-ruin on the rocks.

'the spring of its arch. You will observe that we make 'no pretension to architectural magnificence, but that we 'have abundance of room. And here I am, beholding 'only vines and the sea for days together . . . Good 'Heavens! How I wish you'd come for a week or two, 'and taste the white wine at a penny farthing the pint. 'It is excellent.' . . . Then, after seven days: 'I have got 'my paper and inkstand and figures now (the box from 'Osnaburgh-terrace only came last Thursday), and can 'think—I have begun to do so every morning—with a

Vines and sea.

*Post*, p. 214.

ALBARO: 1844.

Preparing for work.

'business-like air, of the Christmas book. My paper is 'arranged, and my pens are spread out, in the usual form. 'I think you know the form—Don't you? My books have 'not passed the custom-house yet, and I tremble for some 'volumes of Voltaire . . . I write in the best bedroom. 'The sun is off the corner window at the side of the house 'by a very little after twelve; and I can then throw the 'blinds open, and look up from my paper, at the sea, the 'mountains, the washed-out villas, the vineyards, at the 'blistering white hot fort with a sentry on the drawbridge 'standing in a bit of shadow no broader than his own 'musket, and at the sky, as often as I like. It is a very 'peaceful view, and yet a very cheerful one. Quiet as 'quiet can be.'

Work in abeyance.

Not yet however had the time for writing come. A sharp attack of illness befell his youngest little daughter, Kate, and troubled him much. Then, after beginning the Italian grammar himself, he had to call in the help of a master; and this learning of the language took up time. But he had an aptitude for it, and after a month's application told me (24th of August) that he could ask in Italian for whatever he wanted in any shop or coffee-house, and could read it pretty well. 'I wish you could 'see me' (16th of September), 'without my knowing it, 'walking about alone here. I am now as bold as a lion in 'the streets. The audacity with which one begins to speak 'when there is no help for it, is quite astonishing.' The blank impossibility at the outset, however, of getting native meanings conveyed to his English servants, he very humorously described to me; and said the spell was

Learning Italian.

first broken by the cook, 'being really a clever woman, 'and not entrenching herself in that astonishing pride of 'ignorance which induces the rest to oppose themselves 'to the receipt of any information through any channel, 'and which made A. careless of looking out of window, 'in America, even to see the Falls of Niagara.' So that he soon had to report the gain, to all of them, from the fact of this enterprising woman having so primed herself with 'the names of all sorts of vegetables, meats, soups, 'fruits, and kitchen necessaries,' that she was able to order whatever was needful of the peasantry that were trotting in and out all day, basketed and barefooted Her example became at once contagious;* and before the end of the second week of September news reached me that 'the servants are beginning to pick up scraps of 'Italian; some of them go to a weekly conversazione of 'servants at the Governor's every Sunday night, having 'got over their consternation at the frequent introduction 'of quadrilles on these occasions; and I think they begin 'to like their foreigneering life.'

ALBARO: 1844.

The English servants.

Domestic news.

In the tradespeople they dealt with at Albaro he found

Tradespeople.

* Not however, happily for them, in another important particular, for on the eve of their return to England she declared her intention of staying behind and marrying an Italian. 'She will have to go to Florence, I find' (12th of May 1845), 'to be married in Lord Holland's house: and even then is only 'married according to the English law: having no legal rights from such a 'marriage, either in France or Italy. The man hasn't a penny. If there 'were an opening for a nice clean restaurant in Genoa—which I don't believe 'there is, for the Genoese have a natural enjoyment of dirt, garlic, and oil—'it would still be a very hazardous venture; as the priests will certainly 'damage the man, if they can, for marrying a Protestant woman. However, 'the utmost I can do is to take care, if such a crisis should arrive, that she 'shall not want the means of getting home to England. As my father would 'observe, she has sown and must reap.'

May 1845.

ALBARO: 1844.

amusing points of character. Sharp as they were after money, their idleness quenched even that propensity. Order for immediate delivery two or three pounds of tea, and the tea-dealer would be wretched. 'Won't it do 'to-morrow?' 'I want it now,' you would reply; and he would say, 'No, no, there can be no hurry!' He remonstrated against the cruelty. But everywhere there was deference, courtesy, more than civility. 'In a café 'a little tumbler of ice costs something less than three-'pence, and if you give the waiter in addition what you 'would not offer to an English beggar, say, the third of 'a halfpenny, he is profoundly grateful.' The attentions received from English residents were unremitting.* In moments of need at the outset, they bestirred themselves ('large merchants and grave men') as if they were the family's salaried purveyors; and there was in especial one gentleman named Curry whose untiring kindness was long remembered.

Native courtesy.

English residents.

City streets.

The light, eager, active figure soon made itself familiar in the streets of Genoa, and he never went into them with-

* He had carried with him, I may here mention, letters of introduction to residents in all parts of Italy, of which I believe he delivered hardly one. Writing to me a couple of months before he left the country he congratulated himself on this fact. 'We are living very quietly; and I am now more than 'ever glad that I have kept myself aloof from the "receiving" natives always, 'and delivered scarcely any of my letters of introduction. If I had, I should 'have seen nothing and known less. I have observed that the English women 'who have married foreigners are invariably the most audacious in the license 'they assume. Think of one lady married to a royal chamberlain (not 'here) who said at dinner to the master of the house at a place where I was 'dining—that she had brought back his *Satirist*, but didn't think there was 'quite so much "fun" in it as there used to be. I looked at the paper after-'wards, and found it crammed with such vile obscenity as positively made 'one's hair stand on end.

Undelivered letters.

out bringing some oddity away. I soon heard of the strada Nuova and strada Balbi; of the broadest of the two as narrower than Albany-street, and of the other as less wide than Drury-lane or Wych-street; but both filled with palaces of noble architecture and of such vast dimensions that as many windows as there are days in the year might be counted in one of them, and this not covering by any means the largest plot of ground. I heard too of the other streets, none with footways, and all varying in degrees of narrowness, but for the most part like Field-lane in Holborn, with little breathing-places like St. Martin's-court; and the widest only in parts wide enough to enable a carriage and pair to turn. 'Imagine yourself looking down a street of 'Reform Clubs cramped after this odd fashion, the lofty 'roofs almost seeming to meet in the perspective.' In the churches nothing struck him so much as the profusion of trash and tinsel in them that contrasted with their real splendours of embellishment. One only, that of the Cappucini friars, blazed every inch of it with gold, precious stones, and paintings of priceless art; the principal contrast to its radiance being the dirt of its masters, whose bare legs, corded waists, and coarse brown serge never changed by night or day, proclaimed amid their corporate wealth their personal vows of poverty. He found them less pleasant to meet and look at than the country people of their suburb on festa-days, with the Indulgences that gave them the right to make merry stuck in their hats like turnpike-tickets. He did not think the peasant girls in general good-looking, though they carried themselves daintily and walked remarkably well: but the ugliness of the old women, be-

Genoa the Superb.

Church splendours and tinsel.

Friars and peasants.

Old women.

ALBARO: 1844.

gotten of hard work and a burning sun, with porters' knots of coarse grey hair grubbed up over wrinkled and cadaverous faces, he thought quite stupendous. He was never in a street a hundred yards long without getting up perfectly the witch part of *Macbeth.*

Theatres.

With the theatres of course he soon became acquainted, and of that of the puppets he wrote to me again and again with humorous rapture. 'There are other things,' he added, after giving me the account which is published in his book, 'too solemnly surprising to dwell upon. They must be seen. 'They must be seen. The enchanter carrying off the bride 'is not greater than his men brandishing fiery torches and 'dropping their lighted spirits of wine at every shake. Also 'the enchanter himself, when, hunted down and overcome, he 'leaps into the rolling sea, and finds a watery grave. Also 'the second comic man, aged about 55 and like George the 'Third in the face, when he gives out the play for the next 'night. They must all be seen. They can't be told about. 'Quite impossible.' The living performers he did not think so good, a disbelief in Italian actors having been always a heresy with him, and the deplorable length of dialogue to the small amount of action in their plays making them sadly tiresome. The first that he saw at the principal theatre was a version of Balzac's *Père Goriot.* 'The domestic Lear I thought at first was going to be very clever. 'But he was too pitiful—perhaps the Italian reality would 'be. He was immensely applauded, though.' He afterwards saw a version of Dumas' preposterous play of *Kean,* in which most of the representatives of English actors wore red hats with steeple crowns, and very loose blouses with

The puppets.

Italian plays.

Dumas' *Kean.*

broad belts and buckles round their waists. 'There was a 'mysterious person called the Prince of Var-lees' (Wales), 'the youngest and slimmest man in the company, whose 'badinage in Kean's dressing-room was irresistible; and 'the dresser wore top-boots, a Greek skull-cap, a black 'velvet jacket, and leather breeches. One or two of the 'actors looked very hard at me to see how I was touched 'by these English peculiarities—especially when Kean 'kissed his male friends on both cheeks.' The arrangements of the house, which he described as larger than Drury-lane, he thought excellent. Instead of a ticket for the private box he had taken on the first tier, he received the usual key for admission which let him in as if he lived there; and for the whole set-out, 'quite as comfortable 'and private as a box at our opera,' paid only eight and fourpence English. The opera itself had not its regular performers until after Christmas, but in the summer there was a good comic company, and he saw the *Scaramuccia* and the *Barber of Seville* brightly and pleasantly done. There was also a day theatre, beginning at half past four in the afternoon; but beyond the novelty of looking on at the covered stage as he sat in the fresh pleasant air, he did not find much amusement in the Goldoni comedy put before him. There came later a Russian circus, which the unusual rains of that summer prematurely extinguished.

Italian English.

Opera.

Day-theatre.

The Religious Houses he made early and many enquiries about, and there was one that had stirred and baffled his curiosity much before he discovered what it really was. All that was visible from the street was a great high wall, apparently quite alone, no thicker than a party wall, with

Religious houses.

ALBARO: 1844.

grated windows, to which iron screens gave farther protection. At first he supposed there had been a fire; but by degrees came to know that on the other side were galleries, one above another, one above another, and nuns always pacing them to and fro. Like the wall of a racket-ground

Nunnery.

outside, it was inside a very large nunnery; and let the poor sisters walk never so much, neither they nor the passers-by could see anything of each other. It was close upon the Acqua Sola, too; a little park with still young but very pretty trees, and fresh and cheerful fountains, which

Sunday promenade.

the Genoese made their Sunday promenade; and underneath which was an archway with great public tanks, where, at all ordinary times, washerwomen were washing away, thirty or forty together. At Albaro they were worse off in this matter: the clothes there being washed in a pond, beaten with gourds, and whitened with a preparation of lime: 'so that,' he wrote to me (24th of August), 'what 'between the beating and the burning they fall into holes 'unexpectedly, and my white trowsers, after six weeks' 'washing, would make very good fishing-nets. It is such 'a serious damage that when we get into the Peschiere we 'mean to wash at home.'

Winter residence chosen.

Exactly a fortnight before this date, he had hired rooms in the Peschiere from the first of the following October; and so ended the house-hunting for his winter residence, that had taken him so often to the city. The Peschiere was the largest palace in Genoa let on hire, and had the advantage of standing on a height aloof from the town, surrounded by its own gardens. The rooms taken had been occupied by an English colonel, the remainder of whose term was let to Dickens for 500 francs a month (£20); and a few days after (20th of August) he described to me a fellow tenant: 'A Spanish duke has taken the room under me 'in the Peschiere. The duchess was his mistress many 'years, and bore him (I think) six daughters. He always 'promised her that if she gave birth to a son, he would 'marry her; and when at last the boy arrived, he went 'into her bedroom, saying—"Duchess, I am charmed to '"salute you!" And he married her in good earnest, 'and legitimatized (as by the Spanish law he could) all the 'other children.' The beauty of the new abode will justify a little description when he takes up his quarters there. One or two incidents may be related, meanwhile, of the closing weeks of his residence at Albaro.

A fellow tenant.

Lucky arrival.

In the middle of August he dined with the French consul-general, and there will now be no impropriety in printing his agreeable sketch of the dinner. 'There was 'present, among other Genoese, the Marquis di Negri: 'a very fat and much older Jerdan, with the same 'thickness of speech and size of tongue. He was Byron's 'friend, keeps open house here, writes poetry, im-'provises, and is a very good old Blunderbore; just the 'sort of instrument to make an artesian well with, any-'where. Well, sir, after dinner, the consul proposed my 'health, with a little French conceit to the effect that I 'had come to Italy to have personal experience of its 'lovely climate, and that there was this similarity between 'the Italian sun and its visitor, that the sun shone into 'the darkest places and made them bright and happy 'with its benignant influence, and that my books had

Dinner at French consul's.

Compliment to C. D.

ALBARO: 1844.

Verses in his honour.

'done the like with the breasts of men, and so forth. 'Upon which Blunderbore gives his bright-buttoned blue 'coat a great rap on the breast, turns up his fishy eye, 'stretches out his arm like the living statue defying the 'lightning at Astley's, and delivers four impromptu verses 'in my honour, at which everybody is enchanted, and I 'more than anybody—perhaps with the best reason, for 'I didn't understand a word of them. The consul then 'takes from his breast a roll of paper, and says, "I shall '"read them!" Blunderbore then says, "Don't!" But 'the consul does, and Blunderbore beats time to the 'music of the verse with his knuckles on the table; and 'perpetually ducks forward to look round the cap of a 'lady sitting between himself and me, to see what I 'think of them. I exhibit lively emotion. The verses 'are in French—short line—on the taking of Tangiers by

Others in Prince de Joinville's.

'the Prince de Joinville; and are received with great ap-'plause; especially by a nobleman present who is reported 'to be unable to read and write. They end in my mind '(rapidly translating them into prose) thus,—

'The cannon of France
'Shake the foundation
'Of the wondering sea,
'The artillery on the shore
'Is put to silence,
'Honour to Joinville
'And the Brave!
'The Great Intelligence
'Is borne
'Upon the wings of Fame
'To Paris.
'Her national citizens
'Exchange caresses
'In the streets!
'The temples are crowded
'With religious patriots
'Rendering thanks
'To Heaven.
'The King
'And all the Royal Family
'Are bathed
'In tears.
'They call upon the name
'Of Joinville!
'France also
'Weeps, and echoes it.
'Joinville is crowned
'With Immortality;
'And Peace and Joinville,
'And the Glory of France,
'Diffuse themselves
'Conjointly.

'If you can figure to yourself the choice absurdity of 'receiving anything into one's mind in this way, you 'can imagine the labour I underwent in my attempts to 'keep the lower part of my face square, and to lift up one 'eye gently, as with admiring attention. But I am bound 'to add that this is really pretty literal; for I read them 'afterwards.'

ALBARO: 1844.

Tahiti discomforts.

This, too, was the year of other uncomfortable glories of France in the last three years of her Orleans dynasty; among them the Tahiti business, as politicians may remember; and so hot became rumours of war with England at the opening of September that Dickens had serious thoughts of at once striking his tent. One of his letters was filled with the conflicting doubts in which they lived for nigh a fortnight, every day's arrival contradicting the arrival of the day before: so that, as he told me, you met a man in the street to-day, who told you there would certainly be war in a week; and you met the same man in the street to-morrow, and he swore he always knew there would be nothing but peace; and you met him again the day after, and he said it all depended *now* on something perfectly new and unheard of before, which somebody else said had just come to the knowledge of some consul in some dispatch which said something about some telegraph which had been at work somewhere, signalizing some prodigious intelligence. However, it all passed harmlessly away, leaving him undisturbed opportunity to avail himself of a pleasure that arose out of the consul-general's dinner party, and to be present at a great reception given shortly after by the good 'old

Rumours of war with England.

ALBARO: 1844.

'Blunderbore' just mentioned, on the occasion of his daughter's birthday.

Reception at M. di Negri's.

The Marquis had a splendid house, but Dickens found the grounds so carved into grottoes and fanciful walks as to remind him of nothing so much as our old White-conduit-house, except that he would have been well pleased, on the present occasion, to have discovered a waiter crying, 'Give your orders, gents!' it being not easy to him at any time to keep up, the whole night through, on ices and variegated lamps merely. But the scene for awhile was amusing enough, and not rendered less so by the delight of the Marquis himself, 'who was constantly diving out 'into dark corners and then among the lattice-work and 'flower pots, rubbing his hands and going round and round 'with explosive chuckles in his huge satisfaction with the 'entertainment.' With horror it occurred to Dickens, however, that four more hours of this kind of entertainment would be too much; that the Genoa gates closed at twelve; and that as the carriage had not been ordered till the dancing was expected to be over and the gates to reopen, he must make a sudden bolt if he would himself get back to Albaro. 'I had barely time,' he told me, 'to reach the 'gate before midnight; and was running as hard as I could 'go, downhill, over uneven ground, along a new street 'called the strada Sevra, when I came to a pole fastened 'straight across the street, nearly breast high, without any 'light or watchman—quite in the Italian style. I went 'over it, headlong, with such force that I rolled myself 'completely white in the dust; but although I tore my 'clothes to shreds, I hardly scratched myself except in one

Delight of the host.

Flight of the guest.

A tumble.

'place on the knee. I had no time to think of it then, 'for I was up directly and off again to save the gate: but 'when I got outside the wall, and saw the state I was in, 'I wondered I had not broken my neck. I "took it easy" 'after this, and walked home, by lonely ways enough, 'without meeting a single soul. But there is nothing to 'be feared, I believe, from midnight walks in this part of 'Italy. In other places you incur the danger of being 'stabbed by mistake; whereas the people here are quiet 'and good tempered, and very rarely commit any outrage.'

ALBARO: 1844.

Midnight walks.

Such adventures, nevertheless, are seldom without consequences, and there followed in this case a short but sharp attack of illness. It came on with the old 'unspeakable 'and agonizing pain in the side,' for which Bob Fagin had prepared and applied the hot bottles in the old warehouse time; and it yielded quickly to powerful remedies. But for a few days he had to content himself with the minor sights of Albaro. He sat daily in the shade of the ruined chapel on the seashore. He looked in at the festa in the small country church, consisting mainly of a tenor singer, a seraphine, and four priests sitting gaping in a row on one side of the altar 'in flowered satin dresses and 'little cloth caps, looking exactly like the band at a wild-'beast-caravan.' He was interested in the wine-making, and in seeing the country tenants preparing their annual presents for their landlords, of baskets of grapes and other fruit prettily dressed with flowers. The season of the grapes, too, brought out after dusk strong parties of rats to eat them as they ripened, and so many shooting parties of peasants to get rid of these despoilers, that as he first

Page 40 of Vol. I.

Quiet enjoyments.

ALBARO: 1844.

listened to the uproar of the firing and the echoes he half fancied it a siege of Albaro. The flies mustered strong, too, and the mosquitos;* so that at night he had to lie covered up with gauze, like cold meat in a safe.

English visitors and news.

Of course all news from England, and especially visits paid him by English friends who might be travelling in Italy, were a great delight. This was the year when O'Connell was released from prison by the judgment of the Lords on appeal. 'I have no faith in O'Connell taking the great 'position he might upon this: being beleaguered by vanity 'always. Denman delights me. I am glad to think I have 'always liked him so well. I am sure that whenever he 'makes a mistake, it *is* a mistake; and that no man lives 'who has a grander and nobler scorn of every mean and 'dastard action. I would to Heaven it were decorous to 'pay him some public tribute of respect.... O'Connell's 'speeches are the old thing: fretty, boastful, frothy, waspish 'at the voices in the crowd, and all that: but with no true 'greatness... What a relief to turn to that noble letter 'of Carlyle's' (in which a timely testimony had been borne to the truthfulness and honour of Mazzini), 'which I think 'above all praise. My love to him.' Among his English

The O'Connell appeal.

Troubles of little doggy.

* What his poor little dog suffered should not be omitted from the troubles of the master who was so fond of him. 'Timber has had every hair upon 'his body cut off because of the fleas, and he looks like the ghost of a drowned 'dog come out of a pond after a week or so. It is very awful to see him slide 'into a room. He knows the change upon him, and is always turning round 'and round to look for himself. I think he'll die of grief.' Three weeks later: 'Timber's hair is growing again, so that you can dimly perceive him to 'be a dog. The fleas only keep three of his legs off the ground now, and he 'sometimes moves of his own accord towards some place where they don't 'want to go.' His improvement was slow, but after this continuous.

visitors were Mr. Tagart's family, on their way from a scientific congress at Milan; and Peter (now become Lord) Robertson from Rome, of whose talk he wrote very pleasantly. The sons of Burns had been entertained during the summer in Edinburgh at what was called a Burns Festival, of which, through Jerrold who was present, I had sent him no very favourable account; and this was now confirmed by Robertson, whose letters had given him an 'awful' narrative of Wilson's speech, and of the whole business. 'There was one 'man who spoke a quarter of an hour or so, to the toast 'of the navy; and could say nothing more than "the— '"British—navy—always appreciates—" which remark- 'able sentiment he repeated over and over again for that 'space of time; and then sat down. Robertson told me 'also that Wilson's allusion to, or I should rather say 'expatiation upon, the "vices" of Burns, excited but one 'sentiment of indignation and disgust: and added, very 'sensibly, "By God!—I want to know *what Burns did!* '"I never heard of his doing anything that need be '"strange or unaccountable to the Professor's mind. I '"think he must have mistaken the name, and fancied '"it a dinner to the sons of *Burke*"—meaning of course 'the murderer. In short he fully confirmed Jerrold in all 'respects.' The same letter told me, too, something of his reading. Jerrold's *Story of a Feather* he had derived much enjoyment from. 'Gauntwolf's sickness and the 'career of that snuffbox, masterly.* I have been deep in

ALBARO: 1844.

*Ante*, p. 37.

Lord Robertson.

Burns festival.

Professor Wilson's speech.

* A characteristic message for Jerrold came in a later letter (12th of May, 1845): 'I wish you would suggest to Jerrold for me as a Caudle subject (if 'he pursue that idea), "Mr. Caudle has incidentally remarked that the house- '"maid is good-looking."'

Jerrold.

ALBARO: 1844.

His reading.

'Voyages and Travels, and in De Foe. Tennyson I have also 'been reading, again and again. What a great creature 'he is!... What about the *Goldsmith?* Apropos, I am 'all eagerness to write a story about the length of that 'most delightful of all stories, the *Vicar of Wakefield.*'

Visit of his brother.

In the second week of September he went to meet his brother Frederick at Marseilles, and bring him back over the Cornice road to pass a fortnight's holiday at Genoa; and his description of the first inn upon the Alps they slept in is too good to be lost. 'We lay last night,' he wrote (9th of September) 'at the first halting-place 'on this journey, in an inn which is not entitled, as it 'ought to be, The house of call for fleas and vermin in 'general, but is entitled the grand hotel of the Post! I 'hardly know what to compare it to. It seemed something 'like a house in Somers-town originally built for a wine-'vaults and never finished, but grown very old. There 'was nothing to eat in it and nothing to drink. They had 'lost the teapot; and when they found it, they couldn't 'make out what had become of the lid, which, turning up 'at last and being fixed on to the teapot, couldn't be got 'off again for the pouring in of more water. Fleas of 'elephantine dimensions were gambolling boldly in the 'dirty beds; and the mosquitoes!—But here let me draw 'a curtain (as I would have done if there had been any). 'We had scarcely any sleep, and rose up with hands and 'arms hardly human.'

A grand hotel of the Post.

In four days they were at Albaro, and the morning after their arrival Dickens underwent the terrible shock of seeing his brother very nearly drowned in the bay. He swam out into too strong a current,* and was only narrowly saved by the accident of a fishing-boat preparing to leave the harbour at the time. 'It was a world of horror and 'anguish,' Dickens wrote to me, 'crowded into four or 'five minutes of dreadful agitation; and, to complete the 'terror of it, Georgy, Charlotte' (the nurse), 'and the 'children were on a rock in full view of it all, crying, as 'you may suppose, like mad creatures.' His own bathing was from the rock, and, as he had already told me, of the most primitive kind. He went in whenever he pleased, broke his head against sharp stones if he went in with that end foremost, floundered about till he was all over bruises, and then climbed and staggered out again. 'Every-'body wears a dress. Mine extremely theatrical: Masa-'niello to the life: shall be preserved for your inspection 'in Devonshire-terrace.' I will add another personal touch, also Masaniello-like, which marks the beginning of a change which, though confined for the present to his foreign residence and removed when he came to England, was resumed somewhat later, and in a few more years wholly altered the aspect of his face. 'The moustaches 'are glorious, glorious. I have cut them shorter, and 'trimmed them a little at the ends to improve the shape. 'They are charming, charming. Without them, life would 'be a blank.'

His brother in danger.

Sea-bathing.

A change beginning.

* Of the dangers of the bay he had before written to me (10th of August). 'A monk was drowned here on Saturday evening. He was bathing with two 'other monks, who bolted when he cried out that he was sinking—in conse-'quence, I suppose, of his certainty of going to Heaven.'

A monk drowned.

# CHAPTER VI.

## WORK IN GENOA: PALAZZO PESCHIERE.

1844.

GENOA: 1844.

IN the last week of September they moved from Albaro into Genoa, amid a violent storm of wind and wet, 'great 'guns blowing,' the lightning incessant, and the rain driving down in a dense thick cloud. But the worst of the storm was over when they reached the Peschiere. As they passed into it along the stately old terraces, flanked on either side with antique sculptured figures, all the seven fountains were playing in its gardens, and the sun was shining brightly on its groves of camellias and orange-trees.

Palace of the Fish-ponds.

It was a wonderful place, and I soon became familiar with the several rooms that were to form their home for the rest of their stay in Italy. In the centre was the grand sala, fifty feet high, of an area larger than 'the 'dining-room of the Academy,' and painted, walls and ceiling, with frescoes three hundred years old, 'as fresh as 'if the colours had been laid on yesterday.' On the same floor as this great hall were a drawing-room, and a dining-room,* both covered also with frescoes still bright enough

* 'Into which we might put your large room—I wish we could!—away in 'one corner, and dine without knowing it.

to make them thoroughly cheerful, and both so nicely proportioned as to give to their bigness all the effect of snugness.* Out of these opened three other chambers that were turned into sleeping-rooms and nurseries. Adjoining the sala, right and left, were the two best bed-

GENOA: 1844.

Rooms described.

rooms; 'in size and shape like those at Windsor-castle 'but greatly higher;' both having altars, a range of three

* 'Very vast you will say, and very dreary; but it is not so really. The 'paintings are so fresh, and the proportions so agreeable to the eye, that the 'effect is not only cheerful but snug. . . . We are a little incommoded by 'applications from strangers to go over the interior. The paintings were 'designed by Michael Angelo, and have a great reputation . . . Certain of 'these frescoes were reported officially to the Fine Art Commissioners by 'Wilson as the best in Italy . . . I allowed a party of priests to be shown 'the great hall yesterday . . . It is in perfect repair, and the doors almost 'shut—which is quite a miraculous circumstance. I wish you could see it, 'my dear F. Gracious Heavens! if you could only *come back* with me, wouldn't 'I soon flash on your astonished sight.' (6th of October.)

Frescoes.

GENOA: 1844.

Mural paintings.

windows with stone balconies, floors tesselated in patterns of black and white stone, and walls painted every inch: on the left, nymphs pursued by satyrs 'as large as life 'and as wicked;' on the right, 'Phaeton larger than life, 'with horses bigger than Meux and Co.'s, tumbling head-'long down into the best bed.' The right-hand one he occupied with his wife, and of the left took possession as a study; writing behind a big screen he had lugged into it, and placed by one of the windows, from which he could see over the city, as he wrote, as far as the lighthouse in its harbour. Distant little over a mile as the crow flew, flashing five times in four minutes, and on dark nights, as if by magic, illuminating brightly the whole palace-front every time it shone, this lighthouse was one of the wonders of Genoa.

View over city.

When it had all become more familiar to him, he was fond of dilating on its beauties; and even the dreary sound of the chaunting from neighbouring mass-performances, as it floated in at all the open windows, which at first was a sad trouble, came to have its charm for him. I remember a vivid account he gave me of a great festa on the hill behind the house, when the people alternately danced under tents in the open air and rushed to say a prayer or two in an adjoining church bright with red and gold and blue and silver; so many minutes of dancing, and of praying, in regular turns of each. But the view over into Genoa, on clear bright days, was a never failing enjoyment. The whole city then, without an atom of smoke, and with every possible variety of tower and steeple pointing up into the sky, lay stretched out below his

Dancing and praying.

windows. To the right and left were lofty hills, with every indentation in their rugged sides sharply discernible; and on one side of the harbour stretched away into the dim bright distance the whole of the Cornice, its first highest range of mountains hoary with snow. Sitting down one Spring day to write to me, he thus spoke of the sea and of the garden. 'Beyond the town is the wide 'expanse of the Mediterranean, as blue, at this moment, 'as the most pure and vivid prussian blue on Mac's 'palette when it is newly set; and on the horizon there 'is a red flush, seen nowhere as it is here. Immediately 'below the windows are the gardens of the house, with 'gold fish swimming and diving in the fountains; and 'below them, at the foot of a steep slope, the public 'garden and drive, where the walks are marked out by 'hedges of pink roses, which blush and shine through the 'green trees and vines, close up to the balconies of these 'windows. No custom can impair, and no description 'enhance, the beauty of the scene.'

Distant scenery.

Peschiere garden.

All these and other glories and beauties, however, did not come to him at once. They counted for little indeed when he first set himself seriously to write. 'Never did 'I stagger so upon a threshold before. I seem as if I 'had plucked myself out of my proper soil when I left 'Devonshire-terrace; and could take root no more until 'I return to it. . . . Did I tell you how many fountains 'we have here? No matter. If they played nectar, they 'wouldn't please me half so well as the West Middlesex 'water-works at Devonshire-terrace.' The subject for his new Christmas story he had chosen, but he had not

Trying to write.

Difficulties in the way.

GENOA: 1844.

found a title for it, or the machinery to work it with; when, at the moment of what seemed to be his greatest trouble, both reliefs came. Sitting down one morning resolute for work, though against the grain, his hand being out and everything inviting to idleness, such a peal of chimes arose from the city as he found to be 'madden-'ing.' All Genoa lay beneath him, and up from it, with some sudden set of the wind, came in one fell sound the clang and clash of all its steeples, pouring into his ears, again and again, in a tuneless, grating, discordant, jerking, hideous vibration that made his ideas 'spin round and 'round till they lost themselves in a whirl of vexation and 'giddiness, and dropped down dead.' He had never before so suffered, nor did he again; but this was his description to me next day, and his excuse for having failed in a promise to send me his title. Only two days later, however, came a letter in which not a syllable was written but 'We have heard THE CHIMES at midnight, 'Master Shallow!' and I knew he had discovered what he wanted.

A peal of chimes.

A title found.

Other difficulties were still to be got over. He craved for the London streets. He so missed his long night-walks before beginning anything that he seemed, as he said, dumbfounded without them. 'I can't help thinking of 'the boy in the school-class whose button was cut off by 'Walter Scott and his friends. Put me down on Waterloo-'bridge at eight o'clock in the evening, with leave to 'roam about as long as I like, and I would come home, as 'you know, panting to go on. I am sadly strange as it is, 'and can't settle. You will have lots of hasty notes from me

Craving for streets by night.

'while I am at work: but you know your man; and what-'ever strikes me, I shall let off upon you as if I were in 'Devonshire-terrace. It's a great thing to have my title, 'and see my way how to work the bells. Let them clash 'upon me now from all the churches and convents in 'Genoa, I see nothing but the old London belfry I have 'set them in. In my mind's eye, Horatio. I like more 'and more my notion of making, in this little book, a 'great blow for the poor. Something powerful, I think 'I can do, but I want to be tender too, and cheerful; as 'like the *Carol* in that respect as may be, and as unlike 'it as such a thing can be. The duration of the action 'will resemble it a little, but I trust to the novelty of the 'machinery to carry that off; and if my design be any-'thing at all, it has a grip upon the very throat of the 'time.' (8th of October.)

Design for his book.

Thus bent upon his work, for which he never had been in more earnest mood, he was disturbed by hearing that he must attend the levee of the Governor who had unexpectedly arrived in the city, and who would take it as an affront, his eccentric friend Fletcher told him, if that courtesy were not immediately paid. 'It was the 'morning on which I was going to begin, so I wrote 'round to our consul,'—praying, of course, that excuse should be made for him. Don't bother yourself, replied that sensible functionary, for all the consuls and governors alive; but shut yourself up by all means. 'So,' continues Dickens, telling me the tale, 'he went next morning in 'great state and full costume, to present two English 'gentlemen. "Where's the great poet?" said the Governor.

Governor's levee.

GENOA: 1844.

Absence of the poet.

'"I want to see the great poet." "The great poet, your '"excellency," said the consul, "is at work, writing a book, '"and begged me to make his excuses." "Excuses!" said 'the Governor, "I wouldn't interfere with such an occu-'"pation for all the world. Pray tell him that my house '"is open to the honour of his presence when it is perfectly '"convenient for him; but not otherwise. And let no '"gentleman," said the Governor, a surweyin' of his suite 'with a majestic eye, "call upon Signor Dickens till he is '"understood to be disengaged." And he sent somebody 'with his own cards next day. Now I *do* seriously call 'this, real politeness and pleasant consideration—not posi-'tively American, but still gentlemanly and polished. The 'same spirit pervades the inferior departments; and I have 'not been required to observe the usual police regulations, 'or to put myself to the slightest trouble about anything.' (18th of October.)

Governor's message to him.

Subject he is working at.

The picture I am now to give of him at work should be prefaced by a word or two that may throw light on the design he was working at. It was a large theme for so small an instrument; and the disproportion was not more characteristic of the man, than the throes of suffering and passion to be presently undergone by him for results that many men would smile at. He was bent, as he says, on striking a blow for the poor. They had always been his clients, they had never been forgotten in any of his books, but here nothing else was to be remembered. He had become, in short, terribly earnest in the matter. Several months before he left England I had noticed in him the habit of more gravely regarding many things before passed

How originated.

lightly enough; the hopelessness of any true solution of either political or social problems by the ordinary Downing-street methods had been startlingly impressed on him in Carlyle's writings; and in the parliamentary talk of that day he had come to have as little faith for the putting down of any serious evil, as in a then notorious city Alderman's gabble for the putting down of suicide. The latter had stirred his indignation to its depths just before he came to Italy, and his increased opportunities of solitary reflection since had strengthened and extended it. When he came therefore to think of his new story for Christmas time, he resolved to make it a plea for the poor. He did not want it to resemble his *Carol*, but the same kind of moral was in his mind. He was to try and convert Society, as he had converted Scrooge, by showing that its happiness rested on the same foundations as those of the individual, which are mercy and charity not less than justice. Whether right or wrong in these assumptions, need not be questioned here, where facts are merely stated to render intelligible what will follow; he had not made politics at any time a study, and they were always an instinct with him rather than a science; but the instinct was wholesome and sound, and to set class against class never ceased to be as odious to him as he thought it righteous at all times to help each to a kindlier knowledge of the other. And so, here in Italy, amid the grand surroundings of this Palazzo Peschiere, the hero of his imagination was to be a sorry old drudge of a London ticket-porter, who in his anxiety not to distrust or think hardly of the rich, has fallen into the opposite extreme of distrusting the poor.

A plea for the poor.

C. D.'s politics.

Choice of a hero.

Page 145-6 of Vol. I.

GENOA: 1844.

From such distrust it is the object of the story to reclaim him; and, to the writer of it, the tale became itself of less moment than what he thus intended it to enforce. Far beyond mere vanity in authorship went the passionate zeal with which he began, and the exultation with which he finished, this task. When we met at its close, he was fresh from Venice, which had impressed him as 'the wonder' and 'the new sensation' of the world: but well do I remember how high above it all arose the hope that filled his mind. 'Ah!' he said to me, 'when I saw those places, 'how I thought that to leave one's hand upon the time, 'lastingly upon the time, with one tender touch for the mass 'of toiling people that nothing could obliterate, would be to 'lift oneself above the dust of all the Doges in their graves, 'and stand upon a giant's staircase that Sampson couldn't 'overthrow!' In varying forms this ambition was in all his life.

Master-passion.

Religious sentiment.

Another incident of these days will exhibit aspirations of a more solemn import that were not less part of his nature. It was depth of sentiment rather than clearness of faith which kept safe the belief on which they rested against all doubt or question of its sacredness, but every year seemed to strengthen it in him. This was told me in his second letter after reaching the Peschiere; the first having sent me some such commissions in regard to his wife's family as his kindly care for all connected with him frequently led to. 'Let 'me tell you,' he wrote (30th of September), 'of a curious 'dream I had, last Monday night; and of the fragments of 'reality I can collect, which helped to make it up. I have 'had a return of rheumatism in my back, and knotted

*Ante*, pp. 37-8.

'round my waist like a girdle of pain; and had laid awake 'nearly all that night under the infliction, when I fell 'asleep and dreamed this dream. Observe that throughout 'I was as real, animated, and full of passion as Macready '(God bless him!) in the last scene of *Macbeth*. In an 'indistinct place, which was quite sublime in its indistinct-'ness, I was visited by a Spirit. I could not make out the 'face, nor do I recollect that I desired to do so. It wore 'a blue drapery, as the Madonna might in a picture by 'Raphael; and bore no resemblance to any one I have 'known except in stature. I think (but I am not sure) 'that I recognized the voice. Anyway, I knew it was poor 'Mary's spirit. I was not at all afraid, but in a great delight, 'so that I wept very much, and stretching out my arms to 'it called it "Dear." At this, I thought it recoiled; and 'I felt immediately, that not being of my gross nature, I 'ought not to have addressed it so familiarly. "Forgive '"me!" I said. "We poor living creatures are only able '"to express ourselves by looks and words. I have used '"the word most natural to *our* affections; and you know '"my heart." It was so full of compassion and sorrow for 'me—which I knew spiritually, for, as I have said, I didn't 'perceive its emotions by its face—that it cut me to 'the heart; and I said, sobbing, "Oh! give me some '"token that you have really visited me!" "Form a '"wish," it said. I thought, reasoning with myself: "If '"I form a selfish wish, it will vanish." So I hastily dis-'carded such hopes and anxieties of my own as came into 'my mind, and said, "Mrs. Hogarth is surrounded with '"great distresses"—observe, I never thought of saying

GENOA: 1844.

A dream.

Page 98 of Vol. I.

Dialogue in a vision.

GENOA: 1844.

'"your mother" as to a mortal creature—"will you '"extricate her?" "Yes." "And her extrication is to '"be a certainty to me, that this has really happened?" '"Yes." "But answer me one other question!" I said, in 'an agony of entreaty lest it should leave me. "What is '"the True religion?" As it paused a moment without 'replying, I said—Good God in such an agony of haste, lest 'it should go away!—"You think, as I do, that the Form '"of religion does not so greatly matter, if we try to do '"good? or," I said, observing that it still hesitated, and 'was moved with the greatest compassion for me, "perhaps '"the Roman Catholic is the best? perhaps it makes one '"think of God oftener, and believe in him more steadily?" '"For *you*," said the Spirit, full of such heavenly tender- 'ness for me, that I felt as if my heart would break; "for '"*you*, it is the best!" Then I awoke, with the tears 'running down my face, and myself in exactly the condi- 'tion of the dream. It was just dawn. I called up Kate, 'and repeated it three or four times over, that I might 'not unconsciously make it plainer or stronger afterwards. 'It was exactly this. Free from all hurry, nonsense, or 'confusion, whatever. Now, the strings I can gather up, 'leading to this, were three. The first you know, from the 'main subject of my last letter. The second was, that 'there is a great altar in our bed-room, at which some 'family who once inhabited this palace had mass per- 'formed in old time: and I had observed within myself, 'before going to bed, that there was a mark in the wall, 'above the sanctuary, where a religious picture used to 'be; and I had wondered within myself what the subject

'What is 'the True 'religion?'

Close of the vision.

Its fragments of reality.

'might have been, *and what the face was like.* Thirdly, 'I had been listening to the convent bells (which ring at 'intervals in the night), and so had thought, no doubt, of 'Roman Catholic services. And yet, for all this, put the 'case of that wish being fulfilled by any agency in which I 'had no hand; and I wonder whether I should regard it 'as a dream, or an actual Vision!' It was perhaps natural that he should omit, from his own considerations awakened by the dream, the very first that would have risen in any mind to which his was intimately known—that it strengthens other evidences, of which there are many in his life, of his not having escaped those trying regions of reflection which most men of thought and all men of genius have at some time to pass through. In such disturbing fancies during the next year or two, I may add that the book which helped him most was the *Life of Arnold.* 'I respect and 'reverence his memory,' he wrote to me in the middle of October, in reply to my mention of what had most attracted myself in it, 'beyond all expression. I must have 'that book. Every sentence that you quote from it is the 'text-book of my faith.'

Trying regions of thought.

Reverence for Arnold.

He kept his promise that I should hear from him while writing, and I had frequent letters when he was fairly in his work. 'With my steam very much up, I find it a great 'trial to be so far off from you, and consequently to have 'no one (always excepting Kate and Georgy) to whom 'to expatiate on my day's work. And I want a crowded 'street to plunge into at night. And I want to be "on the '"spot" as it were. But apart from such things, the 'life I lead is favourable to work.' In his next letter: 'I

Hard at work.

GENOA: 1844.

'am in regular, ferocious excitement with the *Chimes;* get 'up at seven; have a cold bath before breakfast; and blaze 'away, wrathful and red-hot, until three o'clock or so: when 'I usually knock off (unless it rains) for the day . . I am 'fierce to finish in a spirit bearing some affinity to those 'of truth and mercy, and to shame the cruel and the cant-'ing. I have not forgotten my catechism. "Yes verily, '"and with God's help, so I will!"'

First part finished.

Within a week he had completed his first part, or quarter. 'I send you to-day' (18th of October), 'by mail, 'the first and longest of the four divisions. This is great 'for the first week, which is usually up-hill. I have kept 'a copy in shorthand in case of accidents. I hope to send 'you a parcel every Monday until the whole is done. I do 'not wish to influence you, but it has a great hold upon 'me, and has affected me, in the doing, in divers strong 'ways, deeply, forcibly. To give you better means of 'judgment I will sketch for you the general idea, but pray 'don't read it until you have read this first part of the MS.' I print it here. It is a good illustration of his method in all his writing. His idea is in it so thoroughly, that, by comparison with the tale as printed, we see the strength of its mastery over his first design. Thus always, whether his tale was to be written in one or in twenty numbers, his fancies controlled him. He never, in any of his books, accomplished what he had wholly preconceived, often as he attempted it. Few men of genius ever did. Once at the sacred heat that opens regions beyond ordinary vision, imagination has its own laws; and where characters are so real as to be treated as existences, their creator himself

Anticipation of the close.

cannot help them having their own wills and ways. Fern the farm-labourer is not here, nor yet his niece the little Lilian (at first called Jessie) who is to give to the tale its most tragical scene; and there are intimations of poetic fancy at the close of my sketch which the published story fell short of. Altogether the comparison is worth observing.

Differences from published tale.

'The general notion is this. That what happens to 'poor Trotty in the first part, and what will happen to 'him in the second (when he takes the letter to a 'punctual and a great man of business, who is balancing 'his books and making up his accounts, and complacently 'expatiating on the necessity of clearing off every liability 'and obligation, and turning over a new leaf and starting 'fresh with the new year), so dispirits him, who can't do 'this, that he comes to the conclusion that his class and 'order have no business with a new year, and really are '"intruding." And though he will pluck up for an hour 'or so, at the christening (I think) of a neighbour's child, 'that evening: still, when he goes home, Mr. Filer's 'precepts will come into his mind, and he will say to 'himself, "we are a long way past the proper average of '"children, and it has no business to be born:" and will 'be wretched again. And going home, and sitting there 'alone, he will take that newspaper out of his pocket, and 'reading of the crimes and offences of the poor, especially 'of those whom Alderman Cute is going to put down, will 'be quite confirmed in his misgiving that they are bad; 'irredeemably bad. In this state of mind, he will fancy 'that the Chimes are calling to him; and saying to him-'self "God help me. Let me go up to 'em. I feel as if

First outline of the *Chimes.*

GENOA: 1844.

'"I were going to die in despair—of a broken heart; let '"me die among the bells that have been a comfort to '"me!"—will grope his way up into the tower; and fall 'down in a kind of swoon among them. Then the third 'quarter, or in other words the beginning of the second 'half of the book, will open with the Goblin part of the 'thing: the bells ringing, and innumerable spirits (the 'sound or vibration of them) flitting and tearing in and 'out of the church-steeple, and bearing all sorts of mis- 'sions and commissions and reminders and reproaches, 'and comfortable recollections and what not, to all sorts 'of people and places. Some bearing scourges; and others 'flowers, and birds, and music; and others pleasant faces 'in mirrors, and others ugly ones: the bells haunting 'people in the night (especially the last of the old year) 'according to their deeds. And the bells themselves, who 'have a goblin likeness to humanity in the midst of their 'proper shapes, and who shine in a light of their own, will 'say (the Great Bell being the chief spokesman) Who is 'he that being of the poor doubts the right of poor men 'to the inheritance which Time reserves for them, and 'echoes an unmeaning cry against his fellows? Toby, all 'aghast, will tell him it is he, and why it is. Then the 'spirits of the bells will bear him through the air to 'various scenes, charged with this trust: That they show 'him how the poor and wretched, at the worst—yes, even 'in the crimes that aldermen put down, and he has 'thought so horrible—have some deformed and hunch- 'backed goodness clinging to them; and how they have 'their right and share in Time. Following out the

First outline of the *Chimes*.

GENOA: 1844.

'history of Meg the Bells will show her, that marriage 'broken off and all friends dead, with an infant child; 'reduced so low, and made so miserable, as to be brought 'at last to wander out at night. And in Toby's sight, 'her father's, she will resolve to drown herself and the 'child together. But before she goes down to the water, 'Toby will see how she covers it with a part of her 'own wretched dress, and adjusts its rags so as to make 'it pretty in its sleep, and hangs over it, and smooths 'its little limbs, and loves it with the dearest love that 'God ever gave to mortal creatures; and when she runs 'down to the water, Toby will cry "Oh spare her! '"Chimes, have mercy on her! Stop her!"—and the 'bells will say, "Why stop her? She is bad at heart— '"let the bad die." And Toby on his knees will beg 'and pray for mercy: and in the end the bells will stop 'her, by their voices, just in time. Toby will see, too, what 'great things the punctual man has left undone on the 'close of the old year, and what accounts he has left un-'settled: punctual as he is. And he will see a great 'many things about Richard, once so near being his son-'in-law, and about a great many people. And the moral 'of it all will be, that he has his portion in the new year 'no less than any other man, and that the poor require 'a deal of beating out of shape before their human shape 'is gone; that even in their frantic wickedness there may 'be good in their hearts triumphantly asserting itself, 'though all the aldermen alive say "No," as he has learnt 'from the agony of his own child; and that the truth is 'Trustfulness in them, not doubt, nor putting down, nor

First outline of the *Chimes*.

GENOA: 1844.

'filing them away. And when at last a great sea rises, 'and this sea of Time comes sweeping down, bearing the 'alderman and such mudworms of the earth away to 'nothing, dashing them to fragments in its fury—Toby 'will climb a rock and hear the bells (now faded from his 'sight) pealing out upon the waters. And as he hears 'them, and looks round for help, he will wake up and find 'himself with the newspaper lying at his foot; and Meg 'sitting opposite to him at the table, making up the rib-'bons for her wedding to-morrow; and the window open, 'that the sound of the bells ringing the old year out and 'the new year in may enter. They will just have broken 'out, joyfully; and Richard will dash in to kiss Meg before 'Toby, and have the first kiss of the new year (he'll get 'it too); and the neighbours will crowd round with good 'wishes; and a band will strike up gaily (Toby knows a 'Drum in private); and the altered circumstances, and the 'ringing of the bells, and the jolly musick, will so transport 'the old fellow that he will lead off a country dance forth-'with in an entirely new step, consisting of his old familiar 'trot. Then quoth the inimitable—Was it a dream of Toby's 'after all? Or is Toby but a dream? and Meg a dream? 'and all a dream! In reference to which, and the 'realities of which dreams are born, the inimitable will 'be wiser than he can be now, writing for dear life, 'with the post just going, and the brave C booted . . . Ah 'how I hate myself, my dear fellow, for this lame and 'halting outline of the Vision I have in my mind. But 'it must go to you . . . You will say what is best for the 'frontispiece' . .

First outline of the *Chimes*.

With the second part or quarter, after a week's interval, came announcement of the enlargement of his plan, by which he hoped better to carry out the scheme of the story, and to get, for its following part, an effect for his heroine that would increase the tragic interest. 'I am still in stout 'heart with the tale. I think it well-timed and a good 'thought; and as you know I wouldn't say so to anybody 'else, I don't mind saying freely thus much. It has great 'possession of me every moment in the day; and drags me 'where it will. . . . If you only could have read it all at 'once!—But you never would have done that, anyway, for I 'never should have been able to keep it to myself; so that's 'nonsense. I hope you'll like it. I would give a hundred 'pounds (and think it cheap) to see you read it. . . . 'Never mind.'

Liking for the subject.

That was the first hint of an intention of which I was soon to hear more; but meanwhile, after eight more days, the third part came, with the scene from which he expected so much, and with a mention of what the writing of it had cost him. 'This book (whether in the Hajji 'Baba sense or not I can't say, but certainly in the literal 'one) has made my face white in a foreign land. My 'cheeks, which were beginning to fill out, have sunk 'again; my eyes have grown immensely large; my hair 'is very lank; and the head inside the hair is hot and 'giddy. Read the scene at the end of the third part, 'twice. I wouldn't write it twice, for something. . . You 'will see that I have substituted the name of Lilian for 'Jessie. It is prettier in sound, and suits my music 'better. I mention this, lest you should wonder who and

Third part finished.

What the writing of it cost him.

GENOA: 1844.

'what I mean by that name. To-morrow I shall begin 'afresh (starting the next part with a broad grin, and 'ending it with the very soul of jollity and happiness); 'and I hope to finish by next Monday at latest. Perhaps 'on Saturday. I hope you will like the little book. 'Since I conceived, at the beginning of the second part, 'what must happen in the third, I have undergone as 'much sorrow and agitation as if the thing were real; 'and have wakened up with it at night. I was obliged to 'lock myself in when I finished it yesterday, for my face 'was swollen for the time to twice its proper size, and 'was hugely ridiculous.' . . . His letter ended abruptly. 'I am going for a long walk, to clear my head. I feel that 'I am very shakey from work, and throw down my pen 'for the day. There! (That's where it fell.)' A huge blot represented it, and, as Hamlet says, the rest was silence.

Realities of fictitious sorrow.

Two davs later, answering a letter from me that had reached in the interval, he gave sprightlier account of himself, and described a happy change in the weather. Up to this time, he protested, they had not had more than four or five clear days. All the time he had been writing they had been wild and stormy. 'Wind, hail, rain, thunder 'and lightning. To-day,' just before he sent me his last manuscript, 'has been November slack-baked, the sirocco 'having come back; and to-night it blows great guns with 'a raging storm.' 'Weather worse,' he wrote after three Mondays, 'than any November English weather I have ever 'beheld, or any weather I have had experience of any-'where. So horrible to-day that all power has been rained 'and gloomed out of me. Yesterday, in pure determination

Wild weather.

Mountain rain.

'to get the better of it, I walked twelve miles in mountain 'rain. You never saw it rain. Scotland and America are 'nothing to it.' But now all this was over. 'The weather 'changed on Saturday night, and has been glorious ever 'since. I am afraid to say more in its favour, lest it 'should change again.' It did not. I think there were no more complainings. I heard now of autumn days with the mountain wind lovely, enjoyable, exquisite past expression. I heard of mountain walks behind the Peschiere, most beautiful and fresh, among which, and along the beds of dry rivers and torrents, he could 'pelt away,' in any dress, without encountering a soul but the contadini. I heard of his starting off one day after finishing work, 'fifteen 'miles to dinner—oh my stars! at such an inn!!!' On another day, of a party to dinner at their pleasant little banker's at Quinto six miles off, to which, while the ladies drove, he was able 'to walk in the sun of the middle of 'the day and to walk home again at night.' On another, of an expedition up the mountain on mules. And on another of a memorable tavern-dinner with their merchant friend Mr. Curry, in which there were such successions of surprising dishes of genuine native cookery that they took two hours in the serving, but of the component parts of not one of which was he able to form the remotest conception: the site of the tavern being on the city wall, its name in Italian sounding very romantic and meaning 'the Whistle,' and its bill of fare kept for an experiment to which, before another month should be over, he dared and challenged my cookery in Lincoln's-inn.

A change.

Fifteen-miles' walk to dinner.

Banquet at the Whistle.

A visit from him to London was to be expected almost

GENOA: 1844.

Startling news.

immediately! That all remonstrance would be idle, under the restless excitement his work had awakened, I well knew. It was not merely the wish he had, natural enough, to see the last proofs and the woodcuts before the day of publication, which he could not otherwise do; but it was the stronger and more eager wish, before that final launch, to have a vivider sense than letters could give him of the effect of what he had been doing. 'If I 'come, I shall put up at Cuttris's' (then the Piazza-hotel in Covent-garden) 'that I may be close to you. 'Don't say to anybody, except our immediate friends, 'that I am coming. Then I shall not be bothered. If I 'should preserve my present fierce writing humour, in any 'pass I may run to Venice, Bologna, and Florence, before 'I turn my face towards Lincoln's-inn-fields; and come 'to England by Milan and Turin. But this of course 'depends in a great measure on your reply.' My reply, dwelling on the fatigue and cost, had the reception I foresaw. 'Notwithstanding what you say, I am still in 'the same mind about coming to London. Not because 'the proofs concern me at all (I should be an ass as well 'as a thankless vagabond if they did), but because of that 'unspeakable restless something which would render it 'almost as impossible for me to remain here and not see 'the thing complete, as it would be for a full balloon, left 'to itself, not to go up. I do not intend coming from '*here,* but by way of Milan and Turin (previously going 'to Venice), and so, across the wildest pass of the Alps 'that may be open, to Strasburg. . . As you dislike the 'Young England gentleman I shall knock him out, and

Coming to London.

'Unspeak- 'able rest- 'less some- 'thing.'

GENOA: 1844.

Objections to *Chimes.*

'replace him by a man (I can dash him in at your rooms 'in an hour) who recognizes no virtue in anything but 'the good old times, and talks of them, parrot-like, what- 'ever the matter is. A real good old city tory, in a blue 'coat and bright buttons and a white cravat, and with a 'tendency of blood to the head. File away at Filer, as you 'please; but bear in mind that the *Westminster Review* 'considered Scrooge's presentation of the turkey to Bob 'Cratchit as grossly incompatible with political economy. 'I don't care at all for the skittle-playing.' These were among things I had objected to.

Secret of the visit.

But the close of his letter revealed more than its opening of the reason, not at once so frankly confessed, for the long winter-journey he was about to make; and if it be thought that, in printing the passage, I take a liberty with my friend, it will be found that equal liberty is taken with myself, whom it goodnaturedly caricatures; so that the reader can enjoy his laugh at either or both.

Eager to try effect of the story.

'Shall I confess to you, I particularly want Carlyle above 'all to see it before the rest of the world, when it is done; 'and I should like to inflict the little story on him and 'on dear old gallant Macready with my own lips, and to 'have Stanny and the other Mac sitting by. Now, if you 'was a real gent, you'd get up a little circle for me, one 'wet evening, when I come to town: and would say, "My '"boy (SIR, will you have the goodness to leave those '"books alone and to go downstairs—WHAT the Devil are '"you doing! And mind, sir, I can see nobody—do you '"hear? Nobody. I am particularly engaged with a '"gentleman from Asia)—My boy, would you give us

GENOA: 1844.

Plans a reading at my rooms.

'"that little Christmas book (a little Christmas book of '"Dickens's, Macready, which I'm anxious you should '"hear); and don't slur it, now, or be too fast, Dickens, '"please!"—I say, if you was a real gent, something to 'this effect might happen. I shall be under sailing orders 'the moment I have finished. And I shall produce my-'self (please God) in London on the very day you name. 'For one week: to the hour.'

The tale finished.

The wish was complied with, of course; and that night in Lincoln's-inn-fields led to rather memorable issues. His next letter told me the little tale was done. 'Third 'of November, 1844. Half-past two, afternoon. Thank 'God! I have finished the *Chimes*. This moment. I 'take up my pen again to-day, to say only that much; 'and to add that I have had what women call "a real good '"cry!"' Very genuine all this, it is hardly necessary to say. The little book thus completed was not one of his greater successes, and it raised him up some objectors; but there was that in it which more than repaid the suffering its writing cost him, and the enmity its opinions provoked; and in his own heart it had a cherished corner to the last. The intensity of it seemed always best to represent to himself what he hoped to be longest remembered for; and exactly what he felt as to this, his friend Jeffrey warmly expressed. 'All the tribe of selfishness, and 'cowardice and cant, will hate you in their hearts, and cavil 'when they can; will accuse you of wicked exaggeration, 'and excitement to discontent, and what they pleasantly 'call disaffection! But never mind. The good and the 'brave are with you, and the truth also.'

Jeffrey to C. D.

He resumed his letter on the fourth of November. 'Here 'is the brave courier measuring bits of maps with a carving-'fork, and going up mountains on a tea-spoon. He and I 'start on Wednesday for Parma, Modena, Bologna, Venice, 'Verona, Brescia, and Milan. Milan being within a reason-'able journey from here, Kate and Georgy will come to 'meet me when I arrive there on my way towards England; 'and will bring me all letters from you. I shall be there 'on the 18th. . . . . . Now, you know my punctiwality. 'Frost, ice, flooded rivers, steamers, horses, passports, and 'custom-houses may damage it. But my design is, to 'walk into Cuttris's coffee-room on Sunday the 1st of 'December, in good time for dinner. I shall look for you 'at the farther table by the fire—where we generally go. '. . . . . But the party for the night following? I know 'you have consented to the party. Let me see. Don't 'have any one, this particular night, to dinner, but let it 'be a summons for the special purpose at half-past 6. 'Carlyle, indispensable, and I should like his wife of all 'things: *her* judgment would be invaluable. You will ask 'Mac, and why not his sister? Stanny and Jerrold I should 'particularly wish; Edwin Landseer; Blanchard; perhaps 'Harness; and what say you to Fonblanque and Fox? I 'leave it to you. You know the effect I want to try . . . . 'Think the *Chimes* a letter, my dear fellow, and forgive 'this. I will not fail to write to you on my travels. Most 'probably from Venice. And when I meet you (in sound 'health I hope) oh Heaven! what a week we will have.'

Proposed travel.

Party for the Reading.

# CHAPTER VII.

## ITALIAN TRAVEL.

1844.

FERRARA: 1844.

So it all fell out accordingly. He parted from his disconsolate wife, as he told me in his first letter from Ferrara, on Wednesday the 6th of November: left her shut up in her palace like a baron's lady in the time of the crusades; and had his first real experience of the wonders of Italy. He saw Parma, Modena, Bologna, Ferrara, Venice, Verona, and Mantua. As to all which the impressions conveyed to me in his letters have been more or less given in his published *Pictures*. They are charmingly expressed. There is a sketch of a cicerone at Bologna which will remain in his books among their many delightful examples of his unerring and loving perception for every gentle, heavenly, and tender soul, under whatever conventional disguise it wanders here on earth, whether as poorhouse orphan or lawyer's clerk, architect's pupil at Salisbury or cheerful little guide to graves at Bologna; and there is another memorable description in his Rembrandt sketch, in form of a dream, of the silent, unearthly, watery wonders of Venice. This last, though not written until after his London visit, had been prefigured so vividly

Cities and people.

Venice.

in what he wrote at once from the spot, that those passages from his letter* may be read still with a quite undiminished interest. 'I must not,' he said, 'anticipate 'myself. But, my dear fellow, nothing in the world that 'ever you have heard of Venice, is equal to the magnifi-'cent and stupendous reality. The wildest visions of the 'Arabian Nights are nothing to the piazza of Saint Mark, 'and the first impression of the inside of the church. The 'gorgeous and wonderful reality of Venice is beyond the 'fancy of the wildest dreamer. Opium couldn't build such 'a place, and enchantment couldn't shadow it forth in a 'vision. All that I have heard of it, read of it in truth 'or fiction, fancied of it, is left thousands of miles behind. 'You know that I am liable to disappointment in such 'things from over-expectation, but Venice is above, beyond, 'out of all reach of coming near, the imagination of a man. 'It has never been rated high enough. It is a thing you 'would shed tears to see. When I came *on board* here

VENICE: 1844.

Letter of 12th November.

Rapture of enjoyment.

* 'I began this letter, my dear friend' (he wrote it from Venice on Tuesday night the 12th of November), 'with the intention of describing my travels as 'I went on. But I have seen so much, and travelled so hard (seldom dining, 'and being almost always up by candle light), that I must reserve my crayons 'for the greater leisure of the Peschiere after we have met, and I have again 'returned to it. As soon as I have fixed a place in my mind, I bolt—at such 'strange seasons and at such unexpected angles, that the brave C stares again. 'But in this way, and by insisting on having everything shewn to me whether 'or no, and against all precedents and orders of proceeding, I get on wonder-'fully.' Two days before he had written to me from Ferrara, after the very pretty description of the vineyards between Piacenza and Parma which will be found in the *Pictures from Italy* (pp. 203-4): 'If you want an antidote to this, 'I may observe that I got up, this moment, to fasten the window; and the 'street looked as like some byeway in Whitechapel—or—I look again—like 'Wych Street, down by the little barber's shop on the same side of the way as 'Holywell Street—or—I look again—as like Holywell Street itself—as ever 'street was like to street, or ever will be, in this world.'

Making the most of time.

Homely aspects.

VENICE: 1844.

Aboard the city.

'last night (after a five miles' row in a gondola; which 'somehow or other, I wasn't at all prepared for); when, 'from seeing the city lying, one light, upon the distant 'water, like a ship, I came plashing through the silent and 'deserted streets; I felt as if the houses were reality—the 'water, fever-madness. But when, in the bright, cold, 'bracing day, I stood upon the piazza this morning, by 'Heaven the glory of the place was insupportable! And 'diving down from that into its wickedness and gloom—'its awful prisons, deep below the water; its judgment 'chambers, secret doors, deadly nooks, where the torches 'you carry with you blink as if they couldn't bear the air 'in which the frightful scenes were acted; and coming out 'again into the radiant, unsubstantial Magic of the town; 'and diving in again, into vast churches, and old tombs—'a new sensation, a new memory, a new mind came upon 'me. Venice is a bit of my brain from this time. My 'dear Forster, if you could share my transports (as you 'would if you were here) what would I not give! I feel 'cruel not to have brought Kate and Georgy; positively 'cruel and base. Canaletti and Stanny, miraculous in their 'truth. Turner, very noble. But the reality itself, beyond 'all pen or pencil. I never saw the thing before that I 'should be afraid to describe. But to tell what Venice is, 'I feel to be an impossibility. And here I sit alone, writing 'it: with nothing to urge me on, or goad me to that 'estimate, which, speaking of it to anyone I loved, and 'being spoken to in return, would lead me to form. In 'the sober solitude of a famous inn; with the great bell 'of Saint Mark ringing twelve at my elbow; with three

What he saw and felt.

Beyond pencil or pen.

'arched windows in my room (two stories high) looking 'down upon the grand canal and away, beyond, to where 'the sun went down to-night in a blaze; and thinking over 'again those silent speaking faces of Titian and Tintoretto; 'I swear (uncooled by any humbug I have seen) that 'Venice is *the* wonder and the new sensation of the world! 'If you could be set down in it, never having heard of it, 'it would still be so. With your foot upon its stones, its 'pictures before you, and its history in your mind, it is 'something past all writing of or speaking of—almost past 'all thinking of. You couldn't talk to me in this room, 'nor I to you, without shaking hands and saying "Good '"God my dear fellow, have we lived to see this!"'

VENICE: 1844.

Solitary thoughts.

Five days later, Sunday the 17th, he was at Lodi, from which he wrote to me that he had been, like Leigh Hunt's pig, up 'all manner of streets' since he left his palazzo; that with one exception he had not on any night given up more than five hours to rest; that all the days except two had been bad ('the last two foggy as Blackfriars-bridge 'on Lord Mayor's day'); and that the cold had been dismal. But what cheerful, keen, observant eyes he carried everywhere; and, in the midst of new and unaccustomed scenes, and of objects and remains of art for which no previous study had prepared him, with what a delicate play of imagination and fancy the minuteness and accuracy of his ordinary vision was exalted and refined; I think strikingly shown by the few unstudied passages I am preserving from these friendly letters. He saw everything for himself; and from mistakes in judging for himself which not all the learning and study in the world will save ordinary men,

LODI: 17th November.

Refining influences.

LODI: 1844.

the intuition of genius almost always saved him. Hence there is hardly anything uttered by him, of this much-trodden and wearisomely-visited, but eternally beautiful and interesting country, that will not be found worth listening to.

About paintings.

'I am already brim-full of cant about pictures, and shall 'be happy to enlighten you on the subject of the different 'schools, at any length you please. It seems to me that 'the proposterous exaggeration in which our countrymen 'delight in reference to this Italy, hardly extends to the 'really good things.* Perhaps it is in its nature, that

About engravings.

Private galleries.

* Four months later, after he had seen the galleries at Rome and the other great cities, he sent me a remark which has since had eloquent reinforcement from critics of undeniable authority. 'The most famous of the oil paintings 'in the Vatican you know through the medium of the finest line-engravings 'in the world; and as to some of them I much doubt, if you had seen 'them with me, whether you might not think you had lost little in having 'only known them hitherto in that translation. Where the drawing is poor 'and meagre, or alloyed by time,—it is so, and it must be, often; though no 'doubt it is a heresy to hint at such a thing—the engraving presents the 'forms and the idea to you, in a simple majesty which such defects impair. 'Where this is not the case, and all is stately and harmonious, still it is some-'how in the very grain and nature of a delicate engraving to suggest to you '(I think) the utmost delicacy, finish, and refiriement, as belonging to the 'original. Therefore, though the Picture in this latter case will greatly charm 'and interest you, it does not take you by surprise. You are quite pre-'pared beforehand for the fullest excellence of which it is capable.' In the same letter he wrote of what remained always a delight in his memory, the charm of the more private collections. He found magnificent portraits and paintings in the private palaces, where he thought them seen to greater advantage than in galleries; because in numbers not so large as to distract attention or confuse the eye. 'There are portraits innumerable by Titian, Rubens, 'Rembrandt and Vandyke; heads by Guido, and Domenichino, and Carlo Dolci; 'subjects by Raphael, and Correggio, and Murillo, and Paul Veronese, and Sal-'vator; which it would be difficult indeed to praise too highly, or to praise 'enough. It is a happiness to me to think that they cannot be felt, as they 'should be felt, by the profound connoisseurs who fall into fits upon the longest 'notice and the most unreasonable terms. Such tenderness and grace, such noble

'there it should fall short. I have never seen any praise 'of Titian's great picture of the Transfiguration of the 'Virgin at Venice, which soared half as high as the beautiful and amazing reality. It is perfection. Tintoretto's 'picture too, of the Assembly of the Blest, at Venice also, 'with all the lines in it (it is of immense size and the 'figures are countless) tending majestically and dutifully 'to Almighty God in the centre, is grand and noble in 'the extreme. There are some wonderful portraits there, 'besides; and some confused, and hurried, and slaughterous 'battle pieces, in which the surprising art that presents the 'generals to your eye, so that it is almost impossible you 'can miss them in a crowd though they are in the thick 'of it, is very pleasant to dwell upon. I have seen some 'delightful pictures; and some (at Verona and Mantua) 'really too absurd and ridiculous even to laugh at. 'Hampton-court is a fool to 'em—and oh there are some 'rum 'uns there, my friend. Some werry rum 'uns. . . . 'Two things are clear to me already. One is, that the 'rules of art are much too slavishly followed; making it a 'pain to you, when you go into galleries day after day, to be 'so very precisely sure where this figure will be turning 'round, and that figure will be lying down, and that other

LODI: 1844.

Titian's Transfiguration.

Works of Tintoretto.

Conventionalities.

'elevation, purity, and beauty, so shine upon me from some well-remembered 'spots in the walls of these galleries, as to relieve my tortured memory from 'legions of whining friars and waxy holy families. I forgive, from the 'bottom of my soul, whole orchestras of earthy angels, and whole groves of 'St. Sebastians stuck as full of arrows according to pattern as a lying-in 'pincushion is stuck with pins. And I am in no humour to quarrel even 'with that priestly infatuation, or priestly doggedness of purpose, which 'persists in reducing every mystery of our religion to some literal development 'in paint and canvas, equally repugnant to the reason and the sentiment of 'any thinking man.'

Art wholly satisfactory.

LODI: 1844.

'will have a great lot of drapery twined about him, and so 'forth. This becomes a perfect nightmare. The second is, 'that these great men, who were of necessity very much in 'the hands of the monks and priests, painted monks and 'priests a vast deal too often. I constantly see, in pictures 'of tremendous power, heads quite below the story and 'the painter; and I invariably observe that those heads 'are of the convent stamp, and have their counterparts, 'exactly, in the convent inmates of this hour. I see the 'portraits of monks I know at Genoa, in all the lame parts 'of strong paintings: so I have settled with myself that in 'such cases the lameness was not with the painter, but with 'the vanity and ignorance of his employers, who *would* be 'apostles on canvas at all events.'*

Monks and painters.

The inns.

In the same letter he described the Inns. 'It is a great 'thing—quite a matter of course—with English travellers, 'to decry the Italian inns. Of course you have no com- 'forts that you are used to in England; and travelling 'alone, you dine in your bedroom always. Which is 'opposed to our habits. But they are immeasurably better 'than you would suppose. The attendants are very quick; 'very punctual; and so obliging, if you speak to them 'politely, that you would be a beast not to look cheerful, 'and take everything pleasantly. I am writing this in a 'room like a room on the two-pair front of an unfinished 'house in Eaton-square: the very walls make me feel as 'if I were a bricklayer distinguished by Mr. Cubitt with 'the favour of having it to take care of. The windows

Place of entertainment.

* The last two lines he has printed in the *Pictures*, p. 249, 'certain of' being inserted before 'his employers.'

'won't open, and the doors won't shut; and these latter '(a cat could get in, between them and the floor) have a 'windy command of a colonnade which is open to the night, 'so that my slippers positively blow off my feet, and make 'little circuits in the room—like leaves. There is a very 'ashy wood-fire, burning on an immense hearth which 'has no fender (there is no such thing in Italy); and it 'only knows two extremes—an agony of heat when wood 'is put on, and an agony of cold when it has been on two 'minutes. There is also an uncomfortable stain in the 'wall, where the fifth door (not being strictly indis-'pensable) was walled up a year or two ago, and never 'painted over. But the bed is clean; and I have had 'an excellent dinner; and without being obsequious or 'servile, which is not at all the characteristic of the 'people in the North of Italy, the waiters are so amiably 'disposed to invent little attentions which they suppose 'to be English, and are so lighthearted and goodnatured, 'that it is a pleasure to have to do with them. But so 'it is with all the people. Vetturino-travelling involves 'a stoppage of two hours in the middle of the day, to bait 'the horses. At that time I always walk on. If there 'are many turns in the road, I necessarily have to ask 'my way, very often: and the men are such gentlemen, 'and the women such ladies, that it is quite an inter-'change of courtesies.'

LODI: 1844.

Windows and doors:

Wood fires.

Compensations.

Of the help his courier continued to be to him I had whimsical instances in almost every letter, but he appears too often in the published book to require such celebration here. He is however an essential figure to two little

Brave C of his *Pictures*.

LODI: 1844.

Louis Roche of Avignon.

scenes sketched for me at Lodi, and I may preface them by saying that Louis Roche, a native of Avignon, justified to the close his master's high opinion. He was again engaged for nearly a year in Switzerland, and soon after, poor fellow, though with a jovial robustness of look and breadth of chest that promised unusual length of days, was killed by heart-disease. 'The brave C continues to 'be a prodigy. He puts out my clothes at every inn 'as if I were going to stay there twelve months; calls 'me to the instant every morning; lights the fire before 'I get up; gets hold of roast fowls and produces them 'in coaches at a distance from all other help, in hungry 'moments; and is invaluable to me. He is such a good 'fellow, too, that little rewards don't spoil him. I always

Master and servant.

'give him, after I have dined, a tumbler of Sauterne or 'Hermitage or whatever I may have; sometimes (as 'yesterday) when we have come to a public-house at 'about eleven o'clock, very cold, having started before 'day-break and had nothing, I make him take his break-'fast with me; and this renders him only more anxious 'than ever, by redoubling attentions, to show me that 'he thinks he has got a good master . . . I didn't tell you

Dinner at the Peschiere.

'that the day before I left Genoa, we had a dinner-'party—our English consul and his wife; the banker; 'Sir George Crawford and his wife; the De la Rues; 'Mr. Curry; and some others, fourteen in all. At about 'nine in the morning, two men in immense paper caps 'enquired at the door for the brave C, who presently 'introduced them in triumph as the Governor's cooks, 'his private friends, who had come to dress the dinner!

'Jane wouldn't stand this, however; so we were obliged 'to decline. Then there came, at half-hourly intervals, 'six gentlemen having the appearance of English clergy-'men; other private friends who had come to wait... 'We accepted *their* services; and you never saw anything 'so nicely and quietly done. He had asked, as a special 'distinction, to be allowed the supreme control of the 'dessert; and he had ices made like fruit, had pieces 'of crockery turned upside down so as to look like other 'pieces of crockery non-existent in this part of Europe, 'and carried a case of tooth-picks in his pocket. Then his 'delight was, to get behind Kate at one end of the table, 'to look at me at the other, and to say to Georgy in a 'low voice whenever he handed her anything, "What '"does master think of datter 'rangement? Is he con-'"tĕnt?" . . . . . If you could see what these fellows of 'couriers are when their families are not upon the move, 'you would feel what a prize he is. I can't make out 'whether he was ever a smuggler, but nothing will in-'duce him to give the custom-house-officers anything: 'in consequence of which that portmanteau of mine has 'been unnecessarily opened twenty times. Two of them 'will come to the coach-door, at the gate of a town. "Is '"there anything contraband in this carriage, signore?"—'"No, no. There's nothing here. I am an Englishman, '"and this is my servant." "A buono mano signore?" '"Roche," (in English) "give him something, and get '"rid of him." He sits unmoved. "A buono mano '"signore?" "Go along with you!" says the brave C. '"Signore, I am a custom-house-officer!" "Well, then,

LODI: 1844.

Resources of a courier.

Custom-house officers.

LODI: 1844.

Natural enemies.

'"more shame for you!"—he always makes the same 'answer. And then he turns to me and says in English: 'while the custom-house-officer's face is a portrait of 'anguish framed in the coach-window, from his intense 'desire to know what is being told to his disparagement: '"Datter chip," shaking his fist at him, "is greatest tief— '"and you know it you rascal—as never did en-razh me so, '"that I cannot bear myself!" I suppose chip to mean 'chap, but it may include the custom-house-officer's 'father and have some reference to the old block, for 'anything I distinctly know.'

MILAN: 18th November.

He closed his Lodi letter next day at Milan, whither his wife and her sister had made an eighty miles journey from Genoa, to pass a couple of days with him in Prospero's old Dukedom before he left for London. 'We shall go our 'several ways on Thursday morning, and I am still bent 'on appearing at Cuttris's on Sunday the first, as if I had 'walked thither from Devonshire-terrace. In the mean-'time I shall not write to you again ... to enhance the 'pleasure (if anything *can* enhance the pleasure) of our 'meeting ... I am opening my arms so wide!' One more letter I had nevertheless; written at Strasburg on Monday night the 25th; to tell me I might look for him one day earlier, so rapid had been his progress. He had been in bed only once, at Friburg for two or three hours, since he left Milan; and he had sledged through the snow on the top of the Simplon in the midst of prodigious cold.

STRASBURG.

After passing the Simplon.

'I am sitting here *in* a wood-fire, and drinking brandy and 'water scalding hot, with a faint idea of coming warm in 'time. My face is at present tingling with the frost and

Maclise. R A. C. H. Jeens.

AT 58, LINCOLNS INN FIELDS, MONDAY THE 2ND OF DECEMBER 1844

'wind, as I suppose the cymbals may, when that turbaned 'turk attached to the life guards' band has been newly 'clashing at them in St. James's-park. I am in hopes it 'may be the preliminary agony of returning animation.'

STRASBURG: 1844.

There was certainly no want of animation when we met. I have but to write the words to bring back the eager face and figure, as they flashed upon me so suddenly this wintry Saturday night that almost before I could be conscious of his presence I felt the grasp of his hand. It is almost all I find it possible to remember of the brief, bright, meeting. Hardly did he seem to have come when he was gone. But all that the visit proposed he accomplished. He saw his little book in its final form for publication; and, to a select few brought together on Monday the 2nd of December at my house, had the opportunity of reading it aloud. An occasion rather memorable, in which was the germ of those readings to larger audiences by which, as much as by his books, the world knew him in his later life; but of which no detail beyond the fact remains in my memory, and all are now dead who were present at it excepting only Mr. Carlyle and myself. Among those however who have thus passed away was one, our excellent Maclise, who, anticipating the advice of Captain Cuttle, had 'made a note of' it in pencil, which I am able here to reproduce. It will tell the reader all he can wish to know. He will see of whom the party consisted; and may be assured (with allowance for a touch of caricature to which I may claim to be considered myself as the chief victim), that in the grave attention of Carlyle, the eager interest of Stanfield and Maclise, the keen look of poor Laman

LONDON: 30th November.

A reading in Lincoln's-inn-fields.

Only two survivors.

LONDON: 1844.

Persons present.

Blanchard, Fox's rapt solemnity, Jerrold's skyward gaze, and the tears of Harness and Dyce, the characteristic points of the scene are sufficiently rendered. All other recollection of it is passed and gone; but that at least its principal actor was made glad and grateful, sufficient farther testimony survives. Such was the report made of it, that once more, on the pressing intercession of our friend Thomas Ingoldsby (Mr. Barham), there was a second reading to which the presence and enjoyment of Fonblanque gave new zest; * and when I expressed to Dickens, after he left us, my grief that he had had so tempestuous a journey for such brief enjoyment, he replied that the visit had been one happiness and delight to him. 'I would not recall an 'inch of the way to or from you, if it had been twenty 'times as long and twenty thousand times as wintry. It 'was worth any travel—anything! With the soil of 'the road in the very grain of my cheeks, I swear I 'wouldn't have missed that week, that first night of our 'meeting, that one evening of the reading at your rooms, 'aye, and the second reading too, for any easily stated or 'conceived consideration.'

Barham and Fonblanque.

Success of the visit.

He wrote from Paris, at which he had stopped on his way back to see Macready, whom an engagement to act there with Mr. Mitchell's English company had prevented from joining us in Lincoln's-inn-fields. There had been no such frost and snow since 1829, and he gave dismal report of the city. With Macready he had gone two nights

* I find the evening mentioned in the diary which Mr. Barham's son quotes in his Memoir. 'December 5, 1844. Dined at Forster's with Charles Dickens, 'Stanfield, Maclise, and Albany Fonblanque. Dickens read with remarkable 'effect his Christmas story, the *Chimes*, from the proofs . . . .' (ii. 191.)

before to the Odéon to see Alexandre Dumas' *Christine* played by Madame St. George, once Napoleon's mistress; 'now of an immense size, from dropsy I suppose; and with 'little weak legs which she can't stand upon. Her age, 'withal, somewhere about 80 or 90. I never in my life 'beheld such a sight. Every stage-conventionality she 'ever picked up (and she has them all) has got the 'dropsy too, and is swollen and bloated hideously. The 'other actors never looked at one another, but delivered all 'their dialogues to the pit, in a manner so egregiously un-'natural and preposterous that I couldn't make up my 'mind whether to take it as a joke or an outrage.' And then came allusion to a project we had started on the night of the reading, that a private play should be got up by us on his return from Italy. 'You and I, sir, will 'reform this altogether.' He had but to wait another night, however, when he saw it all reformed at the Italian opera where Grisi was singing in *Il Pirato*, and 'the 'passion and fire of a scene between her, Mario, and 'Fornasari, was as good and great as it is possible for any-'thing operatic to be. They drew on one another, the two 'men—not like stage-players, but like Macready himself: 'and she, rushing in between them; now clinging to this 'one, now to that, now making a sheath for their naked 'swords with her arms, now tearing her hair in distraction 'as they broke away from her and plunged again at each 'other; was prodigious.' This was the theatre at which Macready was immediately to act, and where Dickens saw him next day rehearse the scene before the doge and council in *Othello*, 'not as usual facing the float but

PARIS: 1844.

With Macready at the Odéon.

Origin of our private play.

Acting at the opera.

A Macready rehearsal.

MARSEILLES: 1844.

'arranged on one side,' with an effect that seemed to him to heighten the reality of the scene.

He left Paris on the night of the 13th with the malle poste, which did not reach Marseilles till fifteen hours behind its time, after three days and three nights travelling over horrible roads. Then, in a confusion between the two rival packets for Genoa, he unwillingly detained one of them more than an hour from sailing; and only managed at last to get to her just as she was moving out of harbour. As he went up the side, he saw a strange sensation among the angry travellers whom he had detained so long; heard a voice exclaim 'I am blarmed if it ain't 'DICKENS!' and stood in the centre of a group of *Five Americans!* But the pleasantest part of the story is that they were, one and all, glad to see him; that their chief man, or leader, who had met him in New York, at once introduced them all round with the remark, 'Personally our countrymen, and you, can fix it friendly sir, I do 'expectuate;' and that, through the stormy passage to Genoa which followed, they were excellent friends. For the greater part of the time, it is true, Dickens had to keep to his cabin; but he contrived to get enjoyment out of them nevertheless. The member of the party who had the travelling dictionary wouldn't part with it, though he was dead sick in the cabin next to my friend's; and every now and then Dickens was conscious of his fellow-travellers coming down to him, crying out in varied tones of anxious bewilderment, 'I say, what's French for a pillow?' 'Is 'there any Italian phrase for a lump of sugar? Just look, 'will you?' 'What the devil does echo mean? The

A recognition.

Friendly Americans.

'garsong says echo to everything!' They were excessively curious to know, too, the population of every little town on the Cornice, and all its statistics; 'perhaps the very 'last subjects within the capacity of the human intellect,' remarks Dickens, 'that would ever present themselves to 'an Italian steward's mind. He was a very willing fellow, 'our steward; and, having some vague idea that they 'would like a large number, said at hazard fifty thousand, 'ninety thousand, four hundred thousand, when they asked 'about the population of a place not larger than Lincoln's-'inn-fields. And when they said *Non Possible!* (which 'was the leader's invariable reply), he doubled or trebled 'the amount; to meet what he supposed to be their views, 'and make it quite satisfactory.'

ON BOARD FOR GENOA: 1844.

Information for travellers.

# CHAPTER VIII.

## LAST MONTHS IN ITALY.

1845.

GENOA: 1844.

Jeffrey on the *Chimes*.

ON the 22nd of December he had resumed his ordinary Genoa life; and of a letter from Jeffrey, to whom he had dedicated his little book, he wrote as 'most energetic and 'enthusiastic. Filer sticks in his throat rather, but all the 'rest is quivering in his heart. He is very much struck by 'the management of Lilian's story, and cannot help speak-'ing of that; writing of it all indeed with the freshness 'and ardour of youth, and not like a man whose blue and 'yellow has turned grey.' Some of its words have been already given. 'Miss Coutts has sent Charley, with the best 'of letters to me, a Twelfth Cake weighing ninety pounds, 'magnificently decorated; and only think of the characters, 'Fairburn's Twelfth Night characters, being detained at 'the custom-house for Jesuitical surveillance! But these 'fellows are—— Well! never mind. Perhaps you have 'seen the history of the Dutch minister at Turin, and of the 'spiriting away of his daughter by the Jesuits? It is all 'true; though, like the history of our friend's servant,* al-'most incredible. But their devilry is such that I am

Birthday gift.

Suspicious characters.

* In a previous letter he had told me that history. 'Apropos of servants, I must tell you of a child-bearing handmaiden of some friends of ours, a

'assured by our consul that if, while we are in the south, we 'were to let our children go out with servants on whom we 'could not implicitly rely, these holy men would trot even 'their small feet into churches with a view to their ulti-'mate conversion! It is tremendous even to see them in 'the streets, or slinking about this garden.' Of his purpose to start for the south of Italy in the middle of January, taking his wife with him, his letter the following week told me; dwelling on all he had missed, in that first Italian Christmas, of our old enjoyments of the season in England; and closing its pleasant talk with a postscript at midnight. 'First of January, 1845. Many many many happy returns 'of the day! A life of happy years! The Baby is dressed 'in thunder, lightning, rain, and wind. His birth is most 'portentous here.'

GENOA: 1844.

Jesuit interferences.

Birth of 1845.

It was of ill-omen to me, one of its earliest incidents being my only brother's death; but Dickens had a friend's true helpfulness in sorrow, and a portion of what he then wrote to me I permit myself to preserve in a note* for what

'thorough out and outer, who, by way of expiating her sins, caused herself, 'the other day, to be received into the bosom of the infallible church. She 'had two marchionesses for her sponsors; and she is heralded in the Genoa 'newspapers as Miss B—, an English lady, who has repented of her errors 'and saved her soul alive.'

A conversion.

* 'I feel the distance between us now, indeed. I would to Heaven, my 'dearest friend, that I could remind you in a manner more lively and affec-'tionate than this dull sheet of paper can put on, that you have a Brother 'left. One bound to you by ties as strong as ever Nature forged. By ties 'never to be broken, weakened, changed in any way—but to be knotted 'tighter up, if that be possible, until the same end comes to them as has come 'to these. That end but the bright beginning of a happier union, I believe; 'and have never more strongly and religiously believed (and oh! Forster, with 'what a sore heart I have thanked God for it) than when that shadow has 'fallen on my own hearth, and made it cold and dark as suddenly as in the

Comfort in sorrow.

GENOA: 1845.

Travel southward.

it relates of his own sad experiences and solemn beliefs and hopes. The journey southward began on the 20th January, and five days later I had a letter written from La Scala, at a little inn, 'supported on low brick arches like a 'British haystack,' the bed in their room 'like a mangle,' the ceiling without lath or plaster, nothing to speak of available for comfort or decency, and nothing particular to eat or drink. 'But for all this I have become attached to the 'country and I don't care who knows it.' They had left

CARRARA and PISA.

Pisa that morning and Carrara the day before: at the latter place an ovation awaiting him, the result of the zeal of our eccentric friend Fletcher, who happened to be staying there with an English marble-merchant.* 'There 'is a beautiful little theatre there, built of marble; and

'home of that poor girl you tell me of . . . When you write to me again, the 'pain of this will have passed. No consolation can be so certain and so 'lasting to you as that softened and manly sorrow which springs up from the 'memory of the Dead. I read your heart as easily as if I held it in my hand, 'this moment. And I know—I *know*, my dear friend—that before the 'ground is green above him, you will be content that what was capable of 'death in him, should lie there . . . I am glad to think it was so easy, and 'full of peace. What can we hope for more, when our own time comes!— 'The day when he visited us in our old house is as fresh to me as if it had 'been yesterday. I remember him as well as I remember you . . I have 'many things to say, but cannot say them now. Your attached and loving 'friend for life, and far, I hope, beyond it. C. D.' (8th of January, 1845.)

Yorkshire Italian.

* 'A Yorkshireman, who talks Yorkshire Italian with the drollest and 'pleasantest effect; a jolly, hospitable excellent fellow; as odd yet kindly a 'mixture of shrewdness and simplicity as I have ever seen. He is the only 'Englishman in these parts who has been able to erect an English household out 'of Italian servants, but he has done it to admiration. It would be a capital 'country-house at home; and for staying in "first-rate." (I find myself in'advertently quoting *Tom Thumb.*) Mr. Walton is a man of an extraordi'narily kind heart, and has a compassionate regard for Fletcher to whom his 'house is open as a home, which is half affecting and half ludicrous. He paid 'the other day a hundred pounds for him, which he knows he will never see a 'penny of again.' C. D. to J. F. (25th of January, 1845.)

'they had it illuminated that night, in my honour. 'There was really a very fair opera: but it is curious 'that the chorus has been always, time out of mind, made 'up of labourers in the quarries, who don't know a note 'of music, and sing entirely by ear. It was crammed to 'excess, and I had a great reception; a deputation 'waiting upon us in the box, and the orchestra turning 'out in a body afterwards and serenading us at Mr. 'Walton's.' Between this and Rome they had a somewhat wild journey;* and before Radicofani was reached, there were disturbing rumours of bandits and even uncomfortable whispers as to their night's lodging-place. 'I 'really began to think we might have an adventure; and 'as I had brought (like an ass) a bag of Napoleons with 'me from Genoa, I called up all the theatrical ways of 'letting off pistols that I could call to mind, and was the 'more disposed to fire them from not having any.' It ended in no worse adventure, however, than a somewhat exciting dialogue with an old professional beggar at Radicofani itself, in which he was obliged to confess that he came off second-best. It transpired at a little town hanging on a hill side, of which the inhabitants, being all of them beggars, had the habit of swooping down, like so many birds of prey, upon any carriage that approached it.

CARRARA: 1845.

Marble theatre.

A wild journey.

Birds of prey.

* 'Do you think,' he wrote from Ronciglione on the 29th January, 'in 'your state room, when the fog makes your white blinds yellow, and the wind 'howls in the brick and mortar gulf behind that square perspective, with a 'middle distance of two ladder-tops and a back-ground of Drury-lane sky— 'when the wind howls, I say, as if its eldest brother, born in Lincoln's-inn-'fields, had gone to sea and was making a fortune on the Atlantic—at such 'times do you ever think of houseless Dick?'

'Houseless 'Dick.'

RADICOFANI: 1845.

A beggar and his staff.

'Can you imagine' (he named a first-rate bore, for whose name I shall substitute) 'M. F. G. in a very frowsy brown 'cloak concealing his whole figure, and with very white 'hair and a very white beard, darting out of this place 'with a long staff in his hand, and begging? There he 'was, whether you can or not; out of breath with the 'rapidity of his dive, and staying with his staff all the 'Radicofani boys, that he might fight it out with me alone. 'It was very wet, and so was I: for I had kept, according 'to custom, my box-seat. It was blowing so hard that I 'could scarcely stand; and there was a custom-house on 'the spot, besides. Over and above all this, I had no 'small money; and the brave C never has, when I want 'it for a beggar. When I had excused myself several 'times, he suddenly drew himself up and said, with a 'wizard look (fancy the aggravation of M. F. G. as a 'wizard!) "Do you know what you are doing, my lord? '"Do you mean to go on, to-day?" "Yes," I said, "I '"do." "My lord," he said, "do you know that your '"vetturino is unacquainted with this part of the country; '"that there is a wind raging on the mountain, which '"will sweep you away; that the courier, the coach, and '"all the passengers, were blown from the road last year; '"and that the danger is great and almost certain?" '"No," I said, "I don't." "My lord, you don't under- '"stand me, I think?" "Yes I do, d—— you!" nettled 'by this (you feel it? I confess it). "Speak to my ser- '"vant. It's his business. Not mine"—for he really was 'too like M. F. G. to be borne. If you could have seen 'him!—"Santa Maria, these English lords! It's not

Warning to my lord.

My lord loses temper:

'"their business, if they're killed! They leave it to their '"servants!" He drew off the boys; whispered them to 'keep away from the heretic; and ran up the hill again, 'almost as fast as he had come down. He stopped at a 'little distance as we moved on; and pointing to Roche 'with his long staff cried loudly after me, "It's *his* busi-'"ness if you're killed, is it, my lord? Ha! ha! ha! '"whose business is it, when the English lords are born! '"Ha ha ha!" The boys taking it up in a shrill yell, I 'left the joke and them at this point. But I must confess 'that I thought he had the best of it. And he had so 'far reason for what he urged, that when we got on the 'mountain pass the wind became terrific, so that we were 'obliged to take Kate out of the carriage lest she should 'be blown over, carriage and all, and had ourselves to hang 'on to it, on the windy side, to prevent its going Heaven 'knows where!'

RADICOFANI: 1845.

and has the worst of it.

The first impression of Rome was disappointing. It was the evening of the 30th of January, and the cloudy sky, dull cold rain, and muddy footways, he was prepared for; but he was not prepared for the long streets of common-place shops and houses like Paris or any other capital, the busy people, the equipages, the ordinary walkers up and down. 'It was no more my Rome, degraded and 'fallen and lying asleep in the sun among a heap of ruins, 'than Lincoln's-inn-fields is. So I really went to bed in 'a very indifferent humour.' That all this yielded to later and worthier impressions I need hardly say; and he had never in his life, he told me afterwards, been so moved or overcome by any sight as by that of the Coliseum,

AT ROME.

First thoughts.

ROME: 1845.

Second thoughts.

'except perhaps by the first contemplation of the Falls 'of Niagara.' He went to Naples for the interval before the holy week; and his first letter from it was to say that he had found the wonderful aspects of Rome before he left, and that for loneliness and grandeur of ruin nothing could transcend the southern side of the Campagna. But farther and farther south the weather had become worse; and for a week before his letter (the 11th of February), the only bright sky he had seen was just as

Terracina.

the sun was coming up across the sea at Terracina. 'Of 'which place, a beautiful one, you can get a very good 'idea by imagining something as totally unlike the 'scenery in *Fra Diavolo* as possible.' He thought the

Bay of Naples.

bay less striking at Naples than at Genoa, the shape of the latter being more perfect in its beauty, and the smaller size enabling you to see it all at once, and feel it more like an exquisite picture. The city he conceived the greatest dislike to.* 'The condition of the common

A burial-place.

* He makes no mention in his book of the pauper burial-place at Naples, to which the reference made in his letters is striking enough for preservation. 'In Naples, the burying place of the poor people is a great paved yard with 'three hundred and sixty-five pits in it: every one covered by a square stone 'which is fastened down. One of these pits is opened every night in the 'year; the bodies of the pauper dead are collected in the city; brought out 'in a cart (like that I told you of at Rome); and flung in, uncoffined. 'Some lime is then cast down into the pit; and it is sealed up until a year is 'past, and its turn again comes round. Every night there is a pit opened; 'and every night that same pit is sealed up again, for a twelvemonth. The 'cart has a red lamp attached, and at about ten o'clock at night you see it 'glaring through the streets of Naples: stopping at the doors of hospitals and 'prisons, and such places, to increase its freight: and then rattling off again. 'Attached to the new cemetery (a very pretty one, and well kept: immeasur-'ably better in all respects than Père-la-Chaise) there is another similar yard, 'but not so large.' . . . In connection with the same subject he adds: 'About 'Naples, the dead are borne along the street, uncovered, on an open bier;

NAPLES: 1845.

'people here is abject and shocking. I am afraid the 'conventional idea of the picturesque is associated with 'such misery and degradation that a new picturesque 'will have to be established as the world goes onward. 'Except Fondi, there is nothing on earth that I have 'seen so dirty as Naples. I don't know what to liken the 'streets to where the mass of the lazzaroni live. You 'recollect that favourite pigstye of mine near Broadstairs? 'They are more like streets of such apartments heaped 'up story on story, and tumbled house on house, than 'anything else I can think of, at this moment.' In a later letter he was even less tolerant. 'What would I 'give that you should see the lazzaroni as they really are '—mere squalid, abject, miserable animals for vermin to 'batten on; slouching, slinking, ugly, shabby, scavenging 'scarecrows! And oh the raffish counts and more than 'doubtful countesses, the noodles and the blacklegs, the 'good society! And oh the miles of miserable streets and 'wretched occupants,* to which Saffron-hill or the Borough-'mint is a kind of small gentility, which are found to be

Filth of Fondi and Naples.

Lazzaroni.

'which is sometimes hoisted on a sort of palanquin, covered with a cloth of 'scarlet and gold. This exposure of the deceased is not peculiar to that 'part of Italy; for about midway between Rome and Genoa we encountered 'a funeral procession attendant on the body of a woman, which was presented 'in its usual dress, to my eyes (looking from my elevated seat on the box of 'a travelling carriage) as if she were alive, and resting on her bed. An 'attendant priest was chanting lustily—and as badly as the priests invariably 'do. Their noise is horrible . . .'

Exposure of the dead.

* 'Thackeray praises the people of Italy for being kind to brutes. There is 'probably no country in the world where they are treated with such frightful 'cruelty. It is universal.' (Naples, 2nd Feb. 1845.) Emphatic confirmation of this remark has been lately given by the Naples correspondent of the *Times*, writing under date of February 1872.

Unkindness to brutes.

NAPLES: 1845.

False picturesque.

'so picturesque by English lords and ladies; to whom the 'wretchedness left behind at home is lowest of the low, 'and vilest of the vile, and commonest of all common 'things. Well! well! I have often thought that one of 'the best chances of immortality for a writer is in the

What makes good company.

'Death of his language, when he immediately becomes 'good company; and I often think here,—What *would* 'you say to these people, milady and milord, if they 'spoke out of the homely dictionary of your own "lower '"orders."' He was again at Rome on Sunday the second of March.

Sad English news.

Sad news from me as to a common and very dear friend awaited him there; but it is a subject on which I may not dwell farther than to say that there arose from it much to redeem even such a sorrow, and that this I could not indicate better than by these wise and tender words from Dickens. 'No philosophy will bear these dreadful things, 'or make a moment's head against them, but the practical 'one of doing all the good we can, in thought and deed. 'While we can, God help us! ourselves stray from our-'selves so easily; and there are all around us such fright-'ful calamities besetting the world in which we live; 'nothing else will carry us through it. . . . What a com-

True friends in calamity.

'fort to reflect on what you tell me. Bulwer Lytton's con-'duct is that of a generous and noble-minded man, as I 'have ever thought him. Our dear good Procter too! And 'Thackeray—how earnest they have all been! I am very 'glad to find you making special mention of Charles Lever. 'I am glad over every name you write. It says something 'for our pursuit, in the midst of all its miserable disputes 'and jealousies, that the common impulse of its followers, 'in such an instance as this, is surely and certainly of the 'noblest.'

ROME. 1845.

FLORENCE.

After the ceremonies of the holy week, of which the descriptions sent to me were reproduced in his book, he went to Florence,* which lived always afterwards in his memory with Venice, and with Genoa. He thought these the three great Italian cities. 'There are some places here,†—oh Heaven

* The reader will perhaps think with me that what he noticed, on the roads in Tuscany more than in any others, of wayside crosses and religious memorials, may be worth preserving. . . . 'You know that in the streets and corners of 'roads, there are all sorts of crosses and similar memorials to be seen in Italy. 'The most curious are, I think, in Tuscany. There is very seldom a figure on 'the cross, though there is sometimes a face; but they are remarkable for 'being garnished with little models in wood of every possible object that can 'be connected with the Saviour's death. The cock that crowed when Peter 'had denied his master thrice, is generally perched on the tip-top; and an 'ornithological phenomenon he always is. Under him is the inscription. 'Then, hung on to the cross-beam, are the spear, the reed with the sponge of 'vinegar and water at the end, the coat without seam for which the soldiers 'cast lots, the dice-box with which they threw for it, the hammer that drove 'in the nails, the pincers that pulled them out, the ladder which was set 'against the cross, the crown of thorns, the instrument of flagellation, the 'lantern with which Mary went to the tomb—I suppose; I can think of no 'other—and the sword with which Peter smote the high priest's servant. A 'perfect toyshop of little objects; repeated at every four or five miles all along 'the highway.'

Wayside memorials.

† Of his visit to Fiesole I have spoken in my LIFE OF LANDOR. 'Ten years 'after Landor had lost this home, an Englishman travelling in Italy, his friend 'and mine, visited the neighbourhood for his sake, drove out from Florence to 'Fiesole, and asked his coachman which was the villa in which the Landor 'family lived. "He was a dull dog, and pointed to Boccaccio's. I didn't '"believe him. He was so deuced ready that I knew he lied. I went up to '"the convent, which is on a height, and was leaning over a dwarf wall '"basking in the noble view over a vast range of hill and valley, when a little '"peasant girl came up and began to point out the localities. *Ecco la villa* '"*Landora!* was one of the first half-dozen sentences she spoke. My heart '"swelled as Landor's would have done when I looked down upon it, nestling '"among its olive-trees and vines, and with its upper windows (there are five

Visit to Landor's villa.

FLORENCE: 1845.

'how fine! I wish you could see the tower of the palazzo 'Vecchio as it lies before me at this moment, on the 'opposite bank of the Arno! But I will tell you more 'about it, and about all Florence, from my shady arm-'chair up among the Peschiere oranges. I shall not be 'sorry to sit down in it again. . . . Poor Hood, poor Hood! 'I still look for his death, and he still lingers on. And 'Sydney Smith's brother gone after poor dear Sydney 'himself! Maltby will wither when he reads it; and poor 'old Rogers will contradict some young man at dinner, 'every day for three weeks."

Death of Bobus Smith.

Before he left Florence (on the 4th of April) I heard of a 'very pleasant and very merry day' at Lord Holland's; and I ought to have mentioned how much he was gratified, at Naples, by the attentions of the English Minister there, Mr. Temple, Lord Palmerston's brother, whom he described as a man supremely agreeable, with everything about him in perfect taste, and with that truest gentleman-manner which has its root in kindness and generosity of nature. He was back at home in the Peschiere on Wednesday the ninth of April. Here he continued to write to me every week, for as long as he remained, of whatever he had seen: with no definite purpose as yet, but the pleasure

At Lord Holland's.

Again at Peschiere.

' "above the door) open to the setting sun. Over the centre of these there is ' "another story, set upon the housetop like a tower; and all Italy, except its ' "sea, is melted down into the glowing landscape it commands. I plucked ' "a leaf of ivy from the convent-garden as I looked; and here it is. For ' "Landor. With my love." So wrote Mr. Dickens to me from Florence on 'the 2nd of April 1845; and when I turned over Landor's papers in the same 'month after an interval of exactly twenty years, the ivy-leaf was found care-'fully enclosed, with the letter in which I had sent it.' Dickens had asked him before leaving what he would most wish to have in remembrance of Italy. 'An ivy-leaf from Fiesole,' said Landor.

Ivy-leaf from Fiesole.

of interchanging with myself the impressions and emotions undergone by him. 'Seriously,' he wrote to me on the 13th of April, 'it is a great pleasure to me to find 'that you are really pleased with these shadows in the 'water, and think them worth the looking at. Writing at 'such odd places, and in such odd seasons, I have been 'half savage with myself, very often, for not doing better. 'But d'Orsay, from whom I had a charming letter three 'days since, seems to think as you do of what he has read 'in those shown to him, and says they remind him vividly of 'the real aspect of these scenes. . . . Well, if we should de-'termine, after we have sat in council, that the experiences 'they relate are to be used, we will call B. and E. to their 'share and voice in the matter.' Shortly before he left, the subject was again referred to (7th of June). 'I am in as 'great doubt as you about the letters I have written you 'with these Italian experiences. I cannot for the life of 'me devise any plan of using them to my own satisfaction, 'and yet think entirely with you that in some form I 'ought to use them.' Circumstances not in his contemplation at this time settled the form they ultimately took.

Shadows in the water.

To publish or not?

Two more months were to finish his Italian holiday, and I do not think he enjoyed any part of it so much as its close. He had formed a real friendship for Genoa, was greatly attached to the social circle he had drawn round him there, and liked rest after his travel all the more for the little excitement of living its activities over again, week by week, in these letters to me. And so, from his 'shady arm-chair up among the Peschiere oranges,' I had at regular intervals what he called his rambling talk; went

Weekly letters.

GENOA: 1845.

over with him again all the roads he had taken; and of the more important scenes and cities, such as Venice, Rome, and Naples, received such rich filling-in to the first outlines sent, as fairly justified the title of *Pictures* finally chosen for them. The weather all the time too had been without a flaw. 'Since our return,' he wrote on the 27th April, 'we have had charming spring days. The garden 'is one grove of roses; we have left off fires; and we break-'fast and dine again in the great hall, with the windows 'open. To-day we have rain, but rain was rather wanted I 'believe, so it gives offence to nobody. As far as I have 'had an opportunity of judging yet, the spring is the most 'delightful time in this country. But for all that I am 'looking with eagerness to the tenth of June, impatient 'to renew our happy old walks and old talks in dear old 'home.'

Italy's best season.

Thoughts of home.

Of incidents during these remaining weeks there were few, but such as he mentioned had in them points of humour or character still worth remembering.* Two men were hanged in the city; and two ladies of quality, he told me, agreed to keep up for a time a prayer for the souls of these two miserable creatures so incessant that

American friends.

* One message sent me, though all to whom it refers have now passed away, I please myself by thinking may still, where he might most have desired it, be the occasion of pleasure. ' . . Give my love to Colden, and tell him if 'he leaves London before I return I will ever more address him and speak of 'him as *Colonel* Colden. Kate sends *her* love to him also, and we both entreat 'him to say all the affectionate things he can spare for third parties—using so 'many himself—when he writes to Mrs. Colden: whom you ought to know, 'for she, as I have often told you, is BRILLIANT. I would go five hundred 'miles to see her for five minutes. I am deeply grieved by poor Felton's loss. 'His letter is manly, and of a most rare kind in the dignified composure and 'silence of his sorrow.' (See Vol. I. p. 296).

Heaven should never for a moment be left alone: to which end 'they relieved each other' after such wise, that, for the whole of the stated time, one of them was always on her knees in the cathedral church of San Lorenzo. From which he inferred that 'a morbid sympathy for 'criminals is not wholly peculiar to England, though it 'affects more people in that country perhaps than in any 'other.'

Morbid sympathies.

Of Italian usages to the dead some notices from his letters have been given, and he had an example before he left of the way in which they affected English residents. A gentleman of his friend Fletcher's acquaintance living four miles from Genoa had the misfortune to lose his wife; and no attendance on the dead beyond the city gate, nor even any decent conveyance, being practicable, the mourner, to whom Fletcher had promised nevertheless the sad satisfaction of an English funeral, which he had meanwhile taken enormous secret pains to arrange with a small Genoese upholsterer, was waited upon, on the appointed morning, by a very bright yellow hackney-coach-and-pair driven by a coachman in yet brighter scarlet knee-breeches and waistcoat, who wanted to put the husband and the body inside together. 'They were 'obliged to leave one of the coach-doors open for the 'accommodation even of the coffin; the widower walked 'beside the carriage to the Protestant cemetery; and 'Fletcher followed on a big grey horse.'*

Deaths among English residents.

A funeral.

Scarlet breeches out of place.

* 'It matters little now,' says Dickens, after describing this incident in one of his minor writings, 'for coaches of all colours are alike to poor Kindheart, 'and he rests far north of the little cemetery with the cypress trees, by the 'city walls where the Mediterranean is so beautiful.' What was said on a

GENOA: 1845.

Scarlet breeches reappear, not less characteristically, in what his next letter told of a couple of English travellers who took possession at this time (24th of May) of a portion of the ground floor of the Peschiere. They had with them a meek English footman who immediately confided to Dickens's servants, among other personal grievances, the fact that he was made to do everything, even cooking, in crimson breeches; which in a hot climate, he protested, was 'a grinding of him down.' 'He is a poor soft country 'fellow; and his master locks him up at night, in a base-'ment room with iron bars to the window. Between 'which our servants poke wine in, at midnight. His 'master and mistress buy old boxes at the curiosity shops, 'and pass their lives in lining 'em with bits of parti-'coloured velvet. A droll existence, is it not? We are 'lucky to have had the palace to ourselves until now, 'but it is so large that we never see or hear these people; 'and I should not have known even, if they had not

Complaint of a meek footman.

His employers.

former page (*ante*, 156) may here be completed by a couple of stories told to Dickens by Mr. Walton, suggestive strongly of the comment that it required indeed a kind heart and many attractive qualities (which undoubtedly Fletcher possessed) to render tolerable such eccentricities. Dickens made one of these stories wonderfully amusing. It related the introduction by Fletcher of an unknown Englishman to the marble-merchant's house; the stay there of the Englishman, unasked, for ten days; and finally the walking off of the Englishman in a shirt, pair of stockings, neckcloth, pocket-handkerchief, and other etceteras belonging to Mr. Walton, which never reappeared after that hour. On another occasion, Fletcher confessed to Mr. Walton his having given a bill to a man in Carrara for £30; and the marble-merchant having asked, 'And pray, Fletcher, have you arranged to meet it when it falls due?' Fletcher at once replied, 'Yes,' and to the marble-merchant's farther enquiry 'how?' added, in his politest manner, 'I have arranged to blow my brains 'out the day before!' The poor fellow did afterwards almost as much self-violence without intending it, dying of fever caught in night-wanderings through Liverpool half-clothed amid storms of rain.

Angus Fletcher, Vol. I. p. 237.

GENOA: 1845.

'called upon us, that another portion of the ground floor 'had been taken by some friends of old Lady Holland— 'whom I seem to see again, crying about dear Sydney Smith, 'behind that green screen as we last saw her together.'*

A remembrance of Lady Holland.

Then came a little incident also characteristic. An English ship of war, the Phantom, appeared in the harbour; and from her commander, Sir Henry Nicholson, Dickens received, among attentions very pleasant to him, an invitation to lunch on board and bring his wife, for whom, at a time appointed, a boat was to be sent to the Ponte Reale (the royal bridge). But no boat being there at the time, Dickens sent off his servant in another boat to the ship to say he feared some mistake. 'While we 'were walking up and down a neighbouring piazza in his 'absence, a brilliant fellow in a dark blue shirt with a 'white hem to it all round the collar, regular corkscrew 'curls, and a face as brown as a berry, comes up to me 'and says "Beg your pardon sir—Mr. Dickens?" "Yes." '"Beg your pardon sir, but I'm one of the ship's company '"of the Phantom sir, cox'en of the cap'en's gig sir, '"she's a lying off the pint sir—been there half an hour." '"Well but my good fellow," I said, "you're at the '"wrong place!" "Beg your pardon sir, I was afeerd it '"was the wrong place sir, but I've asked them Genoese '"here sir, twenty times, if it was Port Real; and they '"knows no more than a dead jackass!"—Isn't it a good 'thing to have made a regular Portsmouth name of it?'

Nautical incident.

A touch of Portsmouth.

That was in his letter of the 1st June, which began by telling me it had been twice begun and twice flung into the

* Sydney died on the 22nd of February ('45), in his 77th year.

GENOA: 1845.

basket, so great was his indisposition to write as the time for departure came; and which ended thus. 'The fire-'flies at night now, are miraculously splendid; making 'another firmament among the rocks on the sea-shore, 'and the vines inland. They get into the bedrooms, and 'fly about, all night, like beautiful little lamps.* . . . I have 'surrendered much I had fixed my heart upon, as you 'know, admitting you have had reason for not coming to 'us here: but I stand by the hope that you and Mac will 'come and meet us at Brussels; it being so very easy. A 'day or two there, and at Antwerp, would be very happy 'for us; and we could still dine in Lincoln's-inn-fields on 'the day of arrival.' I had been unable to join him in Genoa, urgently as he had wished it: but what is said here was done, and Jerrold was added to the party.

Fireflies at night.

Plans for meeting.

Last letter.

His last letter from Genoa was written on the 7th of June, not from the Peschiere, but from a neighbouring palace, 'Brignole Rosso,' into which he had fled from the miseries of moving. 'They are all at sixes and sevens up 'at the Peschiere, as you may suppose; and Roche is in a 'condition of tremendous excitement, engaged in settling 'the inventory with the house-agent, who has just told

* A remark on this, made in my reply, elicited what follows in a letter during his travel home: 'Odd enough that remark of yours. I had been wondering 'at Rome that Juvenal (which I have been always lugging out of a bag, on 'all occasions) never used the fire-flies for an illustration. But even now, they 'are only partially seen; and no where I believe in such enormous numbers 'as on the Mediterranean coast-road, between Genoa and Spezzia. I will 'ascertain for curiosity's sake, whether there are any at this time in Rome, 'or between it and the country-house of Mæcenas—on the ground of Horace's 'journey. I know there is a place on the French side of Genoa, where they 'begin at a particular boundary-line, and are never seen beyond it. . . . All 'wild to see you at Brussels! What a meeting we will have, please God!'

Fireflies only in modern Italy.

'me he is the devil himself. I had been appealed to, and 'had contented myself with this expression of opinion. '"Signor Noli, you are an old impostor!" "Illustrissimo," 'said Signor Noli in reply, "your servant is the devil '"himself: sent on earth to torture me." I look occa-'sionally towards the Peschiere (it is visible from this 'room), expecting to see one of them flying out of a 'window. Another great cause of commotion is, that 'they have been paving the lane by which the house is 'approached, ever since we returned from Rome. We 'have not been able to get the carriage up since that 'time, in consequence; and unless they finish to-night, 'it can't be packed in the garden, but the things will 'have to be brought down in baskets, piecemeal, and 'packed in the street. To avoid this inconvenient 'necessity, the Brave made proposals of bribery to the 'paviours last night, and induced them to pledge them-'selves that the carriage should come up at seven this 'evening. The manner of doing that sort of paving 'work here, is to take a pick or two with an axe, and then 'lie down to sleep for an hour. When I came out, the 'Brave had issued forth to examine the ground; and was 'standing alone in the sun among a heap of prostrate 'figures: with a Great Despair depicted in his face, 'which it would be hard to surpass. It was like a 'picture—"After the Battle"—Napoleon by the Brave: 'Bodies by the Paviours.'

GENOA: 1845.

Closing excitements:

and difficulties.

Italians hard at work.

He came home by the Great St. Gothard, and was quite carried away by what he saw of Switzerland. The country was so divine that he should have wondered indeed if its

Returning by Switzerland.

GENOA: 1845.

sons and daughters had ever been other than a patriotic people. Yet, infinitely above the country he had left as he ranked it in its natural splendours, there was something more enchanting than these that he lost in leaving Italy; and he expressed this delightfully in the letter from Lucerne (14th of June) which closes the narrative of his Italian life.

LUCERNE.

'We came over the St. Gothard, which has been open 'only eight days. The road is cut through the snow, 'and the carriage winds along a narrow path between two 'massive snow walls, twenty feet high or more. Vast 'plains of snow range up the mountain-sides above the 'road, itself seven thousand feet above the sea; and 'tremendous waterfalls, hewing out arches for themselves 'in the vast drifts, go thundering down from precipices 'into deep chasms, here and there and everywhere: the 'blue water tearing through the white snow with an 'awful beauty that is most sublime. The pass itself, 'the mere pass over the top, is not so fine, I think, as 'the Simplon; and there is no plain upon the summit, 'for the moment it is reached the descent begins. So 'that the loneliness and wildness of the Simplon are not 'equalled *there*. But being much higher, the ascent and 'the descent range over a much greater space of country; 'and on both sides there are places of terrible grandeur, 'unsurpassable, I should imagine, in the world. The 'Devil's Bridge, terrific! The whole descent between 'Andermatt (where we slept on Friday night) and Altdorf, 'William Tell's town, which we passed through yesterday 'afternoon, is the highest sublimation of all you can

Passage of the St. Gothard.

LUCERNE: 1845.

'imagine in the way of Swiss scenery. Oh God! what 'a beautiful country it is! How poor and shrunken, 'beside it, is Italy in its brightest aspect!

Splendour of Swiss scenery:

'I look upon the coming down from the Great St. 'Gothard with a carriage and four horses and only one 'postilion, as the most dangerous thing that a carriage 'and horses can do. We had two great wooden logs for 'drags, and snapped them both like matches. The road 'is like a geometrical staircase, with horrible depths 'beneath it; and at every turn it is a toss-up, or seems 'to be, whether the leaders shall go round or over. The 'lives of the whole party may depend upon a strap in 'the harness; and if we broke our rotten harness once 'yesterday, we broke it at least a dozen times. The 'difficulty of keeping the horses together in the continual 'and steep circle, is immense. They slip and slide, and 'get their legs over the traces, and are dragged up against 'the rocks; carriage, horses, harness, all a confused heap. 'The Brave, and I, and the postilion, were constantly at 'work, in extricating the whole concern from a tangle, 'like a skein of thread. We broke two thick iron chains, 'and crushed the box of a wheel, as it was; and the 'carriage is now undergoing repair, under the window, 'on the margin of the lake: where a woman in short 'petticoats, a stomacher, and two immensely long tails 'of black hair hanging down her back very nearly to her 'heels, is looking on—apparently dressed for a melodrama, 'but in reality a waitress at this establishment.

dangers of it.

Swiss villages.

'If the Swiss villages looked beautiful to me in winter, 'their summer aspect is most charming: most fascinating:

LUCERNE: 1845.

'most delicious. Shut in by high mountains capped with 'perpetual snow; and dotting a rich carpet of the softest 'turf, overshadowed by great trees; they seem so many 'little havens of refuge from the troubles and miseries of 'great towns. The cleanliness of the little baby-houses of 'inns is wonderful to those who come from Italy. But the 'beautiful Italian manners, the sweet language, the quick 'recognition of a pleasant look or cheerful word; the cap'tivating expression of a desire to oblige in everything; 'are left behind the Alps. Remembering them, I sigh for 'the dirt again: the brick floors, bare walls, unplaistered 'ceilings, and broken windows.'

What is left behind the Alps.

We met at Brussels; Maclise, Jerrold, myself, and the travellers; passed a delightful week in Flanders together; and were in England at the close of June.

# CHAPTER IX.

## AGAIN IN ENGLAND.

### 1845—1846.

HIS first letter after again taking possession of Devonshire-terrace revived a subject on which opinions had been from time to time interchanged during his absence, and to which there was allusion in the agreement executed before his departure. The desire was still as strong with him as when he started *Master Humphrey's Clock* to establish a periodical, that, while relieving his own pen by enabling him to receive frequent help from other writers, might yet retain always the popularity of his name. 'I really think I have an idea, and not a bad 'one, for the periodical. I have turned it over, the last 'two days, very much in my mind: and think it positively 'good. I incline still to weekly; price three halfpence, 'if possible; partly original, partly select; notices of books, 'notices of theatres, notices of all good things, notices of 'all bad ones; *Carol* philosophy, cheerful views, sharp 'anatomization of humbug, jolly good temper; papers 'always in season, pat to the time of year; and a vein 'of glowing, hearty, generous, mirthful, beaming reference

LONDON: 1845.

Old hopes revived.

Notion for a periodical.

LONDON: 1845.

'in everything to Home, and Fireside. And I would call 'it, sir,—

Proposed weekly paper.

| |
|---|
| THE CRICKET. |
| A cheerful creature that chirrups on the Hearth. |
| *Natural History.* |

Prospectus for it.

'Now, don't decide hastily till you've heard what I 'would do. I would come out, sir, with a prospectus 'on the subject of the Cricket that should put every-'body in a good temper, and make such a dash at people's 'fenders and arm-chairs as hasn't been made for many a 'long day. I could approach them in a different mode 'under this name, and in a more winning and imme-'diate way, than under any other. I would at once sit 'down upon their very hobs; and take a personal and 'confidential position with them which should separate 'me, instantly, from all other periodicals periodically 'published, and supply a distinct and sufficient reason 'for my coming into existence. And I would chirp, 'chirp, chirp away in every number until I chirped it up 'to——well, you shall say how many hundred thousand! '. . . Seriously, I feel a capacity in this name and notion 'which appears to give us a tangible starting-point, and a 'real, defined, strong, genial drift and purpose. I seem to 'feel that it is an aim and name which people would 'readily and pleasantly connect with *me*; and that, for a 'good course and a clear one, instead of making circles 'pigeon-like at starting, here we should be safe. I think the

Home confidences.

'general recognition would be likely to leap at it; and 'of the helpful associations that could be clustered round 'the idea at starting, and the pleasant tone of which the 'working of it is susceptible, I have not the smallest doubt. '. . . But you shall determine. What do you think? And 'what do you say? The chances are, that it will either strike 'you instantly, or not strike you at all. Which is it, my dear 'fellow? You know I am not bigoted to the first sugges- 'tions of my own fancy; but you know also exactly how I 'should use such a lever, and how much power I should find 'in it. Which is it? What do you say?—I have not myself 'said half enough. Indeed I have said next to nothing; but 'like the parrot in the negro-story, I "think a dam deal."'

LONDON: 1845.

Chances for and against it.

My objection, incident more or less to every such scheme, was the risk of losing its general advantage by making it too specially dependent on individual characteristics; but there was much in favour of the present notion, and its plan had been modified so far, in the discussions that followed, as to involve less absolute personal identification with Dickens,—when discussion, project, everything was swept away by a larger scheme, in its extent and its danger more suitable to the wild and hazardous enterprises of that prodigious year (1845) of excitement and disaster. In this more tremendous adventure, already hinted at on a previous page, we all became involved; and the chirp of the Cricket, delayed in consequence until Christmas, was heard then in circumstances quite other than those that were first intended. The change he thus announced to me about half way through the summer, in the same letter which told me the success of d'Orsay's kind exertion to procure a fresh

Too dependent on himself.

Swept away by larger venture.

*Ante*, 82.

LONDON: 1845.

Use for its fancy and name.

engagement for his courier Roche.* 'What do you think 'of a notion that has occurred to me in connection with 'our abandoned little weekly? It would be a delicate and 'beautiful fancy for a Christmas book, making the Cricket 'a little household god—silent in the wrong and sorrow of 'the tale, and loud again when all went well and happy.' The reader will not need to be told that thus originated the story of the *Cricket on the Hearth*, a Fairy Tale of Home, which had a great popularity in the Christmas days of 1845. Its sale at the outset doubled that of both its predecessors.

Christmas book of 1845.

But as yet the larger adventure has not made itself known, and the interval was occupied with the private play of which the notion had been started between us at his visit in December, and which cannot now be better introduced than by a passage of autobiography. This belongs to his early life, but I overlooked it when engaged on that portion of the memoir; and the accident gives it now a more appropriate place. For, though the facts related belong to the interval described in the chapter on

Another passage of autobiography.

D'Orsay and the courier.

* Count d'Orsay's note about Roche, replying to Dickens's recommendation of him at his return, has touches of the pleasantry, wit, and kindliness that gave such a wonderful fascination to its writer. 'Gore House, 6 July, 1845. 'MON CHER DICKENS, Nous sommes enchantés de votre retour. Voici, thank 'God, Devonshire Place ressuscité. Venez luncheoner demain à 1 heure, et 'amenez notre brave ami Forster. J'attends la perle fine des couriers. Vous 'l'immortalisez par ce certificat—la difficulté sera de trouver un maître digne de 'lui. J'essayerai de tout mon cœur. La Reine devroit le prendre pour aller en 'Saxe Gotha, car je suis convaincu qu'il est assez intelligent pour pouvoir 'découvrir ce Royaume. Gore House vous envoye un cargo d'amitiés des plus 'sincères. Donnez de ma part 100,000 kind regards à Madame Dickens. 'Toujours votre affectionné, Ce D'ORSAY. J'ai vu le courier, c'est le tableau 'de l'honnêteté, et de la bonne humeur. Don't forget to be here at one to-'morrow, with Forster.'

LONDON: 1845.

his school-days and start in life, when he had to pass nearly two years as a reporter for one of the offices in Doctors' Commons, the influences and character it illustrates had their strongest expression at this later time. I had asked him, after his return to Genoa, whether he continued to think that we should have the play; and this was his reply. It will startle and interest the reader, and I must confess that it took myself by surprise; for I did not thus early know the story of his boyish years, and I thought it strange that he could have concealed from me so much.

More of the story of his early years.

'ARE we to have that play??? Have I spoken of it, 'ever since I came home from London, as a settled thing! 'I do not know if I have ever told you seriously, but I 'have often thought, that I should certainly have been as 'successful on the boards as I have been between them. 'I assure you, when I was on the stage at Montreal (not 'having played for years) I was as much astonished at the 'reality and ease, to myself, of what I did as if I had been 'another man. See how oddly things come about! When 'I was about twenty, and knew three or four successive 'years of Mathews's At Homes from sitting in the pit to 'hear them, I wrote to Bartley who was stage manager 'at Covent-garden, and told him how young I was, and 'exactly what I thought I could do; and that I believed I 'had a strong perception of character and oddity, and 'a natural power of reproducing in my own person what 'I observed in others. There must have been something 'in the letter that struck the authorities, for Bartley wrote 'to me, almost immediately, to say that they were busy 'getting up the *Hunchback* (so they were!) but that they

Page 396 of Vol. I.

Wish to try the stage.

Applies to Covent-garden manager.

LONDON: 1845.

'would communicate with me again, in a fortnight. 'Punctual to the time, another letter came: with an 'appointment to do anything of Mathews's I pleased, 'before him and Charles Kemble, on a certain day at the 'theatre. My sister Fanny was in the secret, and was to 'go with me to play the songs. I was laid up, when the 'day came, with a terrible bad cold and an inflammation 'of the face; the beginning, by the bye, of that annoyance 'in one ear to which I am subject at this day. I wrote 'to say so, and added that I would resume my application 'next season. I made a great splash in the gallery soon 'afterwards; the *Chronicle* opened to me; I had a dis-'tinction in the little world of the newspaper, which made 'me like it; began to write; didn't want money; had 'never thought of the stage, but as a means of getting it; 'gradually left off turning my thoughts that way; and 'never resumed the idea. I never told you this, did I? 'See how near I may have been, to another sort of life.

Sister Fanny in the secret.

Notion dropped.

'This was at the time when I was at Doctors' Commons 'as a shorthand writer for the proctors. And I recollect 'I wrote the letter from a little office I had there, where 'the answer came also. It wasn't a very good living '(though not a *very* bad one), and was wearily uncertain; 'which made me think of the Theatre in quite a busi-'ness-like way. I went to some theatre every night, with 'a very few exceptions, for at least three years: really 'studying the bills first, and going to where there was 'the best acting: and always to see Mathews whenever 'he played. I practised immensely (even such things as 'walking in and out, and sitting down in a chair): often

Page 71 of Vol. I.

Stage studies.

'four, five, six hours a day: shut up in my own room, or 'walking about in the fields. I prescribed to myself, too, 'a sort of Hamiltonian system for learning parts; and 'learnt a great number. I haven't even lost the habit 'now, for I knew my Canadian parts immediately, though 'they were new to me. I must have done a good deal: 'for, just as Macready found me out, they used to challenge 'me at Braham's: and Yates, who was knowing enough 'in those things, wasn't to be parried at all. It was just 'the same, that day at Keeley's, when they were getting 'up the *Chuzzlewit* last June.

LONDON: 1845.

Rehearsing parts.

'If you think Macready would be interested in this 'Strange news from the South, tell it him. Fancy Bartley 'or Charles Kemble *now!* And how little they suspect 'me!' In the later letter from Lucerne written as he was travelling home, he adds: '*Did* I ever tell you the details 'of my theatrical idea, before? Strange, that I should 'have quite forgotten it. I had an odd fancy, when I was 'reading the unfortunate little farce at Covent-garden, that 'Bartley looked as if some struggling recollection and con-'nection were stirring up within him—but it may only 'have been his doubts of that humorous composition.' The last allusion is to the farce of the *Lamplighter* which he read in the Covent-garden green-room, and to which former allusion was made in speaking of his wish to give help to Macready's managerial enterprise.

Strange news for Macready.

Then and now.

Page 160 of Vol. I.

*What Might have Been* is a history of too little profit to be worth anybody's writing, and here there is no call even to regret how great an actor was in Dickens lost. He took to a higher calling, but it included the lower. There

LONDON: 1845.

The lower in the higher calling.

was no character created by him into which life and reality were not thrown with such vividness, that the thing written did not seem to his readers the thing actually done, whether the form of disguise put on by the enchanter was Mrs. Gamp, Tom Pinch, Mr. Squeers, or Fagin the Jew. He had the power of projecting himself into shapes and suggestions of his fancy which is one of the marvels of creative imagination, and what he desired to express he became. The assumptions of the theatre have the same method at a lower pitch, depending greatly on personal accident; but the accident as much as the genius favoured Dickens, and another man's conception underwent in his acting the process which in writing he applied to his own. Into both he flung himself with the passionate fullness of his nature; and though the theatre had limits for him that may be named hereafter, and he was always greater in quickness of assumption than in steadiness of delineation, there was no limit to his delight and enjoyment in the adventures of our theatrical holiday.

An actor's requisites.

Play selected.

In less than three weeks after his return we had selected our play, cast our parts, and all but engaged our theatre; as I find by a note from my friend of the 22nd of July, in which the good natured laugh can give now no offence, since all who might have objected to it have long gone from us. Fanny Kelly, the friend of Charles Lamb, and a genuine successor to the old school of actresses in which the Mrs. Orgers and Miss Popes were bred, was not more delightful on the stage than impracticable when off, and the little theatre in Dean-street which the Duke of

Devonshire's munificence had enabled her to build, and which with any ordinary good sense might handsomely have realized both its uses, as a private school for young actresses and a place of public amusement, was made useless for both by her mere whims and fancies. 'Heavens! 'Such a scene as I have had with Miss Kelly here, this 'morning! She wanted us put off until the theatre 'should be cleaned and brushed up a bit, and she would 'and she would not, for she is eager to have us and 'alarmed when she thinks of us. By the foot of Pharaoh, 'it was a great scene! Especially when she choked, and had 'the glass of water brought. She exaggerates the import'ance of our occupation, dreads the least prejudice against 'the establishment in the minds of any of our company, 'says the place already has quite ruined her, and with 'tears in her eyes protests that any jokes at her additional 'expense in print would drive her mad. By the body of 'Cæsar, the scene was incredible! It's like a preposterous 'dream.' Something of our play is disclosed by the oaths à la Bobadil, and of our actors by 'the jokes' poor Miss Kelly was afraid of. We had chosen EVERY MAN IN HIS HUMOUR, with special regard to the singleness and individuality of the 'humours' portrayed in it; and our company included the leaders of a journal then in its earliest years, but already not more renowned as the most successful joker of jokes yet known in England, than famous for that exclusive use of its laughter and satire for objects the highest or most harmless which makes it still so enjoyable a companion to mirth-loving right-minded men. Maclise took earnest part with us, and was to have acted,

LONDON: 1845.

Fanny Kelly and her theatre.

C. D. and Fanny Kelly.

Every Man in his Humour.

LONDON: 1845.

The company of actors.

Parts cast.

Enjoying a character.

Bobadil to Kitely.

but fell away on the eve of the rehearsals; and Stanfield, who went so far as to rehearse Downright twice, then took fright and also ran away:* but Jerrold, who played Master Stephen, brought with him Lemon, who took Brainworm; Leech, to whom Master Matthew was given; A'Beckett, who had condescended to the small part of William; and Mr. Leigh, who had Oliver Cob. I played Kitely, and Bobadil fell to Dickens, who took upon him the redoubtable Captain long before he stood in his dress at the footlights; humouring the completeness of his assumption by talking and writing Bobadil, till the dullest of our party were touched and stirred to something of his own heartiness of enjoyment. One or two hints of these have been given, and I will only add to them his refusal of my wish that he should go and see some special performance of the *Gamester*. 'Man of the House. *Game-*'*ster!* By the foot of Pharaoh, I will *not* see the *Gamester*. 'Man shall not force, nor horses drag, this poor gentleman-'like carcass into the presence of the *Gamester*. I have 'said it. . . . The player Mac hath bidden me to eat and 'likewise drink with him, thyself, and short-necked Fox 'to-night. An' I go not, I am a hog, and not a soldier.

Troubles of management.

* 'Look here! Enclosed are two packets—a large one and a small one. 'The small one, read first. It contains Stanny's renunciation as an actor!!! 'After receiving it, at dinner time to-day' (22nd of August), 'I gave my 'brains a shake, and thought of George Cruikshank. After much shaking, I 'made up the big packet, wherein I have put the case in the artfullest manner. 'R—r—r—r—ead it! as a certain Captain whom you know observes.' The great artist was not for that time procurable, having engagements away from London, and Mr. Dudley Costello was substituted; Stanfield taking off the edge of his desertion as an actor by doing valuable work in management and scenery.

'But an' thou goest not—Beware citizen! Look to it. . . . 'Thine as thou meritest. BOBADIL (Captain). Unto 'Master Kitely. These.'

LONDON: 1845.

First performance.

The play was played on the 21st of September with a success that out-ran the wildest expectation; and turned our little enterprise into one of the small sensations of the day. The applause of the theatre found so loud an echo in the press, that for the time nothing else was talked about in private circles; and after a week or two we had to yield (we did not find it difficult) to a pressure of demand for more public performance in a larger theatre, by which a useful charity received important help, and its committee showed their gratitude by an entertainment to us at the Clarendon, a month or two later, when Lord Lansdowne took the chair. There was also another performance by us at the same theatre, before the close of the year, of a play by Beaumont and Fletcher. I may not farther indicate the enjoyments that attended the success, and gave always to the first of our series of performances a preeminently pleasant place in memory.

Second performance.

'Elder 'Brother.'

Of the acting.

Of the thing itself, however, it is necessary to be said that a modicum of merit goes a long way in all such matters, and it would not be safe now to assume that ours was much above the average of amateur attempts in general. Lemon certainly had most of the stuff, conventional as well as otherwise, of a regular actor in him, but this was not of a high kind; and though Dickens had the title to be called a born comedian, the turn for it being in his very nature, his strength was rather in the vividness and variety of his assumptions, than in the completeness, finish, or

LONDON: 1845.

C. D. as performer.

ideality he could give to any part of them. It is expressed exactly by what he says of his youthful preference for the representations of the elder Mathews. At the same time this was in itself so thoroughly genuine and enjoyable, and had in it such quickness and keenness of insight, that of its kind it was unrivalled; and it enabled him to present in Bobadil, after a richly coloured picture of bombastical extravagance and comic exaltation in the earlier scenes, a contrast in the later of tragical humility and abasement, that had a wonderful effect. But greatly as his acting contributed to the success of the night, this was nothing

C. D. as manager.

to the service he had rendered as manager. It would be difficult to describe it. He was the life and soul of the entire affair. I never seemed till then to have known his business capabilities. He took everything on himself, and did the whole of it without an effort. He was stage-director, very often stage-carpenter, scene-arranger, property-man, prompter, and band-master. Without offending any one he kept every one in order. For all he had useful suggestions, and the dullest of clays under his potter's hand were transformed into little bits of porcelain. He adjusted scenes, assisted carpenters, invented costumes, devised playbills, wrote out calls, and enforced as well as exhibited in his proper person everything of which he urged the necessity

Everything changed in Dean Street:

on others. Such a chaos of dirt, confusion, and noise, as the little theatre was the day we entered it, and such a cosmos as he made it of cleanliness, order, and silence, before the rehearsals were over! There were only two things left as we found them, bits of humanity both, understood from the first as among the fixtures of the place: a Man in a Straw Hat, tall, and very fitful in his exits and entrances, of whom we never could pierce the mystery, whether he was on guard or in possession, or what he was; and a solitary little girl, who flitted about so silently among our actors and actresses that she might have been deaf and dumb but for sudden small shrieks and starts elicited by the wonders going on, which obtained for her the name of Fireworks. There is such humorous allusion to both in a letter of Dickens's of a year's later date, on the occasion of the straw-hatted mystery revealing itself as a gentleman in training for the tragic stage, that it may pleasantly close for the present our private theatricals.

LONDON: 1845.

except two human mysteries.

'OUR STRAW-HATTED FRIEND from Miss Kelly's! Oh 'my stars! To think of him, all that time—Macbeth in 'disguise; Richard the Third grown straight; Hamlet 'as he appeared on his seavoyage to England. What an 'artful villain he must be, never to have made any sign 'of the melodrama that was in him! What a wicked-'minded and remorseless Iago to have seen you doing 'Kitely night after night! raging to murder you and 'seize the part! Oh fancy Miss Kelly "getting him up" 'in Macbeth. Good Heaven! what a mass of absurdity 'must be shut up sometimes within the walls of that 'small theatre in Dean-street! FIREWORKS will come 'out shortly, depend upon it, in the dumb line; and will 'relate her history in profoundly unintelligible motions 'that will be translated into long and complicated descrip-'tions by a grey-headed father, and a red-wigged country-'man, his son. You remember the dumb dodge of 'relating an escape from captivity? Clasping the left

22 Nov. '46, from Paris.

The mysteries explained.

Training for the stage.

LONDON: 1845.

'wrist with the right hand, and the right wrist with the 'left hand—alternately (to express chains)—and then 'going round and round the stage very fast, and coming 'hand over hand down an imaginary cord: at the end of 'which there is one stroke on the drum, and a kneeling 'to the chandelier? If Fireworks can't do that—and 'won't somewhere—I'm a Dutchman.'

Pantomimic.

Graver things now claim a notice which need not be proportioned to their gravity, because, though they had an immediate effect on Dickens's fortunes, they do not otherwise form part of his story. But first let me say, he was at Broadstairs for three weeks in the autumn;* we

At Broadstairs.

* Characteristic glimpse of this Broadstairs holiday is afforded by a letter of the 19th of August 1845. 'Perhaps it is a fair specimen of the odd 'adventures which befall the inimitable, that the cab in which the children 'and the luggage were (I and my womankind being in the other) got its shafts 'broken in the city, last Friday morning, through the horse stumbling on the 'greasy pavement; *and was drawn to the wharf (about a mile) by a stout 'man*, amid such frightful howlings and derisive yellings on the part of an 'infuriated populace, as I never heard before. Conceive the man in the 'broken shafts with his back towards the cab; all the children looking out 'of the windows; and the muddy portmanteaus and so forth (which were all 'tumbled down when the horse fell) tottering and nodding on the box! The 'best of it was, that *our* cabman, being an intimate friend of the damaged 'cabman, insisted on keeping him company; and proceeded at a solemn walk, 'in front of the procession; thereby securing to me a liberal share of the 'popular curiosity and congratulation . . . . Everything here at Broadstairs 'is the same as of old. I have walked 20 miles a day since I came down, 'and I went to a circus at Ramsgate on Saturday night, where *Mazeppa* was 'played in three long acts without an H in it: as if for a wager. Evven, 'and edds, and orrors, and ands, were as plentiful as blackberries; but the 'letter H was neither whispered in Evven, nor muttered in Ell, nor permitted 'to dwell in any form on the confines of the sawdust.' With this I will couple another theatrical experience of this holiday, when he saw a Giant played by a village comedian with a quite Gargantuesque felicity, and singled out for my admiration his fine manner of sitting down to a hot supper (of children), with the self-lauding exalting remark, by way of grace, 'How pleasant is a 'quiet conscience and an approving mind!'

Ramsgate entertainments.

had the private play on his return; and a month later, on the 28th of October, a sixth child and fourth son, named Alfred Tennyson after his godfathers d'Orsay and Tennyson, was born in Devonshire-terrace. A death in the family followed, the older and more gifted of his ravens having indulged the same illicit taste for putty and paint which had been fatal to his predecessor. Voracity killed him, as it killed Scott's. He died unexpectedly before the kitchen-fire. 'He kept his eye to the last upon the meat 'as it roasted, and suddenly turned over on his back with 'a sepulchral cry of *Cuckoo!*' The letter which told me this (31st of October) announced to me also that he was at a dead lock in his Christmas story: 'Sick, bothered 'and depressed. Visions of Brighton come upon me; and 'I have a great mind to go there to finish my second part, 'or to Hampstead. I have a desperate thought of Jack 'Straw's. I never was in such bad writing cue as I am this 'week, in all my life.' The reason was not far to seek. In the preparation for the proposed new Daily Paper to which reference has been made, he was now actively assisting, and had all but consented to the publication of his name.

His fourth son.

Page 210 of Vol. I.

Second raven's death.

Busy with the *Cricket*.

I entertained at this time, for more than one powerful reason, the greatest misgiving of his intended share in the adventure. It was not fully revealed until later on what difficult terms, physical as well as mental, Dickens held the tenure of his imaginative life; but already I knew enough to doubt the wisdom of what he was at present undertaking. In all intellectual labour, his will prevailed so strongly when he fixed it on any object of desire, that what else its attainment might exact was never duly

My misgiving as to daily paper.

LONDON: 1845.

measured; and this led to frequent strain and unconscious waste of what no man could less afford to spare. To the world gladdened by his work, its production might always have seemed quite as easy as its enjoyment; but it may be doubted if ever any man's mental effort cost him more.

Habits more robust than health.

His habits were robust, but not his health; that secret had been disclosed to me before he went to America; and to the last he refused steadily to admit the enormous price he had paid for his triumphs and successes. The

Disturbing engagements.

morning after his last note I heard again. 'I have been 'so very unwell this morning, with giddiness, and head-'ache, and botheration of one sort or other, that I didn't 'get up till noon: and, shunning Fleet-street' (the office of the proposed new paper), 'am now going for a country 'walk, in the course of which you will find me, if you feel 'disposed to come away in the carriage that goes to you 'with this. It is to call for a pull of the first part of the '*Cricket*, and will bring you, if you like, by way of

Old ways interrupted.

'Hampstead to me, and subsequently to dinner. There 'is much I should like to discuss, if you can manage it. 'It's the loss of my walks, I suppose; but I am as giddy as 'if I were drunk, and can hardly see.' I gave far from sufficient importance at the time to the frequency of complaints of this kind, or to the recurrence, at almost regular periods after the year following the present, of those spasms in the side of which he has recorded an instance in the re-

Page 40 of Vol. I.

collections of his childhood, and of which he had an attack in Genoa; but though not conscious of it to its full extent, this consideration was among those that influenced me in a determination to endeavour to turn him from what could

LONDON: 1845.

My appeal against the enterprise.

not but be regarded as full of peril. His health, however, had no real prominence in my letter; and it is strange now to observe that it appears as an argument in his reply. I had simply put before him, in the strongest form, all the considerations drawn from his genius and fame that should deter him from the labour and responsibility of a daily paper, not less than from the party and political involvements incident to it; and here was the material part of the answer made. 'Many thanks for your affectionate letter, 'which is full of generous truth. These considerations 'weigh with me, *heavily:* but I think I descry in these 'times, greater stimulants to such an effort; greater 'chance of some fair recognition of it; greater means of 'persevering in it, or retiring from it unscratched by any 'weapon one should care for; than at any other period. 'And most of all I have, sometimes, that possibility of 'failing health or fading popularity before me, which 'beckons me to such a venture when it comes within my 'reach. At the worst, I have written to little purpose, if 'I cannot *write myself right* in people's minds, in such a 'case as this.'

Reply to my appeal.

The issue.

And so it went on: but it does not fall within my plan to describe more than the issue, which was to be accounted so far at least fortunate that it established a journal which has advocated steadily improvements in the condition of all classes, rich as well as poor, and has been able, during late momentous occurrences, to give wider scope to its influence by its enterprise and liberality. To that result, the great writer whose name gave its earliest attraction to the *Daily News* was not enabled to contri-

LONDON: 1845.

bute much; but from him it certainly received the first impress of the opinions it has since consistently maintained. Its prospectus is before me in his handwriting, but it bears upon itself sufficiently the character of his hand and mind. The paper would be kept free, it said, from personal influence or party bias; and would be devoted to the advocacy of all rational and honest means by which wrong might be redressed, just rights maintained, and the happiness and welfare of society promoted.

Prospectus written by him.

The day for the appearance of its first number was that which was to follow Peel's speech for the repeal of the corn laws; but, brief as my allusions to the subject are, the remark should be made that even before this day came there were interruptions to the work of preparation, at one time very grave, which threw such 'changes 'of vexation' on Dickens's personal relations to the venture as went far to destroy both his faith and his pleasure in it. No opinion need be offered as to where most of the blame lay, and it would be useless now to apportion the share that might possibly have belonged to himself; but, owing to this cause, his editorial work began with such diminished ardour that its brief continuance could not but be looked for. A little note written 'before 'going home' at six o'clock in the morning of Wednesday the 21st of January 1846, to tell me they had 'been at 'press three quarters of an hour, and were out before the '*Times*,' marks the beginning; and a note written in the night of Monday the 9th of February, 'tired to death and 'quite worn out,' to say that he had just resigned his

Interruption.

Renewal.

The beginning and the end.

LONDON: 1845.

editorial functions, describes the end. I had not been unprepared. A week before (Friday 30th of January) he had written: 'I want a long talk with you. I was 'obliged to come down here in a hurry to give out a 'travelling letter I meant to have given out last night, 'and could not call upon you. Will you dine with us to-'morrow at six sharp? I have been revolving plans in 'my mind this morning for quitting the paper and going 'abroad again to write a new book in shilling numbers. 'Shall we go to Rochester to-morrow week (my birthday) 'if the weather be, as it surely must be, better?' To Rochester accordingly we had gone, he and Mrs. Dickens and her sister, with Maclise and Jerrold and myself; going over the old Castle, Watts's Charity, and Chatham fortifications on the Saturday, passing Sunday in Cobham church and Cobham park; having our quarters both days at the Bull inn made famous in *Pickwick;* and thus, by indulgence of the desire which was always strangely urgent in him, associating his new resolve in life with those earliest scenes of his youthful time. On one point our feeling had been in thorough agreement. If long continuance with the paper was not likely, the earliest possible departure from it was desirable. But as the letters descriptive of his Italian travel (turned afterwards into *Pictures from Italy*) had begun with its first number, his name could not at once be withdrawn; and, for the time during which they were still to appear, he consented to contribute other occasional letters on important social questions. Public executions and Ragged schools were among the subjects chosen by him, and

Forming new resolve.

Back to old scenes.

Craving for early associations.

Editorship ceased: letters continued.

LONDON: 1845.

all were handled with conspicuous ability. But the interval they covered was a short one.

I become editor.

To the supreme control which he had quitted, I succeeded, retaining it very reluctantly for the greater part of that weary, anxious, laborious year; but in little more than four months from the day the paper started, the whole of Dickens's connection with the *Daily News*, even that of contributing letters with his signature, had ceased. As he said in the preface to the republished *Pictures*, it was a mistake to have disturbed the old relations between himself and his readers, in so departing from his old pursuits. It had however been 'a brief mistake;' the departure had been only 'for a moment;' and now those pursuits were 'joyfully' to be resumed in Switzerland. Upon the latter point we had much discussion; but he was bent on again removing himself from London, and his glimpse of the Swiss mountains on his coming from Italy had given him a passion to visit them again. 'I don't think,' he wrote to me, 'I *could* shut out the paper sufficiently, here, to 'write well. No . . . I will write my book in Lausanne 'and in Genoa, and forget everything else if I can; and by 'living in Switzerland for the summer, and in Italy or 'France for the winter, I shall be saving money while I 'write.' So therefore it was finally determined.

New book to be written in Switzerland.

There is not much that calls for mention before he left. The first conceiving of a new book was always a restless time, and other subjects beside the characters that were growing in his mind would persistently intrude themselves into his night-wanderings. With some surprise I heard from him afterwards, for example, of a communication opened

LONDON: 1845.

with a leading member of the Government to ascertain what chances there might be for his appointment, upon due qualification, to the paid magistracy of London: the reply not giving him encouragement to entertain the notion farther. It was of course but an outbreak of momentary discontent; and if the answer had been as hopeful as for others' sake rather than his own one could have wished it to be, the result would have been the same. Just upon the eve of his departure, I may add, he took much interest in the establishment of the General Theatrical Fund, of which he remained a trustee until his death. It had originated in the fact that the Funds of the two large theatres, themselves then disused for theatrical performances, were no longer available for the ordinary members of the profession; and on the occasion of his presiding at its first dinner in April he said, very happily, that now the statue of Shakespeare outside the door of Drury-lane, as emphatically as his bust inside the church of Stratford-on-Avon, *pointed out his grave.* I am tempted also to mention as felicitous a word which I heard fall from him at one of the many private dinners that were got up in those days of parting to give him friendliest farewell. 'Nothing is ever so good as it is thought,' said Lord Melbourne. 'And nothing so bad,' interposed Dickens.

Thought of a magistracy.

General Theatrical Fund.

A happy saying.

A wise one.

The last incidents were that he again obtained Roche for his travelling servant, and that he let his Devonshire-terrace house to Sir James Duke for twelve months, the entire proposed term of his absence. On the 30th of May they all dined with me, and on the following day left England.

Leaves England.

# CHAPTER X.

## A HOME IN SWITZERLAND.

1846.

On the Rhine: 1846.

Halting only at Ostend, Verviers, Coblentz, and Mannheim, they reached Strasburg on the seventh of June: the beauty of the weather* showing them the Rhine at its best. At Mayence there had come aboard their boat a German, who soon after accosted Mrs. Dickens on deck in excellent English: 'Your countryman Mr. Dickens is 'travelling this way just now, our papers say. Do you 'know him, or have you passed him anywhere?' Explanations ensuing, it turned out, by one of the odd chances my friend thought himself always singled out for, that he had with him a letter of introduction to the brother of this gentleman; who then spoke to him of the popularity of his books in Germany, and of the many persons he had seen reading them in the steamboats as he came along. Dickens remarking at this how great his own vexation was not to be able himself to speak a word of German, 'Oh dear! that needn't trouble you,' rejoined the other; 'for even in so small a town as ours, where we are mostly

German fellow-traveller.

* 'We have hardly seen a cloud in the sky since you and I parted at Rams- 'gate, and the heat has been extraordinary.'

'primitive people and have few travellers, I could make a 'party of at least forty people who understand and speak 'English as well as I do, and of at least as many more 'who could manage to read you in the original.' His town was Worms, which Dickens afterwards saw, '... a fine old 'place, though greatly shrunken and decayed in respect of 'its population; with a picturesque old cathedral standing 'on the brink of the Rhine, and some brave old churches 'shut up, and so hemmed in and overgrown with vine-'yards that they look as if they were turning into leaves 'and grapes.'

ON THE RHINE: 1846.

German readers of Dickens.

City of Worms.

He had no other adventure on the Rhine. But, on the same steamer, a not unfamiliar bit of character greeted him in the well-known lineaments, moral and physical, of two travelling Englishmen who had got an immense barouche on board with them, and had no plan whatever of going anywhere in it. One of them wanted to have this barouche wheeled ashore at every little town and village they came to. The other was bent upon 'seeing it 'out,' as he said—meaning, Dickens supposed, the river; though neither of them seemed to have the slightest interest in it. 'The locomotive one would have gone 'ashore without the carriage, and would have been de-'lighted to get rid of it; but they had a joint courier, 'and neither of them would part with *him* for a moment; 'so they went growling and grumbling on together, and 'seemed to have no satisfaction but in asking for impos-'sible viands on board the boat, and having a grim delight 'in the steward's excuses.'

Travelling Englishmen.

Their pleasures.

From Strasburg they went by rail on the 8th to Bâle,

LAUSANNE: 1846.

from which they started for Lausanne next day, in three coaches, two horses to each, taking three days for the journey: its only enlivening incident being an uproar between the landlord of an inn on the road, and one of the voituriers who had libelled Boniface's establishment by complaining of the food. 'After various defiances on both sides, 'the landlord said "Scélérat! Mécréant! Je vous boax-'"erai!" to which the voiturier replied, "Aha! Comment '"dites-vous? Voulez-vous boaxer? Eh? Voulez-vous? '"Ah! Boaxez-moi donc! Boaxez-moi!"—at the same 'time accompanying these retorts with gestures of violent 'significance, which explained that this new verb-active 'was founded on the well-known English verb to boax or 'box. If they used it once, they used it at least a hun-'dred times, and goaded each other to madness with it 'always.' The travellers reached the hotel Gibbon at Lausanne on the evening of Thursday the 11th of June; having been tempted as they came along to rest somewhat short of it, by a delightful glimpse of Neuchâtel. 'On consideration however I thought it best to come on 'here, in case I should find, when I begin to write, that I 'want streets sometimes. In which case, Geneva (which 'I hope would answer the purpose) is only four and twenty 'miles away.'

Boaxing match.

Hotel Gibbon.

He at once began house-hunting, and had two days' hard work of it. He found the greater part of those let to the English like small villas in the Regent's-park, with verandahs, glass-doors opening on lawns, and alcoves overlooking the lake and mountains. One he was tempted by, higher up the hill, 'poised above the town like a ship on

House-hunting.

'a high wave;' but the possible fury of its winter winds deterred him. Greater still was the temptation to him of 'L'Elysée,' more a mansion than a villa; with splendid grounds overlooking the lake, and in its corridors and staircases as well as furniture like an old fashioned country house in England; which he could have got for twelve months for £160. 'But when I came to consider 'its vastness, I was rather dismayed at the prospect of 'windy nights in the autumn, with nobody staying in the 'house to make it gay.' And so he again fell back upon the very first place he had seen, Rosemont, quite a doll's house; with two pretty little salons, a dining-room, hall, and kitchen, on the ground floor; and with just enough bedrooms upstairs to leave the family one to spare. 'It is 'beautifully situated on the hill that rises from the lake, 'within ten minutes' walk of this hotel, and furnished, 'though scantily as all here are, better than others except 'Elysée, on account of its having being built and fitted up '(the little salons in the Parisian way) by the landlady and 'her husband for themselves. They live now in a smaller 'house like a porter's lodge, just within the gate. A 'portion of the grounds is farmed by a farmer, and *he* lives 'close by; so that, while it is secluded, it is not at all 'lonely.' The rent was to be ten pounds a month for half a year, with reduction to eight for the second half, if he should stay so long; and the rooms and furniture were to be described to me, so that according to custom I should be quite at home there, as soon as, also according to a custom well-known, his own ingenious re-arrangements and improvements in the chairs and tables should be

LAUSANNE: 1846.

A mansion tempts him.

A cottage chosen.

Its advantages.

LAUSANNE: 1846.

completed. 'I shall merely observe at present therefore, 'that my little study is upstairs, and looks out, from two 'French windows opening into a balcony, on the lake and 'mountains; and that there are roses enough to smother 'the whole establishment of the *Daily News* in. Likewise, 'there is a pavilion in the garden, which has but two 'rooms in it; in one of which, I think you shall do your 'work when you come. As to bowers for reading and 'smoking, there are as many scattered about the grounds, 'as there are in Chalk-farm tea-gardens. But the Rose-'mont bowers are really beautiful. Will you come to the 'bowers . . ?'

Over the lake and mountains.

Garden bowers and roses.

Very pleasant were the earliest impressions of Switzerland with which this first letter closed. 'The country is delight-'ful in the extreme—as leafy, green, and shady, as England; 'full of deep glens, and branchy places (rather a Leigh 'Huntish expression), and bright with all sorts of flowers 'in profusion.* It abounds in singing birds besides—very 'pleasant after Italy; and the moonlight on the lake is 'noble. Prodigious mountains rise up from its opposite 'shore (it is eight or nine miles across, at this point), and 'the Simplon, the St. Gothard, Mont Blanc, and all the 'Alpine wonders are piled there, in tremendous grandeur. 'The cultivation is uncommonly rich and profuse. There 'are all manner of walks, vineyards, green lanes, corn-'fields, and pastures full of hay. The general neatness is 'as remarkable as in England. There are no priests or

Green lanes and Alpine wonders.

* 'The green woods and green shades about here,' he says in another letter, 'are more like Cobham in Kent, than anything we dream of at the foot of the 'Alpine passes.'

'monks in the streets, and the people appear to be industrious and thriving. French (and very intelligible and pleasant French) seems to be the universal language. I never saw so many booksellers' shops crammed within the same space, as in the steep up-and-down streets of Lausanne.'

LAUSANNE: 1846.

Book-sellers' shops.

Of the little town he spoke in his next letter as having its natural dulness increased by that fact of its streets going up and down hill abruptly and steeply, like the streets in a dream; and the consequent difficulty of getting about it. There are some suppressed churches in it, now 'used as packers' warehouses: with cranes and pulleys 'growing out of steeple-towers; little doors for lowering 'goods through, fitted into blocked-up oriel windows; and 'cart-horses stabled in crypts. These also help to give it 'a deserted and disused appearance. On the other hand, 'as it is a perfectly free place subject to no prohibitions 'or restrictions of any kind, there are all sorts of new 'French books and publications in it, and all sorts of fresh 'intelligence from the world beyond the Jura mountains. 'It contains only one Roman Catholic church, which is 'mainly for the use of the Savoyards and Piedmontese 'who come trading over the Alps. As for the country, it 'cannot be praised too highly, or reported too beautiful. 'There are no great waterfalls, or walks through mountain-'gorges, *close* at hand, as in some other parts of Switzerland; 'but there is a charming variety of enchanting scenery. 'There is the shore of the lake, where you may dip your 'feet, as you walk, in the deep blue water, if you choose. 'There are the hills to climb up leading to the great

Town described.

A free place.

LAUSANNE: 1846.

Varieties of nature.

'heights above the town; or to stagger down, leading to 'the lake. There is every possible variety of deep green 'lanes, vineyard, cornfield, pasture-land, and wood. There 'are excellent country roads that might be in Kent or 'Devonshire: and, closing up every view and vista, is an 'eternally changing range of prodigious mountains—some-'times red, sometimes grey, sometimes purple, sometimes 'black; sometimes white with snow; sometimes close at 'hand; and sometimes very ghosts in the clouds and mist.'

Relish for their enjoyment.

In the heart of these things he was now to live and work for at least six months; and, as the love of nature was as much a passion with him in his intervals of leisure, as the craving for crowds and streets when he was busy with the creatures of his fancy, no man was better qualified to enjoy what was thus open to him from his little farm.

Under his windows.

The view from each side of it was different in character, and from one there was visible the liveliest aspect of Lausanne itself, close at hand, and seeming, as he said, to be always coming down the hill with its steeples and towers, not able to stop itself. 'From a fine long broad balcony 'on which the windows of my little study on the first floor '(where I am now writing) open, the lake is seen to 'wonderful advantage,—losing itself by degrees in the 'solemn gorge of mountains leading to the Simplon pass. 'Under the balcony is a stone colonnade, on which the 'six French windows of the drawing-room open; and 'quantities of plants are clustered about the pillars and 'seats, very prettily. One of these drawing-rooms is fur-'nished (like a French hotel) with red velvet, and the other 'with green; in both, plenty of mirrors and nice white

Villa described.

'muslin curtains; and for the larger one in cold weather 'there is a carpet, the floors being bare now, but inlaid in 'squares with different-coloured woods.' His description did not close until, in every nook and corner inhabited by the several members of the family, I was made to feel myself at home; but only the final sentence need be added. 'Walking out into the balcony as I write, I am suddenly

LAUSANNE: 1846.

'reminded, by the sight of the Castle of Chillon glittering 'in the sunlight on the lake, that I omitted to mention 'that object in my catalogue of the Rosemont beauties. 'Please to put it in, like George Robins, in a line by itself.'

Castle of Chillon.

Regular evening walks of nine or ten miles were named in the same letter (22nd of June) as having been begun;*

* To these the heat interposed occasional difficulties. 'Setting off last 'night' (5th of July) 'at six o'clock, in accordance with my usual custom, for a

LAUSANNE: 1846.

Thoughts of books.

and thoughts of his books were already stirring in him. 'An odd shadowy undefined idea is at work within me, 'that I could connect a great battle-field somehow with 'my little Christmas story. Shapeless visions of the repose 'and peace pervading it in after-time; with the corn and 'grass growing over the slain, and people singing at the 'plough; are so perpetually floating before me, that I 'cannot but think there may turn out to be something 'good in them when I see them more plainly .... I want 'to get Four Numbers of the monthly book done here, 'and the Christmas book. If all goes well, and nothing 'changes, and I can accomplish this by the end of No-'vember, I shall run over to you in England for a few 'days with a light heart, and leave Roche to move the 'caravan to Paris in the meanwhile. It will be just the 'very point in the story when the life and crowd of that 'extraordinary place will come vividly to my assistance in 'writing.' Such was his design; and, though difficulties not now seen started up which he had a hard fight to get through, he managed to accomplish it. His letter ended with a promise to tell me, when next he wrote, of the small colony of English who seemed ready to give him even more than the usual welcome. Two visits had thus early been paid him by Mr. Haldimand, formerly a member of

Design as to work.

'long walk, I was really quite floored when I got to the top of a long steep 'hill leading out of the town—the same by which we entered it. I believe 'the great heats, however, seldom last more than a week at a time; there are 'always very long twilights, and very delicious evenings; and now that there 'is moonlight, the nights are wonderful. The peacefulness and grandeur 'of the Mountains and the Lake are indescribable. There comes a rush of 'sweet smells with the morning air too, which is quite peculiar to the 'country.'

The nights.

the English parliament, an accomplished man, who, with his sister Mrs. Marcet (the well-known authoress), had long made Lausanne his home. He had a very fine seat just below Rosemont, and his character and station had made him quite the little sovereign of the place. 'He has 'founded and endowed all sorts of hospitals and institu- 'tions here, and he gives a dinner to-morrow to introduce 'our neighbours, whoever they are.'

LAUSANNE: 1846.

Mr. Haldimand and Mrs. Marcet.

He found them to be happily the kind of people who rendered entirely pleasant those frank and cordial hospitalities which the charm of his personal intercourse made every one so eager to offer him. The dinner at Mr. Haldimand's was followed by dinners from the guests he met there; from an English lady* married to a Swiss, Mr. and Mrs. Cerjat, clever and agreeable both, far beyond the common; from her sister wedded to an Englishman, Mr. and Mrs. Goff; and from Mr. and Mrs. Watson of Rockingham-castle in Northamptonshire, who had taken the Elysée on Dickens giving it up, and with whom, as with Mr. Haldimand, his relations continued to be very intimate long after he left Lausanne. In his drive to Mr. Cerjat's dinner a whimsical difficulty presented itself. He had set up, for use of his wife and children, an odd little one-horse-carriage; made to hold three persons sideways, so that they should avoid the wind always blowing up or down the

Other English neighbours.

Mr. and Mrs. Watson.

Unaccommodating carriage.

* 'One of her brothers by the bye, now dead, had large property in Ireland '—all Nenagh, and the country about; and Cerjat told me, as we were 'talking about one thing and another, that when he went over there for some 'months to arrange the widow's affairs, he procured a copy of the curse 'which had been read at the altar by the parish priest of Nenagh, against 'any of the flock who didn't subscribe to the O'Connell tribute.'

Spiritual tyranny.

LAUSANNE: 1846.

valley; and he found it attended with one of the drollest consequences conceivable. 'It can't be easily turned; and 'as you face to the side, all sorts of evolutions are neces-'sary to bring you "broad-side to" before the door of the 'house where you are going. The country houses here 'are very like those upon the Thames between Richmond 'and Kingston (this, particularly), with grounds all round. 'At Mr. Cerjat's we were obliged to be carried, like the 'child's riddle, round the house and round the house, 'without touching the house; and we were presented in 'the most alarming manner, three of a row, first to all the 'people in the kitchen, then to the governess who was 'dressing in her bedroom, then to the drawing-room where 'the company were waiting for us, then to the dining-room 'where they were spreading the table, and finally to the 'hall where we were got out—scraping the windows of 'each apartment as we glared slowly into it.'

On the way to dinner.

A dinner party of his own followed of course; and a sad occurrence, of which he and his guests were unconscious, signalised the evening (15th of July). 'While we were 'sitting at dinner, one of the prettiest girls in Lausanne 'was drowned in the lake—in the most peaceful water, 'reflecting the steep mountains, and crimson with the 'setting sun. She was bathing in one of the nooks set 'apart for women, and seems somehow to have entangled 'her feet in the skirts of her dress. She was an accom-'plished swimmer, as many of the girls are here, and 'drifted, suddenly, out of only five feet water. Three or 'four friends who were with her, *ran away*, screaming. 'Our children's governess was on the lake in a boat with

Drowned in the lake.

LAUSANNE: 1846.

M. Verdeil.

'M. Verdeil (my prison-doctor) and his family. They 'ran inshore immediately; the body was quickly got out; 'and M. Verdeil, with three or four other doctors, laboured 'for some hours to restore animation; but she only sighed 'once. After all that time, she was obliged to be borne, 'stiff and stark, to her father's house. She was his only 'child, and but 17 years old. He has been nearly dead 'since, and all Lausanne has been full of the story. I 'was down by the lake, near the place, last night; and 'a boatman *acted* to me the whole scene: depositing 'himself finally on a heap of stones, to represent the 'body.'

Boatman's narrative.

With M. Verdeil, physician to the prison and vice-president of the council of health, introduced by Mr. Haldimand, there had already been much communication; and I could give nothing more characteristic of Dickens than his reference to this, and other similar matters in which his interest was strongly moved during his first weeks at Lausanne.*

'Some years ago, when they set about reforming the

The theatre.

* In a note may be preserved another passage from the same letter. 'I 'have been queer and had trembling legs for the last week. But it has been 'almost impossible to sleep at night. There is a breeze to-day (25th of July) 'and I hope another storm is coming up . . . There is a theatre here; and 'whenever a troop of players pass through the town, they halt for a night and 'act. On the day of our tremendous dinner party of eight, there was an infant 'phenomenon; whom I should otherwise have seen. Last night there was a 'Vaudeville company; and Charley, Roche, and Anne went. The Brave 'reports the performances to have resembled Greenwich Fair . . . There are 'some Promenade Concerts in the open air in progress now; but as they are 'just above one part of our garden we don't go: merely sitting outside the 'door instead, and hearing it all where we are . . . Mont Blanc has been 'very plain lately. One heap of snow. A Frenchman got to the top, the other 'day.'

LAUSANNE: 1846.

Prison systems.

Solitude and silence.

Page 326 of Vol. I.

Terrible sentence.

'prison at Lausanne, they turned their attention, in a 'correspondence of republican feeling, to America; and 'taking the Philadelphian system for granted, adopted it. 'Terrible fits, new phases of mental affection, and horrible 'madness, among the prisoners, were very soon the result; 'and attained to such an alarming height, that M. Verdeil, 'in his public capacity, began to report against the 'system, and went on reporting and working against it 'until he formed a party who were determined not to 'have it, and caused it to be abolished—except in cases 'where the imprisonment does not exceed ten months 'in the whole. It is remarkable that in his notes of the 'different cases, there is *every effect* I mentioned as 'having observed myself at Philadelphia; even down to 'those contained in the description of the man who had 'been there thirteen years, and who *picked his hands* so 'much as he talked. He has only recently, he says, read 'the *American Notes;* but he is so much struck by the 'perfect coincidence that he intends to republish some 'extracts from his own notes, side by side with these 'passages of mine translated into French. I went with 'him over the prison the other day. It is wonderfully 'well arranged for a continental jail, and in perfect order. 'The sentences however, or some of them, are very 'terrible. I saw one man sent there for murder under 'circumstances of mitigation—for 30 years. Upon the 'silent social system all the time! They weave, and 'plait straw, and make shoes, small articles of turnery and 'carpentry, and little common wooden clocks. But the 'sentences are too long for that monotonous and hopeless 'life; and, though they are well-fed and cared for, they 'generally break down utterly after two or three years. 'One delusion seems to become common to three-fourths 'of them after a certain time of imprisonment. Under 'the impression that there is something destructive put 'into their food "pour les guérir de crime" (says M. Ver-'deil), they refuse to eat!'

LAUSANNE: 1846.

It was at the Blind Institution, however, of which Mr. Haldimand was the president and great benefactor, that Dickens's attention was most deeply arrested; and there were two cases in especial of which the detail may be read with as much interest now as when my friend's letters were written, and as to which his own suggestions open up still rather startling trains of thought. The first, which in its attraction for him he found equal even to Laura Bridgman's, was that of a young man of 18: 'born deaf and dumb, and 'stricken blind by an accident when he was about five years 'old. The Director of the institution is a young German, of 'great ability, and most uncommonly prepossessing appear-'ance. He propounded to the scientific bodies of Geneva, 'a year ago (when this young man was under education in 'the asylum), the possibility of teaching him to speak—in 'other words, to play with his tongue upon his teeth and 'palate as if on an instrument, and connect particular 'performances with particular words conveyed to him in 'the finger-language. They unanimously agreed that it 'was quite impossible. The German set to work, and the 'young man now speaks very plainly and distinctly: with-'out the least modulation, of course, but with comparatively 'little hesitation; expressing the words aloud as they are

Blind Institution.

*American Notes*, 18-26.

German Director.

Deaf, dumb, and blind patient.

LAUSANNE: 1846.

'struck, so to speak, upon his hands; and showing the most 'intense and wonderful delight in doing it. This is com'monly acquired, as you know, by the deaf and dumb who 'learn by sight; but it has never before been achieved in 'the case of a deaf, dumb, and blind subject. He is an 'extremely lively, intelligent, good-humoured fellow; an 'excellent carpenter; a first-rate turner; and runs about 'the building with a certainty and confidence which none 'of the merely blind pupils acquire. He has a great many 'ideas, and an instinctive dread of death. He knows of God, 'as of Thought enthroned somewhere; and once told, on 'nature's prompting (the devil's of course), a lie. He was 'sitting at dinner, and the Director asked him whether he 'had had anything to drink; to which he instantly replied '"No," in order that he might get some more, though he 'had been served in his turn. It was explained to him 'that this was a wrong thing, and wouldn't do, and that he 'was to be locked up in a room for it: which was done. 'Soon after this, he had a dream of being bitten in the 'shoulder by some strange animal. As it left a great im'pression on his mind, he told M. the Director that he had 'told another lie in the night. In proof of it he related 'his dream, and added, "It must be a lie you know, because '"there is no strange animal here, and I never was bitten." 'Being informed that this sort of lie was a harmless one, 'and was called a dream, he asked whether dead people 'ever dreamed* while they were lying in the ground.

Interesting case.

Punishment for falsehood.

Falsehood without punishment.

* '. . . Ay, there's the rub;
'For in that sleep of death what dreams may come,
'When we have shuffled off this mortal coil. . .'

LAUSANNE: 1846.

'He is one of the most curious and interesting studies 'possible.'

Blind Institution and inmates.

The second case had come in on the very day that Dickens visited the place. 'When I was there' (8th of July) 'there 'had come in, that morning, a girl of ten years old, born 'deaf and dumb and blind, and so perfectly untaught that 'she has not learnt to have the least control even over 'the performance of the common natural functions . . And 'yet she *laughs sometimes* (good God! conceive what at!) '—and is dreadfully sensitive from head to foot, and very 'much alarmed, for some hours before the coming on of a 'thunder storm. Mr. Haldimand has been long trying to 'induce her parents to send her to the asylum. At last 'they have consented; and when I saw her, some of the 'little blind girls were trying to make friends with her, and 'to lead her gently about. She was dressed in just a loose 'robe from the necessity of changing her frequently, but 'had been in a bath, and had had her nails cut (which 'were previously very long and dirty), and was not at all 'ill-looking—quite the reverse; with a remarkably good 'and pretty little mouth, but a low and undeveloped head 'of course. It was pointed out to me, as very singular, that 'the moment she is left alone, or freed from anybody's 'touch (which is the same thing to her), she instantly 'crouches down with her hands up to her ears, in exactly 'the position of a child before its birth; and so remains. 'I thought this such a strange coincidence with the utter 'want of advancement in her moral being, that it made a 'great impression on me; and conning it over and over, I 'began to think that this is surely the invariable action of

Idiot girl.

Crouching attitudes.

LAUSANNE: 1846.

Blind Institution and inmates.

Suggestive.

'savages too, and that I have seen it over and over again 'described in books of voyages and travels. Not having 'any of these with me, I turned to *Robinson Crusoe;* and 'I find De Foe says, describing the savages who came on 'the island after Will Atkins began to change for the 'better and commanded under the grave Spaniard for the 'common defence, "their posture was generally sitting '"upon the ground, with their knees up towards their '"mouth, and the head put between the two hands, '"leaning down upon the knees"—exactly the same 'attitude!' In his next week's letter he reported further: 'I have not been to the Blind asylum again yet, but they 'tell me that the deaf and dumb and blind child's *face* is 'improving obviously, and that she takes great delight in 'the first effort made by the Director to connect himself 'with an occupation of her time. He gives her, every day, 'two smooth round pebbles to roll over and over between 'her two hands. She appears to have an idea that it is 'to lead to something; distinctly recognizes the hand that 'gives them to her, as a friendly and protecting one; and 'sits for hours quite busy.'

Habits in idiot life and savage.

To one part of his very thoughtful suggestion I objected, and would have attributed to a mere desire for warmth, in her as in the savage, what he supposed to be part of an undeveloped or embryo state explaining also the absence of sentient and moral being. To this he replied (25th of July): 'I do not think that there is reason for 'supposing that the savage attitude originates in the 'desire of warmth, because all naked savages inhabit hot 'climates; and their instinctive attitude, if it had re-

'ference to heat or cold, would probably be the coolest 'possible; like their delight in water, and swimming. I 'do not think there is any race of savage men, however 'low in grade, inhabiting cold climates, who do not kill 'beasts and wear their skins. The girl decidedly im-'proves in face, and, if one can yet use the word as 'applied to her, in manner too. No communication by 'the speech of touch has yet been established with her, 'but the time has not been long enough.' In a later letter he tells me (24th of August): 'The deaf, dumb, and 'blind girl is decidedly improved, and very much im-'proved, in this short time. No communication is yet 'established with her, but that is not to be expected. 'They have got her out of that strange, crouching posi-'tion; dressed her neatly; and accustomed her to have a 'pleasure in society. She laughs frequently, and also claps 'her hands and jumps; having, God knows how, some 'inward satisfaction. I never saw a more tremendous 'thing in its way, in my life, than when they stood her, 't'other day, in the centre of a group of blind children who 'sang a chorus to the piano; and brought her hand, and 'kept it, in contact with the instrument. A shudder per-'vaded her whole being, her breath quickened, her colour 'deepened,—and I can compare it to nothing but returning 'animation in a person nearly dead. It was really awful 'to see how the sensation of the music fluttered and stirred 'the locked-up soul within her.' The same letter spoke again of the youth: 'The male subject is well and jolly as 'possible. He is very fond of smoking. I have arranged 'to supply him with cigars during our stay here; so he

Blind Institution and inmates.

Girl improves.

Effect of music:

LAUSANNE: 1846.

and of kindness.

'and I are in amazing sympathy. I don't know whether 'he thinks I grow them, or make them, or produce them 'by winking, or what. But it gives him a notion that the 'world in general belongs to me.' . . . Before his kind friend left Lausanne the poor fellow had been taught to say, 'Monsieur Dickens m'a donné les cigares,' and at their leavetaking his gratitude was expressed by incessant repetition of these words for a full half-hour.

Attending to the neglected.

Certainly by no man was gratitude more persistently earned, than by Dickens, from all to whom nature or the world had been churlish or unfair. Not to those only made desolate by poverty or the temptations incident to it, but to those whom natural defects or infirmities had placed at a disadvantage with their kind, he gave his first consideration; helping them personally where he could, sympathising and sorrowing with them always, but above all applying himself to the investigation of such alleviation or cure as philosophy or science might be able to apply to their condition. This was a desire so eager as properly to be called one of the passions of his life, visible in him to the last hour of it.

Beginning work.

Only a couple of weeks, themselves not idle ones, had passed over him at Rosemont when he made a dash at the beginning of his real work; from which indeed he had only been detained so long by the non-arrival of a box dispatched from London before his own departure, containing not his proper writing materials only, but certain quaint little bronze figures that thus early stood upon his desk, and were as much needed for the easy flow of his writing as blue ink or quill pens. 'I have not been idle'

(28th of June) 'since I have been here, though at first I was '"kept out" of the big box as you know. I had a good 'deal to write for Lord John about the Ragged schools. 'I set to work and did that. A good deal for Miss Coutts, 'in reference to her charitable projects. I set to work 'and did *that*. Half of the children's New Testament* 'to write, or pretty nearly. I set to work and did *that*. 'Next I cleared off the greater part of such correspond-'ence as I had rashly pledged myself to; and then . . . . .

LAUSANNE: 1846.

*Ante*, p. 36.

'BEGAN DOMBEY!

'I performed this feat yesterday—only wrote the first slip '—but there it is, and it is a plunge straight over head 'and ears into the story. . . Besides all this, I have really 'gone with great vigour at the French, where I find my-'self greatly assisted by the Italian; and am subject to two 'descriptions of mental fits in reference to the Christmas 'book: one, of the suddenest and wildest enthusiasm; one, 'of solitary and anxious consideration. . . . By the way, as 'I was unpacking the big box I took hold of a book, and said 'to "Them,"—"Now, whatever passage my thumb rests on, '"I shall take as having reference to my work." It was 'TRISTRAM SHANDY, and opened at these words, "What a '"work it is likely to turn out! Let us begin it!"'

First slip of new novel.

Sortes Shandyanæ.

The same letter told me that he still inclined strongly to 'the field of battle notion' for his Christmas volume,

* This was an abstract, in plain language for the use of his children, of the narrative in the Four Gospels. Allusion was made, shortly after his death, to the existence of such a manuscript, with expression of a wish that it might be published; but nothing would have shocked himself so much as any suggestion of that kind. The little piece was of a peculiarly private character, written for his children, and exclusively and strictly for their use only.

Children's *Life of Christ*.

LAUSANNE: 1846.

but was not as yet advanced in it; being curious first to see whether its capacity seemed to strike me at all. My only objection was to his adventure of opening two stories at once, of which he did not yet see the full danger; but for the moment the Christmas fancy was laid aside, and not resumed, except in passing allusions, until after the close of August, when the first two numbers of *Dombey* were done. The interval supplied fresh illustration of his life in his new home, not without much interest; and as I have shown what a pleasant social circle, 'wonderfully friendly and hospitable'* to the last, already had grouped itself round him in Lausanne, and how full of 'matter to be heard and learn'd' he found such institutions as its prison and blind school, the picture will receive attractive touches if I borrow from his letters written during this outset of *Dombey*, some farther notices as well of the general progress of his work, as of what was specially interesting or amusing to him at the time, and of how the country and the people impressed him. In all of these his character will be found strongly marked.

The Christmas tale.

Weekly letters to me.

The English colony.

* So he described it. 'I do not think,' he adds, 'we could have fallen on 'better society. It is a small circle certainly, but quite large enough. The 'Watsons improve very much on acquaintance. Everybody is very well 'informed; and we are all as social and friendly as people can be, and very 'merry. We play whist with great dignity and gravity sometimes, interrupted 'only by the occasional facetiousness of the inimitable.'

# CHAPTER XI.

## SWISS PEOPLE AND SCENERY.

### 1846.

WHAT at once had struck him as the wonderful feature in the mountain scenery was its everchanging and yet unchanging aspect. It was never twice like the same thing to him. Shifting and altering, advancing and retreating, fifty times a day, it was unalterable only in its grandeur. The lake itself too had every kind of varying beauty for him. By moonlight it was indescribably solemn; and before the coming on of a storm had a strange property in it of being disturbed, while yet the sky remained clear and the evening bright, which he found to be mysterious and impressive in an especial degree. Such a storm had come among his earliest and most grateful experiences; a degree of heat worse even than in Italy* having disabled him at the outset for all

LAUSANNE: 1846.

The mountains and lake.

A storm.

* 'When it is very hot, it is hotter than in Italy. The over-hanging roofs 'of the houses, and the quantity of wood employed in their construction '(where they use tile and brick in Italy), render them perfect forcing-houses. 'The walls and floors, hot to the hand all the night through, interfere with 'sleep; and thunder is almost always booming and rumbling among the moun'tains.' Besides this, though there were no mosquitoes as in Genoa, there was at first a plague of flies, more distressing even than at Albaro. 'They cover 'everything eatable, fall into everything drinkable, stagger into the wet ink of

Disadvantages.

LAUSANNE: 1846.

After storm.

exertion until the lightning, thunder, and rain arrived. The letter telling me this (5th July) described the fruit as so abundant in the little farm, that the trees of the orchard in front of his house were bending beneath it; spoke of a field of wheat sloping down to the side window of his dining-room as already cut and carried; and said that the roses, which the hurricane of rain had swept away, were come back lovelier and in greater numbers than ever.

The people.

Of the ordinary Swiss people he formed from the first a high opinion which everything during his stay among them confirmed. He thought it the greatest injustice to call them 'the Americans of the Continent.' In his first letters he said of the peasantry all about Lausanne that they were as pleasant a people as need be. He never passed, on any of the roads, man, woman, or child, without a salutation; and anything churlish or disagreeable he never noticed in them. 'They have not,' he continued, 'the sweetness and grace of the Italians, or the agreeable 'manners of the better specimens of French peasantry, but 'they are admirably educated (the schools of this canton 'are extraordinarily good, in every little village), and always 'prepared to give a civil and pleasant answer. There is 'no greater mistake. I was talking to my landlord* about 'it the other day, and he said he could not conceive how 'it had ever arisen, but that when he returned from his 'eighteen years' service in the English navy he shunned

Their manners.

'newly-written words and make tracks on the writing paper, clog their legs 'in the lather on your chin while you are shaving in the morning, and drive 'you frantic at any time when there is daylight if you fall asleep.'

* His preceding letter had sketched his landlord for me . . 'There was

'the people, and had no interest in them until they 'gradually forced their real character upon his observation. 'We have a cook and a coachman here, taken at hazard 'from the people of the town; and I never saw more 'obliging servants, or people who did their work so truly '*with a will*. And in point of cleanliness, order, and 'punctuality to the moment, they are unrivalled. . . .'

LAUSANNE: 1846.

Native cook and coachman.

The first great gathering of the Swiss peasantry which he saw was in the third week after his arrival, when a country fête was held at a place called The Signal; a deep green wood, on the sides and summit of a very high hill overlooking the town and all the country round; and he gave me very pleasant account of it. 'There were 'various booths for eating and drinking, and the selling 'of trinkets and sweetmeats; and in one place there was 'a great circle cleared, in which the common people 'waltzed and polka'd, without cessation, to the music of a 'band. There was a great roundabout for children (oh 'my stars what a family were proprietors of it! A sun-'burnt father and mother, a humpbacked boy, a great 'poodle-dog possessed of all sorts of accomplishments, 'and a young murderer of seventeen who turned the 'machinery); and there were some games of chance and 'skill established under trees. It was very pretty. In

Gathering of peasantry.

Family sketch.

'an annual child's fête at the Signal the other night: given by the town. It 'was beautiful to see perhaps a hundred couple of children dancing in an 'immense ring in a green wood. Our three eldest were among them, presided 'over by my landlord, who was 18 years in the English navy, and is the 'Sous Prefet of the town—a very good fellow indeed; quite an Englishman. 'Our landlady, nearly twice his age, used to keep the Inn (a famous one) at 'Zurich: and having made £50,000 bestowed it on a young husband. She 'might have done worse.'

Child's fête.

LAUSANNE: 1846.

'some of the drinking booths there were parties of 'German peasants, twenty together perhaps, singing na- 'tional drinking-songs, and making a most exhilarating 'and musical chorus by rattling their cups and glasses 'on the table and drinking them against each other, to a 'regular tune. You know it as a stage dodge, but the 'real thing is splendid. Farther down the hill, other

Rifle-shooting.

'peasants were rifle-shooting for prizes, at targets set on 'the other side of a deep ravine, from two to three hun- 'dred yards off. It was quite fearful to see the astonish- 'ing accuracy of their aim, and how, every time a rifle 'awakened the ten thousand echoes of the green glen, 'some men crouching behind a little wall immediately in 'front of the targets, sprung up with large numbers in 'their hands denoting where the ball had struck the 'bull's eye—and then in a moment disappeared again. 'Standing in a ring near these shooters was another 'party of Germans singing hunting-songs, in parts,

Summer-evening picture.

'most melodiously. And down in the distance was 'Lausanne, with all sorts of haunted-looking old towers 'rising up before the smooth water of the lake, and an 'evening sky all red, and gold, and bright green. When 'it closed in quite dark, all the booths were lighted up; 'and the twinkling of the lamps among the forest of trees 'was beautiful. . . .' To this pretty picture, a letter of

Marriage on the farm.

a little later date, describing a marriage on the farm, added farther comical illustration of the rifle-firing pro- pensities of the Swiss, and had otherwise also whimsical touches of character. 'One of the farmer's people—a 'sister, I think—was married from here the other day.

'It is wonderful to see how naturally the smallest girls 'are interested in marriages. Katey and Mamey were as 'excited as if they were eighteen. The fondness of the 'Swiss for gunpowder on interesting occasions, is one of 'the drollest things. For three days before, the farmer 'himself, in the midst of his various agricultural duties, 'plunged out of a little door near my windows, about 'once in every hour, and fired off a rifle. I thought he 'was shooting rats who were spoiling the vines; but he 'was merely relieving his mind, it seemed, on the subject 'of the approaching nuptials. All night afterwards, he 'and a small circle of friends kept perpetually letting off 'guns under the casement of the bridal chamber. A 'Bride is always drest here, in black silk; but this bride 'wore merino of that colour, observing to her mother when she bought it (the old lady is 82, and works on 'the farm), "You know, mother, I am sure to want '"mourning for you, soon; and the same gown will '"do."'*

LAUSANNE: 1846.

Gunpowder festivities.

Bride and mother.

Meanwhile, day by day, he was steadily moving on with his first number; feeling sometimes the want of streets in an 'extraordinary nervousness it would be hardly possible 'to describe,' that would come upon him after he had been writing all day; but at all other times finding the repose of the place very favourable to industry. 'I am writing 'slowly at first, of course' (5th of July), 'but I hope I shall

Progress in work.

* The close of this letter sent family remembrances in characteristic form. 'Kate, Georgy, Mamey, Katey, Charley, Walley, Chickenstalker, and Sampson 'Brass, commend themselves unto your Honour's loving remembrance.' The last but one, who continued long to bear the name, was Frank; the last, who very soon will be found to have another, was Alfred.

Page 159 of Vol. I.

LAUSANNE: 1846.

First chapter of *Dombey*.

'have finished the first number in the course of a fortnight 'at farthest. I have done the first chapter, and begun 'another. I say nothing of the merits thus far, or of the 'idea beyond what is known to you; because I prefer that 'you should come as fresh as may be upon them. I shall 'certainly have a great surprise for people at the end 'of the fourth number;* and I think there is a new and 'peculiar sort of interest, involving the necessity of a little 'bit of delicate treatment whereof I will expound my idea 'to you by and by. When I have done this number, I 'may take a run to Chamounix perhaps . . . My thoughts 'have necessarily been called away from the Christmas 'book. The first *Dombey* done, I think I should fly off to 'that, whenever the idea presented itself vividly before me. 'I still cherish the Battle fancy, though it is nothing but a 'fancy as yet.' A week later he told me that he hoped to finish the first number by that day week or thereabouts, when he should then run and look for his Christmas book in the glaciers at Chamounix. His progress to this point had been pleasing him. 'I think *Dombey* very strong— 'with great capacity in its leading idea; plenty of character 'that is likely to tell; and some rollicking facetiousness, 'to say nothing of pathos. I hope you will soon judge of 'it for yourself, however; and I know you will say what 'you think. I have been very constantly at work.' Six days later I heard that he had still eight slips to write, and for a week had put off Chamounix.

Christmas book.

General idea for *Dombey*.

But though the fourth chapter yet was incomplete, he could repress no longer the desire to write to me of what

* The life of Paul was nevertheless prolonged to the fifth number.

LAUSANNE: 1846.

he was doing (18th of July). 'I think the general idea of '*Dombey* is interesting and new, and has great material 'in it. But I don't like to discuss it with you till you 'have read number one, for fear I should spoil its effect. 'When done—about Wednesday or Thursday, please God '—I will send it in two days' posts, seven letters each day. 'If you have it set at once (I am afraid you couldn't read 'it, otherwise than in print) I know you will impress on 'B. & E. the necessity of the closest secrecy. The very 'name getting out, would be ruinous. The points for 'illustration, and the enormous care required, make me 'excessively anxious. The man for Dombey, if Browne 'could see him, the class man to a T, is Sir A— E—, 'of D—'s. Great pains will be necessary with Miss Tox. 'The Toodle family should not be too much caricatured, 'because of Polly. I should like Browne to think of 'Susan Nipper, who will not be wanted in the first 'number. After the second number, they will all be 'nine or ten years older, but this will not involve much 'change in the characters, except in the children and Miss 'Nipper. What a brilliant thing to be telling you all 'these names so familiarly, when you know nothing about ''em! I quite enjoy it. By the bye, I hope you may like 'the introduction of Solomon Gills.* I think he lives in 'a good sort of house. . . . One word more. What do 'you think, as a name for the Christmas book, of THE 'BATTLE OF LIFE? It is not a name I have conned at 'all, but has just occurred to me in connection with that

Points for illustration.

Hints to artist.

A title for Christmas tale.

* The mathematical-instrument-maker, whom Mr. Taine describes as a marine store dealer.

LAUSANNE: 1846.

'foggy idea. If I can see my way, I think I will take it 'next, and clear it off. If you knew how it hangs about 'me, I am sure you would say so too. It would be an 'immense relief to have it done, and nothing standing in 'the way of *Dombey*.'

First *Dombey* done.

Within the time left for it the opening number was done, but two little incidents preceded still the trip to Chamounix. The first was a visit from Hallam to Mr. Haldimand. 'Heavens! how Hallam did talk yesterday! 'I don't think I ever saw him so tremendous. Very good-'natured and pleasant, in his way, but Good Heavens! 'how he did talk. That famous day you and I remember 'was nothing to it. His son was with him, and his 'daughter (who has an impediment in her speech, as if 'nature were determined to balance that faculty in the 'family), and his niece, a pretty woman, the wife of a 'clergyman and a friend of Thackeray's. It strikes me 'that she must be "the little woman" he proposed to take 'us to drink tea with, once, in Golden-square. Don't you 'remember? His great favourite? She is quite a charming 'person anyhow.' I hope to be pardoned for preserving an opinion which more familiar later acquaintance confirmed, and which can hardly now give anything but pleasure to the lady of whom it is expressed. To the second incident he alludes more briefly. 'As Haldimand and Mrs. Marcet 'and the Cerjats had devised a small mountain expedition 'for us for to-morrow, I didn't like to allow Chamounix to 'stand in the way. So we go with them first, and start on 'our own account on Tuesday. We are extremely pleasant 'with these people.' The close of the same letter (25th of

Henry Hallam.

Friendly residents.

July), mentioning two pieces of local news, gives intimation of the dangers incident to all Swiss travelling, and of such special precautions as were necessary for the holiday among the mountains he was now about to take. 'My 'first news is that a crocodile is said to have escaped from 'the Zoological gardens at Geneva, and to be now "zig-'"zag-zigging" about the lake. But I can't make out 'whether this is a great fact, or whether it is a pious fraud 'to prevent too much bathing and liability to accidents. 'The other piece of news is more serious. An English 'family whose name I don't know, consisting of a father, 'mother, and daughter, arrived at the hotel Gibbon here 'last Monday, and started off on some mountain expedition 'in one of the carriages of the country. It was a mere 'track, the road, and ought to have been travelled only 'by mules, but the Englishman persisted (as Englishmen 'do) in going on in the carriage; and in answer to all the 'representations of the driver that no carriage had ever 'gone up there, said he needn't be afraid he wasn't going 'to be paid for it, and so forth. Accordingly, the coach-'man got down and walked by the horses' heads. It was 'fiery hot; and, after much tugging and rearing, the horses 'began to back, and went down bodily, carriage and all, 'into a deep ravine. The mother was killed on the spot; 'and the father and daughter are lying at some house 'hard by, not expected to recover.'

LAUSANNE: 1846.

Local news.

Sight-seers from England.

His next letter (written on the second of August) described his own first real experience of mountain-travel. 'I begin my letter to-night, but only begin, for we re-'turned from Chamounix in time for dinner just now, and

LAUSANNE: 1846.

Trip to Chamounix.

'are pretty considerably done up. We went by a mountain pass not often crossed by ladies, called the Col de 'Balme, where your imagination may picture Kate and 'Georgy on mules *for ten hours at a stretch*, riding up and 'down the most frightful precipices. We returned by the 'pass of the Tête Noire, which Talfourd knows, and which 'is of a different character, but astonishingly fine too. Mont 'Blanc, and the Valley of Chamounix, and the Mer de Glace, 'and all the wonders of that most wonderful place, are above 'and beyond one's wildest expectations. I cannot imagine 'anything in nature more stupendous or sublime. If I 'were to write about it now, I should quite rave—such pro-'digious impressions are rampant within me. . . . You 'may suppose that the mule-travelling is pretty primitive. 'Each person takes a carpet-bag strapped on the mule be-'hind himself or herself: and that is all the baggage that 'can be carried. A guide, a thorough-bred mountaineer, 'walks all the way, leading the lady's mule; I say the lady's '*par excellence*, in compliment to Kate; and all the rest 'struggle on as they please. The cavalcade stops at a lone 'hut for an hour and a half in the middle of the day, and 'lunches brilliantly on whatever it can get. Going by that 'Col de Balme pass, you climb up and up and up for five 'hours and more, and look—from a mere unguarded ledge of 'path on the side of the precipice—into such awful valleys, 'that at last you are firm in the belief that you have got 'above everything in the world, and that there can be 'nothing earthly overhead. Just as you arrive at this 'conclusion, a different (and oh Heaven! what a free and 'wonderful) air comes blowing on your face; you cross a

Wonders of scenery.

Mule-travelling.

Col de Balme.

'ridge of snow; and lying before you (wholly unseen till 'then), towering up into the distant sky, is the vast range 'of Mont Blanc, with attendant mountains diminished 'by its majestic side into mere dwarfs tapering up into 'innumerable rude Gothic pinnacles; deserts of ice and 'snow; forests of firs on mountain sides, of no account at 'all in the enormous scene; villages down in the hollow, 'that you can shut out with a finger; waterfalls, ava-'lanches, pyramids and towers of ice, torrents, bridges; 'mountain upon mountain until the very sky is blocked 'away, and you must look up, overhead, to see it. Good 'God, what a country Switzerland is, and what a concen-'tration of it is to be beheld from that one spot! And '(think of this in Whitefriars and in Lincoln's-inn!) at noon 'on the second day from here, the first day being but half 'a one by the bye and full of uncommon beauty, you lie 'down on that ridge and see it all! . . . I think I must go 'back again (whether you come or not!) and see it again 'before the bad weather arrives. We have had sunlight, 'moonlight, a perfectly transparent atmosphere with not a 'cloud, and the grand plateau on the very summit of Mont 'Blanc so clear by day and night that it was difficult to 'believe in intervening chasms and precipices, and almost 'impossible to resist the idea that one might sally forth 'and climb up easily. I went into all sorts of places; 'armed with a great pole with a spike at the end of it, like 'a leaping-pole, and with pointed irons buckled on to my 'shoes; and am all but knocked up. I was very anxious 'to make the expedition to what is called "The Garden:" 'a green spot covered with wild flowers, lying across the

LAUSANNE: 1846.

Mont Blanc range.

Effect upon C. D.

Mer de Glace.

LAUSANNE: 1846.

Trip to Chamounix.

'Mer de Glace, and among the most awful mountains: but 'I could find no Englishman at the hotels who was similarly 'disposed, and the Brave *wouldn't go.* No sir! He gave 'in point blank (having been horribly blown in a climbing 'excursion the day before), and couldn't stand it. He is 'too heavy for such work, unquestionably.* In all other 'respects, I think he has exceeded himself on this journey: 'and if you could have seen him riding a very small mule, 'up a road exactly like the broken stairs of Rochester-'castle; with a brandy bottle slung over his shoulder, a 'small pie in his hat, a roast fowl looking out of his pocket, 'and a mountain staff of six feet long carried cross-wise 'on the saddle before him; you'd have said so. He was '(next to me) the admiration of Chamounix, but he utterly 'quenched me on the road.'

The Brave C and his master.

On the road as they returned there had been a small adventure, the day before this letter was written. Dickens was jingling slowly up the Tête Noire pass (his mule having thirty-seven bells on its head), riding at the moment quite alone, when—'an Englishman came bolting out of a little 'châlet in a most inaccessible and extraordinary place, and 'said with great glee "There has been an accident here '"sir!" I had been thinking of anything else you please; 'and, having no reason to suppose him an Englishman 'except his language, which went for nothing in the con-'fusion, stammered out a reply in French and stared at 'him, in a very damp shirt and trowsers, as he stared at 'me in a similar costume. On his repeating the announce-

Tête Noire pass.

* Poor fellow! he had latent disease of the heart, which developed itself rapidly on Dickens's return to England.

'ment, I began to have a glimmering of common sense; 'and so arrived at a knowledge of the fact that a German 'lady had been thrown from her mule and had broken her 'leg, at a short distance off, and had found her way in great 'pain to that cottage, where the Englishman, a Prussian, 'and a Frenchman, had presently come up; and the French'man, by extraordinary good fortune, was a surgeon! They 'were all from Chamounix, and the three latter were walk'ing in company. It was quite charming to see how atten'tive they were. The lady was from Lausanne; where she 'had come from Frankfort to make excursions with her 'two boys, who are at the college here, during the vacation. 'She had no other attendants, and the boys were crying 'and very frightened. The Englishman was in the full glee 'of having just cut up one white dress, two chemises, and 'three pocket handkerchiefs, for bandages; the Frenchman 'had set the leg, skilfully; the Prussian had scoured a neigh'bouring wood for some men to carry her forward; and 'they were all at it, behind the hut, making a sort of hand'barrow on which to bear her. When it was constructed, 'she was strapped upon it; had her poor head covered over 'with a handkerchief, and was carried away; and we all 'went on in company: Kate and Georgy consoling and 'tending the sufferer, who was very cheerful, but had lost 'her husband only a year.' With the same delightful observation, and missing no touch of kindly character that might give each actor his place in the little scene, the sequel is described; but it does not need to add more. It was hoped that by means of relays of men at Martigny the poor lady might have been carried on some twenty

LAUSANNE: 1846.

An accident.

English, French, and Prussian help.

Result of adventure.

LAUSANNE: 1846.

miles, in the cooler evening, to the head of the lake, and so have been got into the steamer; but she was too exhausted to be borne beyond the inn, and there she had to remain until joined by relatives from Frankfort.

Second number of *Dombey*.

A few days' rest after his return were interposed, before he began his second number; and until the latter has been completed, and the Christmas story taken in hand, I do not admit the reader to his full confidences about his writing. But there were other subjects that amused and engaged him up to that date, as well when he was idle as when again he was at work, to which expression so full of character is given in his letters that they properly find mention here.

Between the second and the ninth of August he went down one evening to the lake, five minutes after sunset, when the sky was covered with sullen black clouds reflected in the deep water, and saw the Castle of Chillon.

Castle of Chillon described.

He thought it the best deserving and least exaggerated in repute, of all the places he had seen. 'The insupportable solitude and dreariness of the white walls and towers, the sluggish moat and drawbridge, and the lonely ramparts, I never saw the like of. But there is a courtyard inside; surrounded by prisons, oubliettes, and old chambers of torture; so terrifically sad, that death itself is not more sorrowful. And oh! a wicked old Grand Duke's bedchamber upstairs in the tower, with a secret staircase down into the chapel where the bats were wheeling about; and Bonnivard's dungeon; and a horrible trap whence prisoners were cast out into the lake; and a stake all burnt and crackled up, that still stands 'in the torture-ante-chamber to the saloon of justice (!)— 'what tremendous places! Good God, the greatest mys- 'tery in all the earth, to me, is how or why the world was 'tolerated by its Creator through the good old times, and 'wasn't dashed to fragments.'

LAUSANNE: 1846.

Fête in honour of New Constitution.

On the ninth of August he wrote to me that there was to be a prodigious fête that day in Lausanne, in honour of the first anniversary of the proclamation of the New Constitution:* 'beginning at sunrise with the firing of 'great guns, and twice two thousand rounds of rifles by 'two thousand men; proceeding at eleven o'clock with a 'great service, and some speechifying, in the church; and 'ending to-night with a great ball in the public prome- 'nade, and a general illumination of the town.' The authorities had invited him to a place of honour in the ceremony; and though he did not go ('having been up 'till three o'clock in the morning, and being fast asleep 'at the appointed time'), the reply that sent his thanks expressed also his sympathy. He was the readier with this from having discovered, in the 'old' or 'gentlemanly' party of the place ('including of course the sprinkling of 'English who are always tory, hang ''em!'), so wonderfully sore a feeling about the revolution thus celebrated, that to avoid its fête the majority had gone off by steamer the day before, and those who remained were prophesying

Political celebration.

Domestic excitements.

* Out of the excitements consequent on the public festivities arose some domestic inconveniences. I will give one of them. 'Fanchette the cook, 'distracted by the forthcoming fête, madly refused to buy a duck yesterday 'as ordered by the Brave, and a battle of life ensued between those two 'powers. The Brave is of opinion that "datter woman have went mad." 'But she seems calm to-day; and I suppose won't poison the family . . .'

LAUSANNE: 1846.

Malcontents.

assaults on the unilluminated houses, and other excesses. Dickens had no faith in such predictions. 'The people are 'as perfectly good tempered and quiet always, as people 'can be. I don't know what the last Government may 'have been, but they seem to me to do very well with this, 'and to be rationally and cheaply provided for. If you 'believed what the discontented assert, you wouldn't be-'lieve in one solitary man or woman with a grain of good-'ness or civility. I find nothing *but* civility; and I walk 'about in all sorts of out-of-the-way places, where they 'live rough lives enough, in solitary cottages.' The issue was told in two postscripts to his letter, and showed him to be so far right. 'P.S. 6 o'clock afternoon. The fête 'going on, in great force. Not one of "the old party" to 'be seen. I went down with one to the ground before 'dinner, and nothing would induce him to go within the 'barrier with me. Yet what they call a revolution was 'nothing but a change of government. Thirty-six thou-'sand people, in this small canton, petitioned against the 'Jesuits—God knows with good reason. The Government 'chose to call them "a mob." So, to prove that they were 'not, they turned the Government out. I honour them 'for it. They are a genuine people, these Swiss. There 'is better metal in them than in all the stars and stripes 'of all the fustian banners of the so-called, and falsely 'called, U-nited States. They are a thorn in the sides of 'European despots, and a good wholesome people to live 'near Jesuit-ridden Kings on the brighter side of the 'mountains.' 'P.P.S. August 10th. . . . The fête went off as 'quietly as I supposed it would; and they danced all night.'

Good conduct of the people.

These views had forcible illustration in a subsequent letter, where he describes a similar revolution that occurred at Geneva before he left the country; and nothing could better show his practical good sense in a matter of this kind. The description will be given shortly; and meanwhile I subjoin a comment made by him, not less worthy of attention, upon my reply to his account of the anti-Jesuit celebration at Lausanne. 'I don't know whether I 'have mentioned before, that in the valley of the Simplon 'hard by here, where (at the bridge of St. Maurice, over the 'Rhone) this Protestant canton ends and a Catholic canton 'begins, you might separate two perfectly distinct and 'different conditions of humanity by drawing a line with 'your stick in the dust on the ground. On the Protestant 'side, neatness; cheerfulness; industry; education; con-'tinual aspiration, at least, after better things. On the 'Catholic side, dirt, disease, ignorance, squalor, and misery. 'I have so constantly observed the like of this, since I first 'came abroad, that I have a sad misgiving that the religion 'of Ireland lies as deep at the root of all its sorrows, even 'as English misgovernment and Tory villainy.' Almost the counterpart of this remark is to be found in one of the later writings of Macaulay.

Political good sense.

Protestant and Catholic cantons.

Timely word on Ireland.

# CHAPTER XII.

## SKETCHES CHIEFLY PERSONAL.

1846.

LAUSANNE: 1846.

SOME sketches from the life in his pleasantest vein now claim to be taken from the same series of letters; and I will prefix one or two less important notices, for the most part personal also, that have characteristic mention of his opinions in them.

Home politics.

Home-politics he criticized, in what he wrote on the 24th of August, much in the spirit of his last excellent remark on the Protestant and Catholic cantons; having no sympathy with the course taken by the whigs in regard to Ireland after they had defeated Peel on his coercion bill, and resumed the government. 'I am perfectly appalled 'by the hesitation and cowardice of the whigs. To bring 'in that arms bill, bear the brunt of the attack upon it, 'take out the obnoxious clauses, still retain the bill, and 'finally withdraw it, seems to me the meanest and most 'halting way of going to work that ever was taken. I 'cannot believe in them. Lord John must be helpless 'among them. They seem somehow or other never to 'know what cards they hold in their hands, and to play 'them out blindfold. The contrast with Peel (as he was

The whigs: and Peel.

'last) is, I agree with you, certainly not favourable. I don't 'believe now they ever would have carried the repeal of the 'corn law, if they could.' Referring in the same letter* to the reluctance of public men of all parties to give the needful help to schemes of emigration, he ascribed it to a secret belief in 'the gentle politico-economical principle that 'a surplus population must and ought to starve;' in which for himself he never could see anything but disaster for all who trusted to it. 'I am convinced that its philosophers 'would sink any government, any cause, any doctrine, even 'the most righteous. There is a sense and humanity in 'the mass, in the long run, that will not bear them; and 'they will wreck their friends always, as they wrecked them 'in the working of the Poor-law-bill. Not all the figures 'that Babbage's calculating machine could turn up in 'twenty generations, would stand in the long run against 'the general heart.'

Malthus philosophy.

Of other topics in his letters, one or two have the additional attractiveness derivable from touches of personal interest when these may with propriety be printed. Hardly within the class might have fallen a mention of Mark Lemon, of whom our recent play, and his dramatic adaptation of the *Chimes*, had given him pleasant experiences, if I felt less

Mark Lemon.

* Where he makes remark also on a class of offences which are still most inadequately punished: 'I hope you will follow up your idea about the defec- 'tive state of the law in reference to women, by some remarks on the inade- 'quate punishment of that ruffian flippantly called by the liners the Whole- 'sale Matrimonial Speculator. My opinion is, that in any well-ordered state 'of society, and advanced spirit of social jurisprudence, he would have been 'flogged more than once (privately), and certainly sentenced to transportation 'for no less a term than the rest of his life. Surely the man who threw the 'woman out of window was no worse, if so bad.'

Defective legislation.

LAUSANNE: 1846.

strongly not only that its publication would have been gladly sanctioned by the subject of it, but that it will not now displease another to whom also it refers, herself the member of a family in various ways distinguished on the stage, and to whom, since her husband's death, well-merited sympathy and respect have been paid. 'After turning Mrs. Lemon's 'portrait over, in my mind, I am convinced that there is 'not a grain of bad taste in the matter, and that there 'is a manly composure and courage in the proceeding 'deserving of the utmost respect. If Lemon were one 'of your braggart honest men, he would set a taint of 'bad taste upon that action as upon everything else he 'might say or do; but being what he is, I admire him 'for it greatly, and hold it to be a proof of an exalted 'nature and a true heart. Your idea of him, is mine. 'I am sure he is an excellent fellow. We talk about not 'liking such and such a man because he doesn't look one 'in the face,—but how much we should esteem a man 'who looks the world in the face, composedly, and neither 'shirks it nor bullies it. Between ourselves, I say with 'shame and self-reproach that I am quite sure if Kate 'had been a Columbine her portrait would not be hanging, '"in character," in Devonshire-terrace.'

An incident of character.

Self-comparison.

He speaks thus of a novel by Hood. 'I have been 'reading poor Hood's *Tylney Hall:* the most extra-'ordinary jumble of impossible extravagance, and especial 'cleverness, I ever saw. The man drawn to the life from 'the pirate-bookseller, is wonderfully good; and his recom-'mendation to a reduced gentleman from the university, 'to rise from nothing as he, the pirate, did, and go round

Hood's *Tylney Hall.*

'to the churches and see whether there's an opening, and 'begin by being a beadle, is one of the finest things I ever 'read, in its way.' The same letter has a gentle little trait of the great duke, touching in its simplicity, and worth preserving. 'I had a letter from Tagart the day before 'yesterday, with a curious little anecdote of the Duke of 'Wellington in it. They have had a small cottage at Wal-'mer; and one day—the other day only—the old man 'met their little daughter Lucy, a child about Mamey's age, 'near the garden; and having kissed her, and asked her 'what was her name, and who and what her parents 'were, tied a small silver medal round her neck with a 'bit of pink ribbon, and asked the child to keep it in 'remembrance of him. There is something good, and 'aged, and odd in it. Is there not?'

LAUSANNE: 1846.

Duke of Wellington.

Another of his personal references was to Lord Grey, to whose style of speaking and general character of mind he had always a strongly-expressed dislike, drawn not impartially or quite justly from the days of reaction that followed the reform debates, when the whig leader's least attractive traits were presented to the young reporter. 'He is 'a very intelligent agreeable fellow, the said Watson by the 'bye' (he is speaking of the member of the Lausanne circle with whom he established friendliest after-intercourse); 'he sat for Northamptonshire in the reform bill time, and 'is high sheriff of his county and all the rest of it; but has 'not the least nonsense about him, and is a thorough good 'liberal. He has a charming wife, who draws well, and is 'making a sketch of Rosemont for us that shall be yours 'in Paris.' (It is already, by permission of its present

Lord Grey.

Mr. Watson of Rockingham.

*Ante*, p. 203.

LAUSANNE: 1846.

possessor, the reader's, and all the world's who may take interest in the little doll's house of Lausanne which lodged so illustrious a tenant.) 'He was giving me some good 'recollections of Lord Grey the other evening when we 'were playing at battledore (old Lord Grey I mean), and 'of the constitutional impossibility he and Lord Lansdowne 'and the rest laboured under, of ever personally attaching 'a single young man, in all the excitement of that exciting 'time, to the leaders of the party. It was quite a delight 'to me, as I listened, to recall my own dislike of his style 'of speaking, his fishy coldness, his uncongenial and un-'sympathetic politeness, and his insufferable though most 'gentlemanly artificiality. The shape of his head (I see it 'now) was misery to me, and weighed down my youth . .

A recollection of his reporting days.

It was now the opening of the second week in August; and before he finally addressed himself to the second number of *Dombey*, he had again turned a lingering look in the direction of his Christmas book. 'It would be such a 'great relief to me to get that small story out of the way.' Wisely, however, again he refrained, and went on with *Dombey;* at which he had been working for a little time when he described to me (24th of August) a visit from two English travellers, of one of whom with the slightest possible touch he gives a speaking likeness.*

Christmas book.

Returns to *Dombey.*

* Ten days before there had been a visit from Mr. Ainsworth and his daughters on their way to Geneva. 'I breakfasted with him at the hotel Gibbon next 'morning and they dined here afterwards, and we walked about all day, 'talking of our old days at Kensal-lodge.' The same letter told me: 'We 'had a regatta at Ouchy the other day, mainly supported by the contributions 'of the English handfull. It concluded with a rowing-match by women, 'which was very funny. I wish you could have seen Roche appear on the 'Lake, rowing, in an immense boat, Cook, Anne, two nurses, Katey, Mamey,

Page 158 of Vol. I.

LAUSANNE: 1846.

'Not having your letter as usual, I sat down to write to 'you on speculation yesterday, but lapsed in my uncertainty 'into *Dombey*, and worked at it all day. It was, as it has been 'since last Tuesday morning, incessantly raining regular 'mountain rain. After dinner, at a little after seven o'clock, 'I was walking up and down under the little colonnade in 'the garden, racking my brain about *Dombeys* and *Battles 'of Lives*, when two travel-stained-looking men approached, 'of whom one, in a very limp and melancholy straw hat, 'ducked perpetually to me as he came up the walk. I 'couldn't make them out at all; and it wasn't till I got close 'up to them that I recognised A. and (in the straw hat) N. 'They had come from Geneva by the steamer, and taken a 'scrambling dinner on board. I gave them some fine Rhine 'wine, and cigars innumerable. A. enjoyed himself and was 'quite at home. N. (an odd companion for a man of genius) 'was snobbish, but pleased and good-natured. A. had a five 'pound note in his pocket which he had worn down, by 'careless carrying about, to some two-thirds of its original 'size, and which was so ragged in its remains that when 'he took it out bits of it flew about the table. "Oh Lor '"you know—now really—like Goldsmith you know—or '"any of those great men!" said N, with the very

Two English travellers.

A man of genius and his companion.

'Walley, Chickenstalker, and Baby; no boatmen or other degrading assistance; 'and all sorts of Swiss tubs splashing about them . . . Senior is coming 'here to-morrow, I believe, with his wife; and they talk of Brunel and his 'wife as on their way. We dine at Haldimand's to meet Senior—which 'solitary and most interesting piece of intelligence is all the news I know 'of . . . Take care you don't back out of your Paris engagement; but that 'we really do have (please God) some happy hours there. Kate, Georgy, 'Mamey, Katey, Charley, Walley, Chickenstalker, and Baby, send loves . . . I 'am all anxiety and fever to know what we start *Dombey* with!'

News from the lake.

LAUSANNE: 1846.

'"snatches in his voice and burst of speaking" that reminded Leigh Hunt of Cloten. . . The clouds were lying, as 'they do in such weather here, on the earth, and our friends 'saw no more of Lake Leman than of Battersea. Nor had 'they, it might appear, seen more of the Mer de Glace, on 'their way here; their talk about it bearing much resemblance to that of the man who had been to Niagara and 'said it was nothing but water.'

Ill mood for travel.

Party among the hills.

His next letter described a day's party of the Cerjats, Watsons, and Haldimands, among the neighbouring hills, which, contrary to his custom while at work, he had been unable to resist the temptation of joining. They went to a mountain-lake twelve miles off, had dinner at the public-house on the lake, and returned home by Vevay at which they rested for tea; and where pleasant talk with Mr. Cerjat led to anecdotes of an excellent friend of ours, formerly resident at Lausanne, with which the letter closed. Our friend was a distinguished writer, and a man of many sterling fine qualities, but with a habit of occasional free indulgence in coarseness of speech, which, though his earlier life had made it as easy to acquire as difficult to drop, did always less than justice to a very manly, honest, and really gentle nature. He had as much genuinely admirable stuff in him as any favourite hero of Smollett or Fielding, and I never knew anyone who reminded me of those characters so much. 'It would seem, Mr. Cerjat tells me, that he was, when here, 'infinitely worse in his general style of conversation, than 'now—sermuchser, as Toodle says, that Cerjat describes 'himself as having always been in unspeakable agony when 'he was at his table, lest he should forget himself (or re-

A Smollett hero.

LAUSANNE: 1846.

'member himself, as I suggested) and break out before the 'ladies. There happened to be living here at that time a 'stately English baronet and his wife, who had two milksop 'sons, concerning whom they cherished the idea of accom-'plishing their education into manhood coexistently with 'such perfect purity and innocence, that they were hardly 'to know their own sex. Accordingly, they were sent to 'no school or college, but had masters of all sorts at home, 'and thus reached eighteen years or so, in what Falstaff calls 'a kind of male green-sickness. At this crisis of their in-'nocent existence, our ogre friend encountered these lambs 'at dinner, with their father, at Cerjat's house; and, as if 'possessed by a devil, launched out into such frightful and 'appalling impropriety—ranging over every kind of for-'bidden topic and every species of forbidden word and 'every sort of scandalous anecdote—that years of education 'in Newgate would have been as nothing compared with 'their experience of that one afternoon. After turning paler 'and paler, and more and more stoney, the baronet, with a 'half-suppressed cry, rose and fled. But the sons—intent 'on the ogre—remained behind instead of following him; 'and are supposed to have been ruined from that hour. 'Isn't that a good story? I can SEE our friend and his 'pupils now . . . Poor fellow! He seems to have a hard 'time of it with his wife. She had no interest whatever 'in her children; and was such a fury, that, being dressed 'to go out to dinner, she would sometimes, on no other 'provocation than a pin out of its place or some such thing, 'fall upon a little maid she had, beat her till she couldn't 'stand, then tumble into hysterics, and be carried to bed.

Milksop youths.

Ogre and lambs.

Victims of orthological impropriety.

LAUSANNE: 1846.

A martyr of a husband.

'He suffered martyrdom with her; and seems to have 'been himself, in all good-natured easy-going ways, just 'what we know him now.'

There were at this time some fresh arrivals of travelling English at Lausanne, outside their own little circle, and among them another baronet and his family made amusing appearance. 'We have another English family here, 'one Sir Joseph and his lady, and ten children. Sir 'Joseph, a large baronet something in the Graham style, 'with a little, loquacious, flat-faced, damaged-featured, *old* '*young* wife. They are fond of society, and couldn't well 'have less. They delight in a view, and live in a close 'street at Ouchy, down among the drunken boatmen and 'the drays and omnibuses, where nothing whatever is to be 'seen but the locked wheels of carts scraping down the 'uneven, steep, stone pavement. The baronet plays double-'dummy all day long, with an unhappy Swiss whom he 'has entrapped for that purpose; the baronet's lady pays 'visits; and the baronet's daughters play a Lausanne 'piano, which must be heard to be appreciated . . .'

Sir Joseph and his family.

Another sketch in the same letter touches little more than the eccentricities (but all in good taste and good humour) of the subject of it, who is still gratefully remembered by English residents in Italy for his scholarly munificence, and for very valuable service conferred by it on Italian literature. 'Another curious man is back-'wards and forwards here—a Lord Vernon,* who is well-'informed, a great Italian scholar deep in Dante, and a

Lord Vernon.

* This was the fourth Baron Vernon, who succeeded to the title in 1829, and died seven years after the date of Dickens's description, in his 74th year.

'very good-humoured gentleman, but who has fallen into 'the strange infatuation of attending every rifle-match 'that takes place in Switzerland, accompanied by two men 'who load rifles for him, one after another, which he has 'been frequently known to fire off, two a minute, for four-'teen hours at a stretch, without once changing his position 'or leaving the ground. He wins all kinds of prizes; 'gold watches, flags, teaspoons, teaboards, and so forth; 'and is constantly travelling about with them, from place 'to place, in an extraordinary carriage, where you touch a 'spring and a chair flies out, touch another spring and a 'bed appears, touch another spring and a closet of pickles 'opens, touch another spring and disclose a pantry. While 'Lady Vernon (said to be handsome and accomplished) 'is continually cutting across this or that Alpine pass 'in the night, to meet him on the road, for a minute or 'two, on one of his excursions; these being the only 'times at which she can catch him. The last time he saw 'her, was five or six months ago, when they met and 'supped together on the St. Gothard! It is a monomania 'with him, of course. He is a man of some note; seconded 'one of Lord Melbourne's addresses; and had forty thou-'sand a year, now reduced to ten, but nursing and improving 'every day. He was with us last Monday, and comes back 'from some out-of-the-way place to join another small pic-'nic next Friday. As I have said, he is the very soul of 'good nature and cheerfulness, but one can't help being 'melancholy to see a man wasting his life in such a singu-'lar delusion. Isn't it odd? He knows my books very 'well, and seems interested in everything concerning them;

LAUSANNE: 1846.

Passion for rifle-shooting.

A wonderful carriage.

Wasting life.

LAUSANNE: 1846.

'being indeed accomplished in books generally, and 'attached to many elegant tastes.'

But the most agreeable addition to their own special circle was referred to in his first September letter, just when he was coming to the close of his second number of *Dombey*. 'There are two nice girls here, the Ladies 'Taylor, daughters of Lord Headfort. Their mother was 'daughter (I think) of Sir John Stevenson, and Moore 'dedicated one part of the Irish Melodies to her. They 'inherit the musical taste, and sing very well. A proposal 'is on foot for our all bundling off on Tuesday (16 strong) 'to the top of the Great St. Bernard. But the weather 'seems to have broken, and the autumn rains to have set 'in; which I devoutly hope will break up the party. It 'would be a most serious hindrance to me, just now; but 'I have rashly promised. Do you know young Romilly? 'He is coming over from Geneva when "the reading" 'comes off, and is a fine fellow I am told. There is not a 'bad little theatre here; and by way of an artificial crowd, 'I should certainly have got it open with an amateur 'company, if we were not so few that the only thing we 'want is the audience.' . . . The 'reading' named by him was that of his first number, which was to 'come off' as soon as I could get the proofs out to him; but which the changes needful to be made, and to be mentioned hereafter, still delayed. The St. Bernard holiday, which within sight of his Christmas-book labour he would fain have thrown over, came off as proposed very fortunately for the reader, who might otherwise have lost one of his pleasantest descriptions. But before giving it, one more

The Ladies Taylor.

Proposed trip to Great St. Bernard.

Reading of first *Dombey*.

little sketch of character may be interposed as delicately done as anything in his writings. Steele's observation is in the outline, and Charles Lamb's humour in its touch of colouring.

A sketch from life.

'. . . There are two old ladies (English) living here 'who may serve me for a few lines of gossip—as I have 'intended they should, over and over again, but I have 'always forgotten it. There were originally four old la-'dies, sisters, but two of them have faded away in the 'course of eighteen years, and withered by the side of 'John Kemble in the cemetery. They are very little, and 'very skinny; and each of them wears a row of false 'curls, like little rolling-pins, so low upon her brow, that 'there is no forehead; nothing above the eyebrows but a 'deep horizontal wrinkle, and then the curls. They live 'upon some small annuity. For thirteen years they have 'wanted very much to move to Italy, as the eldest old 'lady says the climate of this part of Switzerland doesn't 'agree with her, and preys upon her spirits; but they 'have never been able to go, because of the difficulty of 'moving "the books." This tremendous library belonged 'once upon a time to the father of these old ladies, and 'comprises about fifty volumes. I have never been able 'to see what they are, because one of the old ladies 'always sits before them; but they look, outside, like 'very old backgammon-boards. The two deceased sisters 'died in the firm persuasion that this precious property 'could never be got over the Simplon without some 'gigantic effort to which the united family was unequal. 'The two remaining sisters live, and will die also, in the

Two sisters and their books: a library too gigantic: to be got over the Simplon.

LAUSANNE: 1846.

'same belief. I met the eldest (evidently drooping) 'yesterday, and recommended her to try Genoa. She 'looked shrewdly at the snow that closes up the moun- 'tain prospect just now, and said that when the spring 'was quite set in, and the avalanches were down, and the 'passes well open, she would certainly try that place, if 'they could devise any plan, in the course of the winter, 'for moving "the books." The whole library will be sold 'by auction here, when they are both dead, for about a 'napoleon; and some young woman will carry it home in 'two journeys with a basket.'

Trip to Great St. Bernard.

The last letter sent me before he fell upon his self-appointed task for Christmas, contained a delightful account of the trip to the Great St. Bernard. It was dated on the sixth of September.

'The weather obstinately clearing, we started off last 'Tuesday for the Great St. Bernard, returning here on 'Friday afternoon. The party consisted of eleven people 'and two servants—Haldimand, Mr. and Mrs. Cerjat and 'one daughter, Mr. and Mrs. Watson, two Ladies Taylor, 'Kate, Georgy, and I. We were wonderfully unanimous 'and cheerful; went away from here by the steamer; 'found at its destination a whole omnibus provided by the 'Brave (who went on in advance everywhere); rode there- 'in to Bex; found two large carriages ready to take us to 'Martigny; slept there; and proceeded up the mountain

Ascent of the mountain.

'on mules next day. Although the St. Bernard convent 'is, as I dare say you know, the highest inhabited spot but 'one in the world, the ascent is extremely gradual and 'uncommonly easy: really presenting no difficulties at all, 'until within the last league, when the ascent, lying 'through a place called the valley of desolation, is very 'awful and tremendous, and the road is rendered toilsome 'by scattered rocks and melting snow. The convent is a 'most extraordinary place, full of great vaulted passages, 'divided from each other with iron gratings; and present- 'ing a series of the most astonishing little dormitories, 'where the windows are so small (on account of the cold 'and snow), that it is as much as one can do to get one's 'head out of them. Here we slept: supping, thirty 'strong, in a rambling room with a great wood-fire in it 'set apart for that purpose; with a grim monk, in a high 'black sugar-loaf hat with a great knob at the top of it, 'carving the dishes. At five o'clock in the morning the 'chapel bell rang in the dismallest way for matins: and I, 'lying in bed close to the chapel, and being awakened by 'the solemn organ and the chaunting, thought for a moment 'I had died in the night and passed into the unknown 'world.

Valley of Desolation.

The convent.

C. D. and the matins bell.

'I wish to God you could see that place. A great 'hollow on the top of a range of dreadful mountains, fenced 'in by riven rocks of every shape and colour: and in the 'midst, a black lake, with phantom clouds perpetually 'stalking over it. Peaks, and points, and plains of eternal 'ice and snow, bounding the view, and shutting out the 'world on every side: the lake reflecting nothing: and 'no human figure in the scene. The air so fine, that it is 'difficult to breathe without feeling out of breath; and 'the cold so exquisitely thin and sharp that it is not to be 'described. Nothing of life or living interest in the

Scene at the mountain top.

Lausanne: 1846.

Trip to Great St. Bernard.

'picture, but the grey dull walls of the convent. No 'vegetation of any sort or kind. Nothing growing, no-'thing stirring. Everything iron-bound, and frozen up. 'Beside the convent, in a little outhouse with a grated 'iron door which you may unbolt for yourself, are the 'bodies of people found in the snow who have never been 'claimed and are withering away—not laid down, or 'stretched out, but standing up, in corners and against 'walls; some erect and horribly human, with distinct 'expressions on the faces; some sunk down on their 'knees; some dropping over on one side; some tumbled 'down altogether, and presenting a heap of skulls and 'fibrous dust. There is no other decay in that atmos-'phere; and there they remain during the short days and 'the long nights, the only human company out of doors, 'withering away by grains, and holding ghastly possession 'of the mountain where they died.

Bodies found in the snow.

'It is the most distinct and individual place I have seen, 'even in this transcendent country. But, for the Saint Ber-'nard holy fathers and convent in themselves, I am sorry 'to say that they are a piece of as sheer humbug as we 'ever learnt to believe in, in our young days. Trashy 'French sentiment and the dogs (of which, by the bye, 'there are only three remaining) have done it all. They 'are a lazy set of fellows; not over fond of going out them-'selves; employing servants to clear the road (which has 'not been important or much used as a pass these hun-'dred years); rich; and driving a good trade in Innkeep-'ing: the convent being a common tavern in everything 'but the sign. No charge is made for their hospitality,

The holy fathers.

Convent a tavern in all but sign.

LAUSANNE: 1846.

Trip to Great St. Bernard.

'to be sure; but you are shown to a box in the chapel, 'where everybody puts in more than could, with any show 'of face, be charged for the entertainment; and from this 'the establishment derives a right good income. As to the 'self-sacrifice of living up there, they are obliged to go 'there young, it is true, to be inured to the climate: but it 'is an infinitely more exciting and various life than any 'other convent can offer; with constant change and com-'pany through the whole summer; with a hospital for in-'valids down in the valley, which affords another change; 'and with an annual begging-journey to Geneva and this 'place and all the places round for one brother or other, 'which affords farther change. The brother who carved 'at our supper could speak some English, and had just 'had *Pickwick* given him!—what a humbug he will think 'me when he tries to understand it! If I had had any other 'book of mine with me, I would have given it him, that I 'might have had some chance of being intelligible . . .'

A holy brother and *Pickwick*.

## CHAPTER XIII.

### LITERARY LABOUR AT LAUSANNE.

1846.

LAUSANNE: 1846.

A picture completed.

Great present want.

SOMETHING of the other side of the medal has now to be presented. His letters enable us to see him amid his troubles and difficulties of writing, as faithfully as in his leisure and enjoyments; and when, to the picture thus given of Dickens's home life in Switzerland, some account has been added of the vicissitudes of literary labour undergone in the interval, as complete a representation of the man will be afforded as could be taken from any period of his career. Of the larger life whereof it is part, the Lausanne life is indeed a perfect microcosm, wanting only the London streets. This was his chief present want, as will shortly be perceived: but as yet the reader does not feel it, and he sees otherwise in all respects at his best the great observer and humourist; interested in everything that commended itself to a thoroughly earnest and eagerly enquiring nature; popular beyond measure with all having intercourse with him; the centre, and very soul, of social enjoyment; letting nothing escape a vision that was not more keen than kindly; and even when apparently most idle, never idle in the sense of his art,

LAUSANNE: 1846.

Daily life.

but adding day by day to experiences that widened its range, and gave freer and healthier play to an imagination always busily at wörk, alert and active in a singular degree, and that seemed to be quite untiring. At his heart there was a genuine love of nature at all times; and strange as it may seem to connect this with such forms of humorous delineation as are most identified with his genius, it is yet the literal truth that the impressions of this noble Swiss scenery were with him during the work of many subsequent years: a present and actual, though it might be seldom a directly conscious, influence. When he said afterwards, that, while writing the book on which he is now engaged, he had not seen less clearly each step of the wooden midshipman's staircase, each pew of the church in which Florence was married, or each bed in the dormitory of Doctor Blimber's establishment, because he was himself at the time by the lake of Geneva, he might as truly have said that he saw them all the more clearly even because of that circumstance. He worked his humour to its greatest results by the freedom and force of his imagination; and while the smallest or commonest objects around him were food for the one, the other might have pined or perished without additional higher aliment. Dickens had little love for Wordsworth, but he was himself an example of the truth the great poet never tired of enforcing, that Nature has subtle helps for all who are admitted to become free of her wonders and mysteries.

Influences of nature.

Imaginative needs.

Another noticeable thing in him is impressed upon these letters, as upon many also heretofore quoted, for indeed all of them are marvellously exact in the reproduction of

LAUSANNE: 1846.

Self-judgments.

his nature. He did not think lightly of his work; and the work that occupied him at the time was for the time paramount with him. But the sense he entertained, whether right or wrong, of the importance of what he had to do, of the degree to which it concerned others that the power he held should be exercised successfully, and of the estimate he was justified in forming as the fair measure of its worth or greatness, does not carry with it of necessity presumption or self-conceit. Few men have had less of either. It was part of the intense individuality by which he effected so much, to set the high value which in general he did upon what he was striving to accomplish; he could not otherwise have mastered one half the work he designed; and we are able to form an opinion, more just now for ourselves than it might have seemed to us then from others, of the weight and truth of such self-judgment. The fussy pretension of small men in great places, and the resolute self-assertion of great men in small places, are things essentially different. *Respice finem.* The exact relative importance of all our pursuits is to be arrived at by nicer adjustments of the Now and the Hereafter than are possible to contemporary judgments; and there have been some indications since his death confirmatory of the belief, that the estimate which he thought himself entitled to form of the labours to which his life was devoted, will be strengthened, not lessened, by time.

Intense individuality.

The now and the hereafter.

Work to be done.

Dickens proposed to himself, it will be remembered, to write at Lausanne not only the first four numbers of his larger book, but the Christmas book suggested to him by his fancy of a battle field; and reserving what is to be said of *Dombey* to a later chapter, this and its successor will deal only with what he finished as well as began in Switzerland, and will show at what cost even so much was achieved amid his other and larger engagements.

He had restless fancies and misgivings before he settled to his first notion. 'I have been thinking this last day 'or two,' he wrote on the 25th of July, 'that good 'Christmas characters might be grown out of the idea of 'a man imprisoned for ten or fifteen years: his imprison- 'ment being the gap between the people and circumstances 'of the first part and the altered people and circumstances 'of the second, and his own changed mind. Though I 'shall probably proceed with the Battle idea, I should like 'to know what you think of this one?' It was afterwards used in a modified shape for the *Tale of Two Cities*. 'I 'shall begin the little story straightway,' he wrote, a few weeks later; 'but I have been dimly conceiving a very 'ghostly and wild idea, which I suppose I must now reserve 'for the *next* Christmas book. *Nous verrons.* It will 'mature in the streets of Paris by night, as well as in 'London.' This took ultimately the form of the *Haunted Man,* which was not written until the winter of 1848. At last I knew that his first slip was done, and that even his eager busy fancy would not turn him back again.

A fancy for Christmas book.

Another Christmas fancy.

But other unsatisfied wants and cravings had meanwhile broken out in him, of which I heard near the close of the second number of *Dombey.* The first he had finished at the end of July; and the second, which he began on the 8th of August, he was still at work upon in the first week of September, when this remarkable

Second number of *Dombey.*

LAUSANNE: 1846.

announcement came to me. It was his first detailed confession of what he felt so continuously, and if that were possible even more strongly, as the years went on, that there is no single passage in any of his letters which throws such a flood of illuminative light into the portions of his life which will always awaken the greatest interest. Very much that is to follow must be read by it.

A personal revelation.

'You can hardly imagine,' he wrote on the 30th of August, 'what infinite pains I take, or what extraordinary 'difficulty I find in getting on FAST. Invention, thank 'God, seems the easiest thing in the world; and I seem 'to have such a preposterous sense of the ridiculous, after

Work after rest.

'this long rest' (it was now over two years since the close of *Chuzzlewit*), 'as to be constantly requiring to restrain 'myself from launching into extravagances in the height 'of my enjoyment. But the difficulty of going at what I 'call a rapid pace, is prodigious: it is almost an impossi-'bility. I suppose this is partly the effect of two years' 'ease, and partly of the absence of streets and numbers

Craving for streets.

'of figures. I can't express how much I want these. It 'seems as if they supplied something to my brain, which 'it cannot bear, when busy, to lose. For a week or a 'fortnight I can write prodigiously in a retired place (as 'at Broadstairs), and a day in London sets me up again 'and starts me. But the toil and labour of writing, day 'after day, without that magic lantern, is IMMENSE!! I 'don't say this, at all in low spirits, for we are perfectly 'comfortable here, and I like the place very much indeed, 'and the people are even more friendly and fond of me than 'they were in Genoa I only mention it as a curious fact, 'which I have never had an opportunity of finding out 'before. *My* figures seem disposed to stagnate without 'crowds about them. I wrote very little in Genoa (only 'the *Chimes*), and fancied myself conscious of some such 'influence there—but Lord! I had two miles of streets 'at least, lighted at night, to walk about in; and a great 'theatre to repair to, every night.' At the close of the letter he told me that he had pretty well matured the general idea of the Christmas book, and was burning to get to work on it. He thought it would be all the better, for a change, to have no fairies or spirits in it, but to make it a simple domestic tale.*

LAUSANNE: 1846.

Food for fancy.

In less than a week from this date his second number was finished, his first slip of the little book done, and his confidence greater. They had had wonderful weather,† so clear that he could see from the Neuchâtel road the whole of Mont Blanc, six miles distant, as plainly as if he were standing close under it in the courtyard of the little

Second *Dombey* done.

* Writing on Sunday he had said: 'I hope to finish the second number to-'morrow, and to send it off bodily by Tuesday's post. On Wednesday I purpose, 'please God, beginning the *Battle of Life*. I shall peg away at that, without 'turning aside to *Dombey* again; and *if* I can only do it within the month!' I had to warn him, on receiving these intimations, that he was trying too much.

Trying too much.

† The storm of rain formerly mentioned by him had not been repeated, but the weather had become unsettled, and he thus referred to the rainfall which made that summer so disastrous in England. 'What a storm that must have 'been in London! I wish we could get something like it, here . . . It is 'thundering while I write, but I fear it don't look black enough for a clear-'ance. The echoes in the mountains are of such a stupendous sort, that a 'peal of thunder five or ten minutes long, is here the commonest of circum-'stances . . .' That was early in August, and at the close of the month he wrote: 'I forgot to tell you that yesterday week, at half-past 7 in the morning, 'we had a smart shock of an earthquake, lasting, perhaps, a quarter of a 'minute. It awoke me in bed. The sensation was so curious and unlike any 'other, that I called out at the top of my voice I was sure it was an earthquake.'

Earthquake.

LAUSANNE: 1846.

inn at Chamounix; and, though again it was raining when he wrote, his 'nailed shoes' were by him and his 'great waterproof cloak' in preparation for a 'fourteen-'mile walk' before dinner. Then, after three days more, came something of a sequel to the confession before made, which will be read with equal interest. 'The absence of 'any accessible streets continues to worry me, now that I 'have so much to do, in a most singular manner. It is 'quite a little mental phenomenon. I should not walk 'in them in the day time, if they were here, I dare say: 'but at night I want them beyond description. I don't 'seem able to get rid of my spectres unless I can lose 'them in crowds. However, as you say, there are streets 'in Paris, and good suggestive streets too: and trips to 'London will be nothing then. WHEN I have finished the 'Christmas book, I shall fly to Geneva for a day or two, 'before taking up with *Dombey* again. I like this place 'better and better; and never saw, I think, more agreeable 'people than our little circle is made up of. It is so little, that 'one is not "bothered" in the least; and their interest in 'the inimitable seems to strengthen daily. I read them the 'first number last night "was a" week, with unrelateable 'success; and old Mrs. Marcet, who is devilish 'cute, guessed 'directly (but I didn't tell her she was right) that little 'Paul would die. They were all so apprehensive that it 'was a great pleasure to read it; and I shall leave here, 'if all goes well, in a brilliant shower of sparks struck out 'of them by the promised reading of the Christmas book.' Little did either of us then imagine to what these readings were to lead, but even thus early they were taking in his

Farther confession.

Curious wants of the mind.

A reading of his first *Dombey*.

LAUSANNE: 1846.

mind the shape of a sort of jest that the smallest opportunity of favour might have turned into earnest. In his very next letter he wrote to me: 'I was thinking the other 'day that in these days of lecturings and readings, a great 'deal of money might possibly be made (if it were not infra 'dig) by one's having Readings of one's own books. It 'would be an *odd* thing. I think it would take immensely. 'What do you say? Will you step to Dean-street, and see 'how Miss Kelly's engagement-book (it must be an im'mense volume!) stands? Or shall I take the St. James's?' My answer is to be inferred from his rejoinder: but even at this time, while heightening and carrying forward his jest, I suspected him of graver desires than he cared to avow; and the time was to come, after a dozen years, when with earnestness equal to his own I continued to oppose, for reasons to be stated in their place, that which he had set his heart upon too strongly to abandon, and which I still can only wish he had preferred to surrender with all that seemed to be its enormous gains! 'I don't think you 'have exercised your usual judgment in taking Covent'garden for me. I doubt it is too large for my purpose. 'However, I shall stand by whatever you propose to the 'proprietors.'

First thought of public readings.

A jesting proposal:

with grave results.

Soon came the changes of trouble and vexation I had too surely seen. 'You remember,' he wrote, 'your objec'tion about the two stories. I made over light of it. I 'ought to have considered that I have never before really 'tried the opening of two together—having always had 'one pretty far ahead when I have been driving a pair of 'them. I know it all now. The apparent impossibility

Two tales in hand.

LAUSANNE: 1846.

'of getting each into its place, coupled with that craving 'for streets, so thoroughly put me off the track, that, up 'to Wednesday or Thursday last, I really contemplated, at 'times, the total abandonment of the Christmas book this 'year, and the limitation of my labours to *Dombey and*

Cancelling.

'*Son!* I cancelled the beginning of a first scene—which 'I have never done before—and, with a notion in my 'head, ran wildly about and about it, and could not get the 'idea into any natural socket. At length, thank Heaven, I

Getting on.

'nailed it all at once; and after going on comfortably up 'to yesterday, and working yesterday from half-past nine 'to six, I was last night in such a state of enthusiasm 'about it that I think I was an inch or two taller. I am 'a little cooler to-day, with a headache to boot; but I 'really begin to hope you will think it a pretty story, 'with some delicate notions in it agreeably presented, and 'with a good human Christmas groundwork. I fancy I 'see a great domestic effect in the last part.'

Less hopeful.

That was written on the 20th of September; but six days later changed the picture, and surprised me not a little. I might grudge the space thus given to one of the least important of his books but that the illustration goes farther than the little tale it refers to, and is a picture of him in his moods of writing, with their weakness as well as strength upon him, of a perfect truth and applicability to every period of his life. Movement and change while he was working were not mere restlessness, as we have seen; it was no impatience of labour, or desire of pleasure, that led at such times to his eager craving for the fresh crowds and faces in which he might lose or find the crea-

LAUSANNE: 1846.

tures of his fancy; and recollecting this, much hereafter will be understood that might else be very far from clear, in regard to the sensitive conditions under which otherwise he carried on these exertions of his brain. 'I am going to 'write you' (26th of September) 'a most startling piece of 'intelligence. I fear there may be NO CHRISTMAS BOOK! 'I would give the world to be on the spot to tell you this. 'Indeed I once thought of starting for London to-night. 'I have written nearly a third of it. It promises to be 'pretty; quite a new idea in the story, I hope; but to 'manage it without the supernatural agency now impos'sible of introduction, and yet to move it naturally within 'the required space, or with any shorter limit than a *Vicar 'of Wakefield*, I find to be a difficulty so perplexing—the 'past *Dombey* work taken into account—that I am fearful of 'wearing myself out if I go on, and not being able to come 'back to the greater undertaking with the necessary fresh'ness and spirit. If I had nothing but the Christmas book 'to do, I WOULD do it; but I get horrified and distressed 'beyond conception at the prospect of being jaded when I 'come back to the other, and making it a mere race against 'time. I have written the first part; I know the end and up'shot of the second; and the whole of the third (there are 'only three in all). I know the purport of each character, 'and the plain idea that each is to work out; and I have 'the principal effects sketched on paper. It cannot end '*quite* happily, but will end cheerfully and pleasantly. But 'my soul sinks before the commencement of the second 'part—the longest—and the introduction of the under-idea. '(The main one already developed, with interest.) I don't

Work under sensitive conditions.

Giving up Christmas book:

in alarm for *Dombey*.

LAUSANNE: 1846.

The old craving.

'know how it is. I suppose it is the having been almost 'constantly at work in this quiet place; and the dread for 'the *Dombey;* and the not being able to get rid of it, in 'noise and bustle. The beginning two books together is 'also, no doubt, a fruitful source of the difficulty; for I am 'now sure I could not have invented the *Carol* at the com-'mencement of the *Chuzzlewit,* or gone to a new book from 'the *Chimes.* But this is certain. I am sick, giddy, and 'capriciously despondent. I have bad nights; am full of 'disquietude and anxiety; and am constantly haunted by 'the idea that I am wasting the marrow of the larger book, 'and ought to be at rest. One letter that I wrote you 'before this, I have torn up. In that the Christmas book 'was wholly given up for this year: but I now resolve to 'make one effort more. I will go to Geneva to-morrow, and 'try on Monday and Tuesday whether I can get on at all 'bravely, in the changed scene. If I cannot, I am convinced 'that I had best hold my hand at once; and not fritter my 'spirits and hope away, with that long book before me. 'You may suppose that the matter is very grave when I 'can so nearly abandon anything in which I am deeply 'interested, and fourteen or fifteen close MS pages of which, 'that have made me laugh and cry, are lying in my desk. 'Writing this letter at all, I have a great misgiving that the 'letter I shall write you on Tuesday night will not make 'it better. Take it, for Heaven's sake, as an extremely 'serious thing, and not a fancy of the moment. Last Sa-'turday after a very long day's work, and last Wednesday 'after finishing the first part, I was full of eagerness and 'pleasure. At all other times since I began, I have been

Doubts and misgivings.

Change of scene to be tried.

'brooding and brooding over the idea that it was a wild 'thing to dream of, ever: and that I ought to be at rest for 'the *Dombey*.'

GENEVA: 1846.

The letter came, written on Wednesday not Tuesday night, and it left the question still unsettled. 'When I 'came here' (Geneva, 30th of September) 'I had a blood- 'shot eye; and my head was so bad, with a pain across the 'brow, that I thought I must have got cupped. I have 'become a great deal better, however, and feel quite myself 'again to-day. . . . I still have not made up my mind as 'to what I CAN do with the Christmas book. I would 'give any money that it were possible to consult with you. 'I have begun the second part this morning, and have 'done a very fair morning's work at it, but I do not feel it '*in hand* within the necessary space and divisions: and I 'have a great uneasiness in the prospect of falling behind 'hand with the other labour, which is so transcendantly im- 'portant. I feel quite sure that unless I (being in reason- 'ably good state and spirits) like the Christmas book 'myself, I had better not go on with it; but had best keep 'my strength for *Dombey*, and keep my number in advance. 'On the other hand I am dreadfully averse to abandoning 'it, and am so torn between the two things that I know 'not what to do. It is impossible to express the wish I 'have that I could take counsel with you. Having begun 'the second part I will go on here, to-morrow and Friday '(Saturday, the Talfourds come to us at Lausanne, leaving 'on Monday morning), unless I see new reason to give it 'up in the meanwhile. Let it stand thus—that my next 'Monday's letter shall finally decide the question. But if

Disquietudes of authorship.

Wanting counsel.

GENEVA: 1846.

At the worst.

'you have not already told Bradbury and Evans of my last 'letter I think it will now be best to do so. . . . This non-'publication of a Christmas book, if it must be, I try to think 'light of with the greater story just begun, and with this '*Battle of Life* story (of which I really think the leading 'idea is very pretty) lying by me, for future use. But I 'would like you to consider, in the event of my not going 'on, how best, by timely announcement, in November's or 'December's *Dombey*, I may seem to hold the ground 'prospectively. . . Heaven send me a good deliverance! If 'I don't do it, it will be the first time I ever abandoned 'anything I had once taken in hand; and I shall not 'have abandoned it until after a most desperate fight.

Shadows from *Dombey*.

'I could do it, but for the *Dombey*, as easily as I did 'last year or the year before. But I cannot help falling 'back on that continually: and this, combined with the 'peculiar difficulties of the story for a Christmas book, 'and my being out of sorts, discourages me sadly. . . . 'Kate is here, and sends her love.' . . . A postscript was added on the following day. 'Georgy has come over from 'Lausanne, and joins with Kate, &c. &c. My head 'remains greatly better. My eye is recovering its old

More hopeful.

'hue of beautiful white, tinged with celestial blue. If 'I hadn't come here, I think I should have had some bad 'low fever. The sight of the rushing Rhone seemed to 'stir my blood again. I don't think I shall want to be 'cupped, this bout; but it looked, at one time, worse than 'I have confessed to you. If I have any return, I will 'have it done immediately.'

He stayed two days longer at Geneva, which he found

to be a very good place; pleasantly reporting himself as quite dismayed at first by the sight of gas in it, and as trembling at the noise in its streets, which he pronounced to be fully equal to the uproar of Richmond in Surrey; but deriving from it some sort of benefit both in health and in writing. So far his trip had been successful, though he had to leave the place hurriedly to welcome his English visitors to Rosemont.

GENEVA: 1846.

Report of the city.

One social and very novel experience he had in his hotel, however, the night before he left, which may be told before he hastens back to Lausanne; for it could hardly now offend any one even if the names were given. 'And now sir I will 'describe, modestly, tamely, literally, the visit to the small 'select circle which I promised should make your hair 'stand on end. In our hotel were Lady A, and Lady B, 'mother and daughter, who came to the Peschiere shortly 'before we left it, and who have a deep admiration for 'your humble servant the inimitable B. They are both 'very clever. Lady B, extremely well-informed in lan'guages, living and dead; books, and gossip; very pretty; 'with two little children, and not yet five and twenty. 'Lady A, plump, fresh, and rosy; matronly, but full of 'spirits and good looks. Nothing would serve them but we '*must* dine with them; and accordingly, on Friday at six, 'we went down to their room. I knew them to be rather 'odd. For instance, I have known Lady A, *full dressed*, 'walk alone through the streets of Genoa, the squalid 'Italian bye streets, to the Governor's soirée; and announce 'herself at the palace of state, by knocking at the door. I 'have also met Lady B, full dressed, without any cap or

A new social experience.

Mother and daughter.

Eccentricities.

GENEVA: 1846.

A ladies' dinner.

'bonnet, walking a mile to the opera, with all sorts of jing-'ling jewels about her, beside a sedan chair in which sat 'enthroned her mama. Consequently, I was not surprised 'at such little sparkles in the conversation (from the 'young lady) as "Oh God what a sermon we had here, '"last Sunday!" "And did you ever read such infernal '"trash as Mrs. Gore's?"—and the like. Still, but for Kate 'and Georgy (who were decidedly in the way, as we agreed 'afterwards), I should have thought it all very funny; and, 'as it was, I threw the ball back again, was mighty free 'and easy, made some rather broad jokes, and was highly 'applauded. "You smoke, don't you?" said the young 'lady, in a pause of this kind of conversation. "Yes," I 'said, "I generally take a cigar after dinner when I am '"alone." "I'll give you a good 'un," said she, "when we '"go up-stairs." Well, sir, in due course we went up stairs, 'and there we were joined by an American lady residing 'in the same hotel, who looked like what we call in old 'England "a reg'lar Bunter"—fluffy face (rouged); con-'siderable development of figure; one groggy eye; blue 'satin dress made low with short sleeves, and shoes of 'the same. Also a daughter; face likewise fluffy; figure 'likewise developed; dress likewise low, with short sleeves, 'and shoes of the same; and one eye not yet actually 'groggy, but going to be. American lady married at six-'teen; daughter sixteen now, often mistaken for sisters, '&c. &c. &c. When that was over, Lady B brought out a 'cigar box, and gave me a cigar, made of negrohead she 'said, which would quell an elephant in six whiffs. The 'box was full of cigarettes—good large ones, made of pretty

American reinforcements.

Elephant-quellers.

GENEVA: 1846.

'strong tobacco; I always smoke them here, and used to 'smoke them at Genoa, and I knew them well. When I 'lighted my cigar, Lady B lighted hers, at mine; leaned 'against the mantelpiece, in conversation with me; put 'out her stomach, folded her arms, and with her pretty 'face cocked up sideways and her cigarette smoking away 'like a Manchester cotton mill, laughed, and talked, and 'smoked, in the most gentlemanly manner I ever beheld. 'Lady A immediately lighted her cigar; American lady 'immediately lighted hers; and in five minutes the room 'was a cloud of smoke, with us four in the centre pulling 'away bravely, while American lady related stories of her '"Hookah" up stairs, and described different kinds of 'pipes. But even this was not all. For presently two 'Frenchmen came in, with whom, and the American lady, 'Lady B sat down to whist. The Frenchmen smoked of 'course (they were really modest gentlemen, and seemed 'dismayed), and Lady B played for the next hour or two 'with a cigar continually in her mouth—never out of it. 'She certainly smoked six or eight. Lady A gave in soon '—I think she only did it out of vanity. American lady 'had been smoking all the morning. I took no more; 'and Lady B and the Frenchmen had it all to them- 'selves.

Feminine smoking party.

Modesty of sex.

'Conceive this in a great hotel, with not only their own 'servants, but half a dozen waiters coming constantly in 'and out! I showed no atom of surprise; but I never *was* 'so surprised, so ridiculously taken aback, in my life; for 'in all my experience of "ladies" of one kind and another, 'I never saw a woman—not a basket woman or a gipsy—

A novel experience.

LAUSANNE: 1846.

'smoke, before!' He lived to have larger and wider experience, but there was enough to startle as well as amuse him in the scene described.

But now Saturday is come; he has hurried back for the friends who are on their way to his cottage; and on his arrival, even before they have appeared, he writes to tell me his better news of himself and his work.

Visit of the Talfourds.

'In the breathless interval' (Rosemont: 3rd of October) 'between our return from Geneva and the arrival of the 'Talfourds (expected in an hour or two), I cannot do 'better than write to you. For I think you will be well 'pleased if I anticipate my promise, and Monday, at the 'same time. I have been greatly better at Geneva, 'though I still am made uneasy by occasional giddiness 'and headache: attributable, I have not the least doubt, 'to the absence of streets. There is an idea here, too, that 'people are occasionally made despondent and sluggish in 'their spirits by this great mass of still water, lake Leman. 'At any rate I have been very uncomfortable: at any rate 'I am, I hope, greatly better: and (lastly) at any rate I hope 'and trust, *now*, the Christmas book will come in due 'course!! I have had three very good days' work at Geneva, 'and trust I may finish the second part (the third is the 'shortest) by this day week. Whenever I finish it, I will 'send you the first two together. I do not think they can 'begin to illustrate it, until the third arrives; for it is a 'single-minded story, as it were, and an artist should know 'the end: which I don't think very likely, unless he reads it.' Then, after relating a superhuman effort he was making to lodge his visitors in his doll's house ('I didn't like the

In better heart.

Christmas book resumed.

Lodging his friends.

'idea of turning them out at night. It is so dark in 'these lanes, and groves, when the moon's not bright'), he sketched for me what he possibly might, and really did, accomplish. He would by great effort finish the small book on the 20th; would fly to Geneva for a week to work a little at *Dombey*, if he felt 'pretty sound;' in any case would finish his number three by the 10th of November; and on that day would start for Paris: 'so that, 'instead of resting unprofitably here, I shall be using my 'interval of idleness to make the journey and get into a 'new house, and shall hope so to put a pinch of salt on 'the tail of the sliding number in advance. . . . . I am 'horrified at the idea of getting the blues (and bloodshots) 'again.' Though I did not then know how gravely ill he had been, I was fain to remind him that it was bad economy to make business out of rest itself; but I received prompt confirmation that all was falling out as he wished. The Talfourds stayed two days: 'and I think they were 'very happy. He was in his best aspect; the manner so 'well known to us, not the less loveable for being laughable; 'and if you could have seen him going round and round 'the coach that brought them, as a preliminary to paying 'the voiturier to whom he couldn't speak, in a currency 'he didn't understand, you never would have forgotten it.' His friends left Lausanne on the 5th; and five days later he sent me two thirds of the manuscript of his Christmas book.

LAUSANNE: 1846.

Intentions and hope.

Thomas Noon Talfourd.

# CHAPTER XIV.

## REVOLUTION AT GENEVA, CHRISTMAS BOOK, AND LAST DAYS IN SWITZERLAND.

1846.

LAUSANNE: 1846.

An arrival of MS.

'I SEND you in twelve letters, counting this as one, the 'first two parts (thirty-five slips) of the Christmas book. 'I have two present anxieties respecting it. One to know 'that you have received it safely; and the second to know 'how it strikes you. Be sure you read the first and 'second parts together . . . . There seems to me to be 'interest in it, and a pretty idea; and it is unlike the 'others . . . There will be some minor points for considera-'tion: as, the necessity for some slight alterations in one or 'two of the Doctor's speeches in the first part; and whether

A title.

'it should be called "The Battle of Life. A Love Story" '—to express both a love story in the common accepta-'tion of the phrase, and also a story of love; with one or 'two other things of that sort. We can moot these by 'and by. I made a tremendous day's work of it yester-'day and was horribly excited—so I am going to rush out, 'as fast as I can: being a little used up, and sick . . But 'never say die! I have been to the glass to look at my 'eye. Pretty bright!'

I made it brighter next day by telling him that the first number of *Dombey* had outstripped in sale the first of *Chuzzlewit* by more than twelve thousand copies; and his next letter, sending the close of his little tale, showed his need of the comfort my pleasant news had given him. 'I really do not know what this story is worth. I am so 'floored: wanting sleep, and never having had my head 'free from it for this month past. I think there are 'some places in this last part which I may bring better 'together in the proof, and where a touch or two may 'be of service; particularly in the scene between Craggs 'and Michael Warden, where, as it stands, the interest 'seems anticipated. But I shall have the benefit of your 'suggestions, and my own then cooler head, I hope; and 'I will be very careful with the proofs, and keep them by 'me as long as I can . . . Mr. Britain must have another 'Christian name, then? "Aunt Martha" is the Sally 'of whom the Doctor speaks in the first part. Martha 'is a better name. What do you think of the concluding 'paragraph? Would you leave it for happiness' sake? 'It is merely experimental . . . I am flying to Geneva to-'morrow morning.' (That was on the 18th of October; and on the 20th he wrote from Geneva.) 'We came here yes-'terday, and we shall probably remain until Katey's birth-'day, which is next Thursday week. I shall fall to work 'on number three of *Dombey* as soon as I can. At present 'I am the worse for wear, but nothing like as much so as 'I expected to be on Sunday last. I had not been able 'to sleep for some time, and had been hammering away, 'morning, noon, and night. A bottle of hock on Monday,

LAUSANNE: 1846.

Large sale of *Dombey*.

Christmas book done.

Points in the story.

GENEVA.

Back to *Dombey*.

GENEVA: 1846.

'when Elliotson dined with us (he went away homeward 'yesterday morning), did me a world of good; the change 'comes in the very nick of time; and I feel in Dombeian 'spirits already . . . But I have still rather a damaged head, 'aching a good deal occasionally, as it is doing now, though 'I have not been cupped—yet . . . I dreamed all last week 'that the *Battle of Life* was a series of chambers impos-'sible to be got to rights or got out of, through which 'I wandered drearily all night. On Saturday night I 'don't think I slept an hour. I was perpetually roaming 'through the story, and endeavouring to dove-tail the 'revolution here into the plot. The mental distress, quite 'horrible.'

Remains of over-work.

Rising against the Jesuits.

Of the 'revolution' he had written to me a week before, from Lausanne; where the news had just reached them, that, upon the Federal Diet decreeing the expulsion of the Jesuits, the Roman Catholic cantons had risen against the decree, the result being that the Protestants had deposed the grand council and established a provisional government, dissolving the Catholic league. His interest in this, and prompt seizure of what really was brought into issue by the conflict, is every way characteristic of Dickens. 'You will know,' he wrote from Lausanne on the 11th of October, 'long before you get this, all about the revo-'lution at Geneva. There were stories of plots against the 'Government when I was there, but I didn't believe them; 'for all sorts of lies are always afloat against the radicals, 'and wherever there is a consul from a Catholic Power 'the most monstrous fictions are in perpetual circulation 'against them: as in this very place, where the Sardinian

LAUSANNE.

LAUSANNE: 1846.

'consul was gravely whispering the other day that a 'society called the Homicides had been formed, whereof 'the president of the council of state, the O'Connell of 'Switzerland and a clever fellow, was a member; who were 'sworn on skulls and cross-bones to exterminate men of 'property, and so forth. There was a great stir here, on the 'day of the fight in Geneva. We heard the guns (they shook 'this house) all day; and seven hundred men marched out 'of this town of Lausanne to go and help the radical party '—arriving at Geneva just after it was all over. There 'is no doubt they had received secret help from here; for 'a powder barrel, found by some of the Genevese populace 'with "Canton de Vaud" painted on it, was carried on a 'pole about the streets as a standard, to show that they 'were sympathized with by friends outside. It was a poor 'mean fight enough, I am told by Lord Vernon, who was 'present and who was with us last night. The Government was afraid; having no confidence whatever, I dare 'say, in its own soldiers; and the cannon were fired everywhere except at the opposite party, who (I mean the revolutionists) had barricaded a bridge with an omnibus 'only, and certainly in the beginning might have been 'turned with ease. The precision of the common men 'with the rifle was especially shown by a small party of '*five*, who waited on the ramparts near one of the gates of 'the town, to turn a body of soldiery who were coming in 'to the Government assistance. They picked out every 'officer and struck him down instantly, the moment the 'party appeared; there were three or four of them; upon 'which the soldiers gravely turned round and walked off.

The fight in Geneva.

An eye-witness.

Rifle against cannon.

LAUSANNE: 1846.

Precision of aim.

'I dare say there are not fifty men in this place who 'wouldn't click your card off a target a hundred and fifty 'yards away, at least. I have seen them, time after time, 'fire across a great ravine as wide as the ornamental 'ground in St. James's-park, and never miss the bull's-'eye.

The true objection to Roman Catholicism.

'It is a horribly ungentlemanly thing to say here, 'though I *do* say it without the least reserve—but my 'sympathy is all with the radicals. I don't know any 'subject on which this indomitable people have so good 'a right to a strong feeling as Catholicity—if not as 'a religion, clearly as a means of social degradation. 'They know what it is. They live close to it. They 'have Italy beyond their mountains. They can compare 'the effect of the two systems at any time in their own 'valleys; and their dread of it, and their horror of the 'introduction of Catholic priests and emissaries into their 'towns, seems to me the most rational feeling in the 'world. Apart from this, you have no conception of the 'preposterous, insolent little aristocracy of Geneva: the 'most ridiculous caricature the fancy can suggest of what 'we know in England. I was talking to two famous 'gentlemen (very intelligent men) of that place, not long 'ago, who came over to invite me to a sort of reception 'there—which I declined. Really their talk about "the '"people" and "the masses," and the necessity they 'would shortly be under of shooting a few of them as 'an example for the rest, was a kind of monstrosity one 'might have heard at Genoa. The audacious insolence 'and contempt of the people by their newspapers, too, is

Genevese 'aristo-'cracy.'

'quite absurd. It is difficult to believe that men of sense 'can be such donkeys politically. It was precisely such a 'state of things that brought about the change here. There 'was a most respectful petition presented on the Jesuit 'question, signed by its tens of thousands of small farmers; 'the regular peasants of the canton, all splendidly taught 'in public schools, and intellectually as well as physically 'a most remarkable body of labouring men. This docu'ment is treated by the gentlemanly party with the most 'sublime contempt, and the signatures are said to be the 'signatures of "the rabble." Upon which, each man of 'the rabble shoulders his rifle, and walks in upon a given 'day agreed upon among them to Lausanne; and the 'gentlemanly party walk out without striking a blow.'

GENEVA: 1846.

Swiss 'rabble.'

A lesson.

Such traces of the 'revolution' as he found upon his present visit to Geneva he described in writing to me from the hotel de l'Ecu on the 20th of October. 'You never 'would suppose from the look of this town that there had 'been anything revolutionary going on. Over the window 'of my old bedroom there is a great hole made by a 'cannon-ball in the house-front; and two of the bridges 'are under repair. But these are small tokens which 'anything else might have brought about as well. The 'people are all at work. The little streets are rife with 'every sight and sound of industry; the place is as quiet 'by ten o'clock as Lincoln's-inn-fields; and the only out'ward and visible sign of public interest in political events 'is a little group at every street corner, reading a public 'announcement from the new Government of the forth'coming election of state-officers, in which the people are

Traces left by revolution.

The streets.

GENEVA: 1846.

The people.

'reminded of their importance as a republican institution, 'and desired to bear in mind their dignity in all their 'proceedings. Nothing very violent or bad could go on 'with a community so well educated as this. It is the 'best antidote to American experiences, conceivable. As 'to the nonsense "the gentlemanly interest" talk about, 'their opposition to property and so forth, there never was

Abettors of revolution.

'such mortal absurdity. One of the principal leaders in 'the late movement has a stock of watches and jewellery 'here of immense value—and had, during the disturb-'ance—perfectly unprotected. James Fahzey has a rich 'house and a valuable collection of pictures; and, I will 'be bound to say, twice as much to lose as half the con-'servative declaimers put together. This house, the liberal 'one, is one of the most richly furnished and luxurious 'hotels on the continent. And if I were a Swiss with a 'hundred thousand pounds, I would be as steady against

Where the shoe pinches.

'the Catholic cantons and the propagation of Jesuitism as 'any radical among 'em: believing the dissemination of 'Catholicity to be the most horrible means of political and 'social degradation left in the world. Which these people, 'thoroughly well educated, know perfectly . . . The boys of 'Geneva were very useful in bringing materials for the con-'struction of the barricades on the bridges; and the enclosed 'song may amuse you. They sing it to a tune that dates 'from the great French revolution—a very good one.'

But revolutions may be small as well as their heroes, and while he thus was sending me his Gamin de Genève I was sending him news of a sudden change in Whitefriars which had quite as vivid interest for him. Not much could be told him at first, but his curiosity instantly arose to fever pitch. 'In reference to that *Daily News* revolu-'tion,' he wrote from Geneva on the 26th, 'I have been 'walking and wandering all day through a perfect Miss 'Burney's Vauxhall of conjectural dark walks. Heaven send 'you enlighten me fully on Wednesday, or number three 'will suffer!' Two days later he resumed, as he was beginning his journey back to Lausanne. 'I am in a great state 'of excitement on account of your intelligence, and despe-'rately anxious to know all about it. I shall be put out to 'an unspeakable extent if I don't find your letter await-'ing me. God knows there has been small comfort for 'either of us in the *D. N.*'s nine months.' There was not much to tell then, and there is less now; but at last the discomfort was over for us both, as I had been unable to reconcile myself to a longer continuance of the service I had given in Whitefriars since he quitted it. The subject may be left with the remark made upon it in his first letter after returning to Rosemont. 'I certainly am very 'glad of the result of the *Daily News* business, though my 'gladness is dashed with melancholy to think that you 'should have toiled there so long, to so little purpose. I 'escaped more easily. However, it is all past now. . . 'As to the undoubted necessity of the course you took, I 'have not a grain of question in my mind. That, being 'what you are, you had only one course to take and have 'taken it, I no more doubt than that the Old Bailey is not 'Westminster Abbey. In the utmost sum at which you 'value yourself, you were bound to leave; and now you '*have* left, you will come to Paris, and there, and at home

LAUSANNE: 1846.

Smaller revolution in Whitefriars.

*Daily News* changes.

His pleasure at my surrender of editorship.

LAUSANNE: 1846.

Thoughts for the future.

'again, we'll have, please God, the old kind of evenings 'and the old life again, as it used to be before those daily 'nooses caught us by the legs and sometimes tripped us 'up. Make a vow (as I have done) never to go down that 'court with the little news-shop at the corner, any more, 'and let us swear by Jack Straw as in the ancient times. . . 'I am beginning to get over my sorrow for your nights up 'aloft in Whitefriars, and to feel nothing but happiness in 'the contemplation of your enfranchisement. God bless 'you!'

Letters about his *Battle of Life*.

The time was now shortening for him at Lausanne; but before my sketches of his pleasant days there close, the little story of his Christmas book may be made complete by a few extracts from the letters that followed immediately upon the departure of the Talfourds. Without comment they will explain its closing touches, his own consciousness of the difficulties in working out the tale within limits too confined not to render its proper development imperfect, and his ready tact in dealing with objection and suggestion from without. His condition while writing it did not warrant me in pressing what I might otherwise have thought necessary; but as the little story finally left his hands, it had points not unworthy of him; and a sketch of its design will render the fragments from his letters more intelligible. I read it lately with a sense that its general tone of quiet beauty deserved well the praise which Jeffrey in those days had given it. 'I like 'and admire the *Battle* extremely,' he said in a letter on its publication, sent me by Dickens and not included in Lord Cockburn's Memoir. 'It is better than any other man

Character of it.

'alive could have written, and has passages as fine as any- 'thing that ever came from the man himself. The dance 'of the sisters in that autumn orchard is of itself worth a 'dozen inferior tales, and their reunion at the close, and 'indeed all the serious parts, are beautiful, some traits of 'Clemency charming.'

LAUSANNE: 1846.

Jeffrey's opinion.

Yet it was probably here the fact, as with the *Chimes*, that the serious parts were too much interwoven with the tale to render the subject altogether suitable to the old mirth-bringing season; but this had also some advantages. The story is all about two sisters, the younger of whom, Marion, sacrifices her own affection to give happiness to the elder, Grace. But Grace had already made the same sacrifice for this younger sister; life's first and hardest battle had been won by her before the incidents begin; and when she is first seen, she is busying herself to bring about her sister's marriage with Alfred Heathfield, whom she has herself loved, and whom she has kept wholly unconscious, by a quiet change in her bearing to him, of what his own still disengaged heart would certainly not have rejected. Marion, however, had earlier discovered this, though it is not until her victory over herself that Alfred knows it; and meanwhile he is become her betrothed. The sisters thus shown at the opening, one believing her love undiscovered and the other bent for the sake of that love on surrendering her own, each practising concealment and both unselfishly true, form a pretty and tender picture. The second part is intended to give to Marion's flight the character of an elopement; and so to manage this as to show her all the time unchanged to the man she is pledged

The *Battle of Life*.

Sketch of story.

LAUSANNE: 1846.

*The Battle of Life.*

to, yet flying from, was the author's difficulty. One Michael Warden is the *deus ex machinâ* by whom it is solved, hardly with the usual skill; but there is much art in rendering his pretensions to the hand of Marion, whose husband he becomes after an interval of years, the means of closing against him all hope of success, in the very hour when her own act might seem to be opening it to him.

Difficulty in plot.

During the same interval Grace, believing Marion to be gone with Warden, becomes Alfred's wife; and not until reunion after six years' absence is the truth entirely known to her. The struggle, to all of them, has been filled and chastened with sorrow; but joy revisits them at its close. Hearts are not broken by the duties laid upon them; nor is life shown to be such a perishable holiday, that amidst noble sorrow and generous self-denial it must lose its capacity for happiness. The tale thus justifies its place in the Christmas series. What Jeffrey says of Clemency, too, may suggest another word. The story would not be Dickens's

Old characteristics.

if we could not discover in it the power peculiar to him of presenting the commonest objects with freshness and beauty, of detecting in the homeliest forms of life much of its rarest loveliness, and of springing easily upward from everyday realities into regions of imaginative thought. To this happiest direction of his art, Clemency and her husband render new tribute; and in her more especially, once again, we recognize one of those true souls who fill so large a space in his writings, for whom the lowest seats at life's feast are commonly kept, but whom he moves and welcomes to a more fitting place among the prized and honoured at the upper tables.

'I wonder whether you foresaw the end of the Christmas 'book! There are two or three places in which I can 'make it prettier, I think, by slight alterations. . . . I trust 'to Heaven you may like it. What an affecting story I 'could have made of it in one octavo volume. Oh to think 'of the printers transforming my kindly cynical old father 'into Doctor Taddler!' (28th of October.)

LAUSANNE: 1846.

The *Battle of Life*.

---

'Do you think it worth while, in the illustrations, to 'throw the period back at all for the sake of anything 'good in the costume? The story may have happened at 'any time within a hundred years. Is it worth having 'coats and gowns of dear old Goldsmith's day? or there- 'abouts? I really don't know what to say. The proba- 'bility is, if it has not occurred to you or to the artists, 'that it is hardly worth considering; but I ease myself 'of it by throwing it out to you. It may be already too 'late, or you may see reason to think it best to "stick to '"the *last*" (I feel it necessary to italicize the joke), and 'abide by the ladies' and gentlemen's spring and winter 'fashions of this time. Whatever you think best, in this 'as in all other things, is best, I am sure . . . I would go, 'in the illustrations, for "beauty" as much as possible; and 'I should like each part to have a general illustration to it 'at the beginning, shadowing out its drift and bearing: 'much as Browne goes at that kind of thing on *Dombey* 'covers. I don't think I should fetter your discretion in 'the matter farther. The better it is illustrated, the better 'I shall be pleased of course.' (29th of October.)

His own comments.

Date of story.

---

LAUSANNE: 1846.

The *Battle of Life.*

'... I only write to say that it is of no use my writing 'at length, until I have heard from you; and that I will 'wait until I shall have read your promised communica-'tion (as my father would call it) to-morrow. I have 'glanced over the proofs of the last part and really don't

Reply to criticism.

'wonder, some of the most extravagant mistakes occur-'ring in Clemency's account to Warden, that the marriage 'of Grace and Alfred should seem rather unsatisfactory to 'you. Whatever is done about that must be done with the 'lightest hand, for the reader MUST take something for 'granted; but I think it next to impossible, without dread-'ful injury to the effect, to introduce a scene between 'Marion and Michael. The introduction must be in the 'scene between the sisters, and must be put, mainly, into 'the mouth of Grace. Rely upon it there is no other way, 'in keeping with the spirit of the tale. With this amend-'ment, and a touch here and there in the last part (I know 'exactly where they will come best), I think it may be 'pretty and affecting, and comfortable too ...' (31st of October.)

---

'... I shall hope to touch upon the Christmas book as 'soon as I get your opinion. I wouldn't do it without. I

Stanfield's offer of illustrations.

'am delighted to hear of noble old Stanny. Give my love 'to him, and tell him I think of turning Catholic. It 'strikes me (it may have struck you perhaps) that another 'good place for introducing a few lines of dialogue, is at the 'beginning of the scene between Grace and her husband, 'where he speaks about the messenger at the gate.' (4th of November.)

---

'Before I reply to your questions I wish to remark generally of the third part that all the passion that can be got into it, through my interpretation at all events, is there. I know that, by what it cost me; and I take it to be, as a question of art and interest, in the very nature of the story that it *should* move at a swift pace after the sisters are in each other's arms again. Anything after that would drag like lead, and must. . . . Now for your questions. I don't think any little scene with Marion and anybody can prepare the way for the last paragraph of the tale: I don't think anything but a printer's line *can* go between it and Warden's speech. A less period than ten years? Yes. I see no objection to six. I have no doubt you are right. Any word from Alfred in his misery? Impossible: you might as well try to speak to somebody in an express train. The preparation for his change is in the first part, and he kneels down beside her in that return scene. He is left alone with her, as it were, in the world. I am quite confident it is wholly impossible for me to alter that. . . . BUT (keep your eye on me) when Marion went away, she left a letter for Grace in which she charged her to encourage the love that Alfred would conceive for her, and FOREWARNED her that years would pass before they met again, &c. &c. This coming out in the scene between the sisters, and something like it being expressed in the opening of the little scene between Grace and her husband before the messenger at the gate, will make (I hope) a prodigious difference; and I will try to put in something with Aunt Martha and the Doctor which shall



The *Battle of Life.*

Doubts of third part.

Strengthening the close.

LAUSANNE: 1846.

The *Battle of Life.*

'carry the tale back more distinctly and unmistakeably to 'the battle-ground. I hope to make these alterations 'next week, and to send the third part back to you before 'I leave here. If you think it can still be improved after 'that, say so to me in Paris and I will go at it again. I 'wouldn't have it limp, if it can fly. I say nothing to you 'of a great deal of this being already expressed in the 'sentiment of the beginning, because your delicate per-'ception knows all that already. Observe for the artists. 'Grace will now only have *one child*—little Marion.' . . . (At night, on same day.) . . 'You recollect that I asked 'you to read it all together, for I knew that I was working 'for that? But I have no doubt of *your* doubts, and will 'do what I have said. . . . I had thought of marking the 'time in the little story, and will do so. . . Think, once 'more, of the period between the second and third parts. 'I will do the same.' (7th of November.)

Farther objection invited.

---

'I hope you will think the third part (when you read 'it in type with these amendments) very much improved. 'I think it so. If there should still be anything wanting, 'in your opinion, pray suggest it to me in Paris. I am 'bent on having it right, if I can. . . . If in going over 'the proofs you find the tendency to blank verse (I *cannot* 'help it, when I am very much in earnest) too strong, 'knock out a word's brains here and there.' (13th of November. Sending the proofs back.)

Tendency to blank verse.

---

'. . . Your Christmas book illustration-news makes me 'jump for joy. I will write you at length to-morrow. I 'should like this dedication: This Christmas Book is cordially inscribed To my English Friends in Switzerland. 'Just those two lines, and nothing more. When I get the 'proofs again I think I may manage another word or two 'about the battle-field, with advantage. I am glad you 'like the alterations. I feel that they make it complete, 'and that it would have been incomplete without your 'suggestions.' (21st of November. From Paris.)

LAUSANNE: 1846.

Dedication.

I had managed, as a glad surprise for him, to enlist both Stanfield and Maclise in the illustration of the story, in addition to the distinguished artists whom the publishers had engaged for it, Leech and Richard Doyle; and among the subjects contributed by Stanfield are three morsels of English landscape which had a singular charm for Dickens at the time, and seem to me still of their kind quite faultless. I may add a curious fact, never mentioned until now. In the illustration which closes the second part of the story, where the festivities to welcome the bridegroom at the top of the page contrast with the flight of the bride represented below, Leech made the mistake of supposing that Michael Warden had taken part in the elopement, and has introduced his figure with that of Marion. We did not discover this until too late for remedy, the publication having then been delayed, for these drawings, to the utmost limit; and it is highly characteristic of Dickens, and of the true regard he had for this fine artist, that, knowing the pain he must give in such circumstances by objection or complaint, he preferred to pass it silently. Nobody made remark upon it, and there the illustration still stands; but any one who reads the tale carefully will

Artists.

Stanfield's designs.

Grave mistake by Leech.

How dealt with by C. D.

Lausanne: 1846.

at once perceive what havoc it makes of one of the most delicate turns in it.

His first impulse.

'When I first saw it, it was with a horror and agony 'not to be expressed. Of course I need not tell *you*, my 'dear fellow, Warden has no business in the elopement 'scene. *He* was never there! In the first hot sweat of 'this surprise and novelty, I was going to implore the 'printing of that sheet to be stopped, and the figure taken 'out of the block. But when I thought of the pain this 'might give to our kind-hearted Leech; and that what 'is such a monstrous enormity to me, as never having 'entered my brain, may not so present itself to others, I 'became more composed: though the fact is wonderful to 'me. No doubt a great number of copies will be printed 'by the time this reaches you, and therefore I shall take 'it for granted that it stands as it is. Leech otherwise is 'very good, and the illustrations altogether are by far the 'best that have been done for any of the Christmas books. 'You know how I build up temples in my mind that are 'not made with hands (or expressed with pen and ink, I 'am afraid), and how liable I am to be disappointed in 'these things. But I really am *not* disappointed in this 'case. Quietness and beauty are preserved throughout. 'Say everything to Mac and Stanny, more than everything! 'It is a delight to look at these little landscapes of the 'dear old boy. How gentle and elegant, and yet how manly 'and vigorous, they are! I have a perfect joy in them.'

Kindly after-thought.

Last days in Switzerland.

Of the few days that remained of his Lausanne life, before he journeyed to Paris, there is not much requiring to be said. His work had continued during the whole of the month before departure to occupy him so entirely as to leave room for little else, and even occasional letters to very dear friends at home were intermitted. Here is one example of many. 'I will write to Landor as soon as I 'can possibly make time, but I really am so much at my 'desk perforce, and so full of work, whether I am there 'or elsewhere, between the Christmas book and *Dombey*, 'that it is the most difficult thing in the world for me to 'make up my mind to write a letter to any one but you. 'I ought to have written to Macready. I wish you would 'tell him, with my love, how I am situated in respect 'of pen, ink, and paper. One of the Lausanne papers, 'treating of free trade, has been very copious lately in 'its mention of LORD GOBDEN. Fact; and I think it a 'good name.' Then, as the inevitable time approached, he cast about him for such comfort as the coming change might bring, to set against the sorrow of it; and began to think of Paris, 'in a less romantic and more homely con-'templation of the picture,' as not wholly undesirable. 'I have no doubt that constant change, too, is indispens-'able to me when I am at work: and at times something 'more than a doubt will force itself upon me whether 'there is not something in a Swiss valley that disagrees 'with me. Certainly, whenever I live in Switzerland again, 'it shall be on the hill-top. Something of the *goître* 'and *cretin* influence seems to settle on my spirits some-'times, on the lower ground.* How sorry, ah yes! how

LAUSANNE: 1846.

Engagements.

Lord Gobden and free trade.

Needs while at work.

* 'I may tell you,' he wrote to me from Paris at the end of November, 'now it is all over. I don't know whether it was the hot summer, or the 'anxiety of the two new books coupled with D. N. remembrances and remin-

LAUSANNE: 1846.

'sorry I shall be to leave the little society nevertheless. 'We have been thoroughly good-humoured and agreeable 'together, and I'll always give a hurrah for the Swiss and 'Switzerland.'

One or two English travelling by Lausanne had meanwhile greeted him as they were passing home, and a few days given him by Elliotson had been an enjoyment without a drawback. It was now the later autumn, very high winds were coursing through the valley, and his last letter but one described the change which these approaches of winter were making in the scene. 'We have had some 'tremendous hurricanes at Lausanne. It is an extra-'ordinary place now for wind, being peculiarly situated 'among mountains—between the Jura, and the Simplon, 'St. Gothard, St. Bernard, and Mont Blanc ranges; and 'at night you would swear (lying in bed) you were at sea. 'You cannot imagine wind blowing so, over earth. It is 'very fine to hear. The weather generally, however, has 'been excellent. There is snow on the tops of nearly all 'the hills, but none has fallen in the valley. On a bright 'day, it is quite hot between eleven and half past two. 'The nights and mornings are cold. For the last two or 'three days, it has been thick weather; and I can see no 'more of Mont Blanc from where I am writing now than 'if I were in Devonshire-terrace, though last week it 'bounded all the Lausanne walks. I would give a great 'deal that you could take a walk with me about Lausanne

Mountain winds.

Pleasures of autumn.

'ders, but I was in that state in Switzerland, when my spirits sunk so, I felt 'myself in serious danger. Yet I had little pain in my side; excepting that 'time at Genoa I have hardly had any since poor Mary died, when it came on 'so badly; and I walked my fifteen miles a day constantly, at a great pace.'

'on a clear cold day. It is impossible to imagine any- 'thing more noble and beautiful than the scene; and the 'autumn colours in the foliage are more brilliant and vivid 'now than any description could convey to you. I took 'Elliotson, when he was with us, up to a ravine I had found 'out in the hills eight hundred or a thousand feet deep! 'Its steep sides dyed bright yellow, and deep red, by the 'changing leaves; a sounding torrent roaring down below; 'the lake of Geneva lying at its foot; one enormous mass 'and chaos of trees at its upper end; and mountain piled 'on mountain in the distance, up into the sky! He really 'was struck silent by its majesty and splendour.'

LAUSANNE: 1846.

A ravine in the hills.

He had begun his third number of *Dombey* on the 26th of October, on the 4th of the following month he was half through it, on the 7th he was in 'the agonies' of its last chapter, and on the 9th, one day before that proposed for its completion, all was done. This was marvellously rapid work, after what else he had undergone; but within a week, Monday the 16th being the day for departure, they were to strike their tents, and troubled and sad were the few days thus left him for preparation and farewell. He included in his leave-taking his deaf, dumb, and blind friends; and, to use his own homely phrase, was yet more terribly 'down in the mouth' at taking leave of his hearing, speaking, and seeing friends. 'I shall see you soon, please 'God, and that sets all to rights. But I don't believe 'there are many dots on the map of the world where we 'shall have left such affectionate remembrances behind us, 'as in Lausanne. It was quite miserable this last night, 'when we left them at Haldimand's.'

Striking tents.

Sadness of leave-taking.

POST FOR PARIS: 1846.

He shall himself describe how they travelled post to Paris, occupying five days. 'We got through the journey 'charmingly, though not quite so quickly as we hoped. The 'children as good as usual, and even Skittles jolly to the 'last. (That name has long superseded Sampson Brass, by 'the bye. I call him so, from something skittle-playing and 'public-housey in his countenance.) We have been up at 'five every morning, and on the road before seven. We were 'three carriages: a sort of wagon, with a cabriolet attached, 'for the luggage; a ramshackle villainous old swing upon 'wheels (hired at Geneva), for the children; and for our'selves, that travelling chariot which I was so kind as to 'bring here for sale. It was very cold indeed crossing the 'Jura—nothing but fog and frost; but when we were out 'of Switzerland and across the French frontier, it became 'warmer, and continued so. We stopped at between six 'and seven each evening; had two rather queer inns, wild 'French country inns; but the rest good. They were three 'hours and a half examining the luggage at the frontier 'custom-house—atop of a mountain, in a hard and biting 'frost; where Anne and Roche had sharp work I assure 'you, and the latter insisted on volunteering the most 'astonishing and unnecessary lies about my books, for the 'mere pleasure of deceiving the officials. When we were 'out of the mountain country, we came at a good pace, 'but were a day late in getting to our hotel here.'

*Ante*, p. 221.

Travelling to Paris.

At PARIS.

They were in Paris when that was written; at the hotel Brighton; which they had reached in the evening of Friday the 20th of November.

# CHAPTER XV.

## THREE MONTHS IN PARIS.

### 1846—1847.

No man enjoyed brief residence in a hotel more than Dickens, but 'several tons of luggage, other tons of 'servants, and other tons of children' are not desirable accompaniments to this kind of life; and his first day in Paris did not close before he had offered for an 'eligible 'mansion.' That same Saturday night he took a 'colossal' walk about the city, of which the brilliancy and brightness almost frightened him; and among other things that attracted his notice was 'rather a good book announced 'in a bookseller's window as *Les Mystères de Londres 'par Sir Trollopp.* Do you know him?' A countryman better known had given him earlier greeting. 'The first 'man who took hold of me in the street, immediately 'outside this door, was Bruffum in his check trousers, and 'without the proper number of buttons on his shirt, who 'was going away this morning, he told me, but coming 'back in two months, when we would go and dine—at 'some place known to him and fame.'

PARIS: 1846.

First day.

Lord Brougham.

Next day he took another long walk about the streets, and lost himself fifty times. This was Sunday, and he

PARIS: 1846.

hardly knew what to say of it, as he saw it there and then. The bitter observance of that day he always sharply resisted, believing a little rational enjoyment to be not opposed to either rest or religion; but here was another matter. 'The dirty churches, and the clattering 'carts and waggons, and the open shops (I don't think I 'passed fifty shut up, in all my strollings in and out), and 'the work-a-day dresses and drudgeries, are not comfortable. 'Open theatres and so forth I am well used to, of course, 'by this time; but so much toil and sweat on what one 'would like to see, apart from religious observances, a 'sensible holiday, is painful.'

French Sunday.

The date of his letter was the 22nd of November, and it had three postscripts.* The first, 'Monday afternoon,' told me a house was taken; that, unless the agreement should break off on any unforeseen fight between Roche and the agent ('a French Mrs. Gamp'), I was to address him at No. 48, Rue de Courcelles, Faubourg St. Honoré; and that he would merely then advert to the premises as in his belief the 'most ridiculous, extraordi-'nary, unparalleled, and preposterous' in the whole world; being something between a baby-house, a 'shades,' a haunted castle, and a mad kind of clock. 'They belong

A house taken.

Thoughts for periodical.

* It had also the mention of another floating fancy for the weekly periodical which was still and always present to his mind, and which settled down at last, as the reader knows, into *Household Words*. 'As to the Review, I strongly 'incline to the notion of a kind of *Spectator* (Addison's)—very cheap, and 'pretty frequent. We must have it thoroughly discussed. It would be a great 'thing to found something. If the mark between a sort of *Spectator*, and a 'different sort of *Athenæum*, could be well hit, my belief is that a deal 'might be done. But it should be something with a marked and distinctive 'and obvious difference, in its design, from any other existing periodical.'

'to a Marquis Castellan, and you will be ready to die of 'laughing when you go over them.' The second P.S. declared that his lips should be sealed till I beheld for myself. 'By Heaven it is not to be imagined by the 'mind of man!' The third P.S. closed the letter. 'One 'room is a tent. Another room is a grove. Another 'room is a scene at the Victoria. The upstairs rooms 'are like fanlights over street-doors. The nurseries—but 'no, no, no, no more! . .'

PARIS: 1846.

His French abode.

His following letter nevertheless sent more, even in the form of an additional protestation that never till I saw it should the place be described. 'I will merely observe 'that it is fifty yards long, and eighteen feet high, and 'that the bedrooms are exactly like opera-boxes. It has 'its little courtyard and garden, and porter's house, and 'cordon to open the door, and so forth; and is a Paris 'mansion in little. There is a gleam of reason in the 'drawing-room. Being a gentleman's house, and not one 'furnished to let, it has some very curious things in it; 'some of the oddest things you ever beheld in your life; 'and an infinity of easy chairs and sofas . . . Bad weather. 'It is snowing hard. There is not a door or window here— 'but that's nothing! there's not a door or window in all 'Paris—that shuts; not a chink in all the billions of 'trillions of chinks in the city that can be stopped to keep 'the wind out. And the cold!—but you shall judge for 'yourself; and also of this preposterous dining-room. The 'invention, sir, of Henry Bulwer, who when he had exe-'cuted it (he used to live here), got frightened at what he 'had done, as well he might, and went away . . . The Brave

Its absurdity.

A former tenant.

PARIS: 1846.

'called me aside on Saturday night, and showed me an im-'provement he had effected in the decorative way. "Which," 'he said, "will very much s'prize Mis'r Fors'er when he '"come." You are to be deluded into the belief that 'there is a perspective of chambers twenty miles in length, 'opening from the drawing-room. . .'

My visit was not yet due, however, and what occupied or interested him in the interval may first be told. He had not been two days in Paris when a letter from his father made him very anxious for the health of his eldest sister. 'I was going to the play (a melodrama in eight 'acts, five hours long), but hadn't the heart to leave home 'after my father's letter,' he is writing on the 30th of November, 'and sent Georgy and Kate by themselves. 'There seems to be no doubt whatever that Fanny is in a 'consumption.' She had broken down in an attempt to sing at a party in Manchester; and subsequent examination by Sir Charles Bell's son, who was present and took much interest in her, too sadly revealed the cause. 'He 'advised that neither she nor Burnett should be told the 'truth, and my father has not disclosed it. In worldly 'circumstances they are very comfortable, and they are 'very much respected. They seem to be happy together, 'and Burnett has a great deal of teaching. You remember 'my fears about her when she was in London the time of 'Alfred's marriage, and that I said she looked to me as if 'she were in a decline? Kate took her to Elliotson, who 'said that her lungs were certainly not affected then. 'And she cried for joy. Don't you think it would be 'better for her to be brought up, if possible, to see Elliot-

Sister Fanny's illness.

Opinion of Elliotson.

'son again? I am deeply, deeply grieved about it.' This course was taken, and for a time there seemed room for hope; but the result will be seen. In the same letter I heard of poor Charles Sheridan, well known to us both, dying of the same terrible disease; and his chief, Lord Normanby, whose many acts of sympathy and kindness had inspired strong regard in Dickens, he had already found 'as informal and good-natured as ever, but not so 'gay as usual, and having an anxious haggard way with 'him, as if his responsibilities were more than he had 'bargained for.' Nor, to account for this, had Dickens far to seek, when a little leisure enabled him to see something of what was passing in Paris in that last year of Louis Philippe's reign. What first impressed him most unfavourably was a glimpse in the Champs Elysées, of the King himself coming in from the country. 'There 'were two carriages. His was surrounded by horseguards. 'It went at a great pace, and he sat very far back in a 'corner of it, I promise you. It was strange to an 'Englishman to see the Prefet of Police riding on horse-'back some hundreds of yards in advance of the cortége, 'turning his head incessantly from side to side, like a 'figure in a Dutch clock, and scrutinizing everybody and 'everything, as if he suspected all the twigs in all the trees 'in the long avenue.'

PARIS: 1846.

The English Ambassador.

The king of the barricades.

But these and other political indications were only, as they generally prove to be, the outward signs of maladies more deeply-seated. He saw almost everywhere signs of canker eating into the heart of the people themselves. 'It 'is a wicked and detestable place, though wonderfully at-

Unhealthy symptoms.

PARIS: 1846.

'tractive; and there can be no better summary of it, after 'all, than Hogarth's unmentionable phrase.' He sent me no letter that did not contribute something of observation or character. He went at first rather frequently to the Morgue, until shocked by something so repulsive that he had not courage for a long time to go back; and on that same occasion he had noticed the keeper smoking a short pipe at his little window, 'and giving a bit of fresh turf to 'a linnet in a cage.' Of the condition generally of the streets he reported badly; the quays on the other side of the Seine were not safe after dark; and here was his own night experience of one of the best quarters of the city. 'I took Georgy out, the night before last, to show her the 'Palais Royal lighted up; and on the Boulevard, a street 'as bright as the brightest part of the Strand or Regent- 'street, we saw a man fall upon another, close before us, 'and try to tear the cloak off his back. It was in a little 'dark corner near the Porte St. Denis, which stands out 'in the middle of the street. After a short struggle, the 'thief fled (there were thousands of people walking about), 'and was captured just on the other side of the road.'

The Morgue.

Incident in streets.

An incident of that kind might mean little or much: but what he proceeded to remark of the ordinary Parisian workpeople and smaller shopkeepers, had a more grave complexion; and may be thought perhaps still to yield some illustration, not without value, to the story of the quarter of a century that has passed since, and even to some of the appalling events of its latest year or two. 'It is extraordinary 'what nonsense English people talk, write, and believe, 'about foreign countries. The Swiss (so much decried) will

Parisian population.

Paris: 1846.

'do anything for you, if you are frank and civil; they are 'attentive and punctual in all their dealings; and may be 'relied upon as steadily as the English. The Parisian work-'people and smaller shopkeepers are more like (and un-'like) Americans than I could have supposed possible. To 'the American indifference and carelessness, they add a 'procrastination and want of the least heed about keeping 'a promise or being exact, which is certainly not surpassed 'in Naples. They have the American semi-sentimental 'independence too, and none of the American vigour or 'purpose. If they ever get free trade in France (as I 'suppose they will, one day), these parts of the population 'must, for years and years, be ruined. They couldn't get 'the means of existence, in competition with the English 'workmen. Their inferior manual dexterity, their lazy 'habits, perfect unreliability, and habitual insubordination, 'would ruin them in any such contest, instantly. They 'are fit for nothing but soldiering—and so far, I believe, 'the successors in the policy of your friend Napoleon have 'reason on their side. Eh bien, mon ami, quand vous venez 'à Paris, nous nous mettrons à quatre épingles, et nous 'verrons toutes les merveilles de la cité, et vous en jugerez. 'God bless me, I beg your pardon! It comes so natural.'

Americans and French.

The Napoleon excuse.

On the 30th he wrote to me that he had got his papers into order and hoped to begin that day. But the same letter told me of the unsettlement thus early of his half-formed Paris plans. Three months sooner than he designed he should be due in London for family reasons; should have to keep within the limit of four months abroad; and as his own house would not be free till July, would have to

Unsettlement of plans.

PARIS: 1846.

hire one from the end of March. 'In these circumstances 'I think I shall send Charley to King's-college after Christ- 'mas. I am sorry he should lose so much French, but 'don't you think to break another half-year's schooling 'would be a pity? Of my own will I would not send him 'to King's-college at all, but to Bruce-castle instead. I 'suppose, however, Miss Coutts is best. We will talk over 'all this when I come to London.' The offer to take charge of his eldest son's education had been pressed upon Dickens by this true friend, to whose delicate and noble consideration for him it would hardly become me to make other allusion here. Munificent as the kindness was, however, it was yet only the smallest part of the obligation which Dickens felt that he owed this lady; to whose generous schemes for the neglected and uncared-for classes of the population, in all which he deeply sympathised, he did the very utmost to render, through many years, unstinted service of his time and his labour, with sacrifice unselfish as her own. His proposed early visit to London, named in this letter, was to see the rehearsal of his Christmas story, dramatised by Mr. Albert Smith for Mr. and Mrs. Keeley at the Lyceum; and my own proposed visit to Paris was to be in the middle of January. 'It will then be the height 'of the season, and a good time for testing the unaccount- 'able French vanity which really does suppose there are no 'fogs here, but that they are all in London.'*

Eldest son's education.

A true friend.

Christmas tale on the stage.

* Some smaller items of family news were in the same letter. 'Mamey 'and Katey have come out in Parisian dresses, and look very fine. They are not 'proud, and send their loves. Skittles is cutting teeth, and gets cross towards 'evening. Frankey is smaller than ever, and Walter very large. Charley in 'statu quo. Everything is enormously dear. Fuel, stupendously so. In

Family news.

The opening of his next letter, which bore date the 6th of December, and its amusing sequel, will sufficiently speak for themselves. 'Cold intense. The water in the 'bedroom-jugs freezes into solid masses from top to bottom, 'bursts the jugs with reports like small cannon, and rolls 'out on the tables and wash-stands, hard as granite. I 'stick to the shower-bath, but have been most hopelessly 'out of sorts—writing sorts; that's all. Couldn't begin, 'in the strange place; took a violent dislike to my study, 'and came down into the drawing-room; couldn't find a 'corner that would answer my purpose; fell into a black 'contemplation of the waning month; sat six hours at a 'stretch, and wrote as many lines, &c. &c. &c. . . . Then, 'you know what arrangements are necessary with the 'chairs and tables; and then what correspondence had to 'be cleared off; and then how I tried to settle to my desk, 'and went about and about it, and dodged at it, like a bird 'at a lump of sugar. In short I have just begun; five 'printed pages finished, I should say; and hope I shall be 'blessed with a better condition this next week, or I shall 'be behind-hand. I shall try to go at it—hard. I can't do 'more. . . . There is rather a good man lives in this street, 'and I have had a correspondence with him which is pre-'served for your inspection. His name is Barthélemy. He 'wears a prodigious Spanish cloak, a slouched hat, an im-'mense beard, and long black hair. He called the other

PARIS: 1846.

Hard frost.

Out of (writing) sorts.

Alarming neighbour.

'airing the house, we burnt five pounds' worth of firewood in one week!! 'We mix it with coal now, as we used to do in Italy, and find the fires much 'warmer. To warm the house thoroughly, this singular habitation requires fires 'on the ground floor. We burn three . . .'

Paris: 1846.

'day, and left his card. Allow me to enclose his card, which 'has originality and merit.

A fellow-littérateur.

'Roche said I wasn't at home. Yesterday, he wrote me 'to say that he too was a "Littérateur"—that he had 'called, in compliment to my distinguished reputation— '"qu'il n'avait pas été reçu—qu'il n'était pas habitué à '"cette sorte de procédé—et qu'il pria Monsieur Dickens '"d'oublier son nom, sa mémoire, sa carte, et sa visite, et '"de considérer qu'elle n'avait pas été rendu!" Of course 'I wrote him a very polite reply immediately, telling him 'good-humouredly that he was quite mistaken, and that 'there were always two weeks in the beginning of every 'month when M. Dickens ne pouvait rendre visite à per-'sonne. He wrote back to say that he was more than 'satisfied; that it was his case too, at the end of every 'month; and that when busy himself, he not only can't 'receive or pay visits, but—"tombe, généralement, aussi, '"dans des humeurs noires qui approchent de l'anthropo-'"phagie!!!" I think that's pretty well.'

Startling blue-devils!

He was in London eight days, from the 15th to the 23rd of December;* and among the occupations of his visit,

* 'I shall bring the Brave, though I have no use for him. He'd die if I 'didn't.'

besides launching his little story on the stage, was the settlement of form for a cheap edition of his writings, which began in the following year. It was to be printed in double columns, and issued weekly in three-halfpenny numbers; there were to be new prefaces, but no illustrations; and for each book something less than a fourth of the original price was to be charged. Its success was very good, but did not come even near to the mark of the later issues of his writings. His own feeling as to this, however, though any failure at the moment affected him on other grounds, was always that of a quiet confidence; and he had expressed this in a proposed dedication of this very edition, which for other reasons was ultimately laid aside. It will be worth preserving here. 'This cheap edition of 'my books is dedicated to the English people, in whose 'approval, if the books be true in spirit, they will live, 'and out of whose memory, if they be false, they will very 'soon die.'



Cheap edition of works.

Suppressed dedication.

Upon his return to Paris I had frequent report of his progress with his famous fifth number, on the completion of which I was to join him. The day at one time seemed doubtful. 'It would be miserable to have to work while 'you were here. Still, I make such sudden starts, and am 'so possessed of what I am going to do, that the fear may 'prove to be quite groundless, and if any alteration would 'trouble you, let the 13th stand at all hazards.' The cold he described as so intense, and the price of fuel so enormous, that though the house was not half warmed ('as 'you'll say, when you feel it') it cost him very near a pound a day. Begging-letter writers had found out 'Mon-

Return to Paris.

PARIS: 1847.

Begging-letter-writers.

'sieur Dickens, le romancier célèbre,' and waylaid him at the door and in the street as numerously as in London: their distinguishing peculiarity being that they were nearly all of them 'Chevaliers de la Garde Impériale de sa Ma-'jesté Napoléon le Grand,' and that their letters bore immense seals with coats of arms as large as five-shilling pieces. His friends the Watsons passed new year's day with him on their way to Rockingham from Lausanne, leaving that country covered with snow and the Bise blowing cruelly over it, but describing it as nothing to the cold of Paris. On the day that closed the old year he had gone into the Morgue and seen an old man with grey head lying there. 'It seemed 'the strangest thing in the world that it should have been 'necessary to take any trouble to stop such a feeble, spent, 'exhausted morsel of life. It was just dusk when I went 'in; the place was empty; and he lay there, all alone, like 'an impersonation of the wintry eighteen hundred and 'forty-six. . . . I find I am getting inimitable, so I'll stop.'

A tenant of the Morgue.

The time for my visit having come, I had grateful proof of the minute and thoughtful provision characteristic of him in everything. My dinner had been ordered to the second at Boulogne, my place in the malle-poste taken, and these and other services announced in a letter, which, by way of doing its part also in the kindly work of preparation, broke out into French. He never spoke that language very well, his accent being somehow defective; but he practised himself into writing it with remarkable ease and fluency. 'I have written to the Hôtel des Bains at Boulogne 'to send on to Calais and take your place in the malle-'poste. . . Of course you know that you'll be assailed with

My visit.

'frightful shouts all along the two lines of ropes from all 'the touters in Boulogne, and of course you'll pass on like 'the princess who went up the mountain after the talk-'ing bird; but don't forget quietly to single out the Hôtel 'des Bains commissionnaire. The following circumstances 'will then occur. My experience is more recent than 'yours, and I will throw them into a dramatic form. . You 'are filtered into the little office, where there are some 'soldiers; and a gentleman with a black beard and a pen 'and ink sitting behind a counter. *Barbe Noire* (to the 'lord of L. I. F.). Monsieur, votre passeport. *Monsieur.* 'Monsieur, le voici! *Barbe Noire.* Où allez-vous, mon-'sieur? *Monsieur.* Monsieur, je vais à Paris. *Barbe* '*Noire.* Quand allez-vous partir, monsieur? *Monsieur.* 'Monsieur, je vais partir aujourd'hui. Avec la malle-poste. '*Barbe Noire.* C'est bien. (To Gendarme.) Laissez sortir 'monsieur! *Gendarme.* Par ici, monsieur, s'il vous plait. 'Le gendarme ouvert une très petite porte. Monsieur se 'trouve subitement entouré de tous les gamins, agents, 'commissionnaires, porteurs, et polissons, en général, de 'Boulogne, qui s'élancent sur lui, en poussant des cris 'épouvantables. Monsieur est, pour le moment, tout-à-fait 'effrayé, et bouleversé. Mais monsieur reprend ses forces 'et dit, de haute voix: "Le Commissionnaire de l'Hôtel des '"Bains!" *Un petit homme* (s'avançant rapidement, et 'en souriant doucement). Me voici, monsieur. Monsieur 'Fors Tair, n'est-ce pas? . . . Alors . . . Alors monsieur se 'promène à l'Hôtel des Bains, où monsieur trouvera qu'un 'petit salon particulier, en haut, est déjà préparé pour 'sa réception, et que son dîner est déjà commandé, aux

Imaginary dialogue.

A Boulogne reception.

PARIS: 1847.

French-English.

'soins du brave Courier, *à midi et demi*. . . . . Monsieur 'mangera son dîner près du feu, avec beaucoup de plaisir, 'et il boirera de vin rouge à la santé de Monsieur de 'Boze, et sa famille intéressante et aimable. La malle-'poste arrivera au bureau de la poste aux lettres à deux 'heures ou peut-être un peu plus tard. Mais monsieur 'chargera le commissionnaire d'y l'accompagner de bonne 'heure, car c'est beaucoup mieux de l'attendre que de la 'perdre. La malle-poste arrivé, monsieur s'assiéra, aussi 'confortablement qu'il le peut, et il y restera jusqu'à 'son arrivé au bureau de la poste aux lettres à Paris. 'Parceque, le convoi (*train*) n'est pas l'affaire de mon-'sieur, qui continuera s'asseoir dans la malle-poste, sur le 'chemin de fer, et après le chemin de fer, jusqu'il se trouve 'à la basse-cour du bureau de la poste aux lettres à Paris, 'où il trouvera une voiture qui a été dépêché de la Rue 'de Courcelles, quarante-huit. Mais monsieur aura la 'bonté d'observer—Si le convoi arriverait à Amiens après 'le départ du convoi à minuit, il faudra y rester jusqu'à 'l'arrivé d'un autre convoi à trois heures moins un quart. 'En attendant, monsieur peut rester au buffet (*refresh-'ment room*), où l'on peut toujours trouver un bon feu, et 'du café chaud, et des très bonnes choses à boire et à 'manger, pendant toute la nuit.—Est-ce que monsieur 'comprend parfaitement toutes ces règles pour sa guidance? '—Vive le Roi des Français! Roi de la nation la plus 'grande, et la plus noble, et la plus extraordinairement 'merveilleuse, du monde! A bas des Anglais!

Cautions to a traveller.

Citizen Dickens.

'CHARLES DICKENS,

'Français naturalisé, et Citoyen de Paris.'

PARIS: 1847.

We passed a fortnight together, and crowded into it more than might seem possible to such a narrow space. With a dreadful insatiability we passed through every variety of sight-seeing, prisons, palaces, theatres, hospitals, the Morgue and the Lazare, as well as the Louvre, Versailles, St. Cloud, and all the spots made memorable by the first revolution. The excellent comedian Regnier, known to us through Macready and endeared by many kindnesses, incomparable for his knowledge of the city and unwearying in friendly service, made us free of the green-room of the Français, where, on the birthday of Molière, we saw his 'Don Juan' revived. At the Conservatoire we witnessed the masterly teaching of Samson; at the Odéon saw a new play by Ponsard, done but indifferently; at the Variétés 'Gentil-Bernard,' with four grisettes as if stepped out of a picture by Watteau; at the Gymnase 'Clarisse Harlowe,' with a death-scene of Rose Cheri which comes back to me, through the distance of time, as the prettiest piece of pure and gentle stage-pathos in my memory; at the Porte St. Martin 'Lucretia Borgia' by Hugo; at the Cirque, scenes of the great revolution, and all the battles of Napoleon; at the Comic Opera, 'Gibby'; and at the Palais Royal the usual new-year's piece, in which Alexandre Dumas was shown in his study beside a pile of quarto volumes five feet high, which proved to be the first tableau of the first act of the first piece to be played on the first night of his new theatre. That new theatre, the Historique, we also saw verging to a very short-lived completeness; and we supped with Dumas himself, and Eugène Sue, and met Théophile Gautier and Alphonse Karr. We saw Lamartine also, and had much

Sight-seeing.

Theatres.

Alexandre Dumas.

PARIS: 1847.

friendly intercourse with Scribe, and with the kind good-natured Amedée Pichot. One day we visited in the Rue du Bac the sick and ailing Chateaubriand, whom we thought like Basil Montagu; found ourselves at the other extreme of opinion in the sculpture-room of David d'Angers; and closed that day at the house of Victor Hugo, by whom Dickens was received with infinite courtesy and grace. The great writer then occupied a floor in a noble corner-house in the Place Royale, the old quarter of Ninon l'Enclos and the people of the Regency, of whom the gorgeous tapestries, the painted ceilings, the wonderful carvings and old golden furniture, including a canopy of state out of some palace of the middle age, quaintly and grandly reminded us. He was himself, however, the best thing we saw; and I find it difficult to associate the attitudes and aspect in which the world has lately wondered at him, with the sober grace and self-possessed quiet gravity of that night of twenty-five years ago. Just then Louis Philippe had ennobled him, but the man's nature was written noble. Rather under the middle size, of compact close-buttoned-up figure, with ample dark hair falling loosely over his close-shaven face, I never saw upon any features so keenly intellectual such a soft and sweet gentility, and certainly never heard the French language spoken with the picturesque distinctness given to it by Victor Hugo. He talked of his childhood in Spain, and of his father having been Governor of the Tagus in Napoleon's wars; spoke warmly of the English people and their literature; declared his preference for melody and simplicity over the music then fashionable at the Conservatoire; referred kindly to

Visits to famous Frenchmen.

Evening with Victor Hugo.

Ponsard, laughed at the actors who had murdered his tragedy at the Odéon, and sympathized with the dramatic venture of Dumas. To Dickens he addressed very charming flattery, in the best taste; and my friend long remembered the enjoyment of that evening.

PARIS: 1847.

There is little to add of our Paris holiday, if indeed too much has not been said already. We had an adventure with a drunken coachman, of which the sequel showed at least the vigour and decisiveness of the police in regard to hired vehicles* in those last days of the Orleans monarchy. At the Bibliothèque Royale we were much interested by seeing, among many other priceless treasures, Gutenberg's types, Racine's notes in his copy of Sophocles, Rousseau's music, and Voltaire's note upon Frederick of Prussia's letter. Nor

At the Bibliothèque Royale.

* Dickens's first letter after my return described it to me. 'Do you re-'member my writing a letter to the prefet of police about that coachman? I 'heard no more about it until this very day' (12th of February), 'when, at 'the moment of your letter arriving, Roche put his head in at the door (I was 'busy writing in the Baronial drawing-room) and said, "Here is datter '"cocher!"—Sir, he had been in prison ever since! and being released this 'morning, was sent by the police to pay back the franc and a half, and to beg 'pardon, and to get a certificate that he had done so, or he could not go on 'the stand again! Isn't this admirable? But the culminating point of the 'story (it could happen with nobody but me) is that he WAS DRUNK WHEN HE 'CAME!! Not very, but his eye was fixed, and he swayed in his sabots, and 'smelt of wine, and told Roche incoherently that he wouldn't have done it '(committed the offence, that is) if the people hadn't made him. He seemed 'to be troubled with a phantasmagorial belief that all Paris had gathered 'round us that night in the Rue St. Honoré, and urged him on with frantic 'shouts. . . . Snow, frost, and cold. . . . The Duke of Bordeaux is very 'well, and dines at the Tuileries to-morrow. . . . *When* I have done, I will write 'you a brilliant letter. . . Loves from all. . . Your blue and golden bed 'looks desolate.' The allusion to the Duc de Bordeaux was to remind me pleasantly of a slip of his own during our talk with Chateaubriand, when, at a loss to say something interesting to the old royalist, he bethought him to enquire with sympathy when he had last seen the representative of the elder branch of Bourbons, as if he were resident in the city then and there!

Adventure with a coachman.

PARIS: 1847.

Premonitory symptoms.

should I omit that in what Dickens then told me, of even his small experience of the social aspects of Paris, there seemed but the same disease which raged afterwards through the second Empire. Not many days after I left, all Paris was crowding to the sale of a lady of the demi-monde, Marie du Plessis, who had led the most brilliant and abandoned of lives, and left behind her the most exquisite furniture and the most voluptuous and sumptuous bijouterie. Dickens wished at one time to have pointed the moral of this life and death of which there was great talk in Paris while we were together. The disease of satiety, which only less often than hunger passes for a broken heart, had killed her. 'What do 'you want?' asked the most famous of the Paris physicians, at a loss for her exact complaint. At last she answered: 'To see my mother.' She was sent for; and there came a simple Breton peasant-woman clad in the quaint garb of her province, who prayed by her bed until she died. Wonderful was the admiration and sympathy; and it culminated when Eugène Sue bought her prayer-book at the sale. Our last talk before I quitted Paris, after dinner at the Embassy, was of the danger underlying all this, and of the signs also visible everywhere of the Napoleon-worship which the Orleanists themselves had most favoured. Accident brought Dickens to England a fortnight later, when again we met together, at Gore-house, the self-contained reticent man whose doubtful inheritance was thus rapidly preparing to fall to him.*

Death of Marie du Plessis.

Napoleon inheritance ready.

At Gore-house, 21st February.

* This was on Sunday, the 21st of February, when a party were assembled of whom I think the French Emperor, his cousin the Prince Napoleon, Doctor Quin, Dickens's eldest son, and myself, are now the only survivors. Lady Blessington had received the day before from her brother Major Power, who held a military appointment in Hobart Town, a small oil-painting of a girl's

The accident was the having underwritten his number of *Dombey* by two pages, which there was not time to supply otherwise than by coming to London to write them.* This was done accordingly; but another greater trouble followed. He had hardly returned to Paris when his eldest son, whom I had brought to England with me and placed in the house of Doctor Major, then head-master of King's-college-school, was attacked by scarlet fever; and this closed prematurely Dickens's residence in Paris. But though he and his wife at once came over, and were followed after some days by the children and their aunt, the isolation of the little invalid could not so soon be broken through. His father at last saw him, nearly a month before the rest, in a lodging in Albany-street, where his grandmother, Mrs. Hogarth, had devoted herself to the charge of him; and

PARIS: 1847.

Illness of eldest son.

Visit of his father.

face by the murderer Wainewright (mentioned on a former page as having been seen by us together in Newgate), who was among the convicts there under sentence of transportation, and who had contrived somehow to put the expression of his own wickedness into the portrait of a nice kind-hearted girl. Major Power knew nothing of the man's previous history at this time, and had employed him on the painting out of a sort of charity. As soon as the truth went back, Wainewright was excluded from houses before open to him, and shortly after died very miserably. What Reynolds said of portrait painting, to explain its frequent want of refinement, that a man could only put into a face what he had in himself, was forcibly shown in this incident. The villain's story altogether moved Dickens to the same interest as it had excited in another profound student of humanity (Sir Edward Lytton), and, as will be seen, he also introduced him into one of his later writings.

The murderer Waine-wright.

* '. . I am horrified to find that the first chapter makes *at least* two 'pages less than I had supposed, and I have a terrible apprehension that there 'will not be copy enough for the number! As it could not possibly come out 'short, and as there would be no greater possibility of sending to me, in this 'short month, to supply what may be wanted, I decide—after the first burst 'of nervousness is gone—*to follow this letter by Diligence to-morrow morning.* 'The malle poste is full for days and days. I shall hope to be with you some 'time on Friday. C. D. to J. F. Paris: Wednesday, 17th February, 1847.

A number under-written.

PARIS: 1847.

an incident of the visit, which amused us all very much, will not unfitly introduce the subject that waits me in my next chapter.

The 'man 'that put 'together '*Dombey.*'

An elderly charwoman employed about the place had shown so much sympathy in the family trouble, that Mrs. Hogarth specially told her of the approaching visit, and who it was that was coming to the sick-room. 'Lawk ma'am!' she said. 'Is the young gentleman upstairs the son of the 'man that put together *Dombey?*' Reassured upon this point, she explained her question by declaring that she never thought there was a man that *could* have put together *Dombey*. Being pressed farther as to what her notion was of this mystery of a *Dombey* (for it was known she could not read), it turned out that she lodged at a snuff-shop kept by a person named Douglas, where there were several other lodgers; and that on the first Monday of every month there was a Tea, and the landlord read the month's number of *Dombey*, those only of the lodgers who subscribed to the tea partaking of that luxury, but all having the benefit of the reading; and the impression produced on the old charwoman revealed itself in the remark with which she closed her account of it. 'Lawk ma'am! I thought that three 'or four men must have put together *Dombey!*'

Snuff-shop readings.

Old charwoman's compliment.

Dickens thought there was something of a compliment in this, and was not ungrateful.

## CHAPTER XVI.

### DOMBEY AND SON.

1846—1848.

THOUGH his proposed new 'book in shilling numbers' had been mentioned to me three months before he quitted England, he knew little himself at that time or when he left excepting the fact, then also named, that it was to do with Pride what its predecessor had done with Selfishness. But this limit he soon overpassed; and the succession of independent groups of character, surprising for the variety of their forms and handling, with which he enlarged and enriched his plan, went far beyond the range of the passion of Mr. Dombey and Mr. Dombey's second wife.

LAUSANNE: 1846.

Drift of the tale.

Obvious causes have led to grave under-estimates of this novel. Its first five numbers forced up interest and expectation so high that the rest of necessity fell short; but it is not therefore true of the general conception that thus the wine of it had been drawn, and only the lees left. In the treatment of acknowledged masterpieces in literature it not seldom occurs that the genius and the art of the master have not pulled together to the close; but if a work of imagination is to forfeit its higher meed of praise because its pace at starting has not been uniformly kept, hard mea-

Why undervalued.

Lausanne: 1846.

sure would have to be dealt to books of undeniable greatness. Among other critical severities it was said here, that Paul died at the beginning not for any need of the story, but only to interest its readers somewhat more; and that Mr. Dombey relented at the end for just the same reason. What is now to be told will show how little ground existed for either imputation. The so-called 'violent change' in the hero has more lately been revived in the notices of Mr. Taine, who says of it that '*it spoils a fine novel;*' but it will be seen that in the apparent change no unnaturalness of change was involved, and certainly the adoption of it was not a sacrifice to 'public morality.' While every other portion of the tale had to submit to such varieties in development as the characters themselves entailed, the design affecting Paul and his father had been planned from the opening, and was carried without alteration to the close. And of the perfect honesty with which Dickens himself repelled such charges as those to which I have adverted, when he wrote the preface to his collected edition, remarkable proof appears in the letter to myself which accompanied the manuscript of his proposed first number. No other line of the tale had at this time been placed on paper.

Mistakes of critics.

Adherence to first design.

When the first chapter only was done, and again when all was finished but eight slips, he had sent me letters formerly quoted. What follows came with the manuscript of the first four chapters on the 25th of July. 'I will now 'go on to give you an outline of my immediate intentions 'in reference to *Dombey.* I design to show Mr. D. with 'that one idea of the Son taking firmer and firmer posses-

*Ante,* p. 223.

'sion of him, and swelling and bloating his pride to a pro- 'digious extent. As the boy begins to grow up, I shall 'show him quite impatient for his getting on, and urging 'his masters to set him great tasks, and the like. But the 'natural affection of the boy will turn towards the despised 'sister; and I purpose showing her learning all sorts of 'things, of her own application and determination, to assist 'him in his lessons: and helping him always. When the 'boy is about ten years old (in the fourth number), he will 'be taken ill, and will die; and when he is ill, and when 'he is dying, I mean to make him turn always for refuge 'to the sister still, and keep the stern affection of the 'father at a distance. So Mr. Dombey—for all his great-'ness, and for all his devotion to the child—will find 'himself at arms' length from him even then; and will 'see that his love and confidence are all bestowed upon 'his sister, whom Mr. Dombey has used—and so has the 'boy himself too, for that matter—as a mere convenience 'and handle to him. The death of the boy is a death-'blow, of course, to all the father's schemes and cherished 'hopes; and "Dombey and Son," as Miss Tox will say 'at the end of the number, "is a Daughter after all." . . 'From that time, I purpose changing his feeling of indif-'ference and uneasiness towards his daughter into a posi-'tive hatred. For he will always remember how the boy 'had his arm round her neck when he was dying, and 'whispered to her, and would take things only from her 'hand, and never thought of him. . . At the same time I 'shall change *her* feeling towards *him* for one of a greater 'desire to love him, and to be loved by him; engendered

LAUSANNE: 1846.

Letter with MS. of first No.

Design as to Paul and sister.

As to Dombey and daughter.

LAUSANNE: 1846.

Proposed course of the story.

'in her compassion for his loss, and her love for the dead 'boy whom, in his way, he loved so well too. So I mean 'to carry the story on, through all the branches and off-'shoots and meanderings that come up; and through the 'decay and downfall of the house, and the bankruptcy of 'Dombey, and all the rest of it; when his only staff and 'treasure, and his unknown Good Genius always, will be 'this rejected daughter, who will come out better than any 'son at last, and whose love for him, when discovered and 'understood, will be his bitterest reproach. For the struggle 'with himself, which goes on in all such obstinate natures, 'will have ended then; and the sense of his injustice, which 'you may be sure has never quitted him, will have at last 'a gentler office than that of only making him more harshly 'unjust. . . . I rely very much on Susan Nipper grown up, 'and acting partly as Florence's maid, and partly as a kind 'of companion to her, for a strong character throughout the 'book. I also rely on the Toodles, and on Polly, who, like 'everybody else, will be found by Mr. Dombey to have 'gone over to his daughter and become attached to her. 'This is what cooks call "the stock of the soup." All 'kinds of things will be added to it, of course.' Admirable is the illustration thus afforded of his way of working, and very interesting the evidence it gives of the genuine feeling for his art with which this book was begun.

Real character of hero.

'The stock 'of the 'soup.'

The close of the letter put an important question affecting gravely a leading person in the tale. . . . 'About the 'boy, who appears in the last chapter of the first number, 'I think it would be a good thing to disappoint all the 'expectations that chapter seems to raise of his happy 'connection with the story and the heroine, and to show 'him gradually and naturally trailing away, from that love 'of adventure and boyish light-heartedness, into negli- 'gence, idleness, dissipation, dishonesty, and ruin. To 'show, in short, that common, every-day, miserable declen- 'sion of which we know so much in our ordinary life; to 'exhibit something of the philosophy of it, in great 'temptations and an easy nature; and to show how the 'good turns into bad, by degrees. If I kept some little 'notion of Florence always at the bottom of it, I think 'it might be made very powerful and very useful. What 'do you think? Do you think it may be done, without 'making people angry? I could bring out Solomon Gills 'and Captain Cuttle well, through such a history; and I 'descry, anyway, an opportunity for good scenes between 'Captain Cuttle and Miss Tox. This question of the boy 'is very important. . . . Let me hear all you think about 'it. Hear! I wish I could.' . . .

Walter Gay.

Question of his fate.

For reasons that need not be dwelt upon here, but in which Dickens ultimately acquiesced, Walter was reserved for a happier future; and the idea thrown out took subsequent shape, amid circumstances better suited to its excellent capabilities, in the striking character of Richard Carstone in the tale of *Bleak House*. But another point had risen meanwhile for settlement not admitting of delay. In the first enjoyment of writing after his long rest, to which a former letter has referred, he had over-written his number by nearly a fifth; and upon his proposal to transfer the fourth chapter to his second number, replacing it by another of fewer pages, I had to object that

Decided in his favour.

*Ante*, p. 254.

LAUSANNE: 1846.

Six pages too much.

this might damage his interest at starting. Thus he wrote on the 7th of August: '. . I have received your letter 'to-day with the greatest delight, and am overjoyed to 'find that you think so well of the number. I thought 'well of it myself, and that it was a great plunge into a 'story; but I did not know how far I might be stimulated 'by my paternal affection. . . . What should you say, for 'a notion of the illustrations, to "Miss Tox introduces the '"Party?" and "Mr. Dombey and family?" meaning 'Polly Toodle, the baby, Mr. Dombey, and little Florence: 'whom I think it would be well to have. Walter, his uncle, 'and Captain Cuttle, might stand over. It is a great 'question with me, now, whether I had not better take 'this last chapter bodily out, and make it the last chapter of 'the second number; writing some other new one to close 'the first number. I think it would be impossible to take 'out six pages without great pangs. Do you think such 'a proceeding as I suggest would weaken number one very 'much? I wish you would tell me, as soon as you can 'after receiving this, what your opinion is on the point. 'If you thought it would weaken the first number, beyond 'the counterbalancing advantage of strengthening the 'second, I would cut down somehow or other, and let it 'go. I shall be anxious to hear your opinion. In the 'meanwhile I will go on with the second, which I have 'just begun. I have not been quite myself since we re-'turned from Chamounix, owing to the great heat.' Two days later: 'I have begun a little chapter to end the first 'number, and certainly think it will be well to keep the ten pages of Wally and Co. entire for number two. But

Omissions proposed.

Danger of weakening number.

'this is still subject to your opinion, which I am very 'anxious to know. I have not been in writing cue all the 'week; but really the weather has rendered it next to 'impossible to work.' Four days later: 'I shall send 'you with this (on the chance of your being favourable to 'that view of the subject) a small chapter to close the 'first number, in lieu of the Solomon Gills one. I have 'been hideously idle all the week, and have done nothing 'but this trifling interloper; but hope to begin again on 'Monday—ding dong. . . The inkstand is to be cleaned 'out to-night, and refilled, preparatory to execution. I 'trust I may shed a good deal of ink in the next fortnight.' Then, the day following, on arrival of my letter, he submitted to a hard necessity. 'I received yours to-day. A 'decided facer to me! I had been counting, alas! with a 'miser's greed, upon the gained ten pages. . . . No matter. 'I have no doubt you are right, and strength is everything. 'The addition of two lines to each page, or something less, '—coupled with the enclosed cuts, will bring it all to bear 'smoothly. In case more cutting is wanted, I must ask 'you to try your hand. I shall agree to whatever you 'propose.' These cuttings, absolutely necessary as they were, were not without much disadvantage; and in the course of them he had to sacrifice a passage foreshadowing his final intention as to Dombey. It would have shown, thus early, something of the struggle with itself that such pride must always go through; and I think it worth preserving in a note.*

LAUSANNE: 1846.

New chapter written.

Chapter rejected.

Sacrifices made.

* 'He had already laid his hand upon the bell-rope to convey his usual 'summons to Richards, when his eye fell upon a writing-desk, belonging to his

LAUSANNE: 1846.

Anxiety as to face of his hero.

Several letters now expressed his anxiety and care about the illustrations. A nervous dread of caricature in the face of his merchant-hero, had led him to indicate by a living person the type of city-gentleman he would have had the artist select; and this is all he meant by his re-iterated urgent request, 'I do wish he could get a glimpse 'of A, for he is the very Dombey.' But as the glimpse of A was not to be had, it was resolved to send for selection by himself glimpses of other letters of the alphabet, actual heads as well as fanciful ones; and the sheetful I sent out, which he returned when the choice was made, I here reproduce in facsimile. In itself amusing, it has now the important use of showing, once for all, in regard to Dickens's intercourse with his artists, that they certainly had not an easy time with him; that, even beyond what is ordinary between author and illustrator, his requirements were exacting; that he was apt, as he has said himself, to build up temples in his mind not always makeable with

Suggested type of city-gentleman.

Passage of original MS. omitted.

'deceased wife, which had been taken, among other things, from a cabinet in 'her chamber. It was not the first time that his eye had lighted on it. He 'carried the key in his pocket; and he brought it to his table and opened it 'now—having previously locked the room door—with a well accustomed hand.

'From beneath a heap of torn and cancelled scraps of paper, he took one letter 'that remained entire. Involuntarily holding his breath as he opened this 'document, and 'bating in the stealthy action something of his arrogant de-'meanour, he sat down, resting his head upon one hand, and read it through.

'He read it slowly and attentively, and with a nice particularity to every 'syllable. Otherwise than as his great deliberation seemed unnatural, and 'perhaps the result of an effort equally great, he allowed no sign of emotion to 'escape him. When he had read it through, he folded and refolded it slowly 'several times, and tore it carefully into fragments. Checking his hand in the 'act of throwing these away, he put them in his pocket, as if unwilling to 'trust them even to the chances of being reunited and deciphered; and instead 'of ringing, as usual, for little Paul, he sat solitary all the evening in his 'cheerless room.' From the original MS. of *Dombey and Son*.

Artist-fancies for Mr. Dombey.

Artist-fancies for Mr. Dombey.

hands; that in the results he had rarely anything but disappointment; and that of all notions to connect with him the most preposterous would be that which directly reversed these relations, and depicted him as receiving from any artist the inspiration he was always vainly striving to give. An assertion of this kind was contradicted in my first volume; but it has since been repeated so explicitly, that to prevent any possible misconstruction from a silence I would fain have persisted in, the distasteful subject is again reluctantly introduced.

LAUSANNE: 1846.

Dickens and his illustrators.

Pages 132-4 of Vol. I.

It originated with a literary friend of the excellent artist by whom *Oliver Twist* was illustrated from month to month, during the earlier part of its monthly issue. This gentleman stated, in a paper written and published in America, that Mr. Cruikshank, by executing the plates before opportunity was afforded him of seeing the letter press, had suggested to the writer the finest effects in his story; and to this, opposing my clear recollection of all the time the tale was in progress, it became my duty to say that within my own personal knowledge the alleged fact was not true. 'Dickens,' the artist is reported as saying to his admirer, 'ferreted out that bundle of drawings, and when he came 'to the one which represents Fagin in the cell, he silently 'studied it for half an hour, and told me he was tempted to 'change the whole plot of his story. . . I consented to let him 'write up to my designs; and that was the way in which 'Fagin, Sikes, and Nancy were created.' Happily I was able to add the complete refutation of this folly by producing a letter of Dickens written at the time, which proved incontestably that the closing illustrations, including the two

Silly story repeated.

Refutation of it.

LAUSANNE: 1846.

specially named in support of the preposterous charge, Sikes and his Dog, and Fagin in his Cell, had not even been seen by Dickens until his finished book was on the eve of appearance. As however the distinguished artist, notwithstanding the refreshment of his memory by this letter, has permitted himself again to endorse the statement of his friend, I can only again print, on the same page which contains the strange language used by him, the words with which Dickens himself repels its imputation on his memory. To some it may be more satisfactory if I print the latter in fac-simile; and so leave for ever a charge in itself so incredible that nothing would have justified farther allusion to it but the knowledge of my friend's old and true regard for Mr. Cruikshank, of which evidence will shortly appear, and my own respect for an original genius well able to subsist of itself without taking what belongs to others.

Why the charge is again noticed.

Resuming the *Dombey* letters I find him on the 30th of August in better heart about his illustrator. 'I shall gladly 'acquiesce in whatever more changes or omissions you 'propose. Browne seems to be getting on well. . . He will 'have a good subject in Paul's christening. Mr. Chick is 'like D, if you'll mention that when you think of it. The 'little chapter of Miss Tox and the Major, which you alas! '(but quite wisely) rejected from the first number, I have 'altered for the last of the second. I have not quite finished 'the middle chapter yet—having, I should say, three good 'days' work to do at it; but I hope it will be all a worthy 'successor to number one. I will send it as soon as finished. Then, a little later: 'Browne is certainly interesting himself,

Hints for artist.

Alterations.

Dickens's words at the time: 1838.

My dear Cruikshank.

I returned suddenly to town yesterday afternoon to look at the ~~last~~ latter pages of Oliver Twist before it was delivered to the booksellers, when I saw the majority of the plates in the last volume for the first time.

With reference to the last one — Rose Maylie and Oliver. Without entering into the question of great haste or ~~[illegible]~~ any other cause which may have led to its being what it is — I am quite sure there can be little difference of opinion between us with ~~[illegible]~~ respect to the result — may

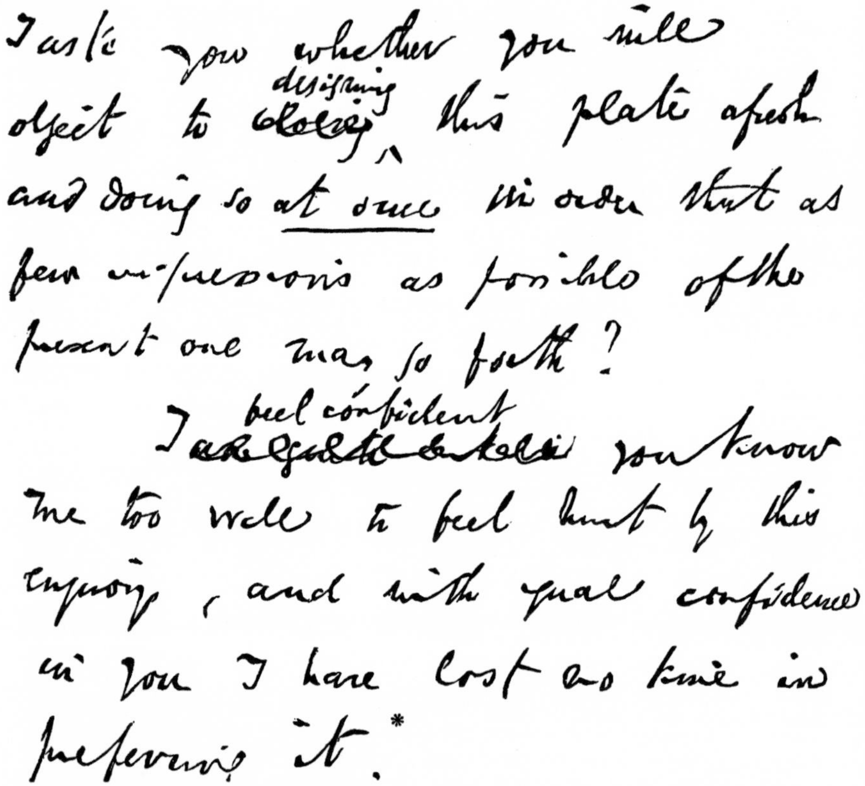
I ask you whether you will object to designing this plate afresh and doing so at once in order that as few impressions as possible of the present one may go forth?

I feel confident you know me too well to feel hurt by this enquiry, and with equal confidence in you I have lost no time in preferring it.*

Mr. Cruikshank's account thirty-four years after.

* 'I will now explain that "Oliver Twist," the ——, the ——, etc' (naming books by another writer), 'were produced in an entirely different manner from 'what would be considered as the usual course; for *I, the Artist, suggested to 'the Authors of those works the original idea, or subject,* for them to write out—'furnishing, at the same time, the *principal characters and the scenes.* And 'then as the tale had to be produced in monthly parts, the *Writer,* or *Author,* 'and the Artist, had every month to arrange and settle what scenes, or subjects, 'and characters were to be introduced, and the Author had to *weave in* such 'scenes as I wished to represent.'—*The Artist and the Author,* by George Cruikshank, p. 15. (Bell & Daldy: 1872.) The italics are Mr. Cruikshank's own.

'and taking pains. I think the cover very good: perhaps with 'a little too much in it, but that is an ungrateful objection.' The second week of September brought me the finished MS. of number two; and his letter of the 3rd of October, noticing objections taken to it, gives additional touches to this picture of him while at work. The matter that engages him is one of his masterpieces. There is nothing in all his writings more perfect, for what it shows of his best qualities, than the life and death of Paul Dombey. The comedy is admirable; nothing strained, everything hearty and wholesome in the laughter and fun; all who contribute to the mirth, Doctor Blimber and his pupils, Mr. Toots, the Chicks and the Toodles, Miss Tox and the Major, Paul and Mrs. Pipchin, up to his highest mark; and the serious scenes never falling short of it, from the death of Paul's mother in the first number, to that of Paul himself in the fifth, which, as a writer of genius with hardly exaggeration said, threw a whole nation into mourning. But see how eagerly this fine writer takes every suggestion, how little of self-esteem and self-sufficiency there is, with what a consciousness of the tendency of his humour to exuberance he surrenders what is needful to restrain it, and of what small account to him is any special piece of work in his care and his considerateness for the general design. I think of Ben Jonson's experience of the greatest of all writers. 'He was 'indeed honest, and of an open and free nature; had an 'excellent phantasy, brave notions and gentle expressions; 'wherein he flowed with that facility, that sometimes it was 'necessary he should be stopped.' Who it was that stopped *him*, and the ease of doing it, no one will doubt. Whether

LAUSANNE: 1846.

Second number done.

A masterpiece of his writing.

Picture of him at work.

An experience of Ben Jonson's.

LAUSANNE: 1846.

he, as well as the writer of later time, might not with more advantage have been left alone, will be the only question.

How objections are taken.

Thus ran the letter of the 3rd of October: 'Miss Tox's 'colony I will smash. Walter's allusion to Carker (would 'you take it *all* out?) shall be dele'd. Of course, you 'understand the man? I turned that speech over in my 'mind; but I thought it natural that a boy should run 'on, with such a subject, under the circumstances: having 'the matter so presented to him. . . I thought of the pos'sibility of malice on christening points of faith, and put 'the drag on as I wrote. Where would you make the 'insertion, and to what effect? *That* shall be done too. 'I want you to think the number sufficiently good stoutly 'to back up the first. It occurs to me—might not your 'doubt about the christening be a reason for not making 'the ceremony the subject of an illustration? Just turn 'this over. Again: if I could do it (I shall have leisure to 'consider the possibility before I begin), do you think it 'would be advisable to make number three a kind of half'way house between Paul's infancy, and his being eight or 'nine years old?—In that case I should probably not kill 'him until the fifth number. Do you think the people so 'likely to be pleased with Florence, and Walter, as to relish 'another number of them at their present age? Other'wise, Walter will be two or three and twenty, straight'way. I wish you would think of this. . . I am sure you 'are right about the christening. It shall be artfully and 'easily amended. . . Eh?'

Should little Paul's life be prolonged?

Meanwhile, two days before this letter, his first number had been launched with a sale that transcended his hopes, and brought back *Nickleby* days. The *Dombey* success 'is BRILLIANT!' he wrote to me on the 11th. 'I had 'put before me thirty thousand as the limit of the most 'extreme success, saying that if we should reach that, I 'should be more than satisfied and more than happy; you 'will judge how happy I am! I read the second number 'here last night to the most prodigious and uproarious 'delight of the circle. I never saw or heard people laugh 'so. You will allow me to observe that my reading of 'the Major has merit.' What a valley of the shadow he had just been passing, in his journey through his Christmas book, has before been told; but always, and with only too much eagerness, he sprang up under pressure. 'A week of perfect idleness,' he wrote to me on the 26th, 'has brought me round again—idleness so rusting and 'devouring, so complete and unbroken, that I am quite 'glad to write the heading of the first chapter of num-'ber three to-day. I shall be slow at first, I fear, in con-'sequence of that change of the plan. But I allow myself 'nearly three weeks for the number; designing, at present, 'to start for Paris on the 16th of November. Full particu-'lars in future bills. Just going to bed. I think I can 'make a good effect, on the after story, of the feeling 'created by the additional number before Paul's death.' . . Five more days confirmed him in this hope. 'I am at 'work at *Dombey* with good speed, thank God. All well 'here. Country stupendously beautiful. Mountains 'covered with snow. Rich, crisp weather.' There was one drawback. The second number had gone out to him, and the illustrations he found to be so 'dreadfully bad' that they

LAUSANNE: 1846.

Sale of the first No.

A reading of the second No.

Beginning third No.

A number to be added to Paul's life.

LAUSANNE: 1846.

made him 'curl his legs up.' They made him also more than usually anxious in regard to a special illustration on which he set much store, for the part he had in hand.

Scene at Mrs. Pipchin's.

The first chapter of it was sent me only four days later (nearly half the entire part, so freely his fancy was now flowing and overflowing), with intimation for the artist: 'The 'best subject for Browne will be at Mrs. Pipchin's; and if 'he liked to do a quiet odd thing, Paul, Mrs. Pipchin, and 'the Cat, by the fire, would be very good for the story. I 'earnestly hope he will think it worth a little extra care. 'The second subject, in case he shouldn't take a second 'from that same chapter, I will shortly describe as soon as 'I have it clearly (to-morrow or next day), and send it to '*you* by post.'

Failure of an illustration.

The result was not satisfactory; but as the artist more than redeemed it in the later course of the tale, and the present disappointment was mainly the incentive to that better success, the mention of the failure here will be excused for what it illustrates of Dickens himself. 'I 'am really *distressed* by the illustration of Mrs. Pipchin 'and Paul. It is so frightfully and wildly wide of the 'mark. Good Heaven! in the commonest and most literal 'construction of the text, it is all wrong. She is described 'as an old lady, and Paul's "miniature arm-chair" is men-'tioned more than once.

What it should have been.

He ought to be sitting in a little 'arm-chair down in the corner of the fireplace, staring up 'at her. I can't say what pain and vexation it is to be so 'utterly misrepresented. I would cheerfully have given a 'hundred pounds to have kept this illustration out of the 'book. He never could have got that idea of Mrs. Pipchin 'if he had attended to the text. Indeed I think he does 'better without the text; for then the notion is made 'easy to him in short description, and he can't help taking 'it in.'

The Mrs. Pipchin of his childhood.

He felt the disappointment more keenly, because the conception of the grim old boarding-house keeper had taken back his thoughts to the miseries of his own child-life, and made her, as her prototype in verity was, a part of the terrible reality.* I had forgotten, until I again read this letter of the 4th of November 1846, that he thus early proposed to tell me that story of his boyish sufferings which a question from myself, of some months later date, so fully elicited. He was now hastening on with the close of his third number, to be ready for departure to Paris.

Finishing third No.

'. . . I hope to finish the number by next Tuesday or 'Wednesday. It is hard writing under these bird-of-passage 'circumstances, but I have no reason to complain, God 'knows, having come to no knot yet. . . . I hope you will 'like Mrs. Pipchin's establishment. It is from the life, 'and I was there—I don't suppose I was eight years old; 'but I remember it all as well, and certainly understood 'it as well, as I do now. We should be devilish sharp in 'what we do to children. I thought of that passage in my 'small life, at Geneva. *Shall I leave you my life in MS.* '*when I die? There are some things in it that would* '*touch you very much, and that might go on the same* '*shelf with the first volume of Holcroft's.*'

First thought of his autobiography.

* I take, from his paper of notes for the number, the various names, beginning with that of her real prototype, out of which the name selected came to him at last. 'Mrs. Roylance . . House at the sea-side. Mrs. Wrychin. Mrs. 'Tipchin. Mrs. Alchin. Mrs. Somching. Mrs. Pipchin.' See Vol. I. p. 35.

PARIS: 1846.

On the Monday week after that was written he left Lausanne for Paris, and my first letter to him there was to say that he had overwritten his number by three pages.

Two pages and a half too much.

'I have taken out about two pages and a half,' he wrote by return from the hotel Brighton, 'and the rest I must 'ask you to take out with the assurance that you will 'satisfy me in whatever you do. The sale, prodigious 'indeed! I am very thankful.' Next day he wrote as to Walter. 'I see it will be best as you advise, to give that 'idea up; and indeed I don't feel it would be reasonable 'to carry it out now. I am far from sure it could be 'wholesomely done, after the interest he has acquired. 'But when I have disposed of Paul (poor boy!) I will 'consider the subject farther.' The subject was never resumed. He was at the opening of his admirable fourth part, when, on the 6th of December, he wrote from the Rue de Courcelles:

Opening fourth No.

'Here am I, writing letters, and 'delivering opinions, politico-economical and otherwise, as 'if there were no undone number, and no undone Dick! 'Well. Cosi va il mondo (God bless me! Italian! I 'beg your pardon)—and one must keep one's spirits up, 'if possible, even under *Dombey* pressure. Paul, I shall 'slaughter at the end of number five. His school ought 'to be pretty good, but I haven't been able to dash at it 'freely, yet. However, I have avoided unnecessary dialogue 'so far, to avoid overwriting; and all I *have* written is 'point.'

At Doctor Blimber's.

And so, in 'point,' it went to the close; the rich humour of its picture of Doctor Blimber and his pupils, alternating with the quaint pathos of its picture of little

Paul; the first a good-natured exposure of the forcing-system and its fruits, as useful as the sterner revelation in *Nickleby* of the atrocities of Mr. Squeers, and the last even less attractive for the sweetness and sadness of its foreshadowing of a child's death, than for those strange images of a vague, deep thoughtfulness, of a shrewd unconscious intellect, of mysterious small philosophies and questionings, by which the young old-fashioned little creature has a glamour thrown over him as he is passing away. It was wonderfully original, this treatment of the part that thus preceded the close of Paul's little life; and of which the first conception, as I have shown, was an afterthought. It quite took the death itself out of the region of pathetic commonplaces, and gave to it the proper relation to the sorrow of the little sister that survives it. It is a fairy vision to a piece of actual suffering; a sorrow with heaven's hues upon it, to a sorrow with all the bitterness of earth.



Paul's school-life.

Paul and Florence.

The number had been finished, he had made his visit to London, and was again in the Rue de Courcelles, when on Christmas day he sent me its hearty old wishes, and a letter of Jeffrey's on his new story of which the first and second part had reached him. 'Many merry 'Christmases, many happy new years, unbroken friend-'ship, great accumulation of cheerful recollections, affec-'tion on earth, and Heaven at last! . . . Is it not a strange 'example of the hazard of writing in parts, that a man 'like Jeffrey should form his notion of Dombey and Miss 'Tox on three months' knowledge? I have asked him the 'same question, and advised him to keep his eye on both

*Ante*, p. 299.

Lord Jeffrey criticizes Nos. 1 & 2.

PARIS: 1846.

'of them as time rolls on.* I do not at heart, however, 'lay much real stress on his opinion, though one is naturally proud of awakening such sincere interest in the 'breast of an old man who has so long worn the blue and 'yellow . . . He certainly did some service in his old criticisms, especially to Crabbe. And though I don't think 'so highly of Crabbe as I once did (feeling a dreary want 'of fancy in his poems), I think he deserved the painstaking and conscientious tracking with which Jeffrey 'followed him' . . . Six days later he described himself sitting down to the performance of one of his greatest achievements, his number five, 'most abominably dull and 'stupid. I have only written a slip, but I hope to get to

Jeffrey on Crabbe.

Beginning fifth No.

* Some passages may be subjoined from the letter, as it does not appear among those printed by Lord Cockburn. 'EDINBURGH, 14*th December*, '46. 'My dear, dear Dickens!—and dearer every day, as you every day give me 'more pleasure and do me more good! You do not wonder at this style? for 'you know that I have been *in love with you*, ever since Nelly! and I do not 'care now who knows it. . . . The Dombeys, my dear D! how can I thank 'you enough for them! The truth, and the delicacy, and the softness and 'depth of the pathos in that opening death-scene, could only come from one 'hand; and the exquisite taste which spares all details, and breaks off just when 'the effect is at its height, is wholly yours. But it is Florence on whom my 'hopes chiefly repose; and in her I see the promise of another Nelly! though 'reserved, I hope, for a happier fate, and destined to let us see what a *grown-up* female angel is like. I expect great things, too, from Walter, who begins 'charmingly, and will be still better I fancy than young Nickleby, to whom as 'yet he bears most resemblance. I have good hopes too of Susan Nipper, who 'I think has great capabilities, and whom I trust you do not mean to drop. 'Dombey is rather too hateful, and strikes me as a mitigated Jonas, without 'his brutal coarseness and ruffian ferocity. I am quite in the dark as to what 'you mean to make of Paul, but shall watch his development with interest. 'About Miss Tox, and her Major, and the Chicks, perhaps I do not care 'enough. But you know I always grudge the exquisite painting you waste on 'such portraits. I love the Captain, tho', and his hook, as much as you can 'wish; and look forward to the future appearances of Carker Junior, with 'expectations which I know will not be disappointed. . . .'

Jeffrey's forecast of the tale.

Jeffrey's anticipations.

'work in strong earnest to-morrow. It occurred to me on 'special reflection, that the first chapter should be with 'Paul and Florence, and that it should leave a pleasant 'impression of the little fellow being happy, before the 'reader is called upon to see him die. I mean to have a 'genteel breaking-up at Doctor Blimber's therefore, for 'the Midsummer vacation; and to show him in a little 'quiet light (now dawning through the chinks of my 'mind), which I hope will create an agreeable impres-'sion.' Then, two days later: '. . I am working very 'slowly. You will see in the first two or three lines of 'the enclosed first subject, with what idea I am ploughing 'along. It is difficult; but a new way of doing it, it 'strikes me, and likely to be pretty.'

What he will do with it.

And then, after three days more, came something of a damper to his spirits, as he thus toiled along. He saw public allusion made to a review that had appeared in the *Times* of his Christmas book, and it momentarily touched what he too truly called his morbid susceptibility to exasperation. 'I see that the "good old Times" are again at 'issue with the inimitable B. Another touch of a blunt 'razor on B.'s nervous system.—Friday morning. Inimit-'able very mouldy and dull. Hardly able to work. Dreamed 'of *Timeses* all night. Disposed to go to New Zealand 'and start a magazine.' But soon he sprang up, as usual, more erect for the moment's pressure; and after not many days I heard that the number was as good as done. His letter was very brief, and told me that he had worked so hard the day before (Tuesday, the 12th of January), and so incessantly, night as well as morning, that he had

A damper to the spirit.

A fancy for New Zealand.

PARIS: 1847.

Close of Paul's life.

breakfasted and lain in bed till midday. 'I hope I have 'been very successful.' There was but one small chapter more to write, in which he and his little friend were to part company for ever; and the greater part of the night of the day on which it was written, Thursday the 14th, he was wandering desolate and sad about the streets of Paris. I arrived there the following morning on my visit; and as I alighted from the malle-poste, a little before eight o'clock, found him waiting for me at the gate of the post-office bureau.

Beginning sixth No.

Its difficulties.

I left him on the 2nd of February with his writing-table in readiness for number six; but on the 4th, enclosing me subjects for illustration, he told me he was 'not under weigh yet. Can't begin.' Then, on the 7th, his birthday, he wrote to warn me he should be late. 'Could not begin before Thursday last, and find it very 'difficult indeed to fall into the new vein of the story. I 'see no hope of finishing before the 16th at the earliest, 'in which case the steam will have to be put on for this 'short month. But it can't be helped. Perhaps I shall 'get a rush of inspiration. . . . I will send the chapters 'as I write them, and you must not wait, of course, for 'me to read the end in type. To transfer to Florence, 'instantly, all the previous interest, is what I am aiming 'at. For that, all sorts of other points must be thrown 'aside in this number. . . . We are going to dine again 'at the Embassy to-day—with a very ill will on my part. 'All well. I hope when I write next I shall report my-'self in better cue. . . . I have had a tremendous outpour-'ing from Jeffrey about the last part, which he thinks the 'best thing past, present, or to come.' * Three more days and I had the MS. of the completed chapter, nearly half the number (in which as printed it stands second, the small middle chapter having been transposed to its place). 'I have taken the most prodigious pains with it; the 'difficulty, immediately after Paul's death, being very 'great. May you like it! My head aches over it now (I 'write at one o'clock in the morning), and I am strange 'to it. . . I think I shall manage Dombey's second wife '(introduced by the Major), and the beginning of that 'business in his present state of mind, very naturally and 'well . . . Paul's death has amazed Paris. All sorts of 'people are open-mouthed with admiration. . . . When 'I have done, I'll write you *such* a letter! Don't cut 'me short in your letters just now, because I'm working 'hard. . . *I*'ll make up. . . Snow—snow—snow—a foot 'thick.' The day after this, came the brief chapter which was printed as the first; and then, on the 16th, which he had fixed as his limit for completion, the close reached me; but I had meanwhile sent him out so much of the proof as

PARIS: 1847.

Thoughts for Edith.

* 'EDINBURGH, 31*st January*, 1847. Oh, my dear, dear Dickens! what a 'No. 5 you have now given us! I have so cried and sobbed over it last night, 'and again this morning; and felt my heart purified by those tears, and 'blessed and loved you for making me shed them; and I never can bless and 'love you enough. Since the divine Nelly was found dead on her humble 'couch, beneath the snow and the ivy, there has been nothing like the actual 'dying of that sweet Paul, in the summer sunshine of that lofty room. And 'the long vista that leads us so gently and sadly, and yet so gracefully and 'winningly, to the plain consummation! Every trait so true, and so touch-'ing—and yet lightened by the fearless innocence which goes *playfully* to the 'brink of the grave, and that pure affection which bears the unstained spirit, 'on its soft and lambent flash, at once to its source in eternity.' . . . In the same letter he told him of his having been reading the *Battle of Life* again, charmed with its sweet writing and generous sentiments.

Jeffrey on Paul's death.

PARIS: 1847.

Two pages too little.

convinced him that he had underwritten his number by at least two pages, and determined him to come to London. The incident has been told which soon after closed his residence abroad, and what remained of his story was written in England.

LONDON.

I shall not farther dwell upon it in any detail. It extended over the whole of the year; and the interest and passion of it, when to himself both became centred in Florence and in Edith Dombey, took stronger hold of him, and more powerfully affected him, than had been the case in any of his previous writings, I think, excepting only the close of the *Old Curiosity Shop*. Jeffrey compared Florence to Little Nell, but the differences from the outset are very marked, and it is rather in what disunites or separates them that we seem to find the purpose aimed at. If the one, amid much strange and grotesque violence surrounding her, expresses the innocent unconsciousness of childhood to such rough ways of the world, passing unscathed as Una to her home beyond it, the other is this character in action and resistance, a brave young resolute heart that will *not* be crushed, and neither sinks nor yields, but from earth's roughest trials works out her own redemption even here. Of Edith from the first Jeffrey judged more rightly; and, when the story was nearly half done, expressed his opinion about her, and about the book itself, in language that pleased Dickens for the special reason that at the time this part of the book had seemed to many to have fallen greatly short of the splendour of its opening. Jeffrey said however quite truly, claiming to be heard with authority as his 'Critic-

Florence and Little Nell.

Jeffrey's judgments.

'laureate,' that of all his writings it was perhaps the most finished in diction, and that it equalled the best in the delicacy and fineness of its touches, 'while it rises to 'higher and deeper passions, not resting, like most of the 'former, in sweet thoughtfulness, and thrilling and attrac-'tive tenderness, but boldly wielding all the lofty and 'terrible elements of tragedy, and bringing before us the 'appalling struggles of a proud, scornful, and repentant 'spirit.' Not that she was exactly this. Edith's worst qualities are but the perversion of what should have been her best. A false education in her, and a tyrant passion in her husband, make them other than Nature meant; and both show how life may run its evil course against the higher dispensations.

LONDON: 1847.

On the Edith scenes.

As the catastrophe came in view, a nice point in the management of her character and destiny arose. I quote from a letter of the 19th of November, when he was busy with his fourteenth part. 'Of course she hates Carker 'in the most deadly degree. I have not elaborated that, 'now, because (as I was explaining to Browne the other 'day) I have relied on it very much for the effect of her 'death. But I have no question that what you suggest 'will be an improvement. The strongest place to put it 'in, would be the close of the chapter immediately before 'this last one. I want to make the two first chapters as 'light as I can, but I will try to do it, solemnly, in that 'place.' Then came the effect of this fourteenth number on Jeffrey; raising the question of whether the end might not come by other means than her death, and bringing with it a more bitter humiliation for her destroyer. While

Edith's first destiny.

Doubts suggested.

LONDON: 1847-8.

engaged on the fifteenth (21st December) Dickens thus wrote to me: 'I am thoroughly delighted that you like 'what I sent. I enclose designs. Shadow-plate, poor. But 'I think Mr. Dombey admirable. One of the prettiest 'things in the book ought to be at the end of the chapter 'I am writing now. But in Florence's marriage, and in 'her subsequent return to her father, I see a brilliant 'opportunity. . . Note from Jeffrey this morning, who 'won't believe (positively refuses) that Edith is Carker's 'mistress. What do you think of a kind of inverted 'Maid's Tragedy, and a tremendous scene of her unde-'ceiving Carker, and giving him to know that she never 'meant that?' So it was done; and when he sent me the chapter in which Edith says adieu to Florence, I had nothing but praise and pleasure to express. 'I need not 'say,' he wrote in reply, 'I can't, how delighted and over-'joyed I am by what you say and feel of it. I propose to 'show Dombey *twice* more; and in the end, leave him 'exactly as you describe.' The end came; and, at the last moment when correction was possible, this note arrived. 'I suddenly remember that I have forgotten Diogenes. 'Will you put him in the last little chapter? After the 'word "favourite" in reference to Miss Tox, you can add, '"except with Diogenes, who is growing old and wilful." 'Or, on the last page of all, after "and with them two '"children: boy and girl" (I quote from memory), you 'might say "and an old dog is generally in their com-'"pany," or to that effect. Just what you think best.'

Disbeliefs of Jeffrey.

Important change.

Diogenes remembered.

That was on Saturday the 25th of March, 1848, and may be my last reference to *Dombey* until the book, in its place with the rest, finds critical allusion when I close. But as the confidences revealed in this chapter have dealt wholly with the leading currents of interest, there is yet room for a word on incidental persons in the story, of whom I have seen other so-called confidences alleged which it will be only right to state have really no authority. And first let me say what unquestionable evidence these characters give of the unimpaired freshness, richness, variety, and fitness of Dickens's invention at this time. Glorious Captain Cuttle, laying his head to the wind and fighting through everything; his friend Jack Bunsby,* with a head too ponderous to lay-to, and so falling victim to the inveterate MacStinger; good-hearted, modest, considerate Toots, whose brains rapidly go as his whiskers come, but who yet gets back from contact with the world, in his shambling way, some fragments of the sense pumped out of him by the forcing Blimbers; breathless Susan Nipper, beaming Polly Toodle, the plaintive Wickham, and the awful Pipchin, each with her duty in the starched Dombey household so nicely appointed as to seem born for only that; simple thoughtful old Gills and his hearty young lad of a nephew; Mr. Toodle and his children, with the charitable grinder's decline and fall; Miss Tox, obsequious flatterer from nothing but good-nature; spectacled and analytic, but not unkind Miss Blimber; and the good droning dull benevolent Doctor himself, withering even the fruits of his well-spread dinner-table with his *It is remarkable, Mr. Feeder,*

LONDON: 1848.

Other characters.

Jack Bunsby.

Dombey household.

Blimber establishment.

* '*Isn't Bunsby good?*' I heard Lord Denman call out, with unmistakable glee and enjoyment, over Talfourd's table—I think to Sir Edward Ryan; one of the few survivors of that pleasant dinner party of May 1847.

LONDON: 1848.

*that the Romans*—'at the mention of which terrible 'people, their implacable enemies, every young gentleman 'fastened his gaze upon the Doctor, with an assumption of 'the deepest interest.' So vivid and life-like were all these people, to the very youngest of the young gentlemen, that it became natural eagerly to seek out for them actual prototypes; but I think I can say with some confidence of them all, that, whatever single traits may have been taken from persons known to him (a practice with all writers, and very specially with Dickens), only two had living originals. His own experience of Mrs. Pipchin has been related; I had myself some knowledge of Miss Blimber; and the Little Wooden Midshipman did actually (perhaps does still) occupy his post of observation in Leadenhall-street. The names that have been connected, I doubt not in perfect good faith, with Sol Gills, Perch the messenger, and Captain Cuttle, have certainly not more foundation than the fancy a courteous correspondent favours me with, that the redoubtable Captain must have sat for his portrait to Charles Lamb's blustering, loud-talking, hook-handed Mr. Mingay. As to the amiable and excellent city-merchant whose name has been given to Mr. Dombey, he might with the same amount of justice or probability be supposed to have originated *Coriolanus* or *Timon of Athens*.

Supposed originals.

Mistaken surmises.

*Ante*, p. 84.

# CHAPTER XVII.

## SPLENDID STROLLING.

1847—1852.

London: 1847.

DEVONSHIRE TERRACE remaining still in possession of Sir James Duke, a house was taken in Chester-place, Regent's-park, where, on the 18th of April, his fifth son, to whom he gave the name of Sydney Smith Haldimand, was born.* Exactly a month before, we had attended together the funeral, at Highgate, of his publisher Mr. William Hall, his old regard for whom had survived the recent temporary cloud, and with whom he had the association as well of his first success, as of much kindly intercourse not forgotten at this sad time. Of the summer

Birth of fifth son.

* He entered the Royal Navy, and survived his father only a year and eleven months. He was a Lieutenant, at the time of his death from a sharp attack of bronchitis; being then on board the P. and O. steamer 'Malta,' invalided from his ship the Topaze, and on his way home. He was buried at sea on the 2nd of May, 1872. Poor fellow! He was the smallest in size of all the children, in his manhood reaching only to a little over five feet; and throughout his childhood was never called by any other name than the 'Ocean Spectre,' from a strange little weird yet most attractive look in his large wondering eyes, very happily caught in a sketch in oils by the good Frank Stone, done at Bonchurch in September 1849 and remaining in his aunt's possession. 'Stone has painted,' Dickens then wrote to me, 'the Ocean 'Spectre, and made a very pretty little picture of him.' It was a strange chance that led his father to invent this playful name for one whom the ocean did indeed take to itself at last.

Death of Lieut. Sydney Dickens.

LONDON: 1847.

months that followed, the greater part was passed by him at Brighton or Broadstairs; and the chief employment of his leisure, in the interyals of *Dombey*, was the management of an enterprise originating in the success of our private play, of which the design was to benefit a great man of letters.

Theatrical benefit for Leigh Hunt.

The purpose and the name had hardly been announced, when, with the statesmanlike attention to literature and its followers for which Lord John Russell has been eccentric among English politicians, a civil-list pension of two hundred a year was granted to Leigh Hunt; but though this modified our plan so far as to strike out of it performances meant to be given in London, so much was still thought necessary as might clear off past liabilities, and enable one of the most genuine of writers better to enjoy the easier future that had at last been opened to him. Reserving therefore anything realized beyond a certain sum for a dramatic author of merit, Mr. John Poole, to whom help had become also important, it was proposed to give, on Leigh Hunt's behalf, two representations of Ben Jonson's comedy, one at Manchester and the other at Liverpool, to be varied by different farces in each place; and with a prologue of Talfourd's which Dickens was to deliver in Manchester, while a similar address by Sir Edward Bulwer Lytton was to be spoken by me in Liverpool. Among the artists and writers associated in the scheme were Mr. Frank Stone, Mr. Augustus Egg, Mr. John Leech, and Mr. George Cruikshank; Mr. Douglas Jerrold, Mr. Mark Lemon, Mr. Dudley Costello, and Mr. George Henry Lewes; the general management and supreme control being given to Dickens.

Proposed performances.

Leading actors.

Leading men in both cities contributed largely to the design, and my friend Mr. Alexander Ireland of Manchester has lately sent me some letters not more characteristic of the energy of Dickens in regard to it than of the eagerness of everyone addressed to give what help they could. Making personal mention of his fellow-sharers in the enterprise he describes the troop, in one of those letters, as 'the most 'easily governable company of actors on earth;' and to this he had doubtless brought them, but not very easily. One or two of his managerial troubles at rehearsals remain on record in letters to myself, and may give amusement still. Comedy and farces are referred to indiscriminately, but the farces were the most recurring plague. 'Good Heaven! 'I find that A. hasn't twelve words, and I am in hourly 'expectation of rebellion!'—'You were right about the 'green baize, that it would certainly muffle the voices; and 'some of our actors, by Jove, haven't too much of that 'commodity at the best.'—'B. shocked me so much the 'other night by a restless, stupid movement of his hands 'in his first scene with you, that I took a turn of an hour 'with him yesterday morning, and I hope quieted his 'nerves a little.'—'I made a desperate effort to get C. to 'give up his part. Yet in spite of all the trouble he gives 'me I am sorry for him, he is so evidently hurt by his own 'sense of not doing well. He clutched the part, however, 'tenaciously; and three weary times we dragged through 'it last night.'—'That infernal E. forgets everything.'—'I 'plainly see that F. when nervous, which he is sure to be, 'loses his memory. Moreover his asides are inaudible, even 'at Miss Kelly's; and as regularly as I stop him to say

The manager.

Troubles at rehearsals.

LONDON: 1847.

'them again, he exclaims (with a face of agony) that "he'll '"speak loud on the night," as if anybody ever did without 'doing it always!'—'G. not born for it at all, and too 'innately conceited, I much fear, to do anything well. I 'thought him better last night, but I would as soon laugh at a kitchen poker.'—'Fancy H, ten days after the cast-'ing of that farce, wanting F.'s part therein! Having 'himself an excellent old man in it already, and a quite 'admirable part in the other farce.' From which it will appear that my friend's office was not a sinecure, and that he was not, as few amateur-managers have ever been, without the experiences of Peter Quince. Fewer still, I suspect, have fought through them with such perfect success, for the company turned out at last would have done credit to any enterprise. They deserved the term applied to them by Maclise, who had invented it first for Macready, on his being driven to 'star' in the provinces when his managements in London closed. They were 'splendid strollers.'*

Managerial exertion.

Its result

* I think it right to place on record here Leigh Hunt's own allusion to the incident (*Autobiography*, p. 432), though it will be thought to have too favourable a tone, and I could have wished that other names had also found mention in it. But I have already (p. 185) stated quite unaffectedly my own opinion of the very modest pretensions of the whole affair, and these kind words of Hunt may stand *valeant quantum*. 'Simultaneous with the 'latest movement about the pension was one on the part of my admirable 'friend Dickens and other distinguished men, Forsters and Jerrolds, who, 'combining kindly purpose with an amateur inclination for the stage, had 'condescended to show to the public what excellent actors they could have 'been, had they so pleased,—what excellent actors, indeed, some of them 'were. . . . They proposed . . . a benefit for myself, . . . and the piece per-'formed on the occasion was Ben Jonson's *Every Man in his Humour*. . . 'If anything had been needed to show how men of letters include actors, on 'the common principle of the greater including the less, these gentlemen would 'have furnished it. Mr. Dickens's Bobadil had a spirit in it of intellectual

Leigh Hunt's account.

On Monday the 26th July we played at Manchester, and on Wednesday the 28th at Liverpool; the comedy being followed on the first night by *A Good Night's Rest* and *Turning the Tables*, and on the second by *Comfortable Lodgings, or Paris in* 1750; and the receipts being, on the first night £440 12*s*, and on the second, £463 8*s*. 6*d*.

MANCHESTER AND LIVERPOOL: 1847.

Receipts and expenses.

'apprehension beyond anything the existing stage has shown . . . and Mr. 'Forster delivered the verses of Ben Jonson with a musical flow and a sense 'of their grace and beauty unknown, I believe, to the recitation of actors at 'present. At least I have never heard anything like it since Edmund Kean's.' . . To this may be added some lines from Lord Lytton's prologue spoken at Liverpool, of which I have not been able to find a copy, if indeed it was printed at the time; but the verses come so suddenly and completely back to me, as I am writing after twenty-five years, that in a small way they recall a more interesting effort of memory told me once by Macready. On a Christmas night at Drury Lane there came a necessity to put up the *Gamester*, which he had not played since he was a youth in his father's theatre thirty years before. He went to rehearsal shrinking from the long and heavy study he should have to undergo, when, with the utterance of the opening sentence, the entire words of the part came back, including even a letter which Beverley has to read, and which it is the property-man's business to supply. My lines come back as unexpectedly; but with pleasanter music than any in Mr. Moore's dreary tragedy, as a few will show.

Lord Lytton's prologue.

Anecdote of Macready.

'Mild amid foes, within a prison free,
'He comes . . our grey-hair'd bard of Rimini!
'Comes with the pomp of memories in his train,
'Pathos and wit, sweet pleasure and sweet pain!
'Comes with familiar smile and cordial tone,
'Our hearths' wise cheerer!—Let us cheer his own!
'Song links her children with a golden thread,
'To aid the living bard strides forth the dead.
'Hark the frank music of the elder age—
'Ben Jonson's giant tread sounds ringing up the stage!
'Hail! the large shapes our fathers loved! again
'Wellbred 's light ease, and Kitely's jealous pain.
'Cob shall have sense, and Stephen be polite,
'Brainworm shall preach, and Bobadil shall fight—
'Each, here, a merit not his own shall find,
'And *Every Man* the *Humour* to be kind.'

LONDON: 1847.

But though the married members of the company who took their wives defrayed that part of the cost, and every one who acted paid three pounds ten to the benefit-fund for his hotel charges, the expenses were necessarily so great that the profit was reduced to four hundred guineas, and, handsomely as this realised the design, expectations had been raised to five hundred. There was just that shade of disappointment, therefore, when, shortly after we came back and Dickens had returned to Broadstairs, I was startled by a letter from him. On the 3rd of August he had written: 'All well. Children' (who had been going through whooping cough) 'immensely 'improved. Business arising out of the late blaze of 'triumph, worse than ever.' Then came what startled me, the very next day. As if his business were not enough, it had occurred to him that he might add the much longed-for hundred pounds to the benefit-fund by a little jeu d'esprit in form of a history of the trip, to be published with illustrations from the artists; and his notion was to write it in the character of Mrs. Gamp. It was to be, in the phraseology of that notorious woman, a new 'Piljians Projiss;" and was to bear upon the title page its description as an Account of a late Expedition into the North, for an Amateur Theatrical Benefit, written by Mrs. Gamp (who was an eye-witness), Inscribed to Mrs. Harris, Edited by Charles Dickens, and published, with illustrations on wood by so and so, in aid of the Benefit-fund. 'What do you think of this idea for it? The 'argument would be, that Mrs. Gamp, being on the eve 'of an excursion to Margate as a relief from her profes-

At Broadstairs.

Appearance of Mrs. Gamp.

Fancy for a jeu d'esprit.

BROADSTAIRS: 1847.

'sional fatigues, comes to the knowledge of the intended 'excursion of our party; hears that several of the ladies 'concerned are in an interesting situation; and decides 'to accompany the party unbeknown, in a second-class 'carriage—"in case." There, she finds a gentleman from 'the Strand in a checked suit, who is going down with 'the wigs'—the theatrical hairdresser employed on these occasions, Mr. Wilson, had eccentric points of character that were a fund of infinite mirth to Dickens—'and to 'his politeness Mrs. Gamp is indebted for much support 'and countenance during the excursion. She will describe 'the whole thing in her own manner: sitting, in each 'place of performance, in the orchestra, next the gentle- 'man who plays the kettle-drums. She gives her critical 'opinion of Ben Jonson as a literary character, and refers 'to the different members of the party, in the course of 'her description of the trip: having always an invincible 'animosity towards Jerrold, for Caudle reasons. She ad- 'dresses herself, generally, to Mrs. Harris, to whom the 'book is dedicated,—but is discursive. Amount of matter, 'half a sheet of *Dombey:* may be a page or so more, 'but not less.' Alas! it never arrived at even that small size, but perished prematurely, as I feared it would, from failure of the artists to furnish needful nourishment. Of course it could not live alone. Without suitable illustration it must have lost its point and pleasantry. 'Mac 'will make a little garland of the ladies for the title- 'page. Egg and Stone will themselves originate some- 'thing fanciful, and I will settle with Cruikshank and 'Leech. I have no doubt the little thing will be droll

Mrs. Gamp at the play.

Artist-failure.

BROADSTAIRS: 1847.

Unfinished fancy.

'and attractive.' So it certainly would have been, if the Thanes of art had not fallen from him; but on their desertion it had to be abandoned after the first few pages were written. They were placed at my disposal then; and, though the little jest has lost much of its flavour now, I cannot find it in my heart to omit them here. There are so many friends of Mrs. Gamp who will rejoice at this unexpected visit from her!

'I. MRS. GAMP'S ACCOUNT OF HER CONNEXION WITH 'THIS AFFAIR.

Mrs. Gamp with the strollers.

'Which Mrs. Harris's own words to me, was these: '"Sairey Gamp," she says, "why not go to Margate? '"Srimps," says that dear creetur, "is to your liking, '"Sairey; why not go to Margate for a week, bring your '"constitootion up with srimps, and come back to them '"loving arts as knows and wallies of you, blooming? '"Sairey," Mrs. Harris says, "you are but poorly. Don't '"denige it, Mrs. Gamp, for books is in your looks. You '"must have rest. Your mind," she says, "is too strong '"for you; it gets you down and treads upon you, Sairey. '"It is useless to disguige the fact—the blade is a wear- '"ing out the sheets." "Mrs. Harris," I says to her, "I '"could not undertake to say, and I will not deceive you '"ma'am, that I am the woman I could wish to be. The '"time of worrit as I had with Mrs. Colliber, the baker's '"lady, which was so bad in her mind with her first, that '"she would not so much as look at bottled stout, and '"kept to gruel through the month, has agued me, Mrs. '"Harris. But ma'am," I says to her, "talk not of Mar-

Confidences with Mrs. Harris.

'"gate, for if I do go anywheres, it is elsewheres and not '"there." "Sairey," says Mrs. Harris, solemn, "whence '"this mystery? If I have ever deceived the hardest- '"working, soberest, and best of women, which her name '"is well beknown is S. Gamp Midwife Kingsgate Street '"High Holborn, mention it. If not," says Mrs. Harris, 'with the tears a standing in her eyes, "reweal your inten- '"tions." "Yes, Mrs. Harris," I says, "I will. Well I '"knows you Mrs. Harris; well you knows me; well we '"both knows wot the characters of one another is. Mrs. '"Harris then," I says, "I *have* heerd as there *is* a expedi- '"tion going down to Manjestir and Liverspool, a play- '"acting. If I goes anywheres for change, it is along with '"that." Mrs. Harris clasps her hands, and drops into a 'chair, as if her time was come—which I know'd it 'couldn't be, by rights, for six weeks odd. "And have I '"lived to hear," she says, "of Sairey Gamp, as always '"kept hersef respectable, in company with play-actors!" '"Mrs. Harris," I says to her, "be not alarmed—not '"reg'lar play-actors—hammertoors." "Thank Evans!" 'says Mrs. Harris, and bustiges into a flood of tears.

BROAD-STAIRS: 1847.

Mrs. Gamp with the strollers.

Alarm of Mrs. Harris.

'When the sweet creetur had compoged hersef (which 'a sip of brandy and water warm, and sugared pleasant, 'with a little nutmeg did it), I proceeds in these words. '"Mrs. Harris, I am told as these hammertoors are lit- '"ter'ry and artistickle." "Sairey," says that best of 'wimmin, with a shiver and a slight relasp, "go on, it '"might be worse." "I likewise hears," I says to her, '"that they're agoin play-acting, for the benefit of two '"litter'ry men; one as has had his wrongs a long time

Leigh Hunt and Poole.

BROADSTAIRS: 1847.

Mrs. Gamp with the strollers.

'"ago, and has got his rights at last, and one as has made '"a many people merry in his time, but is very dull and '"sick and lonely his own sef, indeed." "Sairey," says 'Mrs. Harris, "you're an Inglish woman, and that's no '"business of you'rn."

'"No, Mrs. Harris," I says, "that's very true; I hope I '"knows my dooty and my country. But," I says, "I am '"informed as there is Ladies in this party, and that half a '"dozen of 'em, if not more, is in various stages of a inte'"resting state. Mrs. Harris, you and me well knows what '"Ingeins often does. If I accompanies this expedition, '"unbeknown and second cladge, may I not combine my '"calling with change of air, and prove a service to my '"feller creeturs?" "Sairey," was Mrs. Harris's reply, '"you was born to be a blessing to your sex, and bring 'em '"through it. Good go with you! But keep your distance '"till called in, Lord bless you Mrs. Gamp; for people is '"known by the company they keeps, and litterary and '"artistickle society might be the ruin of you before you '"was aware, with your best customers, both sick and '"monthly, if they took a pride in themselves."

Ticklish society.

'II. MRS. GAMP IS DESCRIPTIVE.

'The number of the cab had a seven in it I think, and 'a ought I know—and if this should meet his eye (which 'it was a black 'un, new done, that he saw with; the other 'was tied up), I give him warning that he'd better take 'that umbereller and patten to the Hackney-coach Office 'before he repents it. He was a young man in a weskit 'with sleeves to it and strings behind, and needn't flatter

Mrs. Gamp's cabman.

'himsef with a suppogition of escape, as I gave this de- 'scription of him to the Police the moment I found he had 'drove off with my property; and if he thinks there an't 'laws enough he's much mistook—I tell him that.

BROAD-STAIRS: 1847.

Mrs. Gamp with the strollers.

'I do assure you, Mrs. Harris, when I stood in the rail- 'ways office that morning with my bundle on my arm and 'one patten in my hand, you might have knocked me down 'with a feather, far less porkmangers which was a lumping 'against me, continual and sewere all round. I was drove 'about like a brute animal and almost worritted into fits, 'when a gentleman with a large shirt-collar and a hook 'nose, and a eye like one of Mr. Sweedlepipes's hawks, and 'long locks of hair, and wiskers that I wouldn't have no 'lady as I was engaged to meet suddenly a turning round 'a corner, for any sum of money you could offer me, says, 'laughing, "Halloa, Mrs. Gamp, what are *you* up to!" I 'didn't know him from a man (except by his clothes); but 'I says faintly, "If you're a Christian man, show me where '"to get a second-cladge ticket for Manjester, and have me '"put in a carriage, or I shall drop!" Which he kindly 'did, in a cheerful kind of a way, skipping about in the 'strangest manner as ever I see, making all kinds of actions, 'and looking and vinking at me from under the brim of 'his hat (which was a good deal turned up), to that extent, 'that I should have thought he meant something but for 'being so flurried as not to have no thoughts at all until I 'was put in a carriage along with a individgle—the politest 'as ever I see—in a shepherd's plaid suit with a long gold 'watch-guard hanging round his neck, and his hand a 'trembling through nervousness worse than a aspian leaf.

George Cruik-shank.

Mr. Wilson the hair-dresser.

BROAD-STAIRS: 1847.

Mrs. Gamp with the strollers.

'"I'm wery appy, ma'am," he says—the politest vice as 'ever I heerd!—"to go down with a lady belonging to our '"party."

'"Our party, sir!" I says.

'"Yes, ma'am," he says, "I'm Mr. Wilson. I'm going '"down with the wigs."

'Mrs. Harris, wen he said he was agoing down with the 'wigs, such was my state of confugion and worrit that I 'thought he must be connected with the Government in 'some ways or another, but directly moment he explains 'himsef, for he says:

'"There's not a theatre in London worth mentioning '"that I don't attend punctually. There's five-and-twenty '"wigs in these boxes, ma'am," he says, a pinting towards 'a heap of luggage, "as was worn at the Queen's Fancy '"Ball. There's a black wig, ma'am," he says, "as was '"worn by Garrick; there's a red one, ma'am," he says, '"as was worn by Kean; there's a brown one, ma'am," 'he says, "as was worn by Kemble; there's a yellow one, '"ma'am," he says, "as was made for Cooke; there's a '"grey one, ma'am," he says, "as I measured Mr. Young for, '"mysef; and there's a white one, ma'am, that Mr. Macready '"went mad in. There's a flaxen one as was got up express '"for Jenny Lind the night she came out at the Italian '"Opera. It was very much applauded was that wig, '"ma'am, through the evening. It had a great reception. '"The audience broke out, the moment they see it."

Wig experiences.

'"Are you in Mr. Sweedlepipes's line, sir?" I says.

In the Sweedlepipes line.

'"Which is that, ma'am?" he says—the softest and 'genteelest vice I ever heerd, I do declare, Mrs. Harris!

'"Hair-dressing," I says.

'"Yes, ma'am," he replies, "I have that honour. Do '"you see this, ma'am?" he says, holding up his right 'hand.

BROAD-STAIRS: 1847.

Mrs. Gamp with the strollers.

'"I never see such a trembling," I says to him. And I 'never did!

'"All along of Her Majesty's Costume Ball, ma'am," he 'says. "The excitement did it. Two hundred and fifty-'"seven ladies of the first rank and fashion had their heads '"got up on that occasion by this hand, and my t'other '"one. I was at it eight-and-forty hours on my feet, '"ma'am, without rest. It was a Powder ball, ma'am. '"We have a Powder piece at Liverpool. Have I not the '"pleasure," he says, looking at me curious, "of addressing '"Mrs. Gamp?"

Fatigues of a powder ball.

'"Gamp I am, sir," I replies. "Both by name and '"natur."

'"Would you like to see your beeograffer's moustache '"and wiskers, ma'am?" he says. "I've got 'em in this '"box."

C. D.'s moustache and whiskers.

'"Drat my beeograffer, sir," I says, "he has given me '"no region to wish to know anythink about him."

'"Oh, Missus Gamp, I ask your parden"—I never see 'such a polite man, Mrs. Harris! "P'raps," he says, "if '"you're not of the party, you don't know who it was that '"assisted you into this carriage!"

'"No, Sir," I says, "I don't, indeed."

'"Why, ma'am," he says, a wisperin', "that was George, '"ma'am."

The great George.

'"What George, sir? I don't know no George," says I.

BROADSTAIRS: 1847.

'"The great George, ma'am," says he. "The Crook-'"shanks."

Mrs. Gamp with the strollers.

'If you'll believe me, Mrs. Harris, I turns my head, 'and see the wery man a making picturs of me on his 'thumb nail, at the winder! while another of 'em—a 'tall, slim, melancolly gent, with dark hair and a bage 'vice—looks over his shoulder, with his head o' one side 'as if he understood the subject, and cooly says, "*I*'ve '"draw'd her several times—in Punch," he says too! 'The owdacious wretch!

John Leech.

'"Which I never touches, Mr. Wilson," I remarks out 'loud—I couldn't have helped it, Mrs. Harris, if you had 'took my life for it!—"which I never touches, Mr. Wilson, '"on account of the lemon!"

'"Hush!" says Mr. Wilson. "There he is!"

Mark Lemon.

'I only see a fat gentleman with curly black hair and 'a merry face, a standing on the platform rubbing his 'two hands over one another, as if he was washing of 'em, 'and shaking his head and shoulders wery much; and I 'was a wondering wot Mr. Wilson meant, wen he says, '"There's Dougladge, Mrs. Gamp!" he says. "There's '"him as wrote the life of Mrs. Caudle!"

Douglas Jerrold.

'Mrs. Harris, wen I see that little willain bodily before 'me, it give me such a turn that I was all in a tremble. 'If I hadn't lost my umbereller in the cab, I must have 'done him a injury with it! Oh the bragian little 'traitor! right among the ladies, Mrs. Harris; looking 'his wickedest and deceitfullest of eyes while he was a 'talking to 'em; laughing at his own jokes as loud as you 'please; holding his hat in one hand to cool his-sef, and

BROAD-STAIRS: 1847.

'tossing back his iron-grey mop of a head of hair with 'the other, as if it was so much shavings—there, Mrs. 'Harris, I see him, getting encouragement from the 'pretty delooded creeturs, which never know'd that sweet 'saint, Mrs. C, as I did, and being treated with as much 'confidence as if he'd never wiolated none of the domestic 'ties, and never showed up nothing! Oh the aggrawation 'of that Dougladge! Mrs. Harris, if I hadn't apologiged to 'Mr. Wilson, and put a little bottle to my lips which was 'in my pocket for the journey, and which it is very rare 'indeed I have about me, I could not have abared the 'sight of him—there, Mrs. Harris! I could not!—I must 'have tore him, or have give way and fainted.

Mrs. Gamp with the strollers.

Dislike of 'Doug-ladge.'

'While the bell was a ringing, and the luggage of the 'hammertoors in great confugion—all a litter'ry indeed—'was handled up, Mr. Wilson demeens his-sef politer than 'ever. "That," he says, "Mrs. Gamp," a pinting to a 'officer-looking gentleman, that a lady with a little basket 'was a taking care on, "is another of our party. He's a '"author too—continivally going up the walley of the '"Muses, Mrs. Gamp. There," he says, alluding to a fine 'looking, portly gentleman, with a face like a amiable full 'moon, and a short mild gent, with a pleasant smile, "is '"two more of our artists, Mrs. G, well beknowed at the '"Royal Academy, as sure as stones is stones, and eggs '"is eggs. This resolute gent," he says, "a coming along '"here as is aperrently going to take the railways by '"storm—him with the tight legs, and his weskit very much '"buttoned, and his mouth very much shut, and his coat a '"flying open, and his heels a giving it to the platform, is

Dudley Costello.

Frank Stone.

Augustus Egg.

J. F.

BROADSTAIRS: 1847.

Mrs. Gamp with the strollers.

C. D.

'"a cricket and beeograffer, and our principal tragegian." '"But who," says I, when the bell had left off, and the 'train had begun to move, "who, Mr. Wilson, is the wild '"gent in the prespiration, that's been a tearing up and '"down all this time with a great box of papers under his '"arm, a talking to everybody wery indistinct, and exciting '"of himself dreadful?" "Why?" says Mr. Wilson, 'with a smile. "Because, sir," I says, "he's being left '"behind." "Good God!" cries Mr. Wilson, turning pale 'and putting out his head, "it's *your* beeograffer—the '"Manager—and he has got the money, Mrs. Gamp!" 'Hous'ever, some one chucked him into the train and we 'went off. At the first shreek of the whistle, Mrs. Harris,

Only the engine!

'I turned white, for I had took notice of some of them 'dear creeturs as was the cause of my being in company, 'and I know'd the danger that—but Mr. Wilson, which is 'a married man, puts his hand on mine, and says, "Mrs. '"Gamp, calm yourself; it's only the Ingein."

Of those of the party with whom these humorous liberties were taken there are only two now living to complain of their friendly caricaturist, and Mr. Cruikshank will perhaps join me in a frank forgiveness not the less heartily for the kind words about himself that reached me from Broadstairs not many days after Mrs. Gamp. 'At Canterbury

Cruikshank's *Bottle*.

'yesterday' (2nd of September) 'I bought George Cruik'shank's *Bottle*. I think it very powerful indeed: the two 'last plates most admirable, except that the boy and girl 'in the very last are too young, and the girl more like 'a circus-phenomenon than that no-phenomenon she is 'intended to represent. I question, however, whether 'anybody else living could have done it so well. There 'is a woman in the last plate but one, garrulous about 'the murder, with a child in her arms, that is as good as 'Hogarth. Also, the man who is stooping down, looking 'at the body. The philosophy of the thing, as a great 'lesson, I think all wrong; because to be striking, and 'original too, the drinking should have begun in sorrow, 'or poverty, or ignorance—the three things in which, in 'its awful aspect, it *does* begin. The design would then 'have been a double-handed sword—but too "radical" for 'good old George, I suppose.'

BROADSTAIRS: 1847.

Profits of *Dombey*.

The same letter made mention of other matters of interest. His accounts for the first half-year of *Dombey* were so much in excess of what had been expected from the new publishing arrangements, that from this date all embarrassments connected with money were brought to a close. His future profits varied of course with his varying sales, but there was always enough, and savings were now to begin. 'The profits of the half-year are brilliant. 'Deducting the hundred pounds a month paid six times, 'I have still to receive two thousand two hundred and 'twenty pounds, which I think is tidy. Don't you? . . . 'Stone is still here, and I lamed his foot by walking him 'seventeen miles the day before yesterday; but otherwise 'he flourisheth. . . Why don't you bring down a carpet-'bag-full of books, and take possession of the drawing-'room all the morning? My opinion is that Goldsmith 'would die more easy by the seaside. Charley and Walley 'have been taken to school this morning in high spirits, 'and at London Bridge will be folded in the arms of

The time come for savings.

BROADSTAIRS: 1847.

Brother-in-law's appointment.

'Blimber. The Government is about to issue a Sanitary 'commission, and Lord John, I am right well pleased to 'say, has appointed Henry Austin secretary.' Mr. Austin, who afterwards held the same office under the Sanitary act, had married his youngest sister Letitia; and of his two youngest brothers I may add that Alfred, also a civil-engineer, became one of the sanitary inspectors, and that Augustus was now placed in a city employment by Mr. Thomas Chapman, which after a little time he surrendered, and then found his way to America.

Younger brothers.

The next Broadstairs letter (5th of September) resumed the subject of Goldsmith, whose life I was then bringing nearly to completion. 'Supposing your *Goldsmith* made 'a general sensation, what should you think of doing a 'cheap edition of his works? I have an idea that we 'might do some things of that sort with considerable effect. 'There is really no edition of the great British novelists 'in a handy nice form, and would it not be a likely move 'to do it with some attractive feature that could not be 'given to it by the Teggs and such people? Supposing 'one wrote an essay on Fielding for instance, and another 'on Smollett, and another on Sterne, recalling how one 'read them as a child (no one read them younger than I, 'I think), and how one gradually grew up into a different 'knowledge of them, and so forth—would it not be in'teresting to many people? I should like to know if you 'descry anything in this. It is one of the dim notions 'fluctuating within me.* . . The profits, brave indeed, are

Design for edition of old novelists.

Another dropped design.

* Another, which for many reasons we may regret went also into the limbo of unrealized designs, is sketched in the subjoined (7th of January,

'four hundred pounds more than the utmost I expected. . . 'The same yearnings have been mine, in reference to the 'Praslin business. It is pretty clear to me, for one thing, 'that the Duchess was one of the most uncomfortable 'women in the world, and that it would have been hard 'work for anybody to have got on with her. It is strange 'to see a bloody reflection of our friends Eugène Sue and 'Dumas in the whole melodrama. Don't you think so. . . 'remembering what we often said of the canker at the 'root of all that Paris life? I dreamed of you, in a wild 'manner, all last night. . . A sea fog here, which prevents 'one's seeing the low-water mark. A circus on the cliff to 'the right, and of course I have a box to-night! Deep 'slowness in the inimitable's brain. A shipwreck on the 'Goodwin sands last Sunday, which WALLY, with a hawk's 'eye, SAW GO DOWN: for which assertion, subsequently 'confirmed and proved, he was horribly maltreated at the 'time.'

BROADSTAIRS: 1847.

The Praslin tragedy in Paris.

Penalty for seeing before others.

Devonshire-terrace meanwhile had been left by his tenant; and coming up joyfully himself to take possession, he brought for completion in his old home an important chapter of *Dombey*. On the way he lost his portmanteau, but 'Thank God! the MS. of the chapter wasn't in it. 'Whenever I travel, and have anything of that valuable 'article, I always carry it in my pocket.'* He had begun

Loss of portmanteau.

1848). 'Mac and I think of going to Ireland for six weeks in the spring, 'and seeing whether anything is to be done there, in the way of a book? I 'fancy it might turn out well.' The Mac of course is Maclise.

* 'Here we are' (23rd of August) 'in the noble old premises; and very nice 'they look, all things considered . . . Trifles happen to me which occur to 'nobody else. My portmanteau "fell off" a cab last night somewhere between

BROADSTAIRS: 1847.

at this time to find difficulties in writing at Broadstairs, of which he told me on his return. 'Vagrant music is getting 'to that height here, and is so impossible to be escaped 'from, that I fear Broadstairs and I must part company 'in time to come. Unless it pours of rain, I cannot write 'half-an-hour without the most excruciating organs, fiddles, 'bells, or glee-singers. There is a violin of the most tor-'turing kind under the window now (time, ten in the 'morning) and an Italian box of music on the steps—both 'in full blast.' He closed with a mention of improvements in the Margate theatre since his memorable last visit. In the past two years it had been managed by a son of the great comedian, Dowton, with whose name it is pleasant to connect this note. 'We went to the manager's benefit 'on Wednesday' (10th of September): '*As You Like It* 'really very well done, and a most excellent house. Mr. 'Dowton delivered a sensible and modest kind of speech 'on the occasion, setting forth his conviction that a means 'of instruction and entertainment possessing such a liter-'ature as the stage in England, could not pass away; and, 'that what inspired great minds, and delighted great men, 'two thousand years ago, and did the same in Shakespeare's 'day, must have within itself a principle of life superior 'to the whim and fashion of the hour. And with that, 'and with cheers, he retired. He really seems a most 'respectable man, and he has cleared out this dust-hole of 'a theatre into something like decency.'

Street-music.

Margate Theatre.

Manager Dowton.

'London-bridge and here. It contained on a moderate calculation £70 worth 'of clothes. I have no shirt to put on, and am obliged to send out to a barber 'to come and shave me.'

He was to be in London at the end of the month: but I had from him meanwhile his preface * for his first completed book in the popular edition (*Pickwick* being now issued in that form, with an illustration by Leslie); and sending me shortly after (12th of Sept.) the first few slips of the story of the *Haunted Man* proposed for his next Christmas book, he told me he must finish it in less than a month if it was to be done at all, *Dombey* having now become very importunate. This prepared me for his letter of a week's later date. 'Have been at work all day, and 'am seedy in consequence. *Dombey* takes so much time, 'and requires to be so carefully done, that I really begin 'to have serious doubts whether it is wise to go on with 'the Christmas book. Your kind help is invoked. What 'do you think? Would there be any distinctly bad effect 'in holding this idea over for another twelvemonth? saying nothing whatever till November; and then announcing in the *Dombey* that its occupation of my entire time 'prevents the continuance of the Christmas series until 'next year, when it is proposed to be renewed. There 'might not be anything in that but a possibility of an 'extra lift for the little book when it did come—eh? On 'the other hand, I am very loath to lose the money. And 'still more so to leave any gap at Christmas firesides which 'I ought to fill. In short I am (forgive the expression)

BROADSTAIRS: 1847.

As to Christmas book.

Suggested delay.

* 'Do you see anything to object to in it? I have never had so much difficulty, I think, in setting about any slight thing; for I really didn't know 'that I had a word to say, and nothing seems to live 'twixt what *I have* said 'and silence. The advantage of it is, that the latter part opens an idea for 'future prefaces all through the series, and may serve perhaps to make a 'feature of them.' (7th of September, 1847.)

BROADSTAIRS: 1847.

A literary Kitely.

'BLOWED if I know what to do. I am a literary Kitely—'and you ought to sympathize and help. If I had no '*Dombey*, I could write and finish the story with the 'bloom on —— but there's the rub . . . Which unfamiliar 'quotation reminds me of a Shakspearian (put an e before 'the s; I like it much better) speculation of mine. What 'do you say to "take arms against a sea of troubles" 'having been originally written "make arms," which is 'the action of swimming. It would get rid of a horrible 'grievance in the figure, and make it plain and apt. I 'think of setting up a claim to live in The House at 'Stratford, rent-free, on the strength of this suggestion. 'You are not to suppose that I am anything but discon-'certed to-day, in the agitation of my soul concerning 'Christmas; but I have been brooding, like Dombey him-'self, over *Dombey* these two days, until I really can't 'afford to be depressed.' To his Shakespearian suggestion I replied that it would hardly give him the claim he thought of setting up, for that swimming through your troubles would not be 'opposing' them. And upon the other point I had no doubt of the wisdom of delay. The result was that the Christmas story was laid aside until the following year.

Emendation for *Hamlet*: of doubtful wisdom.

Public meetings.

The year's closing incidents were his chairmanship at a meeting of the Leeds Mechanics' Society on the 1st of December, and his opening of the Glasgow Athenæum on the 28th; where, to immense assemblages in both,* he

Leeds and Glasgow.

* From his notes on these matters I may quote. 'The Leeds appears to be 'a very important institution, and I am glad to see that George Stephenson will be there, besides the local lights, inclusive of all the Baineses. They

contrasted the obstinacy and cruelty of the Power of ignorance with the docility and gentleness of the Power of knowledge; pointed the use of popular institutes in supplementing what is learnt first in life, by the later education for its employments and equipment for its domesticities and virtues, which the grown person needs from day to day as much as the child its reading and writing; and he closed at Glasgow with allusion to a bazaar set on foot by the ladies of the city, under patronage of the Queen, for adding books to its Athenæum library. 'We never tire of the friendships we form with 'books,' he said, 'and here they will possess the added 'charm of association with their donors. Some neighbour-'ing Glasgow widow will be mistaken for that remoter 'one whom Sir Roger de Coverley could not forget; 'Sophia's muff will be seen and loved, by another than 'Tom Jones, going down the High-street some winter 'day; and the grateful students of a library thus filled 'will be apt, as to the fair ones who have helped to people 'it, to couple them in their thoughts with Principles of 'the Population and Additions to the History of Europe, 'by an author of older date than Sheriff Alison.' At which no one laughed so loudly as the Sheriff himself, who had cordially received Dickens as his guest, and stood with him on the platform.

LEEDS AND GLASGOW: 1847.

Book-friends.

Sheriff Alison.

'talk at Glasgow of 6,000 people.' (26th of November.) 'You have got 'Southey's *Holly Tree*. I have not. Put it in your pocket to-day. It occurs 'to me (up to the eyes in a mass of Glasgow Athenæum papers) that I could 'quote it with good effect in the North.' (24th of December.) 'A most bril-'liant demonstration last night, and I think I never did better. Newspaper 'reports bad.' (29th of December.)

EDINBURGH: 1847-48.

On the last day but one of the old year he wrote to me from Edinburgh. 'We came over this afternoon, leaving 'Glasgow at one o'clock. Alison lives in style in a hand- 'some country house out of Glasgow, and is a capital 'fellow, with an agreeable wife, nice little daughter, 'cheerful niece, all things pleasant in his household. I 'went over the prison and lunatic asylum with him 'yesterday;* at the Lord Provost's had gorgeous state- 'lunch with the Town Council; and was entertained 'at a great dinner-party at night. Unbounded hospi- 'tality and enthoozymoozy the order of the day, and I 'have never been more heartily received anywhere, or 'enjoyed myself more completely. The great chemist, 'Gregory, who spoke at the meeting, returned with us 'to Edinburgh to-day, and gave me many new lights on 'the road regarding the extraordinary pains Macaulay 'seems for years to have taken to make himself disagree- 'able and disliked here. No one else, on that side, would 'have had the remotest chance of being unseated at the 'last election; and, though Gregory voted for him, I 'thought he seemed quite as well pleased as anybody else 'that he didn't come in . . . I am sorry to report the 'Scott Monument a failure. It is like the spire of a 'Gothic church taken off and stuck in the ground.' On the first day of 1848, still in Edinburgh, he wrote again: 'Jeffrey, who is obliged to hold a kind of morning court 'in his own study during the holidays, came up yester-

Stays with Alison.

Friendly reception.

Scott-monument.

* 'Tremendous distress at Glasgow, and a truly damnable jail, exhibiting 'the separate system in a most absurd and hideous form. Governor practical 'and intelligent; very anxious for the associated silent system; and much 'comforted by my fault-finding. (30th of December.)

'day in great consternation, to tell me that a person had 'just been to make and sign a declaration of bankruptcy; 'and that on looking at the signature he saw it was 'James Sheridan Knowles. He immediately sent after, 'and spoke with him; and of what passed I am eager to 'talk with you.' The talk will bring back the main subject of this chapter, from which another kind of strolling has led me away; for its results were other amateur performances, of which the object was to benefit Knowles.

LONDON: 1848.

Jeffrey and Knowles.

This was the year when a committee had been formed for the purchase and preservation of Shakespeare's house at Stratford, and the performances in question took the form of contributions to the endowment of a curatorship to be held by the author of *Virginius* and the *Hunchback*. The endowment was abandoned upon the town and council of Stratford finally (and very properly) taking charge of the house; but the sum realised was not withdrawn from the object really desired, and one of the finest of dramatists profited yet more largely by it than Leigh Hunt did by the former enterprise. It may be proper to remark also, that, like Leigh Hunt, Knowles received soon after, through Lord John Russell, the same liberal pension; and that smaller claims to which attention had been similarly drawn were not forgotten, Mr. Poole, after much kind help from the Bounty Fund, being in 1850 placed on the Civil List for half the amount by the same minister and friend of letters.

Purchase of Shakespeare's house.

Scheme to benefit Knowles.

Civil-list pensions.

Dickens threw himself into the new scheme with all his old energy*; and prefatory mention may be made of

* It would amuse the reader, but occupy too much space, to add to my former illustrations of his managerial troubles; but from an elaborate paper

London: 1848.

our difficulty in selection of a suitable play to alternate with our old Ben Jonson. The *Alchemist* had been such a favourite with some of us, that, before finally laying it aside, we went through two or three rehearsals, in which I recollect thinking Dickens's Sir Epicure Mammon as good as anything he had done; and now the same trouble, with the same result, arising from a vain desire to please everybody, was taken successively with Beaumont and Fletcher's *Beggar's Bush*, and Goldsmith's *Good Natured Man*, with Jerrold's characteristic drama of the *Rent Day*, and Bulwer's masterly comedy of *Money*. Choice was at last made of Shakespeare's *Merry Wives*, in which Lemon played Falstaff, I took again the jealous husband as in Jonson's play, and Dickens was Justice Shallow; to which was added a farce, *Love, Law, and Physick*, in which Dickens took the part he had acted long ago, before his

Plays rehearsed.

*Merry Wives* chosen.

*Ante*, i. 394.

C. D.'s instructions for rehearsals.

of rules for rehearsals, which I have found in his handwriting, I quote the opening and the close. 'Remembering the very imperfect condition of all 'our plays at present, the general expectation in reference to them, the kind 'of audience before which they will be presented, and the near approach of 'the nights of performance, I hope everybody concerned will abide by the 'following regulations, and will aid in strictly carrying them out.' Elaborate are the regulations set forth, but I take only the three last. 'Silence, on 'the stage and in the theatre, to be faithfully observed; the lobbies &c. 'being always available for conversation. No book to be referred to on the 'stage; but those who are imperfect to take their words from the prompter. 'Everyone to act, as nearly as possible, as on the night of performance; every-'one to speak out, so as to be audible through the house. And every mistake 'of exit, entrance, or situation, to be corrected *three times* successively.' He closes thus. 'All who were concerned in the first getting up of *Every Man in* '*his Humour*, and remember how carefully the stage was always kept then, 'and who have been engaged in the late rehearsals of the *Merry Wives*, and 'have experienced the difficulty of getting on, or off: of being heard, or of 'hearing anybody else: will, I am sure, acknowledge the indispensable neces-'sity of these regulations.

LONDON: 1848-50.

days of authorship; and, besides the professional actresses engaged, we had for our Dame Quickly the lady to whom the world owes incomparably the best *Concordance* to Shakespeare that has ever been published, Mrs. Cowden Clarke. The success was undoubtedly very great. At Manchester, Liverpool, and Edinburgh there were single representations; but Birmingham and Glasgow had each two nights, and two were given at the Haymarket, on one of which the Queen and Prince were present. The gross receipts from the nine performances, before the necessary large deductions for London and local charges, were two thousand five hundred and fifty-one pounds and eight-pence.* The first representation was in London on the 15th of April, the last in Glasgow on the 20th of July, and everywhere Dickens was the leading figure. In the enjoyment as in the labour he was first. His animal spirits, unresting and supreme, were the attraction of rehearsal at morning, and of the stage at night. At the quiet early dinner, and the more jovial unrestrained supper, where all engaged were assembled daily, his was the brightest face, the lightest step, the pleasantest word. There seemed to be no rest needed for that wonderful vitality.

Performances.

My allusion to the last of these splendid strollings in aid of what we believed to be the interests of men of letters, shall be as brief as I can make it. Two winters after the present, at the close of November 1850, in the great hall of Lord Lytton's old family mansion in Kneb-

At Knebworth.

* I give the sums taken at the several theatres. Haymarket, £319 14*s.*; Manchester, £266 12*s.* 6*d.*; Liverpool, £467 6*s.* 6*d.*; Birmingham, £327 10*s.*, and £262 18*s.* 6*d.*; Edinburgh, £325 1*s.* 6*d.*; Glasgow, £471 7*s.* 8*d.*, and (at half the prices of the first night) £210 10*s.*

LONDON: 1848-50.

worth-park, there were three private performances by the original actors in Ben Jonson's *Every Man in His Humour.* All the circumstances and surroundings were very brilliant; some of the gentlemen of the county played both in the comedy and farces; our generous host was profuse of all noble encouragement; and amid the general pleasure and excitement hopes rose high. Recent experience had shown what the public interest in this kind of amusement might place within reach of its providers; and there came to be discussed the possibility of making permanent such help as had been afforded to fellow writers, by means of an endowment that should not be mere charity, but should combine indeed something of both pension-list and college-lectureship, without the drawbacks of either. It was not enough considered that schemes for self-help, to be successful, require from those they are meant to benefit, not only a general assent to their desirability, but zealous and active co-operation. Without discussing now, however, what will have to be stated hereafter, it suffices to say that the enterprise was set on foot, and the 'Guild of 'Literature and Art' originated at Knebworth. A five-act comedy was to be written by Sir Edward Lytton, and, when a certain sum of money had been obtained by public representations of it, the details of the scheme were to be drawn up, and appeal made to those whom it addressed more especially. In a very few months everything was ready, except a farce which Dickens was to have written to follow the comedy, and which unexpected cares of management and preparation were held to absolve him from. There

Origin of Guild of Literature and Art.

A thing lost sight of.

Prepara-tions for Guild.

LONDON: 1850.

were other reasons. 'I have written the first scene,' he told me (23rd March, 1851), 'and it has droll points in it, ' "more farcical points than you commonly find in farces,"* 'really better. Yet I am constantly striving, for my repu- 'tation's sake, to get into it a meaning that is impossible 'in a farce; constantly thinking of it, therefore, against the 'grain; and constantly impressed with a conviction that 'I could never act in it myself with that wild abandon- 'ment which can alone carry a farce off. Wherefore I 'have confessed to Bulwer Lytton and asked for absolu- 'tion.' There was substituted a new farce of Lemon's, to which, however, Dickens soon contributed so many jokes and so much Gampish and other fun of his own, that it came to be in effect a joint piece of authorship; and Gabblewig, which the manager took to himself, was one of those personation parts requiring five or six changes of face, voice, and gait in the course of it, from which, as we have seen, he derived all the early theatrical ambition that the elder Mathews had awakened in him. 'You have no 'idea,' he continued, 'of the immensity of the work as the 'time advances, for the Duke even throws the whole of 'the audience on us, or he would get (he says) into all 'manner of scrapes.' The Duke of Devonshire had offered his house in Piccadilly for the first representations, and in his princely way discharged all the expenses attending them. A moveable theatre was built and set up in the

C. D.'s farce not written.

The farce substituted.

Princely help.

* 'Those Rabbits have more nature in them than you commonly find in 'Rabbits'—the self-commendatory remark of an aspiring animal-painter showing his piece to the most distinguished master in that line—was here in my friend's mind.

LONDON AND PROVINCES: 1851-52.

great drawing-room, and the library was turned into a green-room.

Performance of Bulwer Lytton's comedy.

*Not so Bad as We Seem* was played for the first time at Devonshire-house on the 27th of May, 1851, before the Queen and Prince and as large an audience as places could be found for; *Mr. Nightingale's Diary* being the name given to the farce. The success abundantly realised the expectations formed; and, after many representations at the Hanover-square Rooms in London, strolling began in the country, and was continued at intervals for considerable portions of this and the following year. From much of it, illness and occupation disabled me, and substitutes had to be found; but to this I owe the opportunity now of closing with a characteristic picture of the course of the play, and of Dickens amid the incidents and accidents to which his theatrical career exposed him. The company carried with them, it should be said, the theatre constructed for Devonshire-house, as well as the admirable scenes which Stanfield, David Roberts, Thomas Grieve, Telbin, Absolon, and Louis Haghe had painted as their generous free-offerings to the comedy; of which the representations were thus rendered irrespective of theatres or their managers, and took place in the large halls or concert-rooms of the various towns and cities.

Travelling theatre and scenes.

SUNDERLAND.

'The enclosure forgotten in my last' (Dickens writes from Sunderland on the 29th of August 1852), 'was a little 'printed announcement which I have had distributed at 'the doors wherever we go, knocking *Two o'Clock in the 'Morning* bang out of the bills. Funny as it used to 'be, it is become impossible to get anything out of it after 'the scream of *Mr. Nightingale's Diary.* The comedy is 'so far improved by the reductions which your absence 'and other causes have imposed on us, that it acts now 'only two hours and twenty-five minutes, all waits included, 'and goes "like wildfire," as Mr. Tonson* says. We have 'had prodigious houses, though smaller rooms (as to their 'actual size) than I had hoped for. The Duke was at Derby, 'and no end of minor radiances. Into the room at New-'castle (where Lord Carlisle was by the bye) they squeezed 'six hundred people, at twelve and sixpence, into a space 'reasonably capable of holding three hundred. Last night, 'in a hall built like a theatre, with pit, boxes, and gallery, 'we had about twelve hundred—I dare say more. They 'began with a round of applause when Coote's white 'waistcoat appeared in the orchestra, and wound up the 'farce with three deafening cheers. I never saw such 'good fellows. Stanny is their fellow-townsman; was 'born here; and they applauded his scene as if it were 'himself. But what I suffered from a dreadful anxiety 'that hung over me all the time, I can never describe. 'When we got here at noon, it appeared that the hall 'was a perfectly new one, and had only had the slates put 'upon the roof by torchlight over night. Farther, that 'the proprietors of some opposition rooms had declared the 'building to be unsafe, and that there was a panic in the

SUNDERLAND: 1852.

Success of comedy and farce.

At DERBY and NEWCASTLE.

At SUNDERLAND.

Stanfield's fellow-townsmen.

Apprehensions.

* Mr. Tonson was a small part in the comedy entrusted with much appropriateness to Mr. Charles Knight, whose *Autobiography* has this allusion to the first performance, which, as Mr. Pepys says, is 'pretty to observe.' 'The 'actors and the audience were so close together that as Mr. Jacob Tonson sat 'in Wills's Coffee-house he could have touched with his clouded cane the 'Duke of Wellington.' (iii. 116.)

SUNDERLAND: 1852.

'town about it; people having had their money back, and 'being undecided whether to come or not, and all kinds of 'such horrors. I didn't know what to do. The horrible 'responsibility of risking an accident of that awful nature 'seemed to rest wholly upon me; for I had only to say we 'wouldn't act, and there would be no chance of danger. 'I was afraid to take Sloman into council lest the panic 'should infect our men. I asked W. what *he* thought, 'and he consolingly observed that his digestion was so 'bad that death had no terrors for him! I went and 'looked at the place; at the rafters, walls, pillars, and so 'forth; and fretted myself into a belief that they really 'were slight! To crown all, there was an arched iron 'roof without any brackets or pillars, on a new principle! 'The only comfort I had was in stumbling at length on the 'builder, and finding him a plain practical north-country-'man with a foot rule in his pocket. I took him aside, and 'asked him should we, or could we, prop up any weak part 'of the place: especially the dressing-rooms, which were 'under our stage, the weight of which must be heavy on 'a new floor, and dripping wet walls. He told me there 'wasn't a stronger building in the world; and that, to allay 'the apprehension, they had opened it, on Thursday night, 'to thousands of the working people, and induced them to 'sing, and beat with their feet, and make every possible 'trial of the vibration. Accordingly there was nothing 'for it but to go on. I was in such dread, however, lest a 'false alarm should spring up among the audience and 'occasion a rush, that I kept Catherine and Georgina out 'of the front. When the curtain went up and I saw the

Consoling remark.

Troubles of a manager.

SUNDERLAND: 1852.

Acting under difficulties.

'great sea of faces rolling up to the roof, I looked here 'and looked there, and thought I saw the gallery out of 'the perpendicular, and fancied the lights in the ceiling 'were not straight. Rounds of applause were perfect 'agony to me, I was so afraid of their effect upon the 'building. I was ready all night to rush on in case of an 'alarm—a false alarm was my main dread—and implore 'the people for God's sake to sit still. I had our great 'farce-bell rung to startle Sir Geoffrey instead of throwing 'down a piece of wood, which might have raised a sudden 'apprehension. I had a palpitation of the heart, if any of 'our people stumbled up or down a stair. I am sure I 'never acted better, but the anxiety of my mind was so 'intense, and the relief at last so great, that I am half-'dead to-day, and have not yet been able to eat or drink 'anything or to stir out of my room. I shall never forget 'it. As to the short time we had for getting the theatre 'up; as to the upsetting, by a runaway pair of horses, of 'one of the vans at the Newcastle railway station *with all 'the scenery in it, every atom of which was turned over;* 'as to the fatigue of our carpenters, who have now been 'up four nights, and who were lying dead asleep in the en-'trances last night; I say nothing, after the other gigantic 'nightmare, except that Sloman's splendid knowledge of 'his business, and the good temper and cheerfulness of all 'the workmen, are capital. I mean to give them a supper 'at Liverpool, and address them in a neat and appropriate 'speech. We dine at two to-day (it is now one) and go 'to Sheffield at four, arriving there at about ten. I had 'been as fresh as a daisy; walked from Nottingham to

Scenery overturned.

SUNDERLAND: 1852.

'Derby, and from Newcastle here; but seem to have had 'my nerves crumpled up last night, and have an excru- 'ciating headache. That's all at present. I shall never 'be able to bear the smell of new deal and fresh mortar 'again as long as I live.'

Effects of fright.

Manchester and Liverpool closed the trip with enormous success at both places; and Sir Edward Lytton was present at a public dinner which was given in the former city, Dickens's brief word about it being written as he was setting foot in the train that was to bring him to London.

Dinner at Manchester.

'Bulwer spoke brilliantly at the Manchester dinner, and 'his earnestness and determination about the Guild was 'most impressive. It carried everything before it. They 'are now getting up annual subscriptions, and will give 'us a revenue to begin with. I swear I believe that 'people to be the greatest in the world. At Liverpool I 'had a Round Robin on the stage after the play was over, 'a place being left for your signature, and as I am going 'to have it framed, I'll tell Green to send it to Lincoln's- 'inn-fields. You have no idea how good Tenniel, Topham, 'and Collins have been in what they had to do.'

A round robin.

These names, distinguished in art and letters, represent additions to the company who had joined the enterprise; and the last of them, Mr. Wilkie Collins, became, for all the rest of the life of Dickens, one of his dearest and most valued friends.

Mr. Wilkie Collins.

# CHAPTER XVIII.

## SEASIDE HOLIDAYS.

### 1848—1851.

THE portion of Dickens's life over which his adventures of strolling extended was in other respects not without interest; and this chapter will deal with some of his seaside holidays before I pass to the publication in 1848 of the story of *The Haunted Man*, and to the establishment in 1850 of the Periodical which had been in his thoughts for half a dozen years before, and has had foreshadowings nearly as frequent in my pages.

LONDON: 1848.

Among the incidents of 1848 before the holiday season came, were the dethronement of Louis Philippe, and birth of the second French republic: on which I ventured to predict that a Gore-house friend of ours, and *his* friend, would in three days be on the scene of action. The three days passed, and I had this letter. 'Mardi, Février 29, '1848. MON CHER. Vous êtes homme de la plus grande 'pénétration! Ah, mon Dieu, que vous êtes absolument 'magnifique! Vous prévoyez presque toutes les choses 'qui vont arriver; et aux choses qui viennent d'arriver 'vous êtes merveilleusement au-fait. Ah, cher enfant, 'quelle idée sublime vous vous aviez à la tête quand vous

Louis Philippe dethroned.

Letter from C. D.

LONDON: 1848.

French missive from C. D.

'prévîtes si clairement que M. le Comte Alfred d'Orsay 'se rendrait au pays de sa naissance! Quel magicien! 'Mais—c'est tout égal, mais—il n'est pas parti. Il reste 'à Gore-house, où, avant-hier, il y avait un grand diner à 'tout le monde. Mais quel homme, quel ange, néan-'moins! MON AMI, je trouve que j'aime tant la Répu-'blique, qu'il me faut renoncer ma langue et écrire seule-'ment le langage de la République de France—langage des 'Dieux et des Anges—langage, en un mot, des Français! 'Hier au soir je rencontrai à l'Athenæum Monsieur Mack 'Leese, qui me dit que MM. les Commissionnaires des Beaux 'Arts lui avaient écrit, par leur secrétaire, un billet de 'remerciements à propos de son tableau dans la Chambre 'des Députés, et qu'ils lui avaient prié de faire l'autre 'tableau en fresque, dont on y a besoin. Ce qu'il a 'promis. Voici des nouvelles pour les champs de Lincoln's 'Inn! Vive la gloire de France! Vive la République! 'Vive le Peuple! Plus de Royauté! Plus des Bourbons! 'Plus de Guizot! Mort aux traîtres! Faisons couler 'le sang pour la liberté, la justice, la cause populaire! 'Jusqu'à cinq heures et demie, adieu, mon brave! Recevez 'l'assurance de ma considération distinguée, et croyez-'moi, CONCITOYEN! votre tout dévoué, CITOYEN CHARLES 'DICKENS.' I proved to be not quite so wrong, neverthe-less, as my friend supposed.

Aspirations of Citizen Dickens.

At BROADSTAIRS.

Somewhat earlier than usual this summer, on the close of the Shakespeare-house performances, he tried Broad-stairs once more, having no important writing in hand: but in the brief interval before leaving he saw a thing of celebrity in those days, the Chinese Junk; and I had all the details in so good a description that I could not resist the temptation of using some parts of it at the time. 'Drive 'down to the Blackwall railway,' he wrote to me, 'and for 'a matter of eighteenpence you are at the Chinese Empire 'in no time. In half a score of minutes, the tiles and 'chimney-pots, backs of squalid houses, frowsy pieces of 'waste ground, narrow courts and streets, swamps, ditches, 'masts of ships, gardens of dockweed, and unwholesome 'little bowers of scarlet beans, whirl away in a flying 'dream, and nothing is left but China. How the flowery 'region ever came into this latitude and longitude is 'the first thing one asks; and it is not certainly the least 'of the marvel. As Aladdin's palace was transported 'hither and thither by the rubbing of a lamp, so the crew 'of Chinamen aboard the Keying devoutly believed that 'their good ship would turn up, quite safe, at the desired 'port, if they only tied red rags enough upon the mast, 'rudder, and cable. Somehow they did not succeed. 'Perhaps they ran short of rag; at any rate they hadn't 'enough on board to keep them above water; and to the 'bottom they would undoubtedly have gone but for the 'skill and coolness of a dozen English sailors, who brought 'them over the ocean in safety. Well, if there be any 'one thing in the world that this extraordinary craft is 'not at all like, that thing is a ship of any kind. So 'narrow, so long, so grotesque; so low in the middle, so 'high at each end, like a China pen-tray; with no 'rigging, with nowhere to go to aloft; with mats for sails, 'great warped cigars for masts, gaudy dragons and sea-'monsters disporting themselves from stem to stern, and

BROADSTAIRS: 1848.

By rail to China.

The Junk.

How it came over.

What it was like.

BROAD-STAIRS: 1848.

Chinese Junk.

'*on* the stern a gigantic cock of impossible aspect, defying 'the world (as well he may) to produce his equal,—it 'would look more at home at the top of a public building, 'or at the top of a mountain, or in an avenue of trees, or 'down in a mine, than afloat on the water. As for the 'Chinese lounging on the deck, the most extravagant 'imagination would never dare to suppose them to be

Mariners on deck.

'mariners. Imagine a ship's crew, without a profile 'among them, in gauze pinafores and plaited hair; wear-'ing stiff clogs a quarter of a foot thick in the sole; and 'lying at night in little scented boxes, like backgammon 'men or chess-pieces, or mother-of-pearl counters! But 'by Jove! even this is nothing to your surprise when you

In the cabin.

'go down into the cabin. There you get into a torture of 'perplexity. As, what became of all those lanterns hang-'ing to the roof when the Junk was out at sea? Whether 'they dangled there, banging and beating against each 'other, like so many jesters' baubles? Whether the idol 'Chin Tee, of the eighteen arms, enshrined in a celestial 'Punch's Show, in the place of honour, ever tumbled out 'in heavy weather? Whether the incense and the joss-'stick still burnt before her, with a faint perfume and 'a little thread of smoke, while the mighty waves were 'roaring all around? Whether that preposterous tissue-'paper umbrella in the corner was always spread, as being 'a convenient maritime instrument for walking about the

Perplexing questions.

'decks with in a storm? Whether all the cool and shiny 'little chairs and tables were continually sliding about 'and bruising each other, and if not why not? Whether 'anybody on the voyage ever read those two books printed 'in characters like bird-cages and fly-traps? Whether 'the Mandarin passenger, He Sing, who had never been 'ten miles from home in his life before, lying sick on a 'bamboo couch in a private china closet of his own (where 'he is now perpetually writing autographs for inquisitive 'barbarians), ever began to doubt the potency of the 'Goddess of the Sea, whose counterfeit presentment, like 'a flowery monthly nurse, occupies the sailors' joss-house 'in the second gallery? Whether it is possible that the 'said Mandarin, or the artist of the ship, Sam Sing, 'Esquire, R.A. of Canton, *can* ever go ashore without a 'walking-staff of cinnamon, agreeably to the usage of their 'likenesses in British tea-shops? Above all, whether the 'hoarse old ocean could ever have been seriously in earnest 'with this floating toy-shop; or had merely played with it 'in lightness of spirit—roughly, but meaning no harm—'as the bull did with another kind of china-shop on St. 'Patrick's day in the morning.'

BROAD-STAIRS: 1848.

Chinese Junk.

A toy-shop on the seas.

The reply made on this brought back comment and sequel not less amusing. 'Yes, there can be no question 'that this is Finality in perfection; and it is a great ad-'vantage to have the doctrine so beautifully worked out, 'and shut up in a corner of a dock near a fashionable 'white-bait house for the edification of man. Thousands 'of years have passed away since the first junk was built 'on this model, and the last junk ever launched was no 'better for that waste and desert of time. The mimic 'eye painted on their prows to assist them in finding their 'way, has opened as wide and seen as far as any actual 'organ of sight in all the interval through the whole

Type of Finality.

BROADSTAIRS: 1848.

Chinese Junk.

'immense extent of that strange country. It has been set 'in the flowery head to as little purpose for thousands of 'years. With all their patient and ingenious but never 'advancing art, and with all their rich and diligent agri-'cultural cultivation, not a new twist or curve has been 'given to a ball of ivory, and not a blade of experience 'has been grown. There is a genuine finality in that; and 'when one comes from behind the wooden screen that en-'closes the curious sight, to look again upon the river and 'the mighty signs on its banks of life, enterprise, and pro-'gress, the question that comes nearest is beyond doubt 'a home one. Whether *we* ever by any chance, in storms, 'trust to red rags; or burn joss-sticks before idols; or grope 'our way by the help of conventional eyes that have no 'sight in them; or sacrifice substantial facts for absurd 'forms? The ignorant crew of the Keying refused to 'enter on the ships' books, until "a considerable amount '"of silvered-paper, tin-foil, and joss-stick" had been laid 'in by the owners for the purposes of their worship. And 'I wonder whether *our* seamen, let alone our bishops 'and deacons, ever stand out upon points of silvered-paper 'and tin-foil and joss-sticks. To be sure Christianity is 'not Chin-Teeism, and that I suppose is why we never 'lose sight of the end in contemptible and insignificant 'quarrels about the means. There is enough matter for 'reflection aboard the Keying at any rate to last one's 'voyage home to England again.'

A contrast.

Home questions.

*Ante,* pp. 354-5.

Other letters of the summer from Broadstairs will complete what he wrote from the same place last year on Mr. Cruikshank's efforts in the cause of temperance, and will enable me to say, what I know he wished to be remembered in his story, that there was no subject on which through his whole life he felt more strongly than this. No man advocated temperance, even as far as possible its legislative enforcement, with greater earnestness; but he made important reservations. Not thinking drunkenness to be a vice inborn, or incident to the poor more than to other people, he never would agree that the existence of a gin-shop was the alpha and omega of it. Believing it to be *the* 'national horror,' he also believed that many operative causes had to do with having made it so; and his objection to the temperance agitation was that these were left out of account altogether. He thought the gin-shop not fairly to be rendered the exclusive object of attack, until, in connection with the classes who mostly made it their resort, the temptations that led to it, physical and moral, should have been more bravely dealt with. Among the former he counted foul smells, disgusting habitations, bad workshops and workshop-customs, scarcity of light, air, and water, in short the absence of all easy means of decency and health; and among the latter, the mental weariness and languor so induced, the desire of wholesome relaxation, the craving for *some* stimulus and excitement, not less needful than the sun itself to lives so passed, and last, and inclusive of all the rest, ignorance, and the want of rational mental training, generally applied. This was consistently Dickens's 'platform' throughout the years he was known to me; and holding it to be within the reach as well as the scope of legislation, which even our political magnates have been discovering lately, he thought intemperance to be but the



C. D.'s view of temperance agitation.

Temptations to gin-shop.

Necessity of dealing with them.

BROAD-STAIRS: 1848.

Stages anterior to drunkenness.

one result that, out of all of those arising from the absence of legislation, was the most wretched. For him, drunkenness had a teeming and reproachful history anterior to the drunken stage; and he thought it the first duty of the moralist bent upon annihilating the gin-shop, to 'strike 'deep and spare not' at those previous remediable evils. Certainly this was not the way of Mr. Cruikshank, any more than it is that of the many excellent people who take part in temperance agitations. His former tale of the *Bottle*, as told by his admirable pencil, was that of a decent working man, father of a boy and a girl, living in comfort and good esteem until near the middle age, when, happening unluckily to have a goose for dinner one day in the bosom of his thriving family, he jocularly sends out for a bottle of gin, persuades his wife, until then a picture of neatness and good housewifery, to take a little drop after the stuffing, and the whole family from that moment drink themselves to destruction. The sequel, of which Dickens now wrote to me, traced the lives of the boy and girl after the wretched deaths of their drunken parents, through gin-shop, beer-shop, and dancing-rooms, up to their trial for robbery; when the boy is convicted, dying aboard the hulks; and the girl, desolate and mad after her acquittal, flings herself from London-bridge into the night-darkened river.

Cruikshank's *Bottle*: and *Drunkard's Children*.

'I think,' said Dickens, 'the power of that closing scene 'quite extraordinary. It haunts the remembrance like 'an awful reality. It is full of passion and terror, and I 'doubt very much whether any hand but his could so 'have rendered it. There are other fine things too. The 'death-bed scene on board the hulks; the convict who

C. D.'s opinion.

'is composing the face, and the other who is drawing the 'screen round the bed's head; seem to me masterpieces 'worthy of the greatest painter. The reality of the place, 'and the fidelity with which every minute object illustra- 'tive of it is presented, are surprising. I think myself no 'bad judge of this feature, and it is remarkable through- 'out. In the trial scene at the Old Bailey, the eye may 'wander round the Court, and observe everything that is 'a part of the place The very light and atmosphere are 'faithfully reproduced. So, in the gin-shop and the beer- 'shop. An inferior hand would indicate a fragment of 'the fact, and slur it over; but here every shred is 'honestly made out. The man behind the bar in the 'gin-shop, is as real as the convicts at the hulks, or the 'barristers round the table in the Old Bailey. I found it 'quite curious, as I closed the book, to recall the number 'of faces I had seen of individual identity, and to think 'what a chance they have of living, as the Spanish friar 'said to Wilkie, when the living have passed away. But 'it only makes more exasperating to me the obstinate one- 'sidedness of the thing. When a man shows so forcibly 'the side of the medal on which the people in their faults 'and crimes are stamped, he is the more bound to help us 'to a glance at that other side on which the faults and 'vices of the governments placed over the people are not 'less gravely impressed.'

BROADSTAIRS: 1848.

Realities of Cruikshank's pencil.

Its one-sidedness.

This led to some remark on Hogarth's method in such matters, and I am glad to be able to preserve this fine criticism of that great Englishman, by a writer who closely resembled him in genius; as another generation will be

The Hogarth method.

BROAD-STAIRS: 1848.

Dickens on Hogarth.

Cause as well as effect.

Exit of Gin-lane.

probably more apt than our own to discover. 'Hogarth 'avoided the Drunkard's Progress, I conceive, precisely 'because the causes of drunkenness among the poor were 'so numerous and widely spread, and lurked so sorrowfully 'deep and far down in all human misery, neglect, and 'despair, that even *his* pencil could not bring them fairly 'and justly into the light. It was never his plan to be 'content with only showing the effect. In the death of 'the miser-father, his shoe new-soled with the binding of 'his bible, before the young Rake begins his career; in 'the worldly father, listless daughter, impoverished young 'lord, and crafty lawyer, of the first plate of Marriage-à-la 'mode; in the detestable advances through the stages of 'Cruelty; and in the progress downward of Thomas Idle; 'you see the effects indeed, but also the causes. He was 'never disposed to spare the kind of drunkenness that 'was of more "respectable" engenderment, as one sees 'in his midnight modern conversation, the election plates, 'and crowds of stupid aldermen and other guzzlers. But 'after one immortal journey down Gin-lane, he turned 'away in pity and sorrow—perhaps in hope of better 'things, one day, from better laws and schools and poor 'men's homes—and went back no more. The scene of 'Gin-lane, you know, is that just cleared away for the 'extension of Oxford-street, which we were looking at the 'other day; and I think it a remarkable trait of Hogarth's 'picture, that, while it exhibits drunkenness in the most 'appalling forms, it also forces on attention a most neg'lected wretched neighbourhood, and an unwholesome, 'indecent, abject condition of life that might be put as

BROAD-STAIRS: 1848.

Dickens on Hogarth.

'frontispiece to our sanitary report of a hundred years 'later date. I have always myself thought the purpose 'of this fine piece to be not adequately stated even by 'CHARLES LAMB. "The very houses seem absolutely reel-'"ing" it is true; but beside that wonderful picture of 'what follows intoxication, we have indication quite as 'powerful of what leads to it among the neglected classes. 'There is no evidence that any of the actors in the dreary 'scene have ever been much better than we see them 'there. The best are pawning the commonest necessaries, 'and tools of their trades; and the worst are homeless 'vagrants who give us no clue to their having been other-'wise in bygone days. All are living and dying miser-'ably. Nobody is interfering for prevention or for cure, 'in the generation going out before us, or the generation 'coming in. The beadle is the only sober man in the 'composition except the pawnbroker, and he is mightily 'indifferent to the orphan-child crying beside its parent's 'coffin. The little charity-girls are not so well taught or 'looked after, but that they can take to dram-drinking 'already. The church indeed is very prominent and 'handsome; but as, quite passive in the picture, it coldly 'surveys these things in progress under shadow of its 'tower, I cannot but bethink me that it was not until this 'year of grace 1848 that a Bishop of London first came 'out respecting something wrong in poor men's social 'accommodations, and I am confirmed in my suspicion 'that Hogarth had many meanings which have not grown 'obsolete in a century.'

Wisdom of the great painter.

Late, but never too late.

Another art-criticism by Dickens should be added.

BROADSTAIRS: 1848.

Dickens on designs by Leech.

Upon a separate publication by Leech of some drawings on stone called the Rising Generation, from designs done for Mr. Punch's gallery, he wrote at my request a little essay of which a few sentences will find appropriate place with his letter on the other great caricaturist of his time. I use that word, as he did, only for want of a better. Dickens was of opinion that, in this particular line of illustration, while he conceded all his fame to the elder and stronger contemporary, Mr. Leech was the very first Englishman who had made Beauty a part of his art; and he held, that, by striking out this course, and setting the successful

Originality of Leech.

example of introducing always into his most whimsical pieces some beautiful faces or agreeable forms, he had done more than any other man of his generation to refine a branch of art to which the facilities of steam-printing and wood-engraving were giving almost unrivalled diffusion and popularity. His opinion of Leech in a word was that he turned caricature into character; and would leave behind him not a little of the history of his time and its follies, sketched with inimitable grace.

'If we turn back to a collection of the works of Rowland-'son or Gilray, we shall find, in spite of the great humour 'displayed in many of them, that they are rendered weari-'some and unpleasant by a vast amount of personal ugli-

Ugliness or beauty?

'ness. Now, besides that it is a poor device to represent 'what is satirized as being necessarily ugly, which is but 'the resource of an angry child or a jealous woman, it 'serves no purpose but to produce a disagreeable result. 'There is no reason why the farmer's daughter in the old 'caricature who is squalling at the harpsichord (to the 'intense delight, by the bye, of her worthy father, whom 'it is her duty to please) should be squab and hideous. 'The satire on the manner of her education, if there be 'any in the thing at all, would be just as good, if she were 'pretty. Mr. Leech would have made her so. The average 'of farmers' daughters in England are not impossible 'lumps of fat. One is quite as likely to find a pretty girl 'in a farm-house, as to find an ugly one; and we think, 'with Mr. Leech, that the business of this style of art is 'with the pretty one. She is not only a pleasanter object, 'but we have more interest in her. We care more about 'what does become her, and does not become her. Mr. 'Leech represented the other day certain delicate creatures 'with bewitching countenances encased in several varieties 'of that amazing garment, the ladies' paletot. Formerly 'those fair creatures would have been made as ugly and 'ungainly as possible, and then the point would have been 'lost. The spectator, with a laugh at the absurdity of the 'whole group, would not have cared how such uncouth 'creatures disguised themselves, or how ridiculous they 'became. . . . But to represent female beauty as Mr. Leech 'represents it, an artist must have a most delicate percep- 'tion of it; and the gift of being able to realise it to us 'with two or three slight, sure touches of his pencil. This 'power Mr. Leech possesses, in an extraordinary degree. '. . . For this reason, we enter our protest against those of 'the Rising Generation who are precociously in love being 'made the subject of merriment by a pitiless and unsym- 'pathizing world. We never saw a boy more distinctly 'in the right than the young gentleman kneeling on the

BROADSTAIRS: 1848.

Dickens on designs by Leech.

Superiority of his method.

The requisites for it.

BROADSTAIRS: 1848.

Dickens on designs by Leech.

'chair to beg a lock of hair from his pretty cousin, to take 'back to school. Madness is in her apron, and Virgil 'dog's-eared and defaced is in her ringlets. Doubts may 'suggest themselves of the perfect disinterestedness of the 'other young gentleman contemplating the fair girl at 'the piano—doubts engendered by his worldly allusion to '"tin"; though even that may have arisen in his modest 'consciousness of his own inability to support an establish-'ment—but that he should be "deucedly inclined to go '"and cut that fellow out," appears to us one of the most 'natural emotions of the human breast. The young gen-'tleman with the dishevelled hair and clasped hands who 'loves the transcendant beauty with the bouquet, and 'can't be happy without her, is to us a withering and 'desolate spectacle. Who *could* be happy without her? '. . . The growing youths are not less happily observed 'and agreeably depicted than the grown women. The 'languid little creature who "hasn't danced since he was '"quite a boy," is perfect; and the eagerness of the small 'dancer whom he declines to receive for a partner at the 'hands of the glorious old lady of the house (the little feet 'quite ready for the first position, the whole heart pro-'jected into the quadrille, and the glance peeping timidly 'at the desired one out of a flutter of hope and doubt) is 'quite delightful to look at. The intellectual juvenile who 'awakens the tremendous wrath of a Norma of private life 'by considering woman an inferior animal, is lecturing at the 'present moment, we understand, on the Concrete in con-'nexion with the Will. The legs of the young philosopher 'who considers Shakespeare an over-rated man, were seen

Excuses for the rising generation.

Intellectual juvenility.

'by us dangling over the side of an omnibus last Tues-'day. We have no acquaintance with the scowling young 'gentleman who is clear that "if his Governor don't like '"the way he goes on in, why he must have chambers '"and so much a week;" but if he is not by this time in 'Van Diemen's-land, he will certainly go to it through 'Newgate. We should exceedingly dislike to have per-'sonal property in a strong box, to live in the suburb of 'Camberwell, and to be in the relation of bachelor-uncle 'to that youth . . . In all his designs, whatever Mr. Leech 'desires to do, he does. His drawing seems to us charm-'ing; and the expression indicated, though by the simplest 'means, is exactly the natural expression, and is recog-'nised as such immediately. Some forms of our existing 'life will never have a better chronicler. His wit is good-'natured, and always the wit of a gentleman. He has a 'becoming sense of responsibility and self-restraint; he 'delights in agreeable things; he imparts some pleasant air 'of his own to things not pleasant in themselves; he is sug-'gestive and full of matter; and he is always improving. 'Into the tone as well as into the execution of what he 'does, he has brought a certain elegance which is altogether 'new, without involving any compromise of what is true. 'Popular art in England has not had so rich an acquisition.' Dickens's closing allusion was to a remark made by Mr. Ford in a review of *Oliver Twist* formerly referred to. 'It is 'eight or ten years since a writer in the *Quarterly Review*, 'making mention of MR. GEORGE CRUIKSHANK, commented 'on the absurdity of excluding such a man from the Royal 'Academy, because his works were not produced in certain

BROADSTAIRS: 1848.

Dickens on designs by Leech.

A dangerous youth.

What Leech will be remembered for.

Page 161 of Vol. I.

BROADSTAIRS: 1848.

Dickens on Cruikshank and Leech.

'materials, and did not occupy a certain space in its annual 'shows. Will no Associates be found upon its books one 'of these days, the labours of whose oil and brushes will 'have sunk into the profoundest obscurity, when many 'pencil-marks of MR. CRUIKSHANK and of MR. LEECH 'will be still fresh in half the houses in the land?'

Odd adventures. *Ante*, p. 188.

Of what otherwise occupied him at Broadstairs in 1848 there is not much to mention until the close of his holiday. He used to say that he never went for more than a couple of days from his own home without something befalling him that never happened to anyone else, and his Broadstairs adventure of the present summer verged closer on tragedy than comedy. Returning there one day in August after bringing up his boys to school, it had been arranged that his wife should meet him at Margate; but he had walked impatiently far beyond the place for meeting when at last he caught sight of her, not in the small chaise but in a large carriage and pair followed by an excited crowd, and with the youth that should have been driving the little pony bruised and bandaged on the box behind the two prancing horses. 'You may faintly imagine my 'amazement at encountering this carriage, and the 'strange people, and Kate, and the crowd, and the ban-'daged one, and all the rest of it.' And then in a line or two I had the story. 'At the top of a steep hill on the 'road, with a ditch on each side, the pony bolted, upon 'which what does John do but jump out! He says he 'was thrown out, but it cannot be. The reins immediately 'became entangled in the wheels, and away went the pony 'down the hill madly, with Kate inside rending the Isle

Pony-chaise accident.

'of Thanet with her screams. The accident might have 'been a fearful one, if the pony had not, thank Heaven, 'on getting to the bottom, pitched over the side; breaking 'the shaft and cutting her hind legs, but in the most 'extraordinary manner smashing her own way apart. She 'tumbled down, a bundle of legs with her head tucked 'underneath, and left the chaise standing on the bank! 'A Captain Devaynes and his wife were passing in their 'carriage at the moment, saw the accident with no power 'of preventing it, got Kate out, laid her on the grass, and 'behaved with infinite kindness. All's well that ends well, 'and I think she's really none the worse for the fright. 'John is in bed a good deal bruised, but without any 'broken bone, and likely soon to come right; though for 'the present plastered all over, and, like Squeers, a brown-'paper parcel chock-full of nothing but groans. The 'women generally have no sympathy for him whatever; 'and the nurse says, with indignation, how could he go 'and leave an unprotected female in the shay!'

BROADSTAIRS: 1848.

Fortunate escape.

Parallel to Squeers.

Holiday incidents there were many, but none that need detain us. This was really a summer idleness: for it was the interval between two of his important undertakings, there was no periodical yet to make demands on him, and only the task of finishing his *Haunted Man* for Christmas lay ahead. But he did even his nothings in a strenuous way, and on occasion could make gallant fight against the elements themselves. He reported himself, to my horror, thrice wet through on a single day, 'dressed four times,' and finding all sorts of great things, brought out by the rains, among the rocks on the sea-beach. He also sketched now

Strenuous idleness.

BROADSTAIRS: 1848.

French philosophy.

and then morsels of character for me, of which I will preserve one. 'F is philosophical, from sunrise to bedtime: 'chiefly in the French line, about French women going 'mad, and in that state coming to their husbands, and 'saying, "Mon ami, je vous ai trompé. Voici les lettres '"de mon amant!" Whereupon the husbands take the 'letters and think them waste paper, and become extra-'philosophical at finding that they really *were* the lover's 'effusions: though what there is of philosophy in it all, or 'anything but unwholesomeness, it is not easy to see.' (A remark that it might not be out of place to offer to Mr. Taine's notice.) 'Likewise about dark shades coming over 'our wedded Emmeline's face at parties; and about F 'handing her to her carriage, and saying, "May I come in, '"for a lift homeward?" and she bending over him out of 'window, and saying in a low voice, I DARE NOT! And 'then of the carriage driving away like lightning, leaving 'F more philosophical than ever on the pavement.' Not till the close of September I heard of work intruding itself, in a letter twitting me for a broken promise in not joining him: 'We are reasonably jolly, but rurally so; going to 'bed o' nights at ten, and bathing o' mornings at half-past 'seven; and not drugging ourselves with those dirty and 'spoiled waters of Lethe that flow round the base of the 'great pyramid.' Then, after mention of the friends who had left him, Sheriff Gordon, the Leeches, Lemon, Egg and Stone: 'reflection and pensiveness are coming. I have 'NOT

Hint for Mr. Taine.

Shadows of work.

'—seen Fancy write
'With a pencil of light
'On the blotter so solid, commanding the sea!

'but I shouldn't wonder if she were to do it, one of these 'days. Dim visions of divers things are floating around 'me; and I must go to work, head foremost, when I get 'home. I am glad, after all, that I have not been at it 'here; for I am all the better for my idleness, no doubt. '. Roche was very ill last night, and looks like one with 'his face turned to the other world, this morning. When '*are* you coming? Oh what days and nights there have 'been here, this week past!' My consent to a suggestion in his next letter, that I should meet him on his way back, and join him in a walking-excursion home, got me full absolution for broken promises; and the way we took will remind friends of his later life, when he was lord of Gadshill, of an object of interest which he delighted in taking them to see. 'You will come down booked for 'Maidstone (I will meet you at Paddock-wood), and we 'will go thither in company over a most beautiful little 'line of railroad. The eight miles walk from Maidstone 'to Rochester, and the visit to the Druidical altar on the 'wayside, are charming. This could be accomplished on 'the Tuesday; and Wednesday we might look about us 'at Chatham, coming home by Cobham on Thursday. . . .'

BROADSTAIRS: 1848.

Better for his idleness.

A favourite spot.

His first sea-side holiday in 1849 was at Brighton, where he passed some weeks in February; and not, I am bound to add, without the usual *un*usual adventure to signalize his visit. He had not been a week in his lodgings, where Leech and his wife joined him, when both his landlord and the daughter of his landlord went raving mad, and the lodgers were driven away to the Bedford hotel. 'If you 'could have heard the cursing and crying of the two;

At BRIGHTON: 1849.

BRIGHTON: 1849.

With mad people and mad doctors.

'could have seen the physician and nurse quoited out into 'the passage by the madman at the hazard of their lives; 'could have seen Leech and me flying to the doctor's 'rescue; could have seen our wives pulling us back; 'could have seen the M.D. faint with fear; could have 'seen three other M.D.'s come to his aid; with an atmos- 'phere of Mrs. Gamps, strait-waistcoats, struggling friends 'and servants, surrounding the whole; you would have 'said it was quite worthy of me, and quite in keeping 'with my usual proceedings.' The letter ended with a word on what then his thoughts were full of, but for which no name had yet been found. 'A sea-fog to-day, but yes- 'terday inexpressibly delicious. My mind running, like 'a high sea, on names—not satisfied yet, though.' When he next wrote from the sea-side, in the beginning of July, he had found the name; had started his book; and was 'rushing to Broadstairs' to write the fourth number of *David Copperfield.*

A name for his new book.

At BROADSTAIRS.

Revolving No. four.

In this came the childish experiences which had left so deep an impression upon him, and over which he had some difficulty in throwing the needful disguises. 'Fourteen 'miles to-day in the country,' he had written to me on the 21st of June, 'revolving number four!' Still he did not quite see his way. Three days later he wrote: 'On 'leaving you last night, I found myself summoned on a 'special jury in the Queen's Bench to-day. I have taken 'no notice of the document,* and hourly expect to be 'dragged forth to a dungeon for contempt of court. I

Summoned as special juror.

* My friend Mr. Shirley Brooks sends me a 'characteristic cutting from an autograph catalogue in which these few lines are given from an early

'think I should rather like it. It might help me with a 'new notion or two in my difficulties. Meanwhile I shall 'take a stroll to-night in the green fields from 7 to 10, if 'you feel inclined to join.' His troubles ended when he got to Broadstairs, from which he wrote on the tenth of July to tell me that agreeably to the plan we had discussed he had introduced a great part of his MS. into the number. 'I really think I have done it ingeniously, and 'with a very complicated interweaving of truth and fiction. 'Vous verrez. I am getting on like a house afire in point 'of health, and ditto ditto in point of number.'

BROADSTAIRS: 1849.

End of trouble with No. four.

In the middle of July the number was nearly done, and he was still doubtful where to pass his longer summer holiday. Leech wished to join him in it, and both desired a change from Broadstairs. At first he thought of Folkestone,* but disappointment there led to a sudden change.

letter in the Doughty-street days. 'I always pay my taxes when they won't call 'any longer, in order to get a bad name in the parish and so escape all 'honours.' It is a touch of character, certainly; but though his motive in later life was the same, his method was not. He attended to the tax-collector, but of any other parochial or political application took no notice whatever.

A Doughty-street letter.

* Even in the modest retirement of a note I fear that I shall offend the dignity of history, and of biography, by printing the lines in which this intention was announced to me. They were written 'in character;' and the character was that of the 'waterman' at the Charing cross cabstand, first discovered by George Cattermole, whose imitations of him were a delight to Dickens at this time, and adapted themselves in the exuberance of his admiration to every conceivable variety of subject. The painter of the Derby Day will have a fullness of satisfaction in remembering this. 'Sloppy,' the hero in question, had a friend 'Jack' in whom he was supposed to typify his own early and hard experiences before he became a convert to temperance; and Dickens used to point to 'Jack' as the justification of himself and Mrs. Gamp for their portentous invention of Mrs. Harris. It is amazing nonsense to repeat; but to hear Cattermole, in the gruff hoarse accents of what seemed to be the remains of a deep bass voice wrapped up in wet straw, repeat the wild proceedings of Jack, was not to be forgotten. 'Yes sir, Jack went mad

Page 158 of Vol. I.

A male Mrs. Gamp and Mrs. Harris.

BON-CHURCH: 1849.

'I propose' (15th of July) 'returning to town to-morrow by 'the boat from Ramsgate, and going off to Weymouth or 'the Isle of Wight, or both, early the next morning.' A few days after, his choice was made.

James White.

He had taken a house at Bonchurch, attracted there by the friend who had made it a place of interest for him during the last few years, the Reverend James White, with whose name and its associations my mind connects inseparably many of Dickens's happiest hours. To pay him

'sir, just afore he 'stablished hisself by Sir Robert Peel's-s-s, sir. He was 'allis a callin' for a pint o' beer sir, and they brings him water sir. Yes sir. 'And so sir, I sees him dodgin' about one day sir, yes sir, and at last he gits a 'hopportunity sir and claps a pitch-plaster on the mouth o' th' pump sir, 'and says he's done for his wust henemy sir. Yes sir. And then they 'finds him a-sittin' on the top o' the corn-chest sir, yes sir, a crammin' a old 'pistol with wisps o' hay and horse-beans sir, and swearin' he's a goin' to 'blow hisself to hattoms, yes sir, but he doesn't, no sir. For I sees him 'arterwards a lyin' on the straw a manifacktrin' Bengal cheroots out o' corn-'chaff sir and swearin' he'd make 'em smoke sir, but they hulloxed him off 'round by the corner of Drummins's-s-s-s-s-s sir, just afore I come here sir, 'yes sir. And so you never see'd us together sir, no sir.' This was the remarkable dialect in which Dickens wrote from Broadstairs on the 13th of July. 'About Saturday sir?—Why sir, I'm a-going to *Folkestone* a Saturday 'sir!—not on accounts of the manifacktring of Bengal cheroots as there is there 'but for the survayin' o' the coast sir. 'Cos you see sir, bein' here sir, and 'not a finishin' my work sir till to-morrow sir, I couldn't go afore! And if I 'wos to come home, and not go, and come back agin sir, wy it would be na-'t'rally a hulloxing of myself sir. Yes sir. Wy sir, I b'lieve that the gent as 'is a goin' to 'stablish hisself sir, in the autumn, along with me round the 'corner sir (by Drummins's-s-s-s-s-s bank) is a comin' down to Folkestone 'Saturday arternoon—Leech by name sir—yes sir—another Jack sir—and if 'you wos to come down along with him sir by the train as gits to Folkestone 'twenty minutes arter five, you'd find me a smoking a Bengal cheroot (made of 'clover-chaff and horse-beans sir) on the platform. You couldn't spend your 'arternoon better sir. Dover, Sandgate, Herne Bay—they're all to be wisited 'sir, most probable, till sich times as a 'ouse is found sir. Yes sir. Then 'decide to come sir, and say you will, and do it. I shall be here till arter 'post time Saturday mornin' sir. Come on then! SLOPPY

'His × mark.'

Letter from C. D. in character.

fitting tribute would not be easy, if here it were called for. In the kindly shrewd Scotch face, a keen sensitiveness to pleasure and pain was the first thing that struck any common observer. Cheerfulness and gloom coursed over it so rapidly that no one could question the tale they told. But the relish of his life had outlived its more than usual share of sorrows; and quaint sly humour, love of jest and merriment, capital knowledge of books, and sagacious quips at men, made his companionship delightful. Like his life, his genius was made up of alternations of mirth and melancholy. He would be immersed, at one time, in those darkest Scottish annals from which he drew his tragedies; and overflowing, at another, into Sir Frizzle Pumpkin's exuberant farce. The tragic histories may probably perish with the actor's perishable art; but three little abstracts of history written at a later time in prose, with a sunny clearness of narration and a glow of picturesque interest to my knowledge unequalled in books of such small pretension, will find, I hope, a lasting place in literature. They are filled with felicities of phrase, with breadth of understanding and judgment, with manful honesty, quiet sagacity, and a constant cheerful piety, valuable for all and priceless for the young. Another word I permit myself to add. With Dickens, White was popular supremely for his eager good fellowship; and few men brought him more of what he always liked to receive. But he brought nothing so good as his wife. 'He is excellent, but she is better,' is the pithy remark of his first Bonchurch letter; and the true affection and respect that followed is happily still borne her by his daughters.



**Mirth and melancholy.**

*Landmarks of History; and Eighteen Christian Centuries.*

**Mrs. James White.**

BON-CHURCH: 1849.

Of course there is something strange to be recorded of the Bonchurch holiday, but it does not come till nearer the ending; and, with more attention to Mrs. Malaprop's advice to begin with a little aversion, might probably not have come at all. He began with an excess of liking. Of the Undercliff he was full of admiration. 'From the 'top of the highest downs,' he wrote in his second letter (28th of July) 'there are views which are only to be 'equalled on the Genoese shore of the Mediterranean; 'the variety of walks is extraordinary; things are cheap, 'and everybody is civil. The waterfall acts wonderfully, 'and the sea bathing is delicious. Best of all, the place is 'certainly cold rather than hot, in the summer time. The 'evenings have been even chilly. White very jovial, and 'emulous of the inimitable in respect of gin-punch. He 'had made some for our arrival. Ha! ha! not bad for a 'beginner . . . I have been, and am, trying to work this 'morning; but I can't make anything of it, and am going 'out to think. I am invited by a distinguished friend to 'dine with you on the first of August, but I have pleaded 'distance and the being resident in a cave on the sea 'shore; my food, beans; my drink, the water from the 'rock . . . I must pluck up heart of grace to write to Jeffrey, 'of whom I had but poor accounts from Gordon just before 'leaving. Talfourd delightful, and amuses me mightily. 'I am really quite enraptured at his success, and think of 'his happiness with uncommon pleasure.' Our friend was now on the bench; which he adorned with qualities that are justly the pride of that profession, and with accomplishments that have become more rare in its highest

First impressions of the Undercliff.

White's punch.

Talfourd made a judge.

places than they were in former times. His elevation only made those virtues better known. Talfourd assumed nothing with the ermine but the privilege of more frequent intercourse with the tastes and friends he loved, and he continued to be the most joyous and least affected of companions. Such small oddities or foibles as he had made him secretly only dearer to Dickens, who had no friend he was more attached to; and the many happy nights made happier by the voice so affluent in generous words, and the face so bright with ardent sensibility, come back to me sorrowfully now. 'Deaf the prais'd ear, and mute the 'tuneful tongue.' The poet's line has a double application and sadness.

BONCHURCH: 1849.

Dickens's affection for him.

He wrote again on the first of August. 'I have just 'begun to get into work. We are expecting the Queen to 'come by very soon, in grand array, and are going to let off 'ever so many guns. I had a letter from Jeffrey yester-'day morning, just as I was going to write to him. He 'has evidently been very ill, and I begin to have fears for 'his recovery. It is a very pathetic letter, as to his state 'of mind; but only in a tranquil contemplation of death, 'which I think very noble.' His next letter, four days later, described himself as continuing still at work; but also taking part in dinners at Blackgang, and picnics of 'tremendous 'success' on Shanklin Down. 'Two charity sermons for 'the school are preached to-day, and I go to the afternoon 'one. The examination of said school t'other day was 'very funny. All the boys made Buckstone's bow in the '*Rough Diamond*, and some in a very wonderful manner 'recited pieces of poetry, about a clock, and may we be

Touching letter from Jeffrey.

Church-school examination.

BON-CHURCH: 1849.

Doubtful example.

'like the clock, which is always a going and a doing of 'its duty, and always tells the truth (supposing it to be a 'slap-up chronometer I presume, for the American clock 'in the school was lying frightfully at that moment); and 'after being bothered to death by the multiplication table, 'they were refreshed with a public tea in Lady Jane Swin-'burne's garden.' (There was a reference in one of his letters, but I have lost it, to a golden-haired lad of the Swinburnes whom his own boys used to play with, since become more widely known.) 'The rain came in with the 'first tea-pot, and has been active ever since. On Friday

Dinners and pic-nics.

'we had a grand, and what is better, a very good dinner at '"parson" Fielden's, with some choice port. On Tuesday 'we are going on another picnic; with the materials for a 'fire, at my express stipulation; and a great iron pot to boil 'potatoes in. These things, and the eatables, go to the 'ground in a cart. Last night we had some very good 'merriment at White's, where pleasant Julian Young and 'his wife (who are staying about five miles off) showed 'some droll new games'—and roused the ambition in my

A conjuring performance.

friend to give a 'mighty conjuring performance for all the 'children in Bonchurch,' for which I sent him the materials and which went off in a tumult of wild delight. To the familiar names in this letter I will add one more, grieving freshly even now to connect it with suffering. 'A 'letter from Poole has reached me since I began this letter, 'with tidings in it that you will be very sorry to hear.

The comedian Regnier.

'Poor Regnier has lost his only child; the pretty daughter 'who dined with us that nice day at your house, when we 'all pleased the poor mother by admiring her so much.

BON-CHURCH: 1849.

'She died of a sudden attack of malignant typhus. Poole 'was at the funeral, and writes that he never saw, or could 'have imagined, such intensity of grief as Regnier's at the 'grave. How one loves him for it. But is it not always 'true, in comedy and in tragedy, that the more real the 'man the more genuine the actor?'

When acting is genuine.

After a few more days I heard of progress with his writing in spite of all festivities. 'I have made it a rule that 'the inimitable is invisible, until two every day. I shall 'have half the number done, please God, to-morrow. I 'have not worked quickly here yet, but I don't know what 'I *may* do. Divers cogitations have occupied my mind 'at intervals, respecting the dim design.' The design was the weekly periodical so often in his thoughts, of which more will appear in my next chapter. His letter closed with intimations of discomfort in his health; of an obstinate cough; and of a determination he had formed to mount daily to the top of the downs. 'It makes a great 'difference in the climate to get a blow there and come 'down again.' Then I heard of the doctor 'stethoscoping' him, of his hope that all was right in that quarter, and of rubbings 'à la St. John Long' being ordered for his chest. But the mirth still went on. 'There has been a Doctor 'Lankester at Sandown, a very good merry fellow, who 'has made one at the picnics, and whom I went over and 'dined with, along with Danby (I remember your liking 'for Danby, and don't wonder at it), Leech, and White.' A letter towards the close of August resumed yet more of his ordinary tone. 'We had games and forfeits last night 'at White's. Davy Roberts's pretty little daughter is there

Progress in writing.

Doubts as to health.

Personal news.

BON-CHURCH: 1849.

'for a week, with her husband, Bicknell's son. There was 'a dinner first to say good-bye to Danby, who goes to other 'clergyman's-duty, and we were very merry. Mrs. White 'unchanging; White comically various in his moods. Tal-'fourd comes down next Tuesday, and we think of going 'over to Ryde on Monday, visiting the play, sleeping there '(I don't mean at the play), and bringing the Judge back. 'Browne is coming down when he has done his month's 'work. Should you like to go to Alum Bay while you are 'here? It would involve a night out, but I think would 'be very pleasant; and if you think so too, I will arrange 'it sub rosâ, so that we may not be, like Bobadil, "op-'"pressed by numbers." I mean to take a fly over from 'Shanklin to meet you at Ryde; so that we can walk back 'from Shanklin over the landslip, where the scenery is 'wonderfully beautiful. Stone and Egg are coming next 'month, and we hope to see Jerrold before we go.' Such notices from his letters may be thought hardly worth preserving; but a wonderful vitality in every circumstance, as long as life under any conditions remained to the writer, is the picture they contribute to; nor would it be complete without the addition, that fond as he was, in the intervals of his work, of this abundance and variety of enjoyments, to no man were so essential also those quieter hours of thought, and talk, not obtainable when 'oppressed by 'numbers.'

My proposed visit.

Arrivals and departures.

A startling revelation.

My visit was due at the opening of September, but a few days earlier came the full revelation of which only a passing shadow had reached in two or three previous letters. 'Before I think of beginning my next number,

'I perhaps cannot do better than give you an imperfect 'description of the results of the climate of Bonchurch 'after a few weeks' residence. The first salubrious effect 'of which the Patient becomes conscious is an almost con- 'tinual feeling of sickness, accompanied with great prostra- 'tion of strength, so that his legs tremble under him, and 'his arms quiver when he wants to take hold of any object. 'An extraordinary disposition to sleep (except at night, 'when his rest, in the event of his having any, is broken 'by incessant dreams) is always present at the same time; 'and, if he have anything to do requiring thought and at- 'tention, this overpowers him to such a degree that he can 'only do it in snatches: lying down on beds in the fitful 'intervals. Extreme depression of mind, and a disposition 'to shed tears from morning to night, developes itself at 'the same period. If the Patient happen to have been a 'good walker, he finds ten miles an insupportable distance; 'in the achievement of which his legs are so unsteady, that 'he goes from side to side of the road, like a drunken man. 'If he happen to have ever possessed any energy of any 'kind, he finds it quenched in a dull, stupid languor. He 'has no purpose, power, or object in existence whatever. 'When he brushes his hair in the morning, he is so weak 'that he is obliged to sit upon a chair to do it. He is 'incapable of reading, at all times. And his bilious system 'is so utterly overthrown, that a ball of boiling fat appears 'to be always behind the top of the bridge of his nose, 'simmering between his haggard eyes. If he should have 'caught a cold, he will find it impossible to get rid of it, 'as his system is wholly incapable of making any effort.

BONCHURCH: 1849.

Effect on C. D. of Bonchurch climate.

Utter prostration.

BON-CHURCH: 1849.

C. D. and the Undercliff.

'His cough will be deep, monotonous, and constant. "The '"faithful watch-dog's honest bark" will be nothing to it. 'He will abandon all present idea of overcoming it, and 'will content himself with keeping an eye upon his blood-'vessels to preserve them whole and sound. *Patient's 'name, Inimitable B.* . . . It's a mortal mistake!—That's 'the plain fact. Of all the places I ever have been in, I 'have never been in one so difficult to exist in, pleasantly. 'Naples is hot and dirty, New York feverish, Washington 'bilious, Genoa exciting, Paris rainy—but Bonchurch, 'smashing. I am quite convinced that I should die here, 'in a year. It's not hot, it's not close, I don't know what 'it is, but the prostration of it is *awful.* Nobody here 'has the least idea what I think of it; but I find, from all 'sorts of hints from Kate, Georgina, and the Leeches, that 'they are all affected more or less in the same way, and 'find it very difficult to make head against. I make no 'sign, and pretend not to know what is going on. But 'they are right. I believe the Leeches will go soon, and 'small blame to 'em!—For me, when I leave here at the end 'of this September, I must go down to some cold place; as 'Ramsgate for example, for a week or two; or I seriously 'believe I shall feel the effects of it for a long time. . . . 'What do you think of *that?* . . . The longer I live, the 'more I doubt the doctors. I am perfectly convinced, that, 'for people suffering under a wasting disease, this Under-'cliff is madness altogether. The doctors, with the old 'miserable folly of looking at one bit of a subject, take 'the patient's lungs and the Undercliff's air, and settle 'solemnly that they are fit for each other. But the whole

Difficulties of existing there.

Thinking of Ramsgate.

Distrust of doctors.

'influence of the place, never taken into consideration, is 'to reduce and overpower vitality. I am quite confident 'that I should go down under it, as if it were so much 'lead, slowly crushing me. An American resident in Paris 'many years, who brought me a letter from Olliffe, said, 'the day before yesterday, that he had always had a passion 'for the sea never to be gratified enough, but that after 'living here a month, he could not bear to look at it; he 'couldn't endure the sound of it; he didn't know how it 'was, but it seemed associated with the decay of his whole 'powers.' These were grave imputations against one of the prettiest places in England; but of the generally depressing influence of that Undercliff on particular temperaments, I had already enough experience to abate something of the surprise with which I read the letter. What it too bluntly puts aside are the sufferings other than his own, protected and sheltered by what only aggravated his; but my visit gave me proof that he had really very little overstated the effect upon himself. Making allowance, which sometimes he failed to do, for special peculiarities, and for the excitability never absent when he had in hand an undertaking such as *Copperfield*, I observed a nervous tendency to misgivings and apprehensions to the last degree unusual with him, which seemed to make the commonest things difficult; and though he stayed out his time, and brought away nothing that his happier associations with the place and its residents did not long survive, he never returned to Bonchurch.

BONCHURCH: 1849.

An American witness.

Other side of picture.

What I observed at the time.

In the month that remained he completed his fifth number, and with the proof there came the reply to some

BONCHURCH: 1849.

Mr. Dick's original delusion.

questions of which I hardly remember more than that they referred to doubts of mine; one being as to the propriety of the kind of delusion he had first given to poor Mr. Dick,* which I thought a little too farcical for that really touching delineation of character. 'Your suggestion is perfectly 'wise and sound,' he wrote back (22nd of August). 'I 'have acted on it. I have also, instead of the bull and china-'shop delusion, given Dick the idea, that, when the head 'of king Charles the First was cut off, some of the trouble 'was taken out of it, and put into his (Dick's).' When he next wrote, there was news very welcome to me for the pleasure to himself it involved. 'Browne has sketched an 'uncommonly characteristic and capital Mr. Micawber for 'the next number. I hope the present number is a good 'one. I hear nothing but pleasant accounts of the general 'satisfaction.' The same letter told me of an intention to go to Broadstairs, put aside by doubtful reports of its sanitary condition; but it will be seen presently that there was another graver interruption. With his work well off his hands, however, he had been getting on better where he was; and they had all been very merry. 'Yes,' he said, writing after a couple of days (23rd of September), 'we 'have been sufficiently rollicking since I finished the 'number; and have had great games at rounders every

Browne's sketch for Micawber.

From the *Copperfield* MS.

* It stood originally thus: '"Do you recollect the date," said Mr. Dick, 'looking earnestly at me, and taking up his pen to note it down, "when that '"bull got into the china warehouse and did so much mischief?" I was very 'much surprised by the inquiry; but remembering a song about such an oc-'currence that was once popular at Salem House, and thinking he might want 'to quote it, replied that I believed it was on St. Patrick's Day. "Yes, I '"know," said Mr. Dick—"in the morning; but what year?" I could give 'no information on this point.' Original MS. of *Copperfield.*

'afternoon, with all Bonchurch looking on; but I begin 'to long for a little peace and solitude. And now for my 'less pleasing piece of news. The sea has been running 'very high, and Leech, while bathing, was knocked over by 'a bad blow from a great wave on the forehead. He is in 'bed, and had twenty of his namesakes on his temples this 'morning. When I heard of him just now, he was asleep '—which he had not been all night.' He closed his letter hopefully, but next day (24th September) I had less favourable report. 'Leech has been very ill with congestion of the 'brain ever since I wrote, and being still in excessive pain 'has had ice to his head continuously, and been bled in the 'arm besides. Beard and I sat up there, all night.' On the 26th he wrote. 'My plans are all unsettled by Leech's 'illness; as of course I do not like to leave this place 'while I can be of any service to him and his good little 'wife. But all visitors are gone to-day, and Winterbourne 'once more left to the engaging family of the inimitable 'B. Ever since I wrote to you Leech has been seriously 'worse, and again very heavily bled. The night before last 'he was in such an alarming state of restlessness, which 'nothing could relieve, that I proposed to Mrs. Leech to 'try magnetism. Accordingly, in the middle of the night 'I fell to; and, after a very fatiguing bout of it, put him 'to sleep for an hour and thirty-five minutes. A change 'came on in the sleep, and he is decidedly better. I talked 'to the astounded little Mrs. Leech across him, when he 'was asleep, as if he had been a truss of hay. . . . What 'do you think of my setting up in the magnetic line with a 'large brass plate? "Terms, twenty-five guineas per nap."'

BONCHURCH: 1849.

Again making merry.

Accident to Leech.

Its consequences.

C. D. mesmerising.

BON-CHURCH: 1849.

When he wrote again on the 30th, he had completed his sixth number; and his friend was so clearly on the way to recovery that he was next day to leave for Broadstairs with his wife, her sister, and the two little girls. 'I will 'merely add that I entreat to be kindly remembered to 'Thackeray' (who had a dangerous illness at this time); 'that I think I have, without a doubt, *got* the Periodical 'notion; and that I am writing under the depressing and 'discomforting influence of paying off the tribe of bills that 'pour in upon an unfortunate family-young-man on the 'eve of a residence like this. So no more at present from 'the disgusted, though still inimitable, and always affec-'tionate B.'

Depressing influences.

At BROAD-STAIRS.

He stayed at Broadstairs till he had finished his number seven, and what else chiefly occupied him were thoughts about the Periodical of which account will presently be given. 'Such a night and day of rain,' ran his first letter, 'I should think the oldest inhabitant never saw! and yet, 'in the ould formiliar Broadstairs, I somehow or other 'don't mind it much. The change has done Mamey a 'world of good, and I have begun to sleep again. As for 'news, you might as well ask me for dolphins. Nobody in 'Broadstairs—to speak of. Certainly nobody in Ballard's. 'We are in the part, which is the house next door to the 'hotel itself, that we once had for three years running, 'and just as quiet and snug now as it was then. I don't 'think I shall return before the 20th or so, when the 'number is done; but I *may*, in some inconstant freak, 'run up to you before. Preliminary despatches and 'advices shall be forwarded in any case to the fragrant 'neighbourhood of Clare-market and the Portugal-street 'burying-ground.' Such was his polite designation of my whereabouts: for which nevertheless he had secret likings. 'On the Portsmouth railway, coming here, encountered 'Kenyon. On the ditto ditto at Reigate, encountered 'young Dilke, and took him in tow to Canterbury. On 'the ditto ditto at ditto (meaning Reigate), encountered 'Fox, M.P. for Oldham, and his daughter. All within an 'hour. Young Dilke great about the proposed Exposition 'under the direction of H.R.H. Prince Albert, and evinc'ing, very pleasantly to me, unbounded faith in our old 'friend his father.' There was one more letter, taking a rather gloomy view of public affairs in connection with an inflated pastoral from Doctor Wiseman 'given out of the 'Flaminian Gate,' and speaking dolefully of some family matters; which was subscribed, each word forming a separate line, 'Yours Despondently, And Disgustedly, Wilkins 'Micawber.'

BROADSTAIRS: 1849.

Railway travellers.

His visit to the little watering-place in the following year was signalised by his completion of the most famous of his novels, and his letters otherwise were occupied by elaborate managerial preparation for the private performances at Knebworth. But again the plague of itinerant music flung him into such fevers of irritation, that he finally resolved against any renewed attempt to carry on important work here; and the summer of 1851, when he was only busy with miscellaneous writing, was the last of his regular residences in the place. He then let his London house for the brief remainder of its term; ran away at the end of May, when some grave family sorrows had

Again at BROADSTAIRS. 1850.

The Exhibition year. 1851.

BROADSTAIRS: 1851.

Page 182 of Vol. I.

befallen him, from the crowds and excitements of the Great Exhibition; and with intervals of absence, chiefly at the Guild representations, stayed in his favourite Fort-house by the sea until October, when he took possession of Tavistock-house. From his letters may be added a few notices of this last holiday at Broadstairs, which he had always afterwards a kindly word for; and to which he said pleasant adieu in the sketch of 'Our Watering-place,' written shortly before he left.

June by the sea.

'It is more delightful here' (1st of June) 'than I can 'express. Corn growing, larks singing, garden full of 'flowers, fresh air on the sea.—O it is wonderful! Why 'can't you come down next Saturday (bringing work) and 'go back with me on Wednesday for the *Copperfield* 'banquet? Concerning which, of course, I say yes to Tal-'fourd's kind proposal. Lemon by all means. And—don't 'you think? Browne? Whosoever, besides, pleases Talfourd 'will please me.' Great was the success of that banquet.

A *Copperfield* banquet.

The scene was the Star-and-Garter at Richmond; Thackeray and Alfred Tennyson joined in the celebration; and the generous giver was in his best vein. I have rarely seen Dickens happier than he was amid the sunshine of that day. Jerrold and Thackeray returned to town with us; and a little argument between them about money and its uses, led to an avowal of Dickens about himself to which I may add the confirmation of all our years of intercourse.

C. D. on money.

'No man,' he said, 'attaches less importance to the posses-'sion of money, or less disparagement to the want of it, 'than I do.'

Vague mention of a 'next book' escaped in a letter at

the end of July, on which I counselled longer abstinence. 'Good advice,' he replied, 'but difficult: I wish you'd come 'to us and preach another kind of abstinence. Fancy the 'Preventive men finding a lot of brandy in barrels on the 'rocks here, the day before yesterday! Nobody knows any-'thing about the barrels, of course. They were intended 'to have been landed with the next tide, and to have been 'just covered at low water. But the water being unusually 'low, the tops of the barrels became revealed to Preventive 'telescopes, and descent was made upon the brandy. They 'are always at it, hereabouts, I have no doubt. And of 'course B would not have had any of it. O dear no! 'certainly not.'

BROADSTAIRS: 1851.

Smuggling.

His reading was considerable and very various at these intervals of labour, and in this particular summer took in all the minor tales as well as the plays of Voltaire, several of the novels (old favourites with him) of Paul de Kock, Ruskin's *Lamps of Architecture,* and a surprising number of books of African and other travel for which he had insatiable relish: but the notices of all this in his letters were few. 'By the bye, I observe, reading that won-'derful book the *French Revolution* again, for the 500th 'time, that Carlyle, who knows everything, don't know 'what Mumbo Jumbo is. It is not an Idol. It is a se-'cret preserved among the men of certain African tribes, 'and never revealed by any of them, for the punishment 'of their women. Mumbo Jumbo comes in hideous form 'out of the forest, or the mud, or the river, or where not, 'and flogs some woman who has been backbiting, or 'scolding, or with some other domestic mischief disturbing

His reading.

A correction for Carlyle.

Mumbo Jumbo.

BROAD-STAIRS: 1851.

'the general peace. Carlyle seems to confound him with 'the common Fetish; but he is quite another thing. He 'is a disguised man; and all about him is a freemasons' 'secret *among the men.*'—'I finished the *Scarlet Letter* 'yesterday. It falls off sadly after that fine opening scene. 'The psychological part of the story is very much overdone, 'and not truly done I think. Their suddenness of meeting 'and agreeing to go away together, after all those years, 'is very poor. Mr. Chillingworth ditto. The child out of 'nature altogether. And Mr. Dimmisdale certainly never 'could have begotten her.' In Mr. Hawthorne's earlier books he had taken especial pleasure; his *Mosses from an Old Manse* having been the first book he placed in my hands on his return from America, with reiterated injunctions to read it. I will add a word or two of what he wrote of the clever story of another popular writer, because it hits well the sort of ability that has become so common, which escapes the highest point of cleverness, but stops short only at the very verge of it. 'The story extremely good indeed; 'but all the strongest things of which it is capable, missed. 'It shows just how far that kind of power can go. It is 'more like a note of the idea than anything else. It seems 'to me as if it were written by somebody who lived next 'door to the people, rather than inside of 'em.'

Hawthorne's *Scarlet Letter*.

Good criticism.

I joined him for the August regatta and stayed a pleasant fortnight. His paper on 'Our Watering-place' appeared while I was there, and great was the local excitement. His own restlessness with fancies for a new book had now risen beyond bounds, and for the time he was eager to open it in that prettiest quaintest bit of

Thoughts of a new book.

English landscape, Strood valley, which reminded him always of a Swiss scene. I had not left him many days when these lines followed me. 'I very nearly packed up 'a portmanteau and went away, the day before yesterday, 'into the mountains of Switzerland, alone! Still the 'victim of an intolerable restlessness, I shouldn't be at all 'surprised if I wrote to you one of these mornings from 'under Mont Blanc. I sit down between whiles to think 'of a new story, and, as it begins to grow, such a torment 'of a desire to be anywhere but where I am; and to be 'going I don't know where, I don't know why; takes 'hold of me, that it is like being *driven away*. If I had 'had a passport, I sincerely believe I should have gone to 'Switzerland the night before last. I should have remembered our engagement—say, at Paris, and have come 'back for it; but should probably have left by the next 'express train.'

BROADSTAIRS: 1851.

The old restlessness.

*Bleak House* in his mind.

At the end of November, when he had settled himself in his new London abode, the book was begun; and as generally happened with the more important incidents of his life, but always accidentally, begun on a Friday.

Beginning on a Friday.

# CHAPTER XIX.

## HAUNTED MAN AND HOUSEHOLD WORDS.

1848—1850.

LONDON: 1848.

IT has been seen that his fancy for his Christmas book of 1848 first arose to him at Lausanne in the summer of 1846, and that, after writing its opening pages in the autumn of the following year, he laid it aside under the pressure of his *Dombey*. These lines were in the letter that closed his 1848 Broadstairs holiday. 'At last I am 'a mentally matooring of the Christmas book—or, as poor 'Macrone * used to write, "booke," "boke," "buke," &c.'

Leaving Broad-stairs.

Pages 100-103 of Vol. I.

* The mention of this name may remind me to state that I have received, in reference to the account in my first volume of Dickens's repurchase of his *Sketches* from Mr. Macrone, a letter from the solicitor and friend of that gentleman so expressed that I could have greatly wished to revise my narrative into nearer agreement with its writer's wish. But farther enquiry, and an examination of the books of Messrs. Chapman and Hall, have confirmed the statement given. Mr. Hansard is in error in supposing that 'unsold im-'pressions' of the books were included in the transaction (the necessary requirement being simply that the small remainders on hand should be transferred with a view to being 'wasted'): I know myself that it could not have included any supposed right of Mr. Macrone to have a novel written for him, because upon that whole matter, and his continued unauthorised advertisements of the tale, I decided myself the reference against him: and Mr. Hansard may be assured that the £2000 was paid for the copyright alone. For the same copyright, a year before, Dickens had received £250, both the first and second series being included in the payment; and he had already

LONDON: 1848.

It was the first labour to which he applied himself at his return.

Completion of Christmas tale.

In London it soon came to maturity; was published duly as *The Haunted Man, or the Ghost's Bargain;* sold largely, beginning with a subscription of twenty thousand; and had a great success on the Adelphi stage, to which it was rather cleverly adapted by Lemon. He had placed on its title page originally four lines from Tennyson's 'Departure,'

Dropped motto.

> 'And o'er the hills, and far away
>   'Beyond their utmost purple rim,
> 'Beyond the night, across the day,
>   'Thro' all the world IT follow'd him;'

but they were less applicable to the close than to the opening of the tale, and were dropped before publication. The hero is a great chemist, a lecturer at an old foundation, a man of studious philosophic habits, haunted with recollections of the past 'o'er which his melancholy sits on brood,' thinking his knowledge of the present a worthier substitute, and at last parting with that portion of himself which he thinks he can safely cast away. The recollections are of a great wrong done him in early life, and of all the sorrow consequent upon it; and the ghost he holds nightly con-

The hero.

Friendly plea for Mr. Macrone.

had about the same sum as his half share of the profits of sales. I quote the close of Mr. Hansard's letter. 'Macrone no doubt was an adventurer, but 'he was sanguine to the highest degree. He was a dreamer of dreams, putting 'no restraint on his exultant hopes by the reflection that he was not dealing 'justly towards others. But reproach has fallen upon him from wrong 'quarters. He died in poverty, and his creditors received nothing from his 'estate. But that was because he had paid away all he had, and all he had 'derived from trust and credit, *to authors*.' This may have been so, but Dickens was not among the authors so benefited. The *Sketches* repurchased for the high price I have named never afterwards really justified such an outlay.

LONDON: 1848.

The 'ghost' in the story.

The 'bargain.'

A fine contrast.

The Tetterby family.

ference with, is the darker presentiment of himself embodied in those bitter recollections. This part is finely managed. Out of heaped-up images of gloomy and wintry fancies, the supernatural takes a shape which is not forced or violent; and the dialogue which is no dialogue, but a kind of dreary dreamy echo, is a piece of ghostly imagination better than Mrs. Radcliffe. The boon desired is granted and the bargain struck. He is not only to lose his own recollection of grief and wrong, but to destroy the like memory in all whom he approaches. By this means the effect is shown in humble as well as higher minds, in the worst poverty as in competence or ease, always with the same result. The over-thinking sage loses his own affections and sympathy, sees them crushed in others, and is brought to the level of the only creature whom he cannot change or influence, an outcast of the streets, a boy whom the mere animal appetites have turned into a small fiend. Never having had his mind awakened, evil is this creature's good; avarice, irreverence, and vindictiveness, are his nature.; sorrow has no place in his memory; and from his brutish propensities the philosopher can take nothing away. The juxtaposition of two people whom such opposite means have put in the same moral position is a stroke of excellent art. There are plenty of incredibilities and inconsistencies, just as in the pleasant *Cricket on the Hearth*, which one does not care about, but enjoy rather than otherwise; and, as in that charming little book, there were minor characters as delightful as anything in Dickens. The Tetterby group, in whose humble, homely, kindly, ungainly figures there is everything that could suggest itself to a clear eye, a piercing wit, and a loving heart, became enormous favourites. Tilly Slowboy and her little dot of a baby, charging folks with it as if it were an offensive instrument, or handing it about as if it were something to drink, were not more popular than poor Johnny Tetterby staggering under his Moloch of an infant, the Juggernaut that crushes all his enjoyments. The story itself consists of nothing more than the effects of the Ghost's gift upon the various groups of people introduced, and the way the end is arrived at is very specially in Dickens's manner. What the highest exercise of the intellect had missed is found in the simplest form of the affections. The wife of the custodian of the college where the chemist is professor, in whom are all the unselfish virtues that can beautify and endear the humblest condition, is the instrument of the change. Such sorrow as she has suffered had made her only zealous to relieve others' sufferings: and the discontented wise man learns from her example that the world is, after all, a much happier compromise than it seems to be, and life easier than wisdom is apt to think it; that grief gives joy its relish, purifying what it touches truly; and that 'sweet are the uses of 'adversity' when its clouds are not the shadow of dishonour. All this can be shown but lightly within such space, it is true; and in the machinery a good deal has to be taken for granted. But Dickens was quite justified in turning aside from objections of that kind. 'You must suppose,' he wrote to me (21st of November), 'that the Ghost's saving 'clause gives him those glimpses without which it would 'be impossible to carry out the idea. Of course my point

Management of the close.

Teachings of the little story.

LONDON: 1848.

C. D.'s statement of his intention.

'is that bad and good are inextricably linked in remem-'brance, and that you could not choose the enjoyment of 'recollecting only the good. To have all the best of it 'you must remember the worst also. My intention in the 'other point you mention is, that he should not know him-'self how he communicates the gift, whether by look or 'touch; and that it should diffuse itself in its own way in 'each case. I can make this clearer by a very few lines in the second part. It is not only necessary to be so, for the 'variety of the story, but I think it makes the thing wilder 'and stranger.' Critical niceties are indeed out of place, where wildness and strangeness in the means matter less than that there should be clearness in the drift and intention. Dickens leaves no doubt as to this. He thoroughly makes out his fancy, that no man should so far question the mysterious dispensations of evil in this world as to desire to lose the recollection of such injustice or misery as he may suppose it to have done to himself. There may have been sorrow, but there was the kindness that assuaged it; there may have been wrong, but there was the charity that forgave it; and with both are connected inseparably so many thoughts that soften and exalt whatever else is in the sense of memory, that what is good and pleasurable in life would cease to continue so if these were forgotten. The old proverb does not tell you to forget that you may forgive, but to forgive that you may forget. It is forgiveness of wrong, for forgetfulness of the evil that was in it; such as poor old Lear begged of Cordelia.

Moral of the story.

Forgive that you may forget.

The design for his much-thought-of new Periodical was still 'dim,' as we have seen, when the first cogitation of it

BON-CHURCH : 1849.

at Bonchurch occupied him; but the expediency of making it clearer came soon after with a visit from Mr. Evans, who brought his half-year's accounts of sales, and some small disappointment for him in those of *Copperfield.* 'The accounts are rather shy, after *Dombey,* and what 'you said comes true after all. I am not sorry I cannot 'bring myself to care much for what opinions people may 'form; and I have a strong belief, that, if any of my books 'are read years hence, *Dombey* will be remembered as 'among the best of them: but passing influences are im-'portant for the time, and as *Chuzzlewit* with its small sale 'sent me up, *Dombey's* large sale has tumbled me down. 'Not very much, however, in real truth. These accounts 'only include the first three numbers, have of course been 'burdened with all the heavy expenses of number one, 'and ought not in reason to be complained of. But it is clear 'to me that the Periodical must be set agoing in the spring; 'and I have already been busy, at odd half-hours, in shadow-'ing forth a name and an idea. Evans says they have but 'one opinion repeated to them of *Copperfield,* and they feel 'very confident about it. A steady twenty-five thousand, 'which it is now on the verge of, will do very well. The 'back numbers are always going off. Read the enclosed.'

*Copperfield* sales.

*Chuzzlewit* and *Dombey* sales.

Notions and names.

It was a letter from a Russian man of letters, dated from St. Petersburg and signed 'Trinarch Ivansvitch Wreden-'skii,' sending him a translation of *Dombey* into Russian; and informing him that his works, which before had only been translated in the journals, and with certain omissions, had now been translated in their entire form by his correspondent, though even he had found an omission to be neces-

Letter from Russia.

BON-CHURCH: 1849.

C. D. translated into Russian.

sary in his version of *Pickwick*. He adds, with an exquisite courtesy to our national tongue which is yet not forgetful of the claims of his own nationality, that his difficulties (in the Sam Weller direction and others) had arisen from the 'impossibility of portraying faithfully the beauties of the 'original in the Russian language, which, though the 'richest in Europe in its expressiveness, is far from being 'elaborate enough for literature like other civilized lan-'guages.' He had however, he assured Dickens, been unremitting in his efforts to live with his thoughts; and the exalted opinion he had formed of them was attended by only one wish, that such a writer 'could but have expanded 'under a Russian sky!' Still, his fate was an enviable one. 'For the last eleven years your name has enjoyed a wide 'celebrity in Russia, and from the banks of the Neva to 'the remotest parts of Siberia you are read with avidity. 'Your *Dombey* continues to inspire with enthusiasm the 'whole of the literary Russia.' Much did we delight in the good Wredenskii; and for a long time, on anything going 'contrairy' in the public or private direction with him, he would tell me he had ordered his portmanteau to be packed for the more sympathizing and congenial climate of 'the remotest parts of Siberia.'

Complimentary.

Sympathy of Siberia.

The week before he left Bonchurch I again had news of the old and often recurring fancy. 'The old notion of 'the Periodical, which has been agitating itself in my 'mind for so long, I really think is at last gradually grow-'ing into form.' That was on the 24th of September; and on the 7th of October, from Broadstairs, I had something of the form it had been taking. 'I do great injus-

Periodical growing into form.

'tice to my floating ideas (pretty speedily and comfortably 'settling down into orderly arrangement) by saying any-'thing about the Periodical now: but my notion is a 'weekly journal, price either three-halfpence or two-'pence, matter in part original and in part selected, and 'always having, if possible, a little good poetry . . . Upon 'the selected matter, I have particular notions. One is, 'that it should always be *a subject*. For example, a his-'tory of Piracy; in connexion with which there is a vast 'deal of extraordinary, romantic, and almost unknown 'matter. A history of Knight-errantry, and the wild old 'notion of the Sangreal. A history of Savages, showing 'the singular respects in which all savages are like each 'other; and those in which civilised men, under cir-'cumstances of difficulty, soonest become like savages. 'A history of remarkable characters, good and bad, *in* 'history; to assist the reader's judgment in his observation 'of men, and in his estimates of the truth of many charac-'ters in fiction. All these things, and fifty others that I 'have already thought of, would be compilations; through 'the whole of which the general intellect and purpose of 'the paper should run, and in which there would be scarcely 'less interest than in the original matter. The original 'matter to be essays, reviews, letters, theatrical criticisms, '&c, &c, as amusing as possible, but all distinctly and boldly 'going to what in one's own view ought to be the spirit of 'the people and the time . . . Now to bind all this together, 'and to get a character established as it were which any of 'the writers may maintain without difficulty, I want to sup-'pose a certain SHADOW, which may go into any place, by

BROADSTAIRS: 1849.

As to selected matter.

Proposed series of 'histories.

As to original matter.

Connecting link.

BROADSTAIRS: 1849.

'sunlight, moonlight, starlight, firelight, candlelight, and be 'in all homes, and all nooks and corners, and be supposed to 'be cognisant of everything, and go everywhere, without the 'least difficulty. Which may be in the Theatre, the Palace, 'the House of Commons, the Prisons, the Unions, the 'Churches, on the Railroad, on the Sea, abroad and at home: 'a kind of semi-omniscient, omnipresent, intangible crea-'ture. I don't think it would do to call the paper THE 'SHADOW: but I want something tacked to that title, to 'express the notion of its being a cheerful, useful, and 'always welcome Shadow. I want to open the first num-'ber with this Shadow's account of himself and his family. 'I want to have all the correspondence addressed to him. 'I want him to issue his warnings from time to time, that 'he is going to fall on such and such a subject; or to ex-'pose such and such a piece of humbug; or that he may 'be expected shortly in such and such a place. I want 'the compiled part of the paper to express the idea of this 'Shadow's having been in libraries, and among the books 'referred to. I want him to loom as a fanciful thing all 'over London; and to get up a general notion of "What '"will the Shadow say about this, I wonder? What will '"the Shadow say about that? Is the Shadow here?" 'and so forth. Do you understand? . . . I have an enor-'mous difficulty in expressing what I mean, in this stage 'of the business; but I think the importance of the idea 'is, that once stated on paper, there is no difficulty in keep-'ing it up. That it presents an odd, unsubstantial, whim-'sical, new thing: a sort of previously unthought-of Power 'going about. That it will concentrate into one focus all

A Shadow for everywhere.

Hopes of success.

'that is done in the paper. That it sets up a creature 'which isn't the Spectator, and isn't Isaac Bickerstaff, 'and isn't anything of that kind: but in which people 'will be perfectly willing to believe, and which is just mys- 'terious and quaint enough to have a sort of charm for 'their imagination, while it will represent common-sense 'and humanity. I want to express in the title, and in 'the grasp of the idea to express also, that it is the Thing 'at everybody's elbow, and in everybody's footsteps. At 'the window, by the fire, in the street, in the house, from 'infancy to old age, everyone's inseparable companion . . . 'Now do you make anything out of this? which I let off as 'if I were a bladder full of it, and you had punctured me. 'I have not breathed the idea to any one; but I have a 'lively hope that it *is* an idea, and that out of it the whole 'scheme may be hammered.'

BROAD-STAIRS: 1849.

Expected advantages.

Something for every-body.

Excellent the idea doubtless, and so described in his letter that hardly anything more characteristic survives him. But I could not make anything out of it that had a quite feasible look. The ordinary ground of miscellaneous reading, selection, and compilation out of which it was to spring, seemed to me no proper soil for the imaginative produce it was meant to bear. As his fancies grew and gathered round it, they had given it too much of the range and scope of his own exhaustless land of invention and marvel; and the very means proposed for letting in the help of others would only more heavily have weighted himself. Not to trouble the reader now with objections given him in detail, my judgment was clear against his plan; less for any doubt of the effect if its parts could be brought to

My doubts.

Incompati-bilities of design.

LONDON: 1849.

Again at home.

combine, than for my belief that it was not in that view practicable; and though he did not immediately accept my reasons, he acquiesced in them ultimately. 'I do not lay 'much stress on your grave doubts about Periodical, but 'more anon.' The more anon resolved itself into conversations out of which the shape given to the project was that which it finally took.

New design chosen.

It was to be a weekly miscellany of general literature; and its stated objects were to be, to contribute to the entertainment and instruction of all classes of readers, and to help in the discussion of the more important social questions of the time. It was to comprise short stories by others as well as himself; matters of passing interest in the liveliest form that could be given to them; subjects suggested by books that might most be attracting attention; and poetry in every number if possible, but in any case something of romantic fancy. This was to be a cardinal point. There was to be no mere utilitarian spirit; with all familiar things, but especially those repellent on the surface, something was to be connected that should be fanciful or kindly; and the hardest workers were to be taught that their lot is not necessarily excluded from the sympathies and graces of imagination. This was all finally settled by the close of 1849, when a general announcement of the intended adventure was made. There remained only a title and an assistant editor; and I am happy now to remember that for the latter important duty Mr. Wills was chosen at my suggestion. He discharged its duties with admirable patience and ability for twenty years, and Dickens's later life had no more intimate friend.

What it was to comprise.

First announcement made.

Assistant editor appointed.

The title took some time and occupied many letters. One of the first thought-of has now the curious interest of having foreshadowed, by the motto proposed to accompany it, the title of the series of *All the Year Round* which he was led to substitute for the older series in 1859. 'THE 'ROBIN. With this motto from Goldsmith. "*The red-'"breast, celebrated for its affection to mankind, con-'"tinues with us, the year round.*"' That however was rejected. Then came: 'MANKIND. This I think very 'good.' It followed the other nevertheless. After it came: 'And here a strange idea, but with decided advantages. '"CHARLES DICKENS. A weekly journal designed for the '"instruction and entertainment of all classes of readers. '"CONDUCTED BY HIMSELF."' Still, there was something wanting in that also. Next day arrived: 'I really think 'if there *be* anything wanting in the other name, that this 'is very pretty, and just supplies it. THE HOUSEHOLD 'VOICE. I have thought of many others, as—THE HOUSE-'HOLD GUEST. THE HOUSEHOLD FACE. THE COMRADE. 'THE MICROSCOPE. THE HIGHWAY OF LIFE. THE LEVER. 'THE ROLLING YEARS. THE HOLLY TREE (with two lines 'from Southey for a motto). EVERYTHING. But I rather 'think the VOICE is it.' It was near indeed; but the following day came, 'HOUSEHOLD WORDS. This is a very 'pretty name:' and the choice was made.

Selection of title.

Names proposed.

The name chosen.

The first number appeared on Saturday the 30th of March 1850, and contained among other things the beginning of a story by a very original writer, Mrs. Gaskell, for whose powers he had a high admiration, and with whom he had friendly intercourse during many years. Other

Appearance of first number.

LONDON: 1850.

opportunities will arise for mention of those with whom this new labour brought him into personal communication, but I may at once say that of all the writers, before unknown, whom his journal helped to make familiar to a wide world of readers, he had the strongest personal interest in Mr. Sala, and placed at once in the highest rank his capabilities of help in such an enterprise.* An illustrative trait of what I have named as its cardinal point to him will fitly close my account of its establishment. Its first number, still unpublished, had not seemed to him quite to fulfil his promise, 'tenderly to cherish the light of fancy inherent in 'all breasts;' and, as soon as he received the proof of the second, I heard from him. 'Looking over the suggested 'contents of number two at breakfast this morning' (Brighton: 14th of March 1850) 'I felt an uneasy sense 'of there being a want of something tender, which would 'apply to some universal household knowledge. Coming 'down in the railroad the other night (always a wonder-'fully suggestive place to me when I am alone) I was look-'ing at the stars, and revolving a little idea about them. 'Putting now these two things together, I wrote the en-'closed little paper, straightway; and should like you to

First contributors.

At BRIGHTON.

The want first felt by him.

His opinion of Mr. Sala.

* Mr. Sala's first paper appeared in September 1851, and in the same month of the following year I had an allusion in a letter from Dickens which I shall hope to have Mr. Sala's forgiveness for printing. 'That was very good indeed 'of Sala's (some essay he had written). 'He was twenty guineas in advance, 'by the bye, and I told Wills delicately to make him a present of it. I find 'him a very conscientious fellow. When he gets money ahead, he is not 'like the imbecile youth who so often do the like in Wellington-street' (the office of *Household Words*) 'and walk off, but only works more industriously. 'I think he improves with everything he does. He looks sharply at the altera-'tions in his articles, I observe; and takes the hint next time.'

'read it before you send it to the printers (it will not take 'you five minutes), and let me have a proof by return.' This was the child's 'dream of a star,' which opened his second number; and, not appearing among his reprinted pieces, may justify a word or two of description. It is of a brother and sister, constant child-companions, who used to make friends of a star, watching it together until they knew when and where it would rise, and always bidding it good-night; so that when the sister dies the lonely brother still connects her with the star, which he then sees opening as a world of light, and its rays making a shining pathway from earth to heaven; and he also sees angels waiting to receive travellers up that sparkling road, his little sister among them; and he thinks ever after that he belongs less to the earth than to the star where his sister is; and he grows up to youth and through manhood and old age, consoled still under the successive domestic bereavements that fall to his earthly lot by renewal of that vision of his childhood; until at last, lying on his own bed of death, he feels that he is moving as a child to his child-sister, and he thanks his heavenly father that the star had so often opened before to receive the dear ones who awaited him.

BRIGHTON: 1850.

The want supplied.

The child's dream of a star.

His sister Fanny and himself, he told me long before this paper was written, used to wander at night about a churchyard near their house, looking up at the stars; and her early death, of which I am now to speak, had vividly reawakened all the childish associations which made her memory dear to him.

A fancy derived from his childhood.

# CHAPTER XX.

## LAST YEARS IN DEVONSHIRE TERRACE.

### 1848—1851.

LONDON: 1848-51.

Sentiment about places.

EXCEPTING always the haunts and associations of his childhood, Dickens had no particular sentiment of locality, and any special regard for houses he had lived in was not a thing noticeable in him. But he cared most for Devonshire-terrace, perhaps for the bit of ground attached to it; and it was with regret he suddenly discovered, at the close of 1847, that he should have to resign it 'next lady-day 'three years. I had thought the lease two years more.' To that brief remaining time belong some incidents of which I have still to give account; and I connect them with the house in which he lived during the progress of what is generally thought his greatest book, and of what I think were his happiest years.

Confidences.

We had never had such intimate confidences as in the interval since his return from Paris; but these have been used in my narrative of the childhood and boyish experiences, and what remain are incidental only. Of the fragment of autobiography there also given, the origin has been told: but the intention of leaving such a record had been in his mind, we now see, at an earlier date; and it

*Ante*, p. 327.

was the very depth of our interest in the opening of his fragment that led to the larger design in which it became absorbed. 'I hardly know why I write this,' was his own comment on one of his personal revelations, 'but the more 'than friendship which has grown between us seems to 'force it on me in my present mood. We shall speak of 'it all, you and I, Heaven grant, wisely and wonderingly 'many and many a time in after years. In the meanwhile 'I am more at rest for having opened all my heart and 'mind to you. . . This day eleven years, poor dear Mary 'died.' *

Personal revelations.

That was written on the seventh of May 1848, but another sadness impending at the time was taking his thoughts still farther back; to when he trotted about with his little elder sister in the small garden to the house at Portsea. The faint hope for her which Elliotson had given him in Paris had since completely broken down; and I was to hear, in less than two months after the letter just quoted, how nearly the end was come. 'A change took 'place in poor Fanny,' he wrote on the 5th of July, 'about 'the middle of the day yesterday, which took me out there 'last night. Her cough suddenly ceased almost, and, 'strange to say, she immediately became aware of her 'hopeless state; to which she resigned herself, after an 'hour's unrest and struggle, with extraordinary sweetness 'and constancy. The irritability passed, and all hope 'faded away; though only two nights before, she had been

Early memories.

Eldest sister's illness.

* I take the opportunity of saying that there was an omission of three words in the epitaph quoted on a former page (vol. i. p. 99). The headstone at the grave in Kensal-green bears this inscription: 'Young, beautiful, and good, God 'in His mercy numbered her among His angels at the early age of seventeen.'

LONDON: 1848-51.

'planning for "after Christmas." She is greatly changed. 'I had a long interview with her to-day, alone; and when 'she had expressed some wishes about the funeral, and 'her being buried in unconsecrated ground' (Mr. Burnett's family were dissenters), 'I asked her whether she had any 'care or anxiety in the world. She said No, none. It was 'hard to die at such a time of life, but she had no alarm 'whatever in the prospect of the change; felt sure we 'should meet again in a better world; and although they 'had said she might rally for a time, did not really wish it. 'She said she was quite calm and happy, relied upon the 'mediation of Christ, and had no terror at all. She had 'worked very hard, even when ill; but believed that was 'in her nature, and neither regretted nor complained of it. 'Burnett had been always very good to her; they had 'never quarrelled; she was sorry to think of his going 'back to such a lonely home; and was distressed about 'her children, but not painfully so. She showed me how 'thin and worn she was; spoke about an invention she 'had heard of that she would like to have tried, for the 'deformed child's back; called to my remembrance all 'our sister Letitia's patience and steadiness; and, though 'she shed tears sometimes, clearly impressed upon me that 'her mind was made up, and at rest. I asked her very 'often, if she could ever recall anything that she could 'leave to my doing, to put it down, or mention it to some-'body if I was not there; and she said she would, but she 'firmly believed that there was nothing—nothing. Her 'husband being young, she said, and her children infants, 'she could not help thinking sometimes, that it would be

At his sister's sick-bed.

Last thoughts.

Resignation and hope.

'very long in the course of nature before they were re-'united; but she knew that was a mere human fancy, and 'could have no reality after she was dead. Such an affect-'ing exhibition of strength and tenderness, in all that early 'decay, is quite indescribable. I need not tell you how it 'moved me. I cannot look round upon the dear children 'here, without some misgiving that this sad disease will not 'perish out of our blood with her; but I am sure I have 'no selfishness in the thought, and God knows how small 'the world looks to one who comes out of such a sick-'room on a bright summer day. I don't know why I write 'this before going to bed. I only know that in the very 'pity and grief of my heart, I feel as if it were doing 'something.' After not many weeks she died, and the little child who was her last anxiety did not long survive her.

Natural fears.

Sister's death.

In all the later part of the year Dickens's thoughts were turning much to the form his next book should assume. A suggestion that he should write it in the first person, by way of change, had been thrown out by me, which he took at once very gravely; and this, with other things, though as yet not dreaming of any public use of his own personal and private recollections, conspired to bring about that resolve. The determination once taken, with what a singular truthfulness he contrived to blend the fact with the fiction may be shown by a small occurrence of this time. It has been inferred, from the vividness of the boy-impressions of Yarmouth in David's earliest experiences, that the place must have been familiar to his own boyhood: but the truth was that at the close of 1848 he first saw that celebrated

Book to be written in first person.

To tell his early life.

LONDON: 1848-51.

sea-port. One of its earlier months had been signalised by an adventure in which Leech, Lemon, and myself took part with him, when, obtaining horses from Salisbury, we passed the whole of a March day in riding over every part of the Plain; visiting Stonehenge, and exploring Hazlitt's 'hut' at Winterslow, birthplace of some of his finest essays; altogether with so brilliant a success that now (13th of November) he proposed to 'repeat the Salisbury Plain 'idea in a new direction in mid-winter, to wit, Blackgang 'Chine in the Isle of Wight, with dark winter cliffs and 'roaring oceans.' But mid-winter brought with it too much dreariness of its own, to render these stormy accompaniments to it very palatable; and on the last day of the year he bethought him 'it would be better to make an 'outburst to some old cathedral city we don't know, and 'what do you say to Norwich and Stanfield-hall?' Thither accordingly the three friends went, illness at the last disabling me; and of the result I heard (12th of January, 1849) that Stanfield-hall, the scene of a recent frightful tragedy, had nothing attractive unless the term might be applied to 'a murderous look that seemed to invite such 'a crime. We arrived,' continued Dickens, 'between the 'Hall and Potass farm, as the search was going on for the 'pistol in a manner so consummately stupid, that there 'was nothing on earth to prevent any of Rush's labourers 'from accepting five pounds from Rush junior to find the 'weapon and give it to him. Norwich, a disappointment' (one pleasant face transformeth a city,' but he was unable yet to connect it with our delightful friend Elwin); 'all save 'its place of execution, which we found fit for a gigantic

Riding over Salisbury Plain.

Visiting the scene of a tragedy.

'scoundrel's exit. But the success of the trip, for me, was 'to come. Yarmouth, sir, where we went afterwards, is 'the strangest place in the wide world: one hundred and 'forty-six miles of hill-less marsh between it and London. 'More when we meet. I shall certainly try my hand at it.' He made it the home of his 'little Em'ly.'

First sees Yarmouth.

Everything now was taking that direction with him; and soon, to give his own account of it, his mind was upon names 'running like a high sea.' Four days after the date of the last-quoted letter ('all over happily, thank God, by 'four o'clock this morning') there came the birth of his eighth child and sixth son; whom at first he meant to call by Oliver Goldsmith's name, but settled afterwards into that of Henry Fielding; and to whom that early friend Ainsworth who had first made us known to each other, welcome and pleasant companion always, was asked to be godfather. Telling me of the change in the name of the little fellow, which he had made in a kind of homage to the style of work he was now so bent on beginning, he added, 'What should 'you think of this for a notion of a character? "Yes, that '"is very true: but now, *What's his motive?*" I fancy I 'could make something like it into a kind of amusing and 'more innocent Pecksniff. "Well now, yes—no doubt that '"was a fine thing to do! But now, stop a moment, let us '"see—*What's his motive?*"' Here again was but one of the many outward signs of fancy and fertility that accompanied the outset of all his more important books; though, as in their cases also, other moods of the mind incident to such beginnings were less favourable. 'Deepest despon'dency, as usual, in commencing, besets me;' is the open-

Birth of sixth son.

Notion for a character.

Incident to new enterprises.

LONDON: 1848-51.

ing of the letter in which he speaks of what of course was always one of his first anxieties, the selection of a name. In this particular instance he had been undergoing doubts and misgivings to more than the usual degree. It was not until the 23rd of February he got to anything like the shape of a feasible title. 'I should like to know how the 'enclosed (one of those I have been thinking of) strikes 'you, on a first acquaintance with it. It is odd, I think, 'and new; but it may have A's difficulty of being "too '"comic, my boy." I suppose I should have to add, though, 'by way of motto, "And in short it led to the very Mag's '"Diversions. *Old Saying.*" Or would it be better, there 'being equal authority for either, "And in short they all '"played Mag's Diversions. *Old Saying?*"

Choosing a title.

Mag's Diversions.

'*Mag's Diversions.*
'Being the personal history of
'MR. THOMAS MAG THE YOUNGER,
'Of Blunderstone House.'

This was hardly satisfactory, I thought; and it soon became apparent that he thought so too, although within the next three days I had it in three other forms. '*Mag's* '*Diversions,* being the Personal History, Adventures, Ex'perience and Observation of Mr. David Mag the Younger, 'of Blunderstone House.' The second omitted Adventures, and called his hero Mr. David Mag the Younger, of Copperfield House. The third made nearer approach to what the destinies were leading him to, and transformed Mr. David Mag into Mr. David Copperfield the Younger and his great-aunt Margaret; retaining still as his leading

Thomas becomes David.

Blunderstone becomes Copperfield.

title, *Mag's Diversions*. It is singular that it should never have occurred to him, while the name was thus strangely as by accident bringing itself together, that the initials were but his own reversed; but he was much startled when I pointed this out, and protested it was just in keeping with the fates and chances which were always befalling him. 'Why else,' he said, 'should I so obstinately have kept to 'that name when once it turned up?'

Things of destiny.

It was quite true that he did so, as I had curious proof following close upon the heels of that third proposal. 'I 'wish,' he wrote on the 26th of February, 'you would look 'over carefully the titles now enclosed, and tell me to which 'you most incline. You will see that they give up *Mag* 'altogether, and refer exclusively to one name—that which 'I last sent you. I doubt whether I could, on the whole, 'get a better name.

'Copper-'field' chosen.

'1. *The Copperfield Disclosures.* Being 'the personal history, experience, 'and observation, of Mr. David 'Copperfield the Younger, of 'Blunderstone House.

2. *The Copperfield Records.* Being the 'personal history, experience, and 'observation, of Mr. David Cop-'perfield the Younger, of Cop-'perfield Cottage.

'3. *The Last Living Speech and Con-'fession of David Copperfield 'Junior*, of Blunderstone Lodge, 'who was never executed at the 'Old Bailey. Being his personal 'history found among his papers.

'4. *The Copperfield Survey of the 'World as it Rolled.* Being the 'personal history, experience, and 'observation, of David Copper-'field the Younger, of Blunder-'stone Rookery.

'5. *The Last Will and Testament of 'Mr. David Copperfield.* Being 'his personal history left as a 'legacy.

Varieties of it proposed.

'6. *Copperfield, Complete.* Being the 'whole personal history and ex-'perience of Mr. David Copper-'field of Blunderstone House, 'which he never meant to be 'published on any account.

Or, the opening words of No. 6 might be *Copperfield's*

LONDON: 1848-51.

'*Entire;* and *The Copperfield Confessions* might open 'Nos. 1 and 2. Now, WHAT SAY YOU?'

Choice first made.

What I said is to be inferred from what he wrote back on the 28th. 'The *Survey* has been my favourite from 'the first. Kate picked it out from the rest, without my 'saying anything about it. Georgy too. You hit upon it, 'on the first glance. Therefore I have no doubt that it is 'indisputably the best title; and I will stick to it.' There was a change nevertheless. His completion of the second chapter defined to himself, more clearly than before, the character of the book; and the propriety of rejecting everything not strictly personal from the name given to it. The words proposed, therefore, became ultimately these only: 'The Personal History, Adventures, Experience, and Observation of David Copperfield the Younger, of Blunderstone 'Rookery, which he never meant to be published on any 'account.' And the letter which told me that with this name it was finally to be launched on the first of May, told me also (19th April) the difficulties that still beset him at the opening. 'My hand is out in the matter of *Copper-'field.* To-day and yesterday I have done nothing. Though 'I know what I want to do, I am lumbering on like a 'stage-waggon. I can't even dine at the Temple to-day, 'I feel it so important to stick at it this evening, and 'make some head. I am quite aground; quite a literary 'Benedict, as he appeared when his heels wouldn't stay 'upon the carpet; and the long Copperfieldian perspective 'looks snowy and thick, this fine morning.'* The allusion

Title finally determined.

Difficulties of opening.

War and peace.

* From letters of nearly the same date here is another characteristic word: 'Pen and ink before me! Am I not at work on *Copperfield!* Nothing else

was to a dinner at his house the night before; when not only Rogers had to be borne out, having fallen sick at the table, but, as we rose soon after to quit the dining-room, Mr. Jules Benedict had quite suddenly followed the poet's lead, and fallen prostrate on the carpet in the midst of us. Amid the general consternation there seemed a want of proper attendance on the sick: the distinguished musician faring in this respect hardly so well as the famous bard, by whose protracted sufferings in the library, whither he had been removed, the sanitary help available on the establishment was still absorbed; and as Dickens had been eloquent during dinner on the atrocities of a pauper-farming case at Tooting which was then exciting a fury of indignation, Fonblanque now declared him to be no better himself than a second Drouet, reducing his guests to a lamentable state by the food he had given them, and aggravating their sad condition by absence of all proper nursing. The joke was well kept up by Quin and Edwin Landseer, Lord Strangford joining in with a tragic sympathy for his friend the poet; and the banquet so dolefully interrupted ended in uproarious mirth. For nothing really serious had happened. Benedict went laughing away with his wife, and I helped Rogers on with his over-shoes for his usual night-walk home. 'Do you know how 'many waistcoats I wear?' asked the poet of me, as I was doing him this service. I professed my inability to guess. 'Five!' he said: 'and here they are!' Upon which he

LONDON: 1848-51.

Memorable dinner.

Rogers and Benedict.

Wit of Fonblanque.

All's well that ends well.

'would have kept me here until half-past two on such a day . . Indian news 'bad indeed. Sad things come of bloody war. If it were not for Elihu, I 'should be a peace and arbitration man.'

LONDON: 1848-51.

opened them, in the manner of the gravedigger in *Hamlet*, and showed me every one.

That dinner was in the April of 1849, and among others present were Mrs. Procter and Mrs. Macready, dear and familiar names always in his house. No swifter or surer perception than Dickens's for what was solid and beautiful in character; he rated it higher than intellectual effort; and the same lofty place, first in his affection and respect, would have been Macready's and Procter's, if the one had not been the greatest of actors, and the other a poet as genuine as old Fletcher or Beaumont. There were present at this dinner also the American minister and Mrs. Bancroft (it was the year of that visit of Macready to America, which ended in the disastrous Forrest riots); and it had among its guests Lady Graham, the wife of Sir James Graham, than whom not even the wit and beauty of her nieces, Mrs. Norton and Lady Dufferin, better represented the brilliant family of the Sheridans; so many of whose members, and these three above all, Dickens prized among his friends. The table that day will be 'full' if I add the celebrated singer Miss Catherine Hayes, and her homely good-natured Irish mother, who startled us all very much by complimenting Mrs. Dickens on her having had for her father so clever a painter as Mr. Hogarth.

Procter and Macready.

The Sheridans.

Startling compliment.

Others familiar to Devonshire-terrace in these years will be indicated if I name an earlier dinner (3rd of January), for the 'christening' of the *Haunted Man*, when, besides Lemons, Evanses, Leeches, Bradburys, and Stanfields, there were present Tenniel, Topham, Stone, Robert Bell, and Thomas Beard. Next month (24th of March) I

'Christening' dinner.

LONDON: 1848-51.

met at his table, Lord and Lady Lovelace; Milner Gibson, Mowbray Morris, Horace Twiss, and their wives; Lady Molesworth and her daughter (Mrs. Ford); John Hardwick, Charles Babbage, and Doctor Locock. That distinguished physician had attended the poor girl, Miss Abercrombie, whose death by strychnine led to the exposure of Wainewright's murders; and the opinion he had formed of her chances of recovery, the external indications of that poison being then but imperfectly known, was first shaken, he told me, by the gloomy and despairing cries of the old family nurse, that her mother and her uncle had died exactly so! These, it was afterwards proved, had been among the murderer's former victims. The Lovelaces were frequent guests after the return from Italy, Sir George Crawford, so friendly in Genoa, having married Lord Lovelace's sister; and few had a greater warmth of admiration for Dickens than Lord Byron's 'Ada,' on whom Paul Dombey's death laid a strange fascination. They were again at a dinner got up in the following year for Scribe and the composer Halévy, who had come over to bring out the *Tempest* at Her Majesty's-theatre, then managed by Mr. Lumley, who with M. Van de Weyer, Mrs. Gore and her daughter, the Hogarths, and I think the fine French comedian, Samson, were also among those present. Earlier that year there were gathered at his dinner-table the John Delanes, Isambard Brunels, Thomas Longmans (friends since the earliest Broadstairs days, and special favourites always), Lord Mulgrave, and Lord Carlisle, with all of whom his intercourse was intimate and frequent, and became especially so with Delane in later years. Lord

Wainewright murders.

Lord Byron's Ada.

Dinner to Halévy and Scribe.

LONDON: 1848-51.

Brougham and the '*Punch* 'people.'

Carlisle amused us that night, I remember, by repeating what the good old Brougham had said to him of 'those '*Punch* people,' expressing what was really his fixed belief. 'They never get my face, and are obliged' (which, like Pope, he always pronounced obleeged), 'to put up with my 'plaid trousers!' Of Lord Mulgrave, pleasantly associated with the first American experiences, let me add that he now went with us to several outlying places of amusement of which he wished to acquire some knowledge, and which Dickens knew better than any man; small theatres, saloons, and gardens in city or borough, to which the Eagle and Britannia were as palaces; and I think he was of the party one famous night in the summer of 1849 (29th of June), when with Talfourd, Edwin Landseer, and Stanfield, we went to the *Battle of Waterloo* at Vauxhall, and were astounded to see pass in immediately before us, in a bright white overcoat, the great Duke himself, Lady Douro on his arm, the little Ladies Ramsay by his side, and everybody cheering and clearing the way before him. That the old hero enjoyed it all, there could be no doubt, and he made no secret of his delight in 'Young Hernandez;' but the 'Battle' was undeniably tedious, and it was impossible not to sympathize with the repeatedly and very audibly expressed wish of Talfourd, that 'the Prussians would come 'up!'

Expedition with Lord Mulgrave.

The Duke at Vauxhall.

Dinner after first *Copperfield*.

The preceding month was that of the start of *David Copperfield*, and to one more dinner (on the 12th) I may especially refer for those who were present at it. Carlyle and Mrs. Carlyle came, Thackeray and Rogers, Mrs. Gaskell and Kenyon, Jerrold and Hablot Browne, with

Mr. and Mrs. Tagart; and it was a delight to see the enjoyment of Dickens at Carlyle's laughing reply to questions about his health, that he was, in the language of Mr. Peggotty's housekeeper, a lorn lone creature and everything went contrairy with him. Things were not likely to go better, I thought, as I saw the great writer,—kindest as well as wisest of men, but not very patient under sentimental philosophies,—seated next the good Mr. Tagart, who soon was heard launching at him various metaphysical questions in regard to heaven and such like; and the relief was great when Thackeray introduced, with quaint whimsicality, a story which he and I had heard Macready relate in talking to us about his boyish days, of a country actor who had supported himself for six months on his judicious treatment of the 'tag' to the *Castle Spectre.* In the original it stands that you are to do away with suspicion, banish vile mistrust, and, almost in the words we had just heard from the minister to the philosopher, 'Believe there is a 'Heaven nor Doubt that Heaven is just!' in place of which Macready's friend, observing that the drop fell for the most part quite coldly, substituted one night the more telling appeal, 'And give us your Applause, for *that* IS ALWAYS 'JUST!' which brought down the house with rapture.

Carlyle.

Thackeray.

Judicious change of a tag.

This chapter would far outrun its limits if I spoke of other as pleasant gatherings under Dickens's roof during the years which I am now more particularly describing; when, besides the dinners, the musical enjoyments and dancings, as his children became able to take part in them, were incessant. 'Remember that for my Biography!' he said to me gravely on twelfth-day in 1849, after telling me what he

LONDON: 1848-51.

A fact for a biographer.

had done the night before; and as gravely I now redeem my laughing promise that I would. Little Mary and her sister Kate had taken much pains to teach their father the polka, that he might dance it with them at their brother's birthday festivity (held this year on the 7th, as the 6th was a Sunday); and in the middle of the previous night as he lay in bed, the fear had fallen on him suddenly that the step was forgotten, and then and there, in that wintry dark cold night, he got out of bed to practise it. Anything *more* characteristic could certainly not be told; unless I could have shown him dancing it afterwards, and far excelling the youngest performer in untiring vigour and vivacity.

Marryat's delight with children.

There was no one who approached him on these occasions excepting only our attached friend Captain Marryat, who had a frantic delight in dancing, especially with children, of whom and whose enjoyments he was as fond as it became so thoroughly good hearted a man to be. His name would have stood first among those I have been recalling, as he was among the first in Dickens's liking; but in the autumn of 1848 he had unexpectedly passed away. Other names however still reproach me for omission as my memory goes back. With Marryat's on the earliest page of this volume

Monckton Milnes.

stands that of Monckton Milnes, familiar with Dickens over all the time it covers, and still more prominent in Tavistock-house days when with Lady Houghton he brought fresh claims to my friend's admiration and regard. Of Bulwer Lytton's frequent presence in all his houses, and of

Lord Lytton.

Dickens's admiration for him as one of the supreme masters in his art, so unswerving and so often publicly declared, it would be needless again to speak. Nor shall I dwell upon his interchange of hospitalities with distinguished men in the two great professions so closely allied to literature and its followers; Denmans, Pollocks, Campbells, and Chittys; Watsons, Southwood Smiths, Lococks, and Elliotsons. To Alfred Tennyson, through all the friendly and familiar days I am describing, he gave full allegiance and honoured welcome. Tom Taylor was often with him; and there was a charm for him I should find it difficult to exaggerate in Lord Dudley Stuart's gentle yet noble character, his refined intelligence and generous public life, expressed so perfectly in his chivalrous face. Incomplete indeed would be the list if I did not add to it the frank and hearty Lord Nugent, who had so much of his grandfather, Goldsmith's friend, in his lettered tastes and jovial enjoyments. Nor should I forget occasional days with dear old Charles Kemble and one or other of his daughters; with Alexander Dyce; and with Harness and his sister, or his niece and her husband, Mr. and Mrs. Archdale; made especially pleasant by talk about great days of the stage. It was something to hear Kemble on his sister's Mrs. Beverley; or to see Harness and Dyce exultant in recollecting her Volumnia. The enchantment of the Mrs. Beverley, her brother would delightfully illustrate by imitation of her manner of restraining Beverley's intemperance to their only friend, 'You are 'too busy, sir!' when she quietly came down the stage from a table at which she had seemed to be occupying herself, laid her hand softly on her husband's arm, and in a gentle half-whisper 'No, not too busy; mistaken perhaps; 'but—' not only stayed his temper but reminded him of obligations forgotten in the heat of it. Up to where the

LONDON: 1848-51.

Lord Dudley Stuart.

Lord Nugent.

Kemble, Harness, and Dyce.

LONDON: 1848-51.

Mrs. Siddons.

tragic terror began, our friend told us, there was nothing but this composed domestic sweetness, expressed even in the simplicity and neat arrangement of her dress, her cap with the strait band, and her hair gathered up underneath; but all changing when the passion *did* begin; one single disordered lock escaping at the first outbreak, and, in the final madness, all of it streaming dishevelled down her beautiful face. Kemble made no secret of his belief that his sister had the higher genius of the two; but he spoke with rapture of 'John's' Macbeth and parts of his Othello; comparing his 'Farewell the tranquil mind' to the running down of a clock, an image which he did not know that Hazlitt had applied to the delivery of 'To-morrow and to-morrow,' in the other tragedy. In all this Harness seemed to agree; and I thought a distinction was not ill put by him, on the night of which I speak, in his remark that the nature in Kemble's acting only supplemented his magnificent art, whereas, though the artist was not less supreme in his sister, it was on nature she most relied, bringing up the other power only to the aid of it. 'It was in another sense like 'your writing,' said Harness to Dickens, 'the commonest 'natural feelings made great, even when not rendered more 'refined, by art.' Her Constance would have been fishwify, he declared, if its wonderful truth had not overborne every other feeling; and her Volumnia escaped being vulgar only by being so excessively grand. But it was just what was so called 'vulgarity' that made its passionate appeal to the vulgar in a better meaning of the word. When she first entered, Harness said, swaying and surging from side to side with every movement of the Roman crowd itself, as it went

John Kemble.

Good distinction.

A comparison.

out and returned in confusion, she so absorbed her son into herself as she looked at him, so swelled and amplified in her pride and glory for him, that 'the people in the pit blubbered 'all round,' and he could no more help it than the rest.

The pit 'blubber-'ing.'

There are yet some other names that should have place in these rambling recollections, though I by no means affect to remember all. One Sunday evening Mazzini made memorable by taking us to see the school he had established in Clerkenwell for the Italian organ-boys. This was after dining with Dickens, who had been brought into personal intercourse with the great Italian by having given money to a begging impostor who made unauthorized use of his name. Edinburgh friends made him regular visits in the spring time: not Jeffrey and his family alone, but sheriff Gordon and his, with whom he was not less intimate, Lord Murray and his wife, Sir William Allan and his niece, Lord Robertson with his wonderful Scotch mimicries, and Peter Fraser with his enchanting Scotch songs; our excellent friend Liston the surgeon, until his fatal illness came in December 1848, being seldom absent from those assembled to bid such visitors welcome. Allan's name may remind me of other artists often at his house, Eastlakes, Leslies, Friths, and Wards, besides those who have had frequent mention, and among whom I should have included Charles as well as Edwin Landseer, and William Boxall. Nor should I drop from this section of his friends, than whom none were more attractive to him, such celebrated names in the sister arts as those of Miss Helen Faucit, an actress worthily associated with the brightest days of our friend Macready's managements, Mr. Sims Reeves, Mr.

Mazzini.

Edinburgh friends.

Robert Liston.

Artist acquaintance.

LONDON: 1848-51.

John Parry, Mr. Phelps, Mr. Webster, Mr. Harley, Mr. and Mrs. Keeley, Mr. Whitworth, and Miss Dolby. Mr. George Henry Lewes he had an old and great regard for; among other men of letters should not be forgotten the cordial Thomas Ingoldsby, and many-sided true-hearted Charles Knight; Mr. R. H. Horne and his wife were frequent visitors both in London and at seaside holidays; and I have met at his table Mr. and Mrs. S. C. Hall. There were the Duff Gordons too, the Lyells, and, very old friends of us both, the Emerson Tennents; there was the good George Raymond; Mr. Frank Beard and his wife; the Porter Smiths, valued for Macready's sake as well as their own; Mr. and Mrs. Charles Black, near connections by marriage of George Cattermole, with whom there was intimate intercourse both before and during the residence in Italy; Mr. Thompson, brother of Mrs. Smithson formerly named, and his wife, whose sister Frederick Dickens married; Mr. Mitton, his own early companion; and Mrs. Torrens, who had played with the amateurs in Canada. These are all in my memory so connected with Devonshire-terrace, as friends or familiar acquaintance, that they claim this word before leaving it; and visitors from America, I may remark, had always a grateful reception. Of the Bancrofts mention has been made, and with them should be coupled the Abbot Lawrences, Prescott, Hillard, George Curtis, and Felton's brother. Felton himself did not visit England until the Tavistock-house time. In 1847 there was a delightful day with the Coldens and the Wilkses, relatives by marriage of Jeffrey; in the following year, I think at my rooms because of some accident that closed Devonshire-terrace that day

Visitors at his house.

*Ante*, p. 85, and pp. 158 and 205 of Vol. I.

Friends from America.

*Ante*, p. 166.

(25th of April), Dickens, Carlyle, and myself foregathered with the admirable Emerson; and M. Van de Weyer will probably remember a dinner where he took joyous part with Dickens in running down a phrase which the learned in books, Mr. Cogswell, on a mission here for the Astor library, had startled us by denouncing as an uncouth Scotch barbarism—*open up*. You found it constantly in Hume, he said, but hardly anywhere else; and he defied us to find it more than once through the whole of the volumes of Gibbon. Upon this, after brief wonder and doubt, we all thought it best to take part in a general assault upon *open up*, by invention of phrases on the same plan that should show it in exaggerated burlesque, and support Mr. Cogswell's indictment. Then came a struggle who should carry the absurdity farthest; and the victory remained with M. Van de Weyer until Dickens surpassed even him, and 'opened up' depths of almost frenzied absurdity that would have delighted the heart of Leigh Hunt. It will introduce the last and not least honoured name into my list of his acquaintance and friends, if I mention his amusing little interruption one day to Professor Owen's description of a telescope of huge dimensions built by an enterprising clergyman who had taken to the study of the stars; and who was eager, said Owen, to see farther into heaven—he was going to say, than Lord Rosse; if Dickens had not drily interposed, 'than his professional studies had 'enabled him to penetrate.'

'Open up.'

M. Van de Weyer.

Ambition to see into heaven.

Some incidents that belong specially to the three years that closed his residence in the home thus associated with not the least interesting part of his career, will farther show

LONDON: 1848-51.

what now were his occupations and ways of life. In the summer of 1849 he came up from Broadstairs to attend a Mansion-house dinner, which the lord mayor of that day had been moved by a laudable ambition to give to 'litera-'ture and art,' which he supposed would be adequately represented by the Royal Academy, the contributors to *Punch*, Dickens, and one or two newspaper men. On the whole the result was not cheering; the worthy chief magistrate, no doubt quite undesignedly, expressing too much surprise at the unaccustomed faces around him to be altogether complimentary. In general (this was the tone) we are in the habit of having princes, dukes, ministers, and what not for our guests, but what a delight, all the greater for being unusual, to see gentlemen like you! In other words, what could possibly be pleasanter than for people satiated with greatness to get for a while by way of change into the butler's pantry? This in substance was Dickens's account to me next day, and his reason for having been very careful in his acknowledgment of the toast of 'the Novelists.' He was nettled not a little therefore by a jesting allusion to himself in the *Daily News* in connection with the proceedings, and asked me to forward a remonstrance. Having a strong dislike to all such displays of sensitiveness, I suppressed the letter; but it is perhaps worth printing now. Its date is Broadstairs, Wednesday 11th of July 1849. 'I have no other interest in, or concern 'with, a most facetious article on last Saturday's dinner at 'the Mansion-house, which appeared in your paper of yes-'terday, and found its way here to-day, than that it mis-'represents me in what I said on the occasion. If you

Literature and art in the City.

Doubtful compliment.

Jest out of place.

A remonstrance suppressed.

'should not think it at all damaging to the wit of that 'satire to state what I did say, I shall be much obliged to 'you. It was this... That I considered the compliment of 'a recognition of Literature by the citizens of London the 'more acceptable to us because it was unusual in that hall, 'and likely to be an advantage and benefit to them in pro'portion as it became in future less unusual. That, on 'behalf of the novelists, I accepted the tribute as an ap'propriate one; inasmuch as we had sometimes reason 'to hope that our imaginary worlds afforded an occasional 'refuge to men busily engaged in the toils of life, from 'which they came forth none the worse to a renewal of 'its strivings; and certainly that the chief magistrate of 'the greatest city in the world might be fitly regarded as 'the representative of that class of our readers.'

A hint for London citizens.

Of an incident towards the close of the year, though it had important practical results, brief mention will here suffice. We saw the Mannings executed on the walls of Horsemonger-lane gaol; and with the letter which Dickens wrote next day to the *Times* descriptive of what we had witnessed on that memorable morning, there began an active agitation against public executions which never ceased until the salutary change was effected which has worked so well. Shortly after this he visited Rockingham-castle, the seat of Mr. and Mrs. Watson, his Lausanne friends; ar l I must preface by a word or two the amusing letter in which he told me of this visit. It was written in character, and the character was that of an American visitor to England.

The Mannings hanged.

Letter against public executions.

'I knew him, Horatio;' and a very kindly honest man

LONDON: 1848-51.

An American observer in England.

he was, who had come to England authorised to make enquiry into our general agricultural condition, and who discharged his mission by publishing some reports extremely creditable to his good sense and ability, expressed in a plain nervous English that reminded one of the rural writings of Cobbett. But in an evil hour he published also a series of private letters to friends written from the various residences his introductions had opened to him; and these were filled with revelations as to the internal economy of English noblemen's country houses, of a highly startling description. As for example, how, on arrival at a house your 'name is announced, and your portmanteau 'immediately taken into your chamber, which the servant 'shows you, with every convenience.' How 'you are asked 'by the servant at breakfast what you will have, or you 'get up and help yourself.' How at dinner you don't dash at the dishes, or contend for the 'fixings,' but wait till 'his portion is handed by servants to every one.' How all the wines, fruit, glasses, candlesticks, lamps, and plate are 'taken care of' by butlers, who have under-butlers for their 'adjuncts;' how ladies never wear 'white satin shoes 'or white gloves more than once;' how dinner-napkins are 'never left upon the table, but either thrown into your 'chair or on the floor under the table;' how no end of pains are taken to 'empty slops;' and above all what a national propensity there is to brush a man's clothes and polish his boots, whensoever and wheresoever the clothes and boots can be seized without the man.* This was what Dickens good-humouredly laughs at.

At English country-houses.

Marvels of English manners.

* Here is really an only average specimen of the letters as published: 'I

'Rockingham Castle: Friday, thirtieth of November, '1849. Picture to yourself, my dear F, a large old castle, 'approached by an ancient keep, portcullis, &c, &c, filled 'with company, waited on by six-and-twenty servants; 'the slops (and wine-glasses) continually being emptied; 'and my clothes (with myself in them) always being car-'ried off to all sorts of places; and you will have a faint 'idea of the mansion in which I am at present staying. I 'should have written to you yesterday, but for having had 'a very busy day. Among the guests is a Miss B, sister 'of the Honourable Miss B (of Salem, Mass.), whom we 'once met at the house of our distinguished literary coun-'tryman Colonel Landor. This lady is renowned as an 'amateur actress, so last night we got up in the great hall 'some scenes from the *School for Scandal*; the scene 'with the lunatic on the wall, from the *Nicholas Nickleby* 'of Major-General the Hon. C. Dickens (Richmond, Va.); 'some conjuring; and then finished off with country-dances; 'of which we had two admirably good ones, quite new to 'me, though really old. Getting the words, and making 'the preparations, occupied (as you may believe) the 'whole day; and it was three o'clock before I got to bed. 'It was an excellent entertainment, and we were all un-'commonly merry. . . I had a very polite letter from our

Letter from Rockingham.

Private theatricals.

Scenes played.

'forgot to say, if you leave your chamber twenty times a day, after using your 'basin, you would find it clean, and the pitcher replenished on your return, and 'that you cannot take your clothes off, but they are taken away, brushed, folded, 'pressed, and placed in the bureau; and at the dressing-hour, before dinner, 'you find your candles lighted, your clothes laid out, your shoes cleaned, and 'everything arranged for use; . . . the dress-clothes brushed and folded in the 'nicest manner, and cold water, and hot water, and clean napkins in the 'greatest abundance. . . Imagine an elegant chamber, fresh water in basins, 'in goblets, in tubs, and sheets of the finest linen!'

Marked attentions.

LONDON: 1848-51.

Major Bentley.

'enterprising countryman Major Bentley * (of Lexington, 'Ky.), which I shall show you when I come home. We leave 'here this afternoon, and I shall expect you according to 'appointment, at a quarter past ten A.M. to-morrow. Of 'all the country-houses and estates I have yet seen in Eng-'land, I think this is by far the best. Everything undertaken 'eventuates in a most magnificent hospitality; and you 'will be pleased to hear that our celebrated fellow citizen 'General Boxall (Pittsburg, Penn.) is engaged in handing 'down to posterity the face of the owner of the mansion 'and of his youthful son and daughter. At a future time 'it will be my duty to report on the turnips, mangel-'wurzel, ploughs, and live stock; and for the present I 'will only say that I regard it as a fortunate circumstance 'for the neighbouring community that this patrimony 'should have fallen to my spirited and enlightened host. 'Every one has profited by it, and the labouring people in 'especial are thoroughly well cared-for and looked after.

General Boxall.

A family scene.

'To see all the household, headed by an enormously fat 'housekeeper, occupying the back benches last night, laugh-'ing and applauding without any restraint; and to see a 'blushing sleek-headed footman produce, for the watch-'trick, a silver watch of the most portentous dimensions, 'amidst the rapturous delight of his brethren and sister-'hood; was a very pleasant spectacle, even to a conscientious 'republican like yourself or me, who cannot but contem-'plate the parent country with feelings of pride in our 'own land, which (as was well observed by the Honor-

* From this time to his death there was always friendly intercourse with his old publisher Mr. Bentley.

'able Elias Deeze, of Hertford, Conn.) is truly the land of 'the free. Best remembrances from Columbia's daughters. 'Ever thine, my dear F, — C. H." Dickens, during the too brief time this excellent friend was spared to him, often repeated his visits to Rockingham, always a surpassing enjoyment; and in the winter of 1851 he accomplished there, with help of the country carpenter, 'a very elegant little 'theatre,' of which he constituted himself manager, and had among his actors a brother of the lady referred to in his letter, 'a very good comic actor, but loose in words;' poor Augustus Stafford 'more than passable;' and 'a son 'of Vernon Smith's, really a capital low comedian.' It will be one more added to the many examples I have given of his untiring energy both in work and play, if I mention the fact that this theatre was opened at Rockingham for their first representation on Wednesday the 15th of January; that after the performance there was a country dance which lasted far into the morning; and that on the next evening, after a railway journey of more than 120 miles, he dined in London with the prime minister, Lord John Russell.



Visit to Rockingham.

Later visits.

Doing too much.

A little earlier in that winter we had together taken his eldest son to Eton, and a little later he had a great sorrow. 'Poor dear Jeffrey!' he wrote to me on the 29th January, 1850. 'I bought a *Times* at the station 'yesterday morning, and was so stunned by the announcement, that I felt it in that wounded part of me, almost 'directly; and the bad symptoms (modified) returned 'within a few hours. I had a letter from him in extra-'ordinary good spirits within this week or two—he was 'better, he said, than he had been for a long time—

Death of Francis Jeffrey.

LONDON: 1848-51.

Dickens on Jeffrey's death.

'and I sent him proof-sheets of the number only last 'Wednesday. I say nothing of his wonderful abilities and 'great career, but he was a most affectionate and devoted 'friend to me; and though no man could wish to live 'and die more happily, so old in years and yet so young 'in faculties and sympathies, I am very very deeply 'grieved for his loss.' He was justly entitled to feel pride in being able so to word his tribute of sorrowing affection. Jeffrey had completed with consummate success, if ever man did, the work appointed him in this world; and few, after a life of such activities, have left a memory so unstained and pure. But other and sharper sorrows awaited Dickens.

Progress of his work.

The chief occupation of the past and present year, *David Copperfield*, will have a chapter to itself, and in this may be touched but lightly. Once fairly in it, the story bore him irresistibly along; certainly with less trouble to himself in the composition, beyond that ardent sympathy with the creatures of the fancy which always made so absolutely real to him their sufferings or sorrows; and he was probably never less harassed by interruptions or breaks in his invention. His principal hesitation occurred in connection with the child-wife Dora, who had become a great favourite as he went on; and it was shortly after her fate had been decided, in the early autumn of 1850,* but before she

The child-wife.

* It may be proper to record the fact that he had made a short run to Paris, with Maclise, at the end of June, of which sufficient farther note will have been taken if I print the subjoined passages from a letter to me dated 24th June, 1850, Hôtel Windsor, Rue de Rivoli. 'There being no room in the 'Hôtel Brighton, we are lodged (in a very good apartment) here. The heat 'is absolutely frightful. I never felt anything like it in Italy. Sleep is next

breathed her last, that a third daughter was born to him, to whom he gave his dying little heroine's name. On these and other points, without forestalling what waits to be said of the composition of this fine story, a few illustrative words from his letters will properly find a place here. '*Copperfield* half done,' he wrote of the second number on the 6th of June. 'I feel, thank God, quite confident in 'the story. I have a move in it ready for this month; 'another for next; and another for the next.' 'I think it 'is necessary' (15th of November) 'to decide against the 'special pleader. Your reasons quite suffice. I am not 'sure but that the banking house might do. I will con- 'sider it in a walk.' 'Banking business impracticable' (17th of November) 'on account of the confinement: 'which would stop the story, I foresee. I have taken, for

Banker or proctor?

'to impossible, except in the day, when the room is dark, and the patient 'exhausted. We purpose leaving here on Saturday morning and going to 'Rouen, whence we shall proceed either to Havre or Dieppe, and so arrange 'our proceedings as to be home, please God, on Tuesday evening. We are 'going to some of the little theatres to-night, and on Wednesday to the Fran- 'çais, for Rachel's last performance before she goes to London. There does 'not seem to be anything remarkable in progress, in the theatrical way. Nor 'do I observe that out of doors the place is much changed, except in respect 'of the carriages which are certainly less numerous. I also think the Sunday 'is even much more a day of business than it used to be. As we are going 'into the country with Regnier to-morrow, I write this after letter time and 'before going out to dine at the Trois Frères, that it may come to you by to- 'morrow's post. The twelve hours' journey here is astounding—marvellously 'done, except in respect of the means of refreshment, which are absolutely 'none. Mac is very well (extremely loose as to his waistcoat, and otherwise 'careless in regard of buttons) and sends his love. De Fresne proposes a dinner 'with all the notabilities of Paris present, but I WON'T stand it! I really 'have undergone so much fatigue from work, that I am resolved not even to 'see him, but to please myself. I find, my child (as Horace Walpole would 'say), that I have written you nothing here, but you will take the will for 'the deed.'

A run to Paris.

LONDON: 1848-51.

'the present at all events, the proctor. I am wonderfully 'in harness, and nothing galls or frets.' '*Copperfield* done' (20th of November) 'after two days' very hard work indeed; 'and I think a smashing number. His first dissipation I 'hope will be found worthy of attention, as a piece of gro- 'tesque truth.' 'I feel a great hope' (23rd of January, 1850) 'that I shall be remembered by little Em'ly, a good 'many years to come.' 'I begin to have my doubts of 'being able to join you' (20th of February), 'for *Copper-* '*field* runs high, and must be done to-morrow. But I'll 'do it if possible, and strain every nerve. Some beautiful 'comic love, I hope, in the number.' 'Still undecided 'about Dora' (7th of May), 'but MUST decide to-day.'* 'I 'have been' (Tuesday, 20th of August) 'very hard at work 'these three days, and have still Dora to kill. But with 'good luck, I may do it to-morrow. Obliged to go to 'Shepherd's-bush to-day, and can consequently do little this 'morning. Am eschewing all sorts of things that present 'themselves to my fancy—coming in such crowds!' 'Work 'in a very decent state of advancement' (13th of August) 'domesticity notwithstanding. I hope I shall have a

David's first fall.

Little Em'ly.

Doubts as to Dora settled.

* The rest of the letter may be allowed to fill the corner of a note. The allusions to Rogers and Landor are by way of reply to an invitation I had sent him. 'I am extremely sorry to hear about Fox. Shall call to enquire, as I 'come by to the Temple. And will call on you (taking the chance of finding 'you) on my way to that Seat of Boredom. I wrote my paper for *H. W.* 'yesterday, and have begun *Copperfield* this morning. Still undecided about 'Dora, but MUST decide to-day. La difficulté d'écrire l'Anglais m'est extrême- 'ment ennuyeuse. Ah, mon Dieu! si l'on pourrait toujours écrire cette belle 'langue de France! Monsieur Rogere! Ah! qu'il est homme d'esprit, homme 'de génie, homme des lettres! Monsieur Landore! Ah qu'il parle Français— 'pas parfaitement comme un ange—un peu (peut-être) comme un diable! 'Mais il est bon garçon—sérieusement, il est un de la vraie noblesse de la 'nature. Votre tout dévoué, CHARLES. À Monsieur Monsieur Fos-tere.'

'splendid number. I feel the story to its minutest point.' 'Mrs. Micawber is still' (15th of August), 'I regret to say, 'in statu quo. Ever yours, WILKINS MICAWBER.' The little girl was born the next day, the 16th, and received the name of Dora Annie. The most part of what remained of the year was passed away from home.

Third daughter born.

The year following did not open with favourable omen, both the child and its mother having severe illness. The former rallied however, and 'little Dora is getting on 'bravely, thank God!' was his bulletin of the early part of February. Soon after, it was resolved to make trial of Great Malvern for Mrs. Dickens; and lodgings were taken there in March, Dickens and her sister accompanying her, and the children being left in London. 'It is a most beauti-'ful place,' he wrote to me (15th of March). 'O Heaven, to 'meet the Cold Waterers (as I did this morning when I 'went out for a shower-bath) dashing down the hills, with 'severe expressions on their countenances, like men doing 'matches and not exactly winning! Then, a young lady 'in a grey polka going *up* the hills, regardless of legs; and 'meeting a young gentleman (a bad case, I should say) 'with a light black silk cap on under his hat, and the 'pimples of I don't know how many douches under that. 'Likewise an old man who ran over a milk-child, rather 'than stop!—with no neckcloth, on principle; and with his 'mouth wide open, to catch the morning air.' This was the month, as we have seen, when the performances for the Guild were in active preparation, and it was also the date of the farewell dinner to our friend Macready on his quitting the stage. Dickens and myself came up for it from Mal-

At Great Malvern.

Cold Waterers.

*Ante*, pp. 366-8.

LONDON: 1848-51.

Macready's farewell.

vern, to which he returned the next day; and from the spirited speech in which he gave the health of the chairman at the dinner, I will add a few words for the sake of the truth expressed in them. 'There is a popular prejudice, 'a kind of superstition, that authors are not a particularly 'united body, and I am afraid that this may contain half a 'grain or so of the veracious. But of our chairman I have 'never in my life made public mention without adding 'what I can never repress, that in the path we both tread 'I have uniformly found him to be, from the first, the 'most generous of men; quick to encourage, slow to disparage, and ever anxious to assert the order of which he 'is so great an ornament. That we men of letters are, or 'have been, invariably or inseparably attached to each other, 'it may not be possible to say, formerly or now; but there 'cannot now be, and there cannot ever have been, among 'the followers of literature, a man so entirely without the 'grudging little jealousies that too often disparage its 'brightness, as Sir Edward Bulwer Lytton.' That was as richly merited as it is happily said.

Experience of a brother author.

Lord Lytton.

Dickens had to return to London after the middle of March for business connected with a charitable Home established at Shepherd's-bush by Miss Coutts, in the benevolent hope of rescuing fallen women by testing their fitness for emigration, of which future mention will be made, and which largely and regularly occupied his time for several years. On this occasion his stay was prolonged by the illness of his father. His health had been failing latterly, and graver symptoms were now spoken of. 'I saw my poor father twice yesterday,' he wrote to me on the 27th, 'the second

The Home at Shepherd's-bush.

'time between ten and eleven at night. In the morning 'I thought him not so well. At night, as well as any one 'in such a situation could be.' Next day he was so much better that his son went back to Malvern, and even gave us grounds for hope that we might yet have his presence in Hertfordshire to advise on some questions connected with the comedy which Sir Edward Lytton had written for the Guild. But the end came suddenly. I returned from Knebworth to London, supposing that some accident had detained him at Malvern; and at my house this letter waited me. 'Devonshire-terrace, Monday, thirty-first of March '1851. . . . My poor father died this morning at five and 'twenty minutes to six. They had sent for me to Malvern, 'but I passed John on the railway; for I came up with the 'intention of hurrying down to Bulwer Lytton's to-day 'before you should have left. I arrived at eleven last 'night, and was in Keppel-street at a quarter past eleven. 'But he did not know me, nor any one. He began to sink 'at about noon yesterday, and never rallied afterwards. I 'remained there until he died—O so quietly. . . I hardly 'know what to do. I am going up to Highgate to get the 'ground. Perhaps you may like to go, and I should like 'it if you do. I will not leave here before two o'clock. I 'think I must go down to Malvern again, at night, to know 'what is to be done about the children's mourning; and as 'you are returning to Bulwer's I should like to have gone 'that way, if *Bradshaw* gave me any hope of doing it. I 'wish most particularly to see you, I needn't say. I must 'not let myself be distracted by anything—and God knows 'I have left a sad sight!—from the scheme on which so

Father's illness.

Death of John Dickens.

LONDON: 1848-51.

'much depends. Most part of the alterations proposed I 'think good.' Mr. John Dickens was laid in Highgate Cemetery on the 5th of April; and the stone placed over him by the son who has made his name a famous one in England, bore tribute to his 'zealous, useful, cheerful 'spirit.' What more is to be said of him will be most becomingly said in speaking of *David Copperfield*. While the book was in course of being written, all that had been best in him came more and more vividly back to its author's memory; as time wore on, nothing else was remembered; and five years before his own death, after using in one of his letters to me a phrase rather out of the common with him, this was added: 'I find this looks like my poor father, 'whom I regard as a better man the longer I live.'

Tribute by his son.

Theatrical-fund dinner.

He was at this time under promise to take the chair at the General Theatrical Fund on the 14th of April. Great efforts were made to relieve him from the promise; but such special importance was attached to his being present, and the Fund so sorely then required help, that, no change of day being found possible for the actors who desired to attend, he yielded to the pressure put upon him; of which the result was to throw upon me a sad responsibility. The reader will understand why, even at this distance of time, my allusion to it is brief.

Claims of the Fund to support.

The train from Malvern brought him up only five minutes short of the hour appointed for the dinner, and we first met that day at the London Tavern. I never heard him to greater advantage than in the speech that followed. His liking for this Fund was the fact of its not confining its benefits to any special or exclusive body of actors, but opening them generously to all; and he gave a description of the kind of actor, going down to the infinitesimally small, not omitted from such kind help, which had a half-pathetic humour in it that makes it charming still. 'In our Fund,' he said, 'the word exclusiveness is 'not known. We include every actor, whether he be 'Hamlet or Benedict: the ghost, the bandit, or the court 'physician; or, in his one person, the whole king's army. 'He may do the light business, or the heavy, or the 'comic, or the eccentric. He may be the captain who 'courts the young lady, whose uncle still unaccountably 'persists in dressing himself in a costume one hundred 'years older than his time. Or he may be the young 'lady's brother in the white gloves and inexpressibles, 'whose duty in the family appears to be to listen to the 'female members of it whenever they sing, and to shake 'hands with everybody between all the verses. Or he may 'be the baron who gives the fête, and who sits uneasily on 'the sofa under a canopy with the baroness while the fête 'is going on. Or he may be the peasant at the fête who 'comes on the stage to swell the drinking chorus, and who, 'it may be observed, always turns his glass upside down 'before he begins to drink out of it. Or he may be the 'clown who takes away the doorstep of the house where 'the evening party is going on. Or he may be the gentle'man who issues out of the house on the false alarm, and 'is precipitated into the area. Or, if an actress, she may 'be the fairy who resides for ever in a revolving star with 'an occasional visit to a bower or a palace. Or again, if an 'actor, he may be the armed head of the witch's cauldron;

Absence of exclusiveness.

Plea for small actors.

Remembering the forgotten.

LONDON: 1848-51.

'or even that extraordinary witch, concerning whom I 'have observed in country places, that he is much less like 'the notion formed from the description of Hopkins than 'the Malcolm or Donalbain of the previous scenes. This 'society, in short, says, "Be you what you may, be you '"actor or actress, be your path in your profession never '"so high or never so low, never so haughty or never so '"humble, we offer you the means of doing good to your- '"selves, and of doing good to your brethren."'

The Fund and its subscribers.

Half an hour before he rose to speak I had been called out of the room. It was the servant from Devonshire-terrace to tell me his child Dora was suddenly dead. She had not been strong from her birth; but there was just at this time no cause for special fear, when unexpected convulsions came, and the frail little life passed away. My decision had to be formed at once; and I satisfied myself that it would be best to permit his part of the proceedings to close before the truth was told to him. But as he went on, after the sentences I have quoted, to speak of actors having to come from scenes of sickness, of suffering, aye, even of death itself, to play their parts before us, my part was very difficult. 'Yet how often is it with all of us,' he proceeded to say, and I remember to this hour with what anguish I listened to words that had for myself alone, in all the crowded room, their full significance: 'how often is 'it with all of us, that in our several spheres we have to 'do violence to our feelings, and to hide our hearts in 'carrying on this fight of life, if we would bravely discharge 'in it our duties and responsibilities.' In the disclosure that followed when he left the chair, Mr. Lemon, who was

Death of his little daughter.

Difficult tasks in life.

present, assisted me; and I left this good friend with him next day, when I went myself to Malvern and brought back Mrs. Dickens and her sister. The little child lies in a grave at Highgate near that of Mr. and Mrs. John Dickens; and on the stone which covers her is now written also her father's name, and those of two of her brothers.

Dora's grave.

One more public discussion he took part in, before quitting London for the rest of the summer; and what he said (it was a meeting, with Lord Carlisle in the chair, in aid of Sanitary reform) very pregnantly illustrates what was remarked by me on a former page. He declared his belief that neither education nor religion could do anything really useful in social improvement until the way had been paved for their ministrations by cleanliness and decency. He spoke warmly of the services of Lord Ashley in connection with ragged schools, but he put the case of a miserable child tempted into one of those schools out of the noisome places in which his life was passed, and he asked what a few hours' teaching could effect against the ever-renewed lesson of a whole existence. 'But give him, and his, a 'glimpse of heaven through a little of its light and air; 'give them water; help them to be clean; lighten the 'heavy atmosphere in which their spirits flag, and which 'makes them the callous things they are; take the body 'of the dead relative from the room where the living live 'with it, and where such loathsome familiarity deprives 'death itself of awe; and then, but not before, they will 'be brought willingly to hear of Him whose thoughts were 'so much with the wretched, and who had compassion for 'all human sorrow.' He closed by proposing Lord Ashley's

*Ante*, p. 379.

*Ante*, p. 36.

Advocating sanitary reform.

LONDON: 1848-51.

Page 258 of Vol. I.

health as having preferred the higher ambition of labouring for the poor to that of pursuing the career open to him in the service of the State; and as having also had 'the 'courage on all occasions to face the cant which is the worst 'and commonest of all, the cant about the cant of philan-'thropy.' Lord Shaftesbury first dined with him in the following year at Tavistock-house.

Lord Shaftesbury.

Shortly after the Sanitary meeting came the first Guild performances; and then Dickens left Devonshire-terrace, never to return to it. What occupied him in the interval before he took possession of his new abode, has before been told; but two letters were overlooked in describing his progress in the labour of the previous year, and brief extracts from them will naturally lead me to the subject of my next chapter. 'I have been' (15th of September) 'tremendously at work these two days; eight hours at a 'stretch yesterday, and six hours and a half to-day, with 'the Ham and Steerforth chapter, which has completely 'knocked me over—utterly defeated me!' 'I am' (21st of October) 'within three pages of the shore; and am 'strangely divided, as usual in such cases, between sorrow 'and joy. Oh, my dear Forster, if I were to say half of 'what *Copperfield* makes me feel to-night, how strangely, 'even to you, I should be turned inside out! I seem to 'be sending some part of myself into the Shadowy World.'

Realities of his books to Dickens.

END OF THE SECOND VOLUME.

BRADBURY, EVANS, AND CO., PRINTERS, WHITEFRIARS.

Lightning Source UK Ltd.
Milton Keynes UK
UKOW051857181111

182311UK00001B/3/P